Dr. Carl B. Montano
Economics Department
Lamar University
P.O. Box 10045
Beaumont, Texas 77710
Tel. (409) 880-8651

Environmental and Natural Resource Economics
A Contemporary Approach

Jonathan M. Harris

Global Development and Environment Institute
Tufts University

HOUGHTON MIFFLIN COMPANY   Boston   New York

Sponsoring Editor: Ann West
Assistant Editor: Michael Kerns
Editorial Assistant: Tonya Lobato
Senior Project Editor: Cathy Labresh Brooks
Editorial Assistant: Lindsay Frost
Senior Manufacturing Coordinator: Florence Cadran
Marketing Manager: Amy Dhillon

Cover image: © Gary Braasch/CORBIS

Photo Credits: Page 3: Johnson Space Center/NASA; Page 11: © Norbert Wu/Peter Arnold, Inc.; Page 17: © Michael S. Yamashita/CORBIS; Page 24: © William E. Ferguson; Page 37: © 2002 PhotoDisc, Inc.; Page 52: Bob Daemmrich/Stock Boston; Page 61: Stephanie S. Ferguson/© William E. Ferguson; Page 62: Ulrike Welsch/Photo Researchers; Page 76: AP/Wide World Photos; Page 83: Anthony Mercleca/Photo Researchers; Page 93: Joe Munroe/Photo Researchers; Page 105: A. Ramey/PhotoEdit; Page 121: © Kevin R. Morris/CORBIS; Page 127: © 2002 PhotoDisc, Inc.; Page 136: AP/Wide World Photos; Page 147: Spencer Grant/Stock Boston; Page 159: © Japack Company/CORBIS; Page 166: Reuters NewMedia/CORBIS; Page 175: AP/Wide World Photos; Page 191: Sean Sprague/Stock Boston; Page 201: Susan Van Etten/PhotoEdit; Page 222: Richard E. Ferguson/© William E. Ferguson; Page 231: © Michael S. Yamashita/CORBIS; Page 242: Mark C. Burnett/Photo Researchers; Page 253: Christopher Morris/Corbis SABA; Page 267: Peter Menzel/Stock Boston; Page 277: Michael S. Yamashita/CORBIS; Page 291: © David Samuel Robbins/CORBIS; Page 298: Keith Gunnar/Photo Researchers; Page 315: Nicholas Sapieha/Stock Boston; Page 327: AP/Wide World Photos; Page 336: © Marilyn Humphries/The Image Works; Page 351: John Giordono/Corbis SABA; Page 363: © Michael S. Yamashita/CORBIS; Page 374: © Roman Soumar/CORBIS; Page 384: © AFP/CORBIS; Page 405: Richard Hansen/Photo Researchers; Page 413: AP/Wide World Photos; Page 424: Charles Kennard/Stock Boston; Page 431: © Bill Gentile/CORBIS.

Printed in the U.S.A.

Library of Congress Control Number: 2001131505
ISBN: 0-618-13392-5

123456789-QF-06 05 04 03 02

Contents

Preface

iii

PART THREE

Ecological Economics and Environmental Accounting   119

PREFACE

This text is a product of twelve years of teaching environmental and natural resource economics at the undergraduate and graduate levels. It reflects the conviction that environmental issues are of fundamental importance, and that a broad approach to understanding the relationship of the human economy and the natural world is essential.

Typically, students come to an environmental economics course with an awareness that environmental problems are serious, and that local, national, and global policy solutions are needed. Some students may be interested in careers in environmental policy, others in gaining an understanding of issues that are likely to be relevant in their careers, personal lives, and communities. In either case, the current importance of the topics gives the course that special spark of enthusiasm which is a heaven-sent boon to any instructor trying to breathe life into marginal cost and benefit curves.

There is a distinct danger, however, that this initial enthusiasm can rather quickly be dampened by the use of a strictly conventional approach to environmental economics. A major limitation of this approach is its almost exclusive use of microeconomic techniques. This has a number of serious, sometimes crippling, implications for the understanding of environmental issues. The microeconomic perspective strongly implies that anything of importance can be expressed in terms of price — but many important environmental functions cannot be fully captured in dollar terms. Also, a microeconomic perspective also makes it very difficult to focus on the inherently "macro" environmental issues such as global climate change, ocean pollution, ozone depletion, population growth, and global carbon, nitrogen, and water cycles.

Standard environmental economics may also fall into the trap of excessive abstraction and quantitative analysis. Both of these, of course, have their place. But when environmental economics becomes a course *only* in the calculation of present values, inter-temporal equilibrium prices, and "optimal" pollution levels, with the blackboard or the PowerPoint slides full of complex diagrams and equations, that original student enthusiasm that is so valuable is in danger of being lost.

For these reasons, I have tried to develop an alternative approach that presents the broader perspective that has come to be known as ecological economics as a complement to standard economic theory. Many elements of standard microeconomic analysis are essential for analyzing resource and environmental issues. At the same time, it is important to recognize the limitations of a strictly economic approach, and to introduce ecological and biophysical perspectives on the interactions of human and natural systems.

The text is structured so as to be appropriate for a variety of courses. It assumes a background in basic economics, and could be used in an upper-level undergraduate course or a policy-oriented masters-level course. Part One provides a broad overview of different approaches to economic analysis of resources and environment, and discusses fundamental issues of economy/environment interactions. Part Two covers the basics of standard environmental and resource economics including the theory of externalities, resource allocation over time, common property resources, public goods, and valuation. Part Three offers an introduction to the ecological economics approach, including "greening" national accounts and economic/ecological modeling.

Parts Four and Five apply these analytical approaches to fundamental environmental and resource issues. Part Four focuses on population, agriculture, and the environment, reviewing different theories of population, giving an overview of the environmental impacts of world agricultural systems, and discussing policy responses to population and food supply issues. Part Five deals with the economics of renewable and nonrenewable resources at both the microeconomic and macroeconomic levels.

Part Six provides both a standard analysis of the economics of pollution control, and a broader view of industrial ecology and global climate change. Part Seven brings together some of the themes from the specific topics of the earlier parts in a consideration of trade and development issues.

Each chapter has discussion questions and the more quantitative chapters have numerical problems. A list of key terms and concepts from each chapter corresponds to an extensive glossary. Useful web sites are also listed. Instructors and students are urged to make full use of the text's supporting web site. The instructor web site includes teaching tips and objectives, answers to text problems, and test questions. The student site includes chapter review questions and web-based exercises, and will be updated periodically with bulletins on topical environmental issues.

The preparation of a text covering such an extensive area, in addition to the supporting materials, is a vast enterprise, and my indebtedness to all those who have contributed to the effort is accordingly great. Credit for the preparation of the web materials and glossary goes to Brian Roach, Research Associate at the Tufts University Global Development and Environment Institute, who has also provided valuable comments on the text. Other colleagues at the Institute have supplied essential help and inspiration. Research Associate Anne-Marie Codur co-authored the original version of Chapter 18 on global climate change, and contributed material to the chapters on renewable resources. Especially significant has been the unwavering support of the Institute's co-Director, Neva Goodwin, who has long championed the importance of educational materials bringing broader perspectives to economics teaching.

Colleagues Frank Ackerman, Timothy Wise, and Kevin Gallagher provided insights on specific issues both directly and through our work together editing the volume *A Survey of Sustainable Development* (Island Press, 2001). Invaluable research assistance was provided by Chaminda Rajapakse, Sucharita Kuchibhotla, Nathan Monash, Nancy Liu, Nicole Palacz, Jordana Fish, and Dan Allen, and administrative support by Sam Milton.

The book has greatly benefited from the comments of several reviewers, including George K. Criner, University of Maine; Ronald L. Friesen, Bluffton College; Reza Ramazani, Saint Michael's College; Barbara Street, Chaminade University; and James Tober, Marlboro College. It also reflects much that I have learned from the work of colleagues at Tufts University and elsewhere, especially William Moomaw, Sheldon Krimsky, Molly Anderson, Paul Kirshen, and Richard Wetzler. Others whose work has provided special inspiration for this text include Herman Daly, Richard Norgaard, Robert Costanza, Glenn-Marie Lange, John Proops, and many other members of the International Society for Ecological Economics. Lance Taylor showed faith in my as-yet unproven work by using the text in a pre-publication version; Matthew Kahn, Fred Curtis, and many other faculty members at colleges in the U.S. and worldwide have used pre-publication chapters in a modular form in their courses.

I hope that the book will be of use to many faculty and students from a wide variety of backgrounds. Throughout my teaching career I have felt that the best insights come from students who approach topics with an open mind and can judge the relevance and usefulness of different perspectives and techniques. As many instructors are aware, "you really learn it when you teach it," being forced to confront easy assumptions and unwarranted conclusions when challenged by intelligent students. My intention is to continue this process through the use of this text and its supporting web site, which will provide an opportunity for feedback and comments on the text. Updates to the web site will reflect input from instructors and students, as well as the ever-changing, ever-fascinating world of environmental and resource issues.

Jonathan M. Harris
Global Development and Environment Institute
Tufts University

Introduction: The Economy and the Environment

CHAPTER FOCUS QUESTIONS

- What major environmental issues do we face in the twenty-first century?
- How can economics help us understand these issues?
- How do economic and ecological perspectives differ, and how can we combine them to address environmental issues?

CHAPTER

1

Changing Perspectives on the Environment

Economics and the Environment

Over the past three decades, we have become increasingly aware of environmental problems facing communities, nations, and the world. During this period, natural resource and environmental issues have grown in scope and urgency. In 1970, the Environmental Protection Agency was created in the United States to respond to what was at that time a relatively new public concern with air and water pollution. Since then, growing worldwide attention has been devoted to the environment.

In 1992 the United Nations Conference on Environment and Development (UNCED) focused on major global isssues including: depletion of the earth's protective ozone layer, destruction of tropical and old-growth forests and wetlands, species extinction, and the steady buildup of carbon dioxide and other "greenhouse" gases causing global warming and climate change. More recently, the United Nations Environmental Programme (UNEP) report *Global Environmental Outlook 2000* found that "environmental gains from new technology and policies are being overtaken by the pace and scale of population growth and economic development."[1]

---

[1]UNEP 1999.

3

With the exception of ozone depletion, an area in which major reduction in emissions has been achieved by international agreement, the UNEP report offers evidence that the global environmental problems identified at UNCED in 1992 have continued or worsened. In addition, UNEP points to nitrogen pollution in freshwater and oceans, exposure to toxic chemicals and hazardous wastes, forest and freshwater ecosystem damage, water contamination and declining groundwater supplies, urban air pollution and wastes, and overexploitation of major ocean fisheries. Underlying all these problems is global population growth, adding nearly 80 million people a year. The world population, which had passed 6 billion by the year 2000, is expected to grow to around 8 billion by 2030.

Scientists, policymakers, and the general public have begun to grapple with questions such as What will the future look like? and Can we respond to these multiple threats adequately and in time to prevent irreversible damage to the planetary systems that support life? One of the most important components of the problem that rarely receives sufficient attention is the economic analysis of environmental issues.

Some may argue that environmental issues transcend economics and should be judged in different terms from the money values used in economic analysis. Indeed, this assertion holds some truth. We find, however, that policies for environmental protection are often measured—and sometimes rejected—in terms of their economic costs. For example, it is extremely difficult to preserve open land that has high commercial development value. Either large sums must be raised to purchase the land, or strong political opposition to "locking up" land must be overcome. Environmental protection organizations face a continued battle with ever-increasing economic development pressures.

Often public policy issues are framed in terms of a conflict between development and the environment. The battle over logging of old-growth forest in the U.S. Northwest was typified as "jobs versus owls." Opponents of international agreements to reduce carbon dioxide emissions argue that the economic costs of such measures are too high. Supporters of increased oil production clash with advocates of protecting the Arctic National Wildlife Refuge. In developing nations, the tension between the urgency of human needs and environmental protection is even greater.

Does economic development necessarily require a high environmental price? Although all economic development must affect the environment to some degree, is "environment-friendly" development possible? If we must make a trade-off between development and environment, how shall we decide the proper balance? Questions such as these highlight the importance of environmental economics.

Two Approaches

In this book we describe two approaches in addressing natural resource and environmental economics. The first, or traditional, approach uses a set of models and techniques rooted within the standard *neoclassical mainstream* of economic thought[2] to

---

[2]Neoclassical price theory, based on the concepts of marginal utility and marginal productivity, emphasizes the essential function of market price in achieving an equilibrium between supply and demand.

apply economic concepts to the environment. The second approach, known as **ecological economics,**[3] takes a slightly different perspective. Rather than applying economic concepts *to* the environment, ecological economics seeks to place economic activity *in the context of* the biological and physical systems that support life, including all human activities.

The Traditional Economic Approach

Several models in economic theory specifically address environmental issues. One important application of neoclassical economic theory deals with the allocation of **nonrenewable resources** over time. This analysis is important in understanding such issues as depletion of oil and mineral resources, and also has applications to **renewable resources** such as agricultural soils. Economic analyses also address **common property resources** such as the atmosphere and oceans and **public goods** such as national parks and wildlife preserves. Because these resources are not privately owned, the economic principles governing their use differ from those affecting goods traded in the market.

Another central concept in neoclassical economic analysis of the environment is that of **externalities,** or **external costs and benefits.** The theory of externalities provides an economic framework for analyzing the costs of environmental damage caused by economic activities or the social benefits created by economic activity that improves the environment. Externalities are also sometimes referred to as **third-party effects,** because a market transaction that involves two parties—for example, someone buying gasoline from a filling station—also affects other people, such as those exposed to pollution from producing and burning the gas.

Modern environmental economic theory, built on this foundation, addresses many issues ranging from overfishing to fossil fuel depletion to parkland conservation.[4] In this text we will investigate how these economic concepts can help frame environmental questions and provide guidance for environmental policymaking.

The Ecological Economics Approach

Ecological economics takes a broader perspective in framing environmental questions by incorporating laws derived from the natural sciences. For example, to understand the collapse of many important ocean fisheries, ecological economics refers to population biology and ecology as well as to the economic view of fish as a resource for production.

Ecological economics theorists emphasize the importance of energy resources, especially fossil fuels, in current economic systems. All ecological systems depend on en-

---

[3]For an overview of many key articles in ecological economics, see Costanza, 1991, and Krishnan et al., 1995.

[4]See Bromley, 1995; Markandya and Richardson, 1993; and Stavins, 2000, for collections of articles on environmental economics.

ergy inputs, but natural systems rely almost entirely on **solar energy.** The rapid growth of economic production during the twentieth century required enormous energy inputs, and global economic systems will make even greater energy demands in the twenty-first century. Energy availability and environmental implications of energy use are central issues for ecological economics.

A fundamental principle of ecological economics is that human economic activity must be limited by the environment's **carrying capacity.** Carrying capacity is defined as the population level and consumption activities, whether of humans or animals, that the available natural resource base can sustain without depletion. For example, when a herd of grazing animals exceeds a certain size, rangeland overgrazing will diminish the potential food supply, leading inevitably to a population decline.

For the human population, the issue is more complex. The issue of food supplies is certainly relevant as the world population, more than six billion by 2000, grows toward a projected eight to ten billion. But ecological economists also point to energy supplies, scarce natural resources, and cumulative environmental damage as constraints on economic growth. They argue that the standard theory gives these factors insufficient weight, and that major structural changes in the nature of economic activity are required to adapt to environmental limits.

In this text we will consider insights from both the standard and the ecological versions of environmental economics. Sometimes the theories show significant agreement or overlap, and sometimes they produce widely differing implications. The best way to judge which approaches are most fruitful is to apply them to specific environmental issues, as we do throughout this book. First, however, we must understand the relationship between the economic system, natural resources, and the environment.

A Framework for Understanding the Ecological Perspective

How can we best conceptualize the relationship between economic activities and the environment? One way is to start with the traditional **circular flow** diagram, used in most economics courses to depict the economic process.

The Circular Flow Model

Figure 1-1 shows a simplified model of relationships between households and business firms in two markets: the market for goods and services and the market for factors of production. Production factors are generally defined under the headings of land, labor, and capital. The services these factors provide are "inputs" to the production of goods and services, which in turn provide the basis for households' consumption needs. Goods, services, and factors flow clockwise; their economic values are reflected in the flows of money used to pay for them, moving counterclockwise. In both mar-

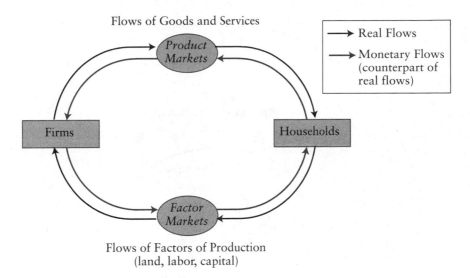

FIGURE 1-1 *The Standard Circular Flow Model*

kets the interaction of supply and demand determines a market-clearing price and establishes an equilibrium level of output.

Where do natural resources and the environment fit in this diagram? **Natural resources,** including minerals, water, fossil fuels, forests, fisheries, and farmland, generally fall under the inclusive category of "land." The two other major production factors, labor and capital, continually regenerate through the economic circular flow process, but by what processes do natural resources regenerate for future economic use? To answer this question, we construct a larger "circular flow" that takes in ecosystem processes as well as economic activity (Figure 1-2).

Taking this broader view, we also notice that the standard circular flow diagram also omits effects of wastes and pollution generated in the production process. These wastes from both firms and households must somewhere flow back into the ecosystem, either through land disposal or as air and water pollution.

In addition to the simple processes of extracting resources from the ecosystem and returning wastes to it, economic activities also affect broader natural systems in more subtle and pervasive ways. For example, modern intensive agriculture changes the composition and ecology of soil and water systems, as well as affecting nitrogen and carbon cycles in the environment.

Figure 1-2, although still quite simple, provides a broader framework for placing the economic system in its ecological context. As you can see, the ecological system has its own circular flow, determined by physical and biological rather than economic laws. This broader flow has only one net "input"—solar energy—and only one net "output"—waste heat. Everything else must somehow be recycled or contained within the planetary ecosystem.

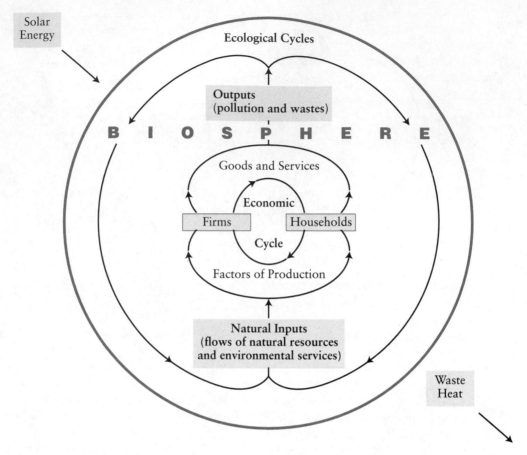

FIGURE 1-2 *A Broader Circular Flow Model*

Points of Contact Between Economic and Ecological Flows

Understanding the relationships between economic systems, natural resources, and the environment begins with defining the different functions natural systems serve.

- The environment's **source function** is its ability to make services and raw materials available for human use. Degradation of the source function can occur for two reasons: (1) **Resource depletion:** the resource declines in quantity because humans have drawn on it more rapidly than it could be regenerated; and (2) Pollution: contamination of the resource reduces its quality and usefulness.
- The environment's **sink function** is its ability to absorb and render harmless the waste by-products of human activity. The sink function is overtaxed when waste volume is too great in a given time period or when wastes are too toxic. When that happens, aspects of the environment on which we depend (most often soil, water, and atmosphere) become damaged, polluted, or poisoned.

These relationships between human activity and the environment define the points of contact between the inner circle of economic flows and the outer circle of ecological flows. Natural resource and environmental economics analyzes the relationships between the two circular flows: the economic system and the ecosystem.

The Economic Valuation Approach

One approach to the analysis of natural resource and waste flows uses the same kind of **economic valuation** applied to factors of production, goods, and services. In this approach, an economic analyst puts a price on each natural resource and environmental input to the economy, including an estimated price for inputs not usually included in market transactions, such as clean air and water. Economic techniques can also be used to assess the money value of the damages done by pollution and waste disposal.

By placing a money value on natural resources and environmental functions, we can include them in the inner, or economic, circular flow. This is the goal of much standard resource and environmental analysis. As we will see, a variety of methods can serve this end, including redefining or reassigning property rights, creating new institutions such as markets for pollution permits, or implicit valuation through surveys and other techniques. If we can be satisfied that these pricing mechanisms accurately reflect the "true value" of resources and of environmental damages, we can relatively easily include these factors in a market-oriented economic analysis.

The Ecological Economics Approach

The ecological economics approach views the economic system as a subset of the broader ecosystem. In this perspective, an economic valuation expressed in prices can only imperfectly capture the complexity of ecological processes, and indeed will sometimes result in serious conflict with ecosystem requirements.

Ecological economists have often argued that standard economic pricing and valuation techniques must either be altered to reflect ecosystem realities, or must be supplemented by other forms of analysis focusing on energy flows, the carrying capacity of the environment, and the requirements of ecological balance. As we will see in our discussion of analytical techniques and of specific issues in population, energy, resources, and pollution, the standard and ecological economics perspectives will sometimes have similar practical implications, but in other cases the two approaches may lead to significantly different conclusions about appropriate resource and environmental policies.

Environmental Microeconomics and Macroeconomics

Another way of viewing the difference between standard and ecological approaches is in terms of a tension between microeconomic and macroeconomic perspectives on the environment.

Standard environmental economic analysis relies largely on microeconomic theory. **Environmental macroeconomics,** however, can help place the economic system in its broader ecological context.

A microeconomic perspective focuses on individual resource and environmental issues. The macroeconomic view is concerned with the interrelationship of economic growth and ecosystems.

Microeconomic and Valuation Techniques

To the extent that we can succeed in putting a price on natural resources and the environment, extensions of standard microeconomic theory can help explain the process of achieving equilibrium in markets for natural resources and for **environmental services**—the capacity of the environment to absorb wastes and pollutants, capture solar energy, and in other ways provide the basis for economic activity. Analytical techniques that play an important role in **environmental microeconomics** include:

- *Measuring* **external costs and benefits.** This means, for example, estimating a money value for damage caused by acid rain pollution. This value can then be compared to the costs of correcting the problem through pollution control technology or reduced output of polluting activities. We can **internalize externalities** through, for example, a tax on the polluting activity.
- *Valuing resources and the environment as assets, whether privately owned or public.* This involves considering **intertemporal resource allocation,** the choice between using a resource now or conserving it for future use. The standard economic technique to balance present and future benefits and costs is to use a **discount rate.** In this technique, a present benefit or cost receives a somewhat higher value than a future benefit or cost—how much higher depends on the discount rate employed and on how far into the future the comparison extends.
- *Devising appropriate property rights rules for environmental resources and establishing rules for use of common property resources and for provision of public goods.*[5] For example, a fishery may be privately owned, or it may be public with access limited by government sale of fishing licenses. Similarly, a wildlife preserve may be privately owned and managed or may be maintained as a public park.
- *Balancing economic costs and benefits through some form of cost-benefit analysis.* This often involves a combination of values observable in the market, such as values of land or goods, and estimates of nonmarket values, such as natural beauty and maintenance of species diversity. For example, deciding whether or not to permit construction of a ski resort on a previously undeveloped hillside would require some estimate of the recreational value of skiing,

---

[5]*Public goods* are resources and goods available to the public without restriction. For a more precise definition, see Chapter 5.

In complex ecosystems such as rainforests, solar energy drives the cycles of life. Many such ecosystems are threatened by expansion of human activities.

the value of alternative land uses, as well as less easily quantifiable concerns such as impact on water supplies, wildlife, and on the rural character of the area.

In the context of the double circular flow shown in Figure 1-2, the above analytical techniques are derived from the smaller "economic" circle: in effect, they apply pricing concepts drawn from the economic system to the intermediate flows of natural resources and wastes that connect the two circles. These approaches seem most appropriate when we focus on a specific, quantifiable problem, such as figuring the appropriate fee to charge for a license to cut timber on government land or appropriate limits on factory air pollutant emissions.

Environmental Macroeconomics

Valuation techniques are less effective in handling important unquantifiable values such as aesthetics, ethical issues, and **biodiversity** (the maintenance of many different interrelated species in an ecological community). They may also fail to capture the scope of **global environmental problems** that have become increasingly important in recent years. Issues such as global climate change, ozone depletion, loss of species, widespread degradation of agricultural lands, regional water shortages, forest and ocean ecosystem damage, and other large-scale environmental issues require a broader perspective. For this reason, ecological economist Herman Daly has called for development of an environmental macroeconomics,[6] which requires a different approach from the standard economic techniques discussed earlier.

Developing such a macroeconomic perspective on environmental issues requires placing the economic system in its broader ecological context. As Figure 1-2 shows, the economic circular flow is really part of a larger ecological circular flow. This ecological flow is actually made up of many cycles. **Ecological cycles** include:

- The *carbon cycle*, in which green plants break down atmospheric carbon dioxide (CO_2) into carbon and oxygen. The carbon is stored in the plants, some of which are eaten by animals. Carbon is recombined with oxygen by animal respiration and by decay or burning of organic matter and is thus returned to the atmosphere.
- The *nitrogen cycle*, in which soil bacteria "fix," or chemically combine nitrogen from the atmosphere with oxygen and make this essential nutrient available for plant growth.
- The *water cycle*, including precipitation, runoff, and evaporation, which continually make fresh water available for plant and animal life.
- Other *organic cycles* of growth, death, decay, and new growth whereby essential nutrients are recycled through the soils to provide a continuing basis for plant and animal life.

All of these cycles rely on solar energy and operate in a complex balance that has evolved through millennia.

Seen in this context, economic activity is a process of speeding up the **throughput** of materials from the ecological cycles. The term "throughput" denotes the total use of energy and materials as both inputs and outputs of a process.

Modern agriculture, for example, applies vast quantities of artificially derived nitrogen fertilizer to obtain higher crop yields. Runoff of excess nitrogen creates environmental problems and water contamination. Both agriculture and industry make heavy demands on water supplies. Together with household use this demand can exceed the capacity of the natural water cycle depleting reservoirs and underground aquifers.

The most important way of speeding up resource throughput is using more energy to drive the economic system. More than 80 percent of the energy used in the global economic system is derived from fossil fuels. Carbon emissions from burning these fuels unbalances the global carbon cycle. Excessive amounts of CO_2 accumulate in the atmosphere, alter the processes that determine the planet's climate, and thereby affect many global ecosystems.

---

[6]See Daly, 1991.

As economic growth proceeds, the demands of the economic system on the ecological cycles grow. Energy use, resource and water use, and waste generation increase. Thus the environmental macroeconomic issue is how to balance the size of the economic system, or **macroeconomic scale,** with the supporting ecosystem. Viewing the problem in this way represents a significant paradigm shift for economic analysis, which until recently has not usually considered overall ecosystem limitations.

Implications of Ecologically Oriented Economics

An ecologically oriented macroeconomics involves new concepts of national income measurement that explicitly reckon environmental pollution and natural resource depletion in calculating national income. In addition, ecological economists have introduced new forms of analysis at both microeconomic and macroeconomic levels. These new analytical techniques are based on the physical laws that govern energy and materials flows in ecosystems. Applying these laws to the economic process offers a contrasting perspective to the standard microeconomic analysis of environmental issues.

Seeking a balance between economic growth and ecosystem health has given rise to the concept of **sustainable development.** Forms of economic development that preserve rather than degrade the environment include renewable energy use, organic and low-input agriculture, and resource-conserving technologies. On a global scale, the promotion of sustainable development responds to the many resource and environmental issues outlined at the beginning of the chapter, viewing these issues in terms of ecosystem impacts rather than as individual problems.[7]

A Look Ahead

How can we best use these two approaches to economic analysis of environmental issues? In the following chapters we will find out by applying the tools and methods of each to specific issues. In preparation, Chapter 2 provides an overview of the relationship between economic development and the environment. The microeconomic elements of resource and environmental economics are explored in detail in Chapters 3–6. Chapters 7–9 cover the concepts of ecological economics, environmental accounting, and ecosystem modeling.

In the core of the text, Chapters 10–18, we apply techniques of standard economic analysis and of ecological analysis to the major issues of population, food supply, energy use, natural resource management, and pollution control. Chapters 19 and 20 bring together many of these topics to focus on questions of trade, economic growth, and development as they relate to the environment.

---

[7]For surveys of the relationship between environmental economics and sustainable development, see Opschoor et al., 1999 and Harris et al., 2001. For a discussion of global ecosystem impacts of human activity, see World Resources Institute, 2000.

SUMMARY

National and global environmental issues are major challenges in the twenty-first century. Response to these challenges requires understanding the economics of the environment. Policies aimed at environmental protection have economic costs and benefits, and this economic dimension is often crucial in determining which policies we adopt. Some cases may require trade-offs between economic and environmental goals; in other cases these goals may prove compatible and mutually reinforcing.

Two different approaches address economic analysis of environmental issues. The standard approach applies economic theory to the environment using concepts of money valuation and economic equilibrium. This approach aims for efficient management of natural resources and proper valuation of waste and pollution impact on the environment. The ecological economic approach views the economic system as a whole as a subset of a broader biophysical system. This approach emphasizes the need for economic activity that conforms to physical and biological limits.

Much of the analysis drawn from the standard approach is microeconomic, based on the workings of markets. Variations of standard market analysis can be applied to cases where economic activity has damaging environmental effects or uses up scarce resources. Other economic analyses provide insight into the use of common property resources and public goods.

Environmental macroeconomics, a relatively new field, emphasizes the relationship between economic production and the major natural cycles of the planet. In many cases, significant conflicts arise between the operations of the economic system and these natural systems, creating regional and global problems such as global climate change from excess carbon dioxide accumulation. This broader approach requires new ways to measure economic activity, as well as analysis of how the scale of economic activity affects environmental systems.

This text outlines both analytical perspectives and draws on both to help understand the major issues of population, food supply, energy use, natural resource management, and pollution. The combination of these analyses can help to formulate policies that address specific environmental problems as well as promote a broader vision of environmentally sustainable development.

KEY TERMS AND CONCEPTS

assets
biodiversity
carrying capacity
circular flow
common property resources
cost-benefit analysis
discount rate
ecological cycles

ecological economics
economic valuation
environmental macroeconomics
environmental microeconomics
environmental services
external costs and benefits
externalities
global environmental problems

internalizing externalities
intertemporal resource allocation
macroeconomic scale
natural resources
nonrenewable resources
property rights
public goods

renewable resources
resource depletion
solar energy
source and sink functions
sustainable development
third-party effects
throughput

DISCUSSION QUESTIONS

1. Do economic growth and sound environmental policy necessarily conflict? Identify some areas where a choice must be made between economic growth and environmental preservation and others where the two are compatible.

2. Can we put a money price on environmental resources? How? Is this impossible in any cases? Identify specific situations of valuing the environment with which you are familiar or have read about.

3. In what ways do the principles of ecological circular flow resemble those of the economic circular flow? How do they differ? Consider specific examples in the areas of agriculture, water, and energy systems.

REFERENCES

Bromley, Daniel W. *The Handbook of Environmental Economics*. Blackwell Handbooks in Economics series. Oxford, England, and Cambridge, U.S.: Basil Blackwell, 1995.

Costanza, Robert, ed. *Ecological Economics: The Science and Management of Sustainability*. New York: Columbia University Press, 1991.

Daly, Herman. "Elements of Environmental Macroeconomics," in Costanza, ed., 1991.

Harris, Jonathan M., Timothy A. Wise, Kevin P. Gallagher, and Neva R. Goodwin, *A Survey of Sustainable Development: Social and Economic Dimensions*. Washington, D.C.: Island Press, 2001.

Krishnan, Rajaram, Jonathan M. Harris, and Neva R. Goodwin, eds. *A Survey of Ecological Economics*. Washington, D.C.: Island Press, 1995.

Markandya, Anil, and Julie Richardson. *Environmental Economics: A Reader*. New York: St. Martin's Press, 1993.

Opschoor, J. B., Kenneth Button, and Peter Nijkamp, eds. *Environmental Economics and Development*. Cheltenham, England: Elgar, 1999.

Stavins, Robert N., ed. *Economics of the Environment: Selected Readings*, 4th ed. New York: Norton, 2000.

World Resources Institute, United Nations Development Programme, United Nations Environment Programme, and World Bank. *World Resources 2000-2001: People and Ecosystems: the Fraying Web of Life.* Washington, D.C.: World Resources Institute, 2000.

World Commission on Environment and Development. *Our Common Future.* New York: Oxford University Press, 1987.

United Nations Environment Programme. *Global Environmental Outlook 2000: UNEP's Millennium Report on the Environment.* London, U.K.: Earthscan Publications, 1999.

WEB SITES

1. **http://www.worldwatch.org/** The home page for the Worldwatch Institute, an organization that conducts a broad range of research on environmental issues. They publish an annual "State of the World" report that presents detailed analyses of current environmental issues.
2. **http://www.cnie.org/stateof.htm** Web site for the National Council for Science and the Environment, with links to various sites with state, national, and international data on environmental quality.
3. **http://www.emagazine.com/** Web site for E/The Environmental Magazine. The site includes many archived articles on all environmental topics.
4. **http://www.unep.org/unep/eia/geo1/ch/toc.htm** Web site for the Global Environment Outlook-1, a United Nations publication. The report is an extensive analysis of the global environmental situation.

CHAPTER FOCUS QUESTIONS

- What is the relationship between economic growth and the environment?
- Will economic growth encounter planetary limits?
- How can economic development become environmentally sustainable?

CHAPTER **2**

Resources, Environment, and Economic Development

A Brief History of Economic Growth and the Environment

Human population and economic activity have remained fairly stable during much of recorded history. Prior to the Industrial Revolution of the nineteenth century, Europe's population grew slowly and standards of living changed little. The advent of the market economy and rapid technological progress altered this pattern dramatically. Populations in Europe entered a period of rapid growth that led British classical economist Thomas Malthus to theorize that populations would outgrow food supplies, keeping the mass of people perpetually at a subsistent standard of living.

Malthus's *Essay on the Principle of Population as It Affects the Future Improvement of Society,* published in 1798, initiated a long and continuing debate on the impact of population growth. History has proved the simple Malthusian hypothesis wrong: both population and living standards in Europe rose rapidly throughout the two centuries following Malthus's *Essay.* But if we consider a more sophisticated argument, that a growing human population and economic system will eventually outrun its biophysical support systems, the debate turns out to have strong current relevance.

The controversy over population growth is intimately intertwined with resource and environmental issues. In the twenty-first century these issues, rather than the simple race between population and food supply, will strongly affect the course of economic development. It is unlikely that we will see major shortfalls in food supply on a global scale. But it is very likely that the environmental stresses associated with a

17

growing population and rising resource demands will require sweeping changes in the nature of economic systems.

Measuring Growth Rates

In approaching complex growth issues, we can start with a simple economic analysis of the relationship between population and economic activity. Measuring economic output in conventional terms as gross national product (GNP), we have the simple identity:

$$GNP = (Population) \times (Per\ Capita\ GNP)$$

which can then be expressed in terms of rates of growth as a relationship among **GNP growth rate**, **population growth rate**, and **per capita GNP growth rate**:

$$GNP\ Growth\ Rate = (Population\ Growth\ Rate)$$
$$+ (Per\ Capita\ GNP\ Growth\ Rate).[1]$$

To correct for the effects of inflation, we should use **real GNP** rather than **nominal GNP** in this equation.[2] Real per capita GNP will rise steadily, as long as real GNP growth remains consistently higher than population growth. For this to occur, productivity must also rise steadily. This increasing productivity is, of course, the key to escaping the Malthusian trap.

Increased agricultural productivity means that the portion of the population working in farming decreases, freeing labor for industrial development. Increased industrial productivity brings higher living standards. Broadly speaking, economic development has unfolded along these lines in Europe, the United States, and other industrialized nations.

Factors Essential to Economic Growth

What determinants of increased productivity make this steady growth possible? One is accumulation of capital. Investment allows growth of **capital stock** over time: as capital stock per worker increases, the productivity of each worker increases. In addition **technological innovation** raises the productivity of both capital and labor. Standard economic growth models place no limits on this process. Provided investment continues at adequate rates, productivity and per capita consumption can continue rising far into the future.

The ecological economics perspective focuses on three additional factors as essential to economic growth. One is energy supply. Europe's economic growth in the nine-

---

[1]This relationship is derived from the mathematical rule of natural logarithms stating that if $A = BC$, then $\ln A = \ln B + \ln C$. The rates of growth of B and C can be expressed in terms of natural logarithms, and when added together they give the rate of growth of A.

[2]Nominal GNP is measured using current prices. Real GNP corrects for inflation by using a price index to calculate the constant dollar value of production.

teenth century depended heavily on coal as an energy source, and some writers at the time expressed concern that coal supplies might run out. In the twentieth century, oil displaced coal as the prime energy source for industry.

Currently oil, natural gas, and coal provide more than 85 percent of energy supplies for the United States, Europe, Japan, and other industrial economies, and about the same proportion of industrial energy for the world as a whole. To a great extent, economic growth both in agriculture and industry has been a process of substituting fossil fuel energy for human labor. This substitution has important resource and environmental implications, which in turn affect projections of future growth.

A second fundamental factor is supplies of land and natural resources, sometimes referred to as **natural capital.** Almost all economic activities require some land use. As these activities grow, pressures increase to convert land from a natural state to agricultural, industrial, and residential uses. Some uses conflict: housing may compete with farming for rural land, and industry or road building may make land less suitable for either residential or agricultural use.

Land, of course, is fixed in supply. Except in limited cases such as the diked areas of the Netherlands, human technology cannot create more land. Natural resources vary in abundance, but mineral resources and the regenerative capacity of forests and other living resources have physical limits.

The third important factor is the **absorptive capacity of the environment** for the waste products of industrial development. This issue is not so critical when the scale of economic activity is small relative to the environment. But as national and global economic activity accelerates, the flow of waste products increases and may threaten to overwhelm environmental systems. Flows of solid wastes, sewage and liquid wastes, toxic and radioactive wastes, and atmospheric emissions all pose specific environmental problems that require local, regional, and global solutions.

Growth Optimists and Pessimists

There is an ongoing debate concerning resource and environmental factors that contribute to, and could eventually limit, economic growth. In 1972 a Massachusetts Institute of Technology research team published *The Limits to Growth,* a study that used computer modeling to project drastic resource and environmental problems looming as a result of continued economic growth (see Box 2-1).[3] This report touched off a vigorous debate between growth "optimists" and "pessimists."

For the most part, the optimists placed faith in future technological progress to tap new sources of energy, overcome any resource limitations, and control pollution problems. The pessimists pointed to the rapid growth of population and GNP, together with the already formidable array of existing environmental problems, to warn that humanity was in danger of overshooting the earth's capacity to sustain economic activity. In effect, the question was whether the successful experience of economic growth over the past two centuries can be sustained in the next century.

_____

[3]Meadows, 1972.

2-1   The Limits to Growth Model

The *Limits to Growth* model, presented by an MIT research team in 1972, addressed the issue of physical limits to economic growth. The study employed a model called World 3, which attempted to capture interrelationships between population, agricultural output, economic growth, resource use, and pollution. At the time, public attention was just beginning to focus on environmental issues, and the MIT study's message had a powerful impact. The team concluded that we would reach the environmental limits to global growth within a century, and that without drastic changes there was a strong likelihood of an "overshoot/collapse" outcome: "a sudden and uncontrollable decline in both population and industrial capacity."[1]

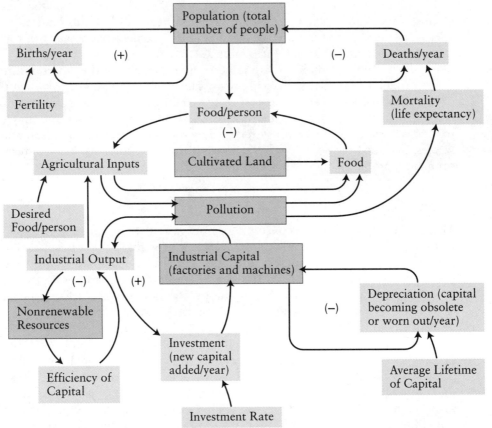

FIGURE 2-1 *Feedback Loops of Population, Capital, Resources, Agriculture, and Pollution*

[1]Meadows et al., 1972.

(continued on following page)

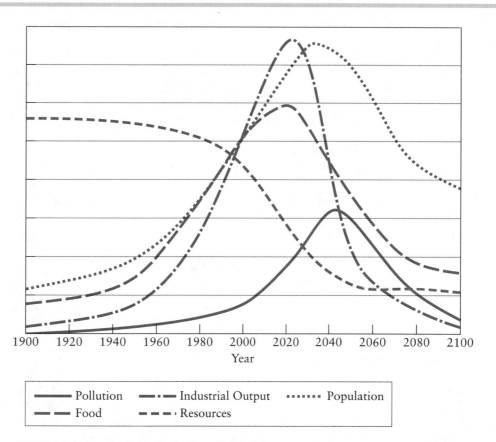

FIGURE 2-2 *The Basic Limits to Growth Model*

Source for figures: *Beyond the Limits: Confronting Global Collapse, Envisioning a Sustainable Future.* By Donnella Meadows et al., copyright 1992, Chelsea Green Publishing, White River Junction, Vt., 1-800-639-4099, www.chelseagreen.com. Reprinted by permission of Chelsea Green Publishing.

The model relied heavily on exponential growth patterns and feedback effects. Exponential growth occurs when population, economic production, resource use, or pollution increases by a certain percentage each year. Feedback effects occur when two variables interact, for example, when capital accumulation increases economic output, which in turn leads to a more rapid accumulation of capital. Positive feedback effects strengthen growth trends, whereas negative feedback effects moderate them. Negative feedback effects, however, may be undesirable, for example, when limits on food supply cause population decline through malnutrition and disease.

Figure 2-1 shows a portion of the complex pattern of feedback effects in the World 3 model. The results of the model's "standard run" are shown in Figure 2-2. Exponential growth in population, industrial output, and food demand generate

(continued on following page)

declines in resources and increasing pollution, which force a catastrophic reversal of growth by the mid-twenty-first century.

The report also emphasized that aggressive policies to moderate population growth, resource consumption, and pollution could avoid this disastrous result, leading instead to a smooth transition to global economic and ecological stability. This conclusion received far less attention than the catastrophic predictions. The report was widely criticized for failing to recognize the flexibility and adaptability of the economic system and for overstating the danger of resource exhaustion.

In 1992, the authors of the 1972 report published another book reasserting their conclusions but with more emphasis on environmental problems such as ozone layer destruction and global climate change. Once again they stated that catastrophe was not inevitable, but warned of an even more urgent need for major policy changes to achieve sustainability, with some ecological systems already being forced beyond their limits.[2]

---

[2]Meadows et al., 1992.

A Summary of Recent Growth

It is worth noting that the economic growth experienced following World War II has been extraordinary in its scope and character. In historical terms, world population and economic growth during the period from 1800 to 1950 represented a significant increase over previous slow growth rates. Even so, the rates since 1950 have been truly remarkable.

Between 1950 and 2000, world population more than doubled; world agricultural production tripled; and world GNP and energy use quadrupled (Figure 2-3 shows trends since 1961). This, of course, has raised demands on resources and the environment to unprecedented levels. The growth process, however, is far from completed. Global population, at more than six billion by 2000, continues to increase by 1.3 percent per year, a net addition of over 70 million people (more than the entire population of France) every year.

Together with population growth, the demand for improved living standards continues to drive overall production steadily upwards. Global GNP growth continues at between 2 and 3 percent per year in both developing and developed countries, with much higher rates in many developing nations such as China. At this rate, the World Bank projects that by 2030 world GNP will be 3.5 times 1990 levels—or approximately 15 times the 1950 level of GNP.[4]

---

[4]World Bank, 1992 and 1999.

Growth Index (1961 = 1.0)

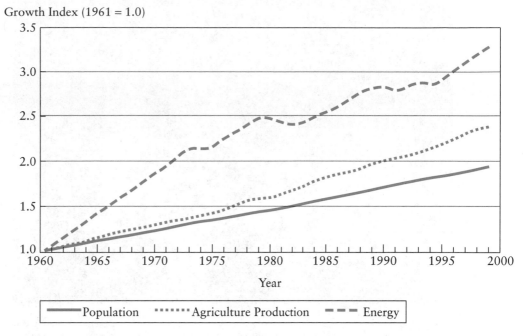

FIGURE 2-3 *Growth in Population, Agricultural Production, and Energy Use, 1961–1999*
Source: Food and Agriculture Organization of the United Nations, FAOSTAT database, 2000; United States Department of Energy, 1999. Indices based on 1961 = 1.0.

Will we have enough energy, resources, and environmental capacity to sustain this level of output? We will examine many specific aspects of this question in future chapters. As an introduction, we can review some of the main dimensions of the problem and suggest some approaches to their analysis.

The Future of Economic Growth and the Environment

In the economic history of the twentieth century, environmental issues have loomed large only recently. During the Great Depression of the 1930s soil erosion drew attention, and in the 1950s and 1960s concerns about pesticide use and air pollution emerged. Only in the last decades of the twentieth century, however, did environmental degradation gain recognition as a fundamental challenge to the whole economic growth process. In the global economy of the twenty-first century, by contrast, environmental considerations will be a determining factor in shaping economic development.

Growing populations require more space for urban and residential development. Here a housing tract covers farmland in the United States. In densely-populated developing countries such as China and India, prime cropland is also being converted to urban, industrial, transportation, and residential uses.

Population Growth

The first essential fact of this new global economy is our dramatically increased population. The phenomenon of **population momentum,** discussed in Chapter 10, guarantees growing populations in most countries over the next half-century. Unlike many predictions that may be quickly disproved by events, this one is virtually certain; the largest generation of children in global history has already been born. We know that these children will grow to be adults and have children of their own. Even if they have small families (and large families are now the norm in much of the world), their children will significantly outnumber the present older generations they will replace.

Thus only a huge increase in the death rate could alter the prediction of significantly higher population. Even the global AIDS crisis, despite its horrifying global spread, is unlikely to affect population projections except in a few regions. The lowest projections for the year 2030 show a 50 percent increase in global population over 1990 levels; higher-range projections show a doubling over 1990 levels to around 10 billion. More than 95 percent of this increase will occur in currently developing nations.

Although global population growth rates have been falling since the 1970s, a decline projected to continue, the total number of people added to world population (a smaller percentage of a larger total) will remain over 60 million per year over the next several decades.

Such population growth raises the question of whether or not we can feed the world. Will agricultural capacity supply the needs of an extra two, three, or four billion people? We can examine this problem in several ways. The simplest question is if it is physically possible to produce sufficient grain and other foodstuffs to provide adequate nutrition for eight to ten billion people, given the limited global land area suitable for agriculture. The more difficult problem is whether or not it is possible to satisfy ever-growing per capita demand, including demand for "luxury" foods and meat-centered diets.

Global inequality means that widespread hunger persists even when the *average* food production on a national or global basis is adequate. Economic growth may improve the standard of living of the poorest (though this is not always true by any means), but it also encourages increased per capita consumption by the relatively affluent. Taking this into account, food consumption is likely to grow significantly faster than population.

Increasing global food production will require **intensification of production**. This means that each acre of land must produce significantly higher food output. The stresses imposed on land and water supplies, the increased fertilizer requirements, as well as the problems of erosion, chemical runoff, and pesticide pollution represent the real limits to agricultural expansion.

In Chapter 11 we will examine in more detail this interplay between population, social inequality, food consumption, food production, and environmental impacts. Certainly a focus on productive capacity alone is insufficient. Resource and environmental factors, as well as issues of equity, will be central in responding to the challenge of feeding much larger populations with limited resources.

In addition to agricultural land requirements, expanding populations require more space for urban, residential, and industrial development. These needs will tend to encroach on farmland, forests, and natural ecosystems. This population pressure on land is acute in countries such as India (794 people per square mile) or Bangladesh (2,320 people per square mile). In less densely populated areas such as the United States (74 people per square mile), land use remains a central environmental issue, with ever-increasing pressure from suburban developments on farmland and natural areas, and continual conflict between large scale agriculture or forestry and wilderness preservation.

Rising Resource Use

Resource use issues also surround the question of future population and economic growth. The original argument of the 1972 *Limits to Growth* report stressed limited supplies of key **nonrenewable resources** such as metal ores and other minerals. Since then, the focus of debate has shifted. Critics of the pessimistic position on growth limits have pointed out that new resource discoveries, new technologies for extraction and the development of substitute resources as well as expanded recycling all extend the horizon of resource use. As with food supply, the real issue may not be absolute limits on availability but rather the environmental impacts of increased **resource recovery** (mining or extraction of resources for economic use).

Mining operations, for example, are notoriously damaging to the environment. If the "average" global consumer's demand for steel rises toward the current U.S. consumption level at the same time as world population rises, requirements for iron ore will rise drastically. Plenty of iron ore remains to be extracted from the earth's crust—but at what environmental cost?

Common sense and economic theory both tell us that the highest-quality ores will be exploited first.[5] As we fall back on lower-quality ores, the energy requirements to obtain processed metal, as well as the volume of related industrial waste, rise steadily. Our present mining operations have left a legacy of scarred earth and polluted water—how will we deal with future higher-impact requirements?

Increasing Energy Use

Expansion of resource use, like expansion of agricultural output, depends on energy supply. Energy is fundamental to economic activity and to life itself, making possible the use of all other resources. Energy resource issues are therefore of special importance. Nineteenth-century economic development relied largely on coal, and twentieth-century development on oil. Our current heavy dependence on fossil fuel resources (more than 85 percent of energy use for developed economies) poses major problems for the twenty-first-century economy.

In part these issues arise from limited supplies of fossil fuels. Currently known reserves of oil and gas will be mostly exhausted within 50 years. Coal reserves will last much longer—but coal is the "dirtiest" of all fossil fuels. Coal, oil, and gas burning all contribute to ground-level air pollution as well as to global carbon emissions, an important cause of **global climate change.**

Increased population and rising living standards are projected to require significantly increased energy use over the next 40 years.[6] New less-polluting sources of energy, as well as reduction in present per capita energy use in developed nations, appear essential. The economics of this transition to alternative energy sources will be discussed in Chapter 13.

Dwindling Resources

Worldwide pressure on **renewable resources** such as forests and fisheries has become increasingly evident. **Over-harvesting of renewable resources** has caused serious environmental losses. World forest cover has declined steadily, with particularly rapid loss of tropical forest during the past several decades. After many years of steady increase, global fish catch appears close to maximum, with major fisheries now in decline.

---

[5]The economic theory of nonrenewable resources is explained in detail in Chapter 12.

[6]As we have noted, world energy use has quadrupled during the period since World War II. A 2 percent annual rate of growth in energy use, barely sufficient to keep ahead of growing population, would double it again in 35 years. Energy use, especially in developing nations, will more likely increase at least 4 percent per annum to supply industrial growth.

Exploitation of natural resources is also causing an increasing rate of species loss, posing unknown ecological hazards and diminishing the natural "inheritance" of future generations. Clearly, these pressures will only increase with rising demands for food, fuel, wood products, and fiber.

Economic theory offers an explanation for the over-harvesting phenomenon, as we will see in Chapter 5. Prescribing solutions is more difficult. Such prescriptions will certainly require a conceptual shift from regarding forests and fisheries as unrestricted **open-access resources** to perceiving them as part of a **global commons.** ("Commons" refers to resources not privately owned but managed for the social good.) Future economic development cannot simply take advantage of "free" resources such as undeveloped land and open oceans, but must be adjusted to ecological limits. In some cases, private property rights can create incentives for individual owners to conserve resources. Other situations require the development of effective regional or global common-property management policies.

Pollution

Economic growth also brings the problem of growing volumes of **cumulative pollutants** (pollutants that neither dissipate nor degrade significantly over time) and of toxic and nuclear wastes. Controls on emissions, the traditional focus of pollution policy, are of limited use in dealing with these more insidious problems. When we deal with cumulative pollutants such as chlorofluorocarbons (CFCs), organochlorides such as DDT, or radioactive wastes, we must grapple with the legacy of all previous pollution and waste production as well as consider how our present activities will affect the future environment. This greatly complicates any economic evaluation of costs and benefits.

Air and water pollutants that are not cumulative can be controlled through specific regulatory policies. But economic growth often leads to an increased volume of such pollutants. In the area of emissions control, improved technology continually races against increased consumption (automobile use is a prime example). The economic analysis of pollution control offers policy solutions for specific emissions problems, whereas the newer theory of **industrial ecology,** explored in Chapter 17, offers an overview of the relationship of pollution-generating activities to the natural environment.

An Ecological Approach to Economic Growth and the Environment

Chapters 10–18 will provide more detailed attention to the above issues. Although in each case specific policies may address individual problems, the issues together suggest a common need for a different kind of economic analysis, one that addresses a global economy in which resource and environmental considerations are much more prominent than in the past.

Rather than approaching environmental questions as an afterthought once we have dealt with the basic economic issues of production, employment, and output growth, our concept of economics must consider the environment as fundamental to the productive process. Of course, economic production has always depended on the environment, but the scale of economic activity makes a difference. So long as human activity remained on a small scale relative to the ecosystem, we could make do with an economic theory that analyzed production and consumption without regard to their environmental impacts. Now that economic production produces such widespread environmental effects, it is essential to integrate our views of economics and environment.

If we adopt a broader perspective, we must adapt the goals of economic activity themselves to ecological realities. Traditionally, the main goals of economic activity have been seen as increased production and rising per capita consumption. But in the many ways presented above, these goals pose a threat to the **environmental sustainability** of our economic system. Either the goals or the methods we choose to achieve them must be modified as population and environmental pressures increase.

The effort to balance economic and environmental goals is addressed in the theory of a **sustainable development**—economic development that provides for human needs without undermining global ecosystems and depleting essential resources. Some have complained that sustainable development is just a buzzword devoid of specific content. Others have quickly moved to appropriate the term "sustainable" to characterize only slightly modified forms of traditional economic growth. Nevertheless, the outlines of a new concept that would indeed redefine economic goals have begun to emerge.[7]

Sustainable Development

Recall that the standard view of economic growth is defined in terms of per capita GNP, meaning that total GNP must rise faster than population. Sustainable development requires different measures. Increased output of goods and services can certainly be part of the desired outcome, but equally important is the maintenance of the ecological base of the economy—fertile soils, natural ecosystems, forests, fisheries, and water systems.

As we will see in Chapter 8, techniques for modifying the measurement of national income can take such factors into account. Even so, sustainable development means more than simply a different yardstick. It also implies a different analysis of the process of production and consumption.

Sustainable Development Versus Standard Views of Economic Growth

On the production side, it is important to differentiate between renewable and nonrenewable resources. Every economy must use some nonrenewable resources, but sustainable development implies conservation or recycling of these resources and greater

---

[7]For a review of recent theory and practice in the area of sustainable development, see Harris et al., 2001.

reliance on renewables. On the consumption side, an important distinction must be drawn between wants and needs. In contrast to the standard economic paradigm, in which "dollar votes" command the marketplace and determine which goods are to be produced, sustainable development implies putting a priority on supplying basic needs before luxury goods.[8]

Also in contrast to standard economic growth theory, sustainability implies some limits to **macroeconomic scale.** Rather than projecting rates of growth indefinitely into the future, some maximum level is postulated based on the **carrying capacity** of the area (and ultimately of the planet). This in turn implies some maximum level of population above which carrying capacity—the level of population and consumption that can be sustained by the available natural resource base—will be exceeded and living standards must fall.[9]

Population and Sustainable Development

This introduction of population as a key variable in determining the limits of economic growth has implications for both developing and currently industrialized economies. For developing economies with rapid population growth rates, it means that limiting population growth is a critical element in successful development.

For industrialized economies, the role of population is different. In much of Europe and in Japan, population has stabilized, and for some countries such as Germany and Russia concern has shifted to an emerging pattern of population decline. In the United States, however, population increase continues to put pressure on both national and global ecosystems. Although the U.S. population growth rate is less dramatic than that in many developing nations (0.6 percent per annum as opposed to 2–3 percent in much of Latin America, Africa, and Asia), the much larger U.S. per capita consumption means that each additional U.S. resident creates several times the additional resource demand of, for example, an additional resident of India.

This means that population policy must be an essential element of sustainable development. Population policy must include elements of education, social policy, economic policy, and health care, including contraceptive availability, and often runs into conflict with established religious and social mores. Still, this difficult area, generally little considered in standard economic development models, is crucial for sustainability.

Agriculture and Sustainable Development

When we consider agricultural production systems, the general principle of relying as much as possible on renewable resources runs counter to much of standard agricultural "modernization." Modern food production is based on **input-intensive agriculture,** meaning that it depends heavily on additional fertilizer, pesticides, water for irrigation, and mechanization. All of these in turn depend on fossil fuel energy.

---

[8]The "basic needs" approach to development, first set forth by Streeten et al. (1981), has been further developed by Stewart (1985), Sen (1999), and UNDP (1990–2000).

[9]See Daly, 1991 and 1996, on limits to macroeconomic scale.

Traditional agriculture, based on solar energy, animal power, and human labor, has generally produced lower yields than modern agriculture.

The concept of **sustainable agriculture** combines elements of traditional and modern techniques. It emphasizes maximum use of renewable resources such as crop wastes and animal manure, as well as crop rotation, intercropping of different plant types, agroforestry, efficient irrigation, minimum-till techniques, and integrated pest management (discussed in Chapter 11). It is still an open question whether this form of agriculture can equal the yields achieved with input-intensive techniques, but its environmental impacts are less damaging, or even beneficial to the environment.

Energy and Sustainable Development

A similar issue arises as to whether **renewable energy sources** (including **solar energy**) have the capacity to replace fossil fuel dependence. The challenge is a daunting one, because renewables now supply less than 10 percent of energy in the industrialized nations. The picture is different in developing nations, where a large portion of current energy supply comes from **biomass** (wood, plant, and animal wastes). Efficient use of biomass and maintenance of forest resources can thus play an important role in energy policy. Technological advances in solar, wind, and biomass energy systems have lowered the prices of these renewable sources, and their potential for future expansion is significant both in developed and developing nations.

A huge, often unrecognized potential, lies in conservation and improved efficiency—by some estimates the developed world could reduce its energy use by at least 30 percent through these techniques with little or no effect on living standards. The traditional emphasis on **energy supply augmentation** (such as building new power plants) could thus give way to a focus on **demand-side management** (increasing efficiency and reducing energy consumption).

Because the industrialized nations now account for three quarters of global energy use (though only one quarter of global population), increased energy consumption in developing nations could possibly be offset by reductions in rich nation energy use. Negotiations over global climate policy (discussed in Chapter 18) suggest that such a tradeoff may be essential to reduce overall human impacts on the world's climate.

Sustainable Management for Natural Resources

Sustainable natural resource management implies a combination of economic and ecological perspectives. The economic theory of natural resource management, set forth in Chapters 14 and 15, shows how many management systems for resources such as forests and fisheries can lead to depletion or even extinction of the resource. Proper incentives and institutions can promote sustainable management. Current management systems for many of the world's fisheries and forests, however, are far from sustainable.

In the area of industrial pollution management the standard economic approach is to analyze the costs and benefits of various forms of pollution control to determine an economically optimal policy. This approach has its merits, fully considered in

Chapter 16, but it is insufficient for sustainability. The best pollution control policy can be overwhelmed by growth in pollution-generating activities, especially those that produce cumulative pollutants.

Attention has therefore begun to focus on the new concept of industrial ecology as a more comprehensive approach to pollution control. Using the analogy of a natural ecosystem's capacity to recycle its own wastes, this approach attempts to analyze industrial systems as a whole to identify ways in which to minimize or avoid generating pollutants and maximize resource recycling. The application of industrial ecology techniques, discussed in Chapter 17, has potential both for restructuring existing industrial systems and for economic development in Latin America, Asia, and Africa.

In all these areas, sustainable development offers a new **theoretical paradigm** different from the standard economic approach. Considering a new paradigm of thought is justified because the global reality has changed radically from an earlier period when economic policy could be formulated with little regard to environmental impacts.

Following this logic, we might roughly distinguish three periods of economic history. In the preindustrial period, human population and economic activity remained at fairly stable levels, placing only limited demands on the planetary ecosystem. During the past two hundred years of rapid industrial and population growth, economic growth has had increasingly heavy environmental impact. The process has not been uniform; in some cases improved technology or changing industrial patterns have lessened pollution and resource demand. Still, the increasing pressures already discussed suggest that we are entering a third period during which population growth and economic activity must align with ecological carrying capacity.

The tools of economic analysis we study in Part 2 are drawn from standard economic theory, and the perspectives presented in Part 3 respond to the issues of ecological limits on economic growth. The two in combination provide a powerful toolbox of analytical techniques with which to address the multifaceted questions of the interrelationship between environment and economy.

SUMMARY

Economic growth over time reflects both population and per capita GNP growth. This growth depends on increases in capital stock and technological progress, as well as increased supplies of energy, natural resources, and the capacity of the environment to absorb wastes.

A simple model of the relationship between population, industrial output, resources, and pollution indicates that unlimited economic growth will lead to exhaustion of resources, rising pollution, and eventual collapse of economic systems and ecosystems. However, such a model depends on assumptions about technological progress and feedback patterns among the variables in the model. A more optimistic view considers increased efficiency, pollution control, and a transition to alternative, more sustainable technologies.

During the second half of the twentieth century, unprecedented rates of growth roughly doubled population, tripled world agricultural production, and quadrupled world GNP and energy use. Continuing population and economic growth will exert even greater demands on resources and the environment during the first half of the twenty-first century. Food production, nonrenewable resource recovery, energy supply, atmospheric pollution, toxic wastes, and renewable resource management are all major issues requiring detailed analysis and policy solutions. In addition, the nature of economic growth itself must adapt to environmental and resource constraints.

The concept of sustainable development attempts to combine economic and environmental goals. Sustainable techniques for agricultural production, energy use, natural resource management, and industrial production have significant potential, but have yet to be widely adopted. A sustainable global economy also implies some limits on population and material consumption. The question of the sustainability of economic activity has already become a major issue, and will be even more important in coming decades.

KEY TERMS AND CONCEPTS

absorptive capacity of the environment
biomass
capital stock
carrying capacity
cumulative pollutants
demand-side management
energy supply augmentation
environmental sustainability
global climate change
global commons
GNP growth rate
industrial ecology
input-intensive agriculture
intensification of production
macroeconomic scale
natural capital
nominal GNP
nonrenewable resources

open-access resources
over-harvesting of renewable resources
per capita GNP growth rate
population growth rate
population momentum
productivity per capita
real GNP
renewable energy sources
renewable resources
resource recovery
solar energy
sustainable agriculture
sustainable development
sustainable natural resource management
technological innovation
theoretical paradigm

DISCUSSION QUESTIONS

1. Can we safely say that the Malthusian hypothesis has been refuted by history? What main factors have worked against Malthus's perspective? How might that perspective still be relevant today?

2. Over the past several decades, people have worried about the world running out of oil or natural resources. Ample oil remains for current needs, however, and no important resources have run short. Have these fears been exaggerated? How would you evaluate them, considering both past experience and future prospects?

3. Does an improved standard of living necessarily mean more consumption? Is it possible to envision a future in which consumption of many goods and natural resources would decline? If this happened would it mean an end to economic growth? How might perception of these questions differ between, for example, a citizen of the United States and a citizen of India?

REFERENCES

Daly, Herman E. *Beyond Growth: The Economics of Sustainable Development.* Boston: Beacon Press, 1996.

Daly, Herman E. "Elements of Environmental Macroeconomics," in Robert Costanza, ed., *Ecological Economics: The Science and Management of Sustainability.* New York: Columbia University Press, 1991.

Food and Agriculture Organization of the United Nations (FAO), *Production Report.* Rome: FAO, 1996, 1998.

Food and Agriculture Organization of the United Nations, FAOSTAT database, 2000.

Harris, Jonathan M. "Carrying Capacity in Agriculture: Global and Regional Issues," *Ecological Economics* 29 no. 3 (June 1999): 443–461.

Harris, Jonathan M., Timothy A. Wise, Kevin Gallagher, and Neva R. Goodwin, eds. *A Survey of Sustainable Development.* Washington, D.C.: Island Press, 2001.

Malthus, Thomas Robert. *Essay on the Principle of Population as It Affects the Future Improvement of Society.* Original publication 1798.

Meadows, Donnella H. et al., *The Limits to Growth.* New York: Universe Books, 1972.

Meadows, Donnella, et al., *Beyond The Limits: Confronting Global Collapse, Envisioning a Sustainable Future.* White River Junction, Vt.: Chelsea Green, 1992.

Sen, Amartya. *Development as Freedom.* New York: Knopf, 2000.

Stewart, Frances. *Basic Needs in Developing Countries.* Baltimore: Johns Hopkins University Press, 1985.

Streeten, Paul, et al., *First Things First: Meeting Basic Needs in Developing Countries.* New York: Oxford University Press, 1981.

United Nations Development Programme (UNDP). *Human Development Report 1990–2000.* New York: Oxford University Press, 1990–2000.

United States Department of Energy. *International Energy Outlook.* Washington, D.C.: Energy Information Administration, 1999.

World Bank. *World Development Report 1992: Development and the Environment.* (New York, Oxford University Press, 1992).

World Bank. *World Development Report 1998/1999: Knowledge for Development.* (New York: Oxford University Press, 1999).

WEB SITES

1. **http://www.iisd.org/** The home page for the International Institute for Sustainable Development, an organization that conducts policy research towards the goal of integrating environmental stewardship and economic development.
2. **http://www.epa.gov/economics/** The web site for the National Center for Environmental Economics, a division of the U.S. Environmental Protection Agency that conducts and supervises research on environmental economics. Their web site includes links to many research reports.
3. **http://www.ase.tufts.edu/gdae/** The home page for the Global Development and Environment Institute at Tufts University, "dedicated to promoting a new understanding of how societies can pursue their economic goals in an environmentally and socially sustainable manner." The site includes links to many research publications.
4. **http://www.foe.org/** The home page for Friends of the Earth, an "environmental organization dedicated to preserving the health and diversity of the planet for future generations." The web site includes links to many publications on environmental issues as well as an "Economics for the Earth" program.

TWO

Economic Analysis of Environmental Issues

CHAPTER FOCUS QUESTIONS

- How can pollution and environmental damage be represented in economics?
- What economic policies effectively respond to environmental problems?
- How do property rights and market processes relate to environmental issues?

CHAPTER **3**

The Theory of Environmental Externalities

External Costs and Benefits

Economic theory deals with costs and benefits. For most goods and services, economic theory represents benefits by a demand curve and costs by a supply curve. The demand and supply curves show us the **marginal benefits** and **marginal costs**—that is, the benefits and costs of producing or consuming one more unit.

Consider, for example, the automobile industry. The **market demand schedule** for automobiles shows how many automobiles consumers are willing to purchase, generally indicating that more will be purchased at lower prices. The **market supply schedule** shows how many automobiles the producers will be willing to put on the market at various prices, reflecting their costs of production. Combining the two schedules gives a **market equilibrium,** which shows the price and quantity traded. So far so good. But, as we know, automobile production and operation have significant environmental effects. Where do these appear in economic analysis?

The answer is that they do not appear in basic supply and demand analysis, nor are they reflected in the real-world market equilibrium of automobile price and quantity

37

produced, unless specific laws and institutions are created to address them. They are what economists call **environmental externalities.**

Automobiles are a major contributor to air pollution, including both urban smog and regional problems such as acid rain. In addition, their carbon dioxide emissions contribute to global warming, and coolants escaping from older-model automobile air conditioners contribute to depletion of the ozone layer. Automobile oil is a significant cause of groundwater pollution. Automobile production involves toxic materials that may be released to the environment or may remain as toxic wastes. Road systems pave over many acres of rural and open land, and salt runoff from roads damages watersheds.

Accounting for Environmental Costs

Clearly, automobile production and use incur many real costs not included in the manufacturer's cost schedule.[1] Neglecting these costs produces a distorted picture of reality. To improve our supply and demand analysis so as to include them, we must look for ways of **internalizing externalities**—bringing these environmental costs into our market analysis.

Our first problem in doing this is assigning a money value to environmental damages. How can we reduce the complex environmental effects we have identified to a single dollar value? There is no clear-cut answer to this question. In some cases, economic damages may be identifiable: for example, if road runoff pollutes a town's water supply, the cost of water treatment gives at least one estimate of environmental damage—but this excludes less tangible factors such as damage to lake and river ecosystems.

Identifying health problems related to air pollution and their resulting medical expenses furnishes another monetary damage estimate—but this ignores the aesthetic damage done by air pollution. Smoggy air is unpleasant, regardless of any measurable effect it has on your health. Such issues are difficult to compress into a monetary indicator. Yet if we fail to assign some value to environmental damage, the market will automatically assign a value of zero, because none of these issues are directly reflected in consumer and producer decisions about automobiles.

Various techniques exist for estimation of environmental externalities. We will examine some of these in more detail in Chapter 6. But suppose we agree for now that some significant costs exist, even if we can't measure them precisely. It is clearly important to account for these costs in economic analysis.

Figure 3-1 shows a simple way of introducing these costs into supply and demand analysis. The supply curve for automobiles (S) already embodies all the production costs of automobiles, including labor, capital, and raw materials. Together with the demand curve (D), it determines a market equilibrium e, with price P_1 and quantity Q_1. We simply add to these costs an estimate of the **external costs** associated with environmental damage. This gives us a new, higher curve showing the combination of market costs and external costs. This curve S' depicts a **social cost** schedule—it shows

---

[1]See, for example, Cobb, 1998.

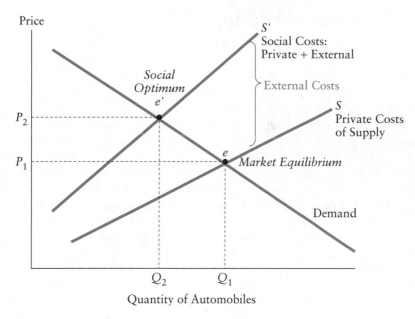

FIGURE 3-1 *Automobile Market with External Costs*

the real costs to society of operating automobiles, taking into account both production costs and environmental externalities.

We could also include in social costs other externalities not strictly environmental—for example, the costs of congestion as more automobiles fill the roads. We could use the value of time wasted in traffic jams in forming a money estimate of this externality. Congestion will also raise the air pollution costs as cars idle in traffic. S' reflects the impact of all these unintended but significant effects associated with the production and use of automobiles.

Now let's consider how the introduction of externalities into supply and demand analysis affects economic equilibrium. Of course, drawing a new curve on a graph has no effect on real-world decisions to produce and purchase automobiles, but it affects our understanding of market equilibrium. In neoclassical price theory, market equilibrium, shown here at e, is generally considered to achieve **economic efficiency** in the automobile market. Once we introduce external costs into our analysis, this concept of efficient equilibrium changes.

Because the market process automatically balances benefits to consumers (reflected in the demand curve) and costs of production (reflected in the supply curve), it ensures that the "right amount" of cars will be produced at a price that accurately reflects production costs. But if we believe the market process misses significant extra costs—environmental externalities—we can no longer consider the equilibrium reached through the market efficient. From this point of view, the *wrong* quantity of cars is being produced at a price that *fails* to reflect true costs.

Internalizing Environmental Costs

If significant externalities exist, what can correct this inefficient market equilibrium? Internalizing externalities can occur in several ways. One example would be a tax on automobiles. We could call this a **pollution tax,** whose object is not primarily to raise revenue for the government (though that will be one result), but to bring home to the purchaser of automobiles the real environmental costs of his or her actions.

Figure 3-2 shows the impact of such a tax on the market for automobiles. At the new equilibrium e', the price rises to P_2, and the quantity consumed decreases to Q_2. From the point of view of economic efficiency, these are good effects. Consumers may complain about higher prices, but these prices reflect the real costs of automobile use to society. Fewer cars will be sold, which reduces pollution. We are now closer to a truly efficient equilibrium, or **social optimum,** than we were at the unmodified market equilibrium e.

Other issues, however, remain to be considered. What if the tax is too high? or too low? Will the same tax apply to compact cars and gas guzzlers? Might it not be better to measure and tax automobile emissions directly, rather than place a tax on automobile sales? How about taxing gasoline instead? Automobiles and gasoline are **complementary goods,** meaning that they tend to be used together. Thus we could internalize the effects of automobile pollution either by taxing cars themselves, or by taxing gas, or by taxing emissions.

Regardless of the exact mechanism we use, the idea of internalizing environmental costs through some kind of tax is well supported by economic theory. We determine the size of the tax by some process of **environmental valuation,** the topic of

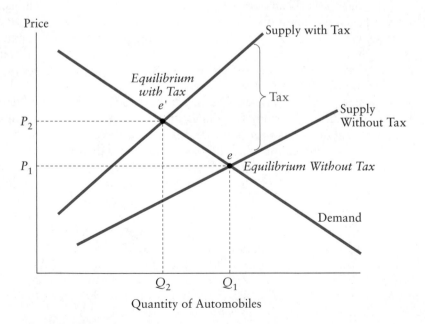

FIGURE 3-2 *Automobile Market with Pollution Tax*

Chapter 6. If we are satisfied with this valuation process, a tax may be the best tool to accomplish the goal of environmental protection.

Other policies, however, may sometimes prove preferable to a pollution tax. **Government regulation,** such as tailpipe emission standards or the CAFE standards[2] requiring certain levels of average fuel efficiency, have a similar effect. They reduce total fuel consumption and total pollution. Such requirements for more efficient and less polluting engines also tend to drive up the purchase price of automobiles (although greater fuel efficiency will reduce operating costs).

Positive Externalities

Just as it is in society's interest to internalize the social costs of pollution, it is also socially beneficial to internalize the **social benefits** of activities that generate positive externalities. For example, many suburban and rural towns have instituted open land preservation programs. Using tax incentives or public purchases, they seek to maintain or increase the amount of open and rural land. Why do they do this?

Regardless of a private landowner's particular reasons for keeping land open or using it as farmland, significant **external benefits** accrue from such uses: Others who live in town may enjoy the sight of natural areas and farmland close to their homes. A beautiful setting may significantly increase surrounding property values, whereas an industrial or residential development nearby would lower them. External benefits are not limited to town residents. Passers-by, hikers, bicyclists, and out-of-state tourists may all gain satisfaction, or **utility,** from the pleasant scenery.

Figure 3-3 on page 44 shows an economic analysis of the situation. Marginal social benefits exceed marginal private benefits because they include gains to neighbors and passers-by as well as to private landowners. The market demand curve for rural uses of land will reflect private, but not social benefits, leading to an equilibrium at the **private optimum.** At the social optimum Q_p, including the benefits to nonowners, a larger quantity of land remains as open and rural land than at the private market equilibrium Q_s.

Internalizing Environmental Benefits

From an economic point of view, policies such as tax incentives are **subsidies** for the protection of open land. It is in the social interest to encourage landowners, by lowering their costs through tax rebates or purchase of development rights,[3] to keep land in an undisturbed state. The subsidy is shown in Figure 3-4 on page 44 as a downward shift in marginal private costs, increasing the quantity of open land to Q_s. The principle parallels the use of a tax to discourage economic activities that create negative ex-

---

[2]Corporate Average Fuel Economy (CAFE) refers to average standards that major automobile manufacturers must meet. For discussion of the use of standards versus taxes, see Baumol and Oates, 1993 and Tietenberg, 2000.

[3]In development-rights purchase programs, a town or state buys the rights to development on private land. The landowner retains ownership of the land, but cannot use it for industrial or residential development. For further discussion of this issue see Hodge, 1995.

| 3-1 | The External Costs of Motor Vehicle Use |

Driving a motor vehicle in the United States incurs not only direct costs but also external, or social, costs. Gasoline taxes cover only some external costs, others we pay in higher healthcare costs, decreased environmental quality, and higher personal taxes.

Annually in the United States, motor vehicles emit about fifty million tons of carbon monoxide, seven million tons of nitrogen oxides, as well as other toxins including formaldehyde and benzene. Annually, U.S. motor vehicle accidents kill more than forty thousand people and injure more than three million. Additional external costs include natural habitat destruction from building roads and parking lots, vehicle and parts disposal, costs associated with national security in securing petroleum supplies, and noise pollution.

Delucchi's 1997 twenty-volume study is perhaps the most ambitious attempt to monetize the external costs of motor vehicle use. The report estimates costs associated with air pollution, crop losses, reduced visibility, national security, noise pollution, and so forth. The public sector pays some of these costs; others become external social losses.

The study used low-estimate assumptions to figure total annual monetary and nonmonetary externality costs at $99 billion and high-estimate assumptions for a figure of $879 billion. Annual public sector costs for motor vehicle infrastructure and services were estimated as $132 billion and $241 billion. Total public sector and social costs were $231 billion or $1,120 billion per year depending on the set of assumptions.

A comparable analysis (Cobb, 1998) figured at least $184 billion per year in U.S. public sector and social costs for motor vehicle use. Free parking subsidies and cross-subsidies caused by congestion amounted to another $50–$100 billion per year.

Cobb suggests an additional gasoline tax of $1.60 per gallon to internalize more social costs, although some costs would still remain. Delucchi notes that fully internalizing all costs associated with motor vehicle use would require a range of policy approaches. For example, air pollution externalities should be internalized based on a vehicle's emissions level rather than on gasoline consumption.

Although scientific and economic uncertainty render even the best attempt to internalize motor vehicle use externalities imperfect, failure to try sends a signal to consumers that the external costs are effectively zero. Delucchi and Cobb's results suggest that although fully internalizing costs may be impractical, implementing cost-internalizing policies could increase economic efficiency.

(continued on following page)

Selected Public Sector and Social Costs of Motor Vehicle Use, 1991
(Billions of 1991 dollars)

Cost Category	Low Estimate	High Estimate
Public Sector Costs		
Highways and parking	$109.7	$196.7
Pollution regulation and control	$3.2	$8.1
Highway patrol and safety	$7.4	$8.4
National security costs associated with Persian Gulf oil	$0.6	$7.0
Other public sector costs	$11.2	$27.7
Externality Costs		
Imposed travel delays	$33.9	$135.5
Accident costs—pain, death, lost productivity, damages	$23.3	$169.0
Air pollution—human mortality and morbidity	$24.3	$450.0
Air pollution—loss of visibility	$5.1	$36.9
Air pollution—damage to crops, materials, and forests	$2.7	$13.9
Global warming	$0.5	$9.2
Noise pollution	$0.5	$15.0
Water pollution	$2.8	$7.2
Other externality costs	$6.4	$42.6
Total public sector and externality costs	$231.0	$1,120.2

Source: Delucchi, 1997.

SOURCES

Cobb, Clifford W. *The Roads Aren't Free: Estimating the Full Social Costs of Driving and the Effects of Accurate Pricing.* Resource Incentives Program Working Paper No. 3. San Francisco: Redefining Progress, 1998.

Delucchi, Mark A. *The Annualized Social Cost of Motor Vehicle Use in the U.S., 1990–1991: Summary of Theory, Data, Methods, and Results.* Report #1 in series: The Annualized Social Cost of Motor Vehicle Use in the United States, based on 1990–1991 data. Report number UCD-ITS-RR-96-3(1). Davis, Calif.: Institute of Transportation Studies, University of California, 1997.

ICF Incorporated. *Opportunities to Improve Air Quality through Transportation Pricing Programs.* Report prepared for the Office of Mobile Sources, U.S. Environmental Protection Agency, 1997.

U.S. Department of Transportation. *Transportation Statistics Annual Report 1999.* Report number BTS99-03, 1999.

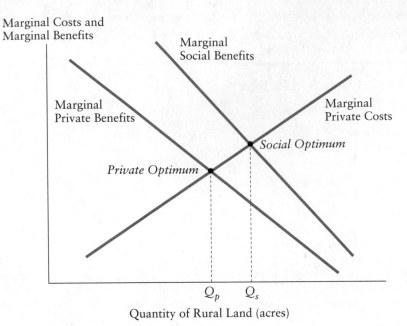

FIGURE 3-3 *A Positive Externality*

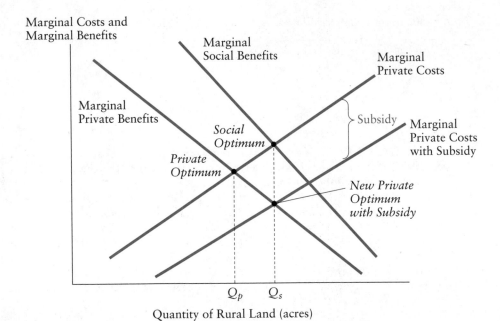

FIGURE 3-4 *A Subsidy for Open and Rural Land Use*

ternalities—except that in this case we want to encourage economic uses of land that have socially beneficial side effects.

Welfare Analysis of Externalities

We can use a form of economic theory called **welfare analysis** to show why it is socially preferable to internalize externalities. The idea, as shown in Figure 3-5, is that *areas* on a supply and demand graph can be used to measure total benefits and costs.[4] The area under the demand curve shows total benefit; the area under the supply curve shows total cost. For each unit purchased, the demand curve measures the value of that unit to consumers, while the supply curve reflects the cost to suppliers.

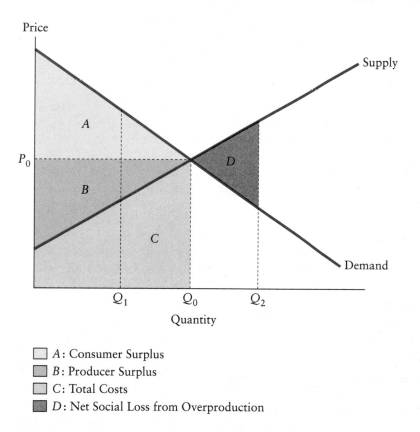

□ A: Consumer Surplus
□ B: Producer Surplus
□ C: Total Costs
■ D: Net Social Loss from Overproduction

FIGURE 3-5 *Welfare Analysis of the Automobile Market*

---

[4]The supply and demand schedules show the *marginal* benefits and costs for each individual unit produced. Therefore, the areas under these curves in effect sum up the *total* benefits and costs for all units produced.

Welfare Analysis Without Externalities

The total value of Q_0 units purchased is shown by areas $A + B + C$. The total cost of producing these units is area C. $A + B$ is the **net social benefit** from the production and consumption of Q_0 units—in other words, the amount by which total benefit exceeds total cost. Part A of this net social benefit goes to consumers as **consumer surplus**—it represents the difference between their benefits from consumption of automobiles, as shown by the demand curve, and the price they pay, as shown by the horizontal line at P_0. Part B goes to producers as **producer surplus**—the difference between their production costs, shown by the supply curve, and the price P_0 that they receive.

Economists call market equilibrium efficient because it maximizes net social benefit. If we were to produce less than Q_0 units, or more, net benefit would be less than at Q_0. At Q_1, for example, the net benefit is only part of the area $A + B$. At Q_2, we realize the full net benefit $A + B$, but we also experience some **net social loss,** shown here by area D. The overall social benefit, then, is $A + B - D$, a lower amount than at Q_0. Thus Q_0, as we have argued, is in some sense the "right" amount to produce.

Welfare Analysis with Externalities

If we introduce external costs (Figure 3-6), the combination of private and external costs gives a social cost curve S', which lies above the ordinary supply curve. The market equilibrium Q_0 no longer maximizes net social benefit. With the new higher total social cost curve, social benefit is only $A' + B'$. The area D' is social loss, so that the overall net social benefit is $A' + B' - D'$. We would do better to lower production to Q_1, avoiding the net social loss D'. And of course this is exactly what we seek to accomplish with a pollution tax.

Notice that in this example the area $C' + D'$ indicates the **total cost of pollution** at point Q_0. But of this total cost, only D' is considered net social loss. According to this analysis, some pollution costs are justifiable—provided they are outweighed by social benefits from production. Only when the combined costs of production and of pollution $(C + C' + D')$ rise above the benefits shown by the demand curve do we produce "too much" pollution.

Optimal Pollution

This analysis leads to a concept that to some seems paradoxical: the doctrine of **optimal pollution.** At our socially optimal equilibrium Q_1, we still have some pollution costs (the part of C' to the left of Q_1). According to our analysis, this is the "optimal" amount of pollution, given current production costs and technologies. But, you might object, isn't the optimal amount of pollution *zero*? How can we call any amount of pollution "optimal"?

The economist's answer would be that the only way to achieve zero pollution is to have zero production. If we want to produce virtually any manufactured good, some pollution will result. We as a society must decide what level of pollution we are willing to accept. Of course, we can strive to reduce this level over time, especially through better pollution-reducing technology, but as long as we have production, we will have an "optimal" pollution level.

Some people remain uneasy with the concept of optimal pollution. Note, for example, that if demand for automobiles increases, the demand curve will shift to the right, and the "optimal" pollution level will increase. This suggests that as global demand for automobiles rises steadily, ever-rising levels of pollution will in some sense be acceptable. Does society have a right to increase pollution just because we want more goods? This analysis would seem to imply that the answer is yes.

The issue is by no means a purely academic one. During the past thirty years, improvements in automotive technology have reduced pollution per car as well as total automotive pollution in the United States. Nevertheless, with ever more cars on the road, total pollution levels for at least some major pollutants may soon start to rise again, after a period of decline. Carbon dioxide emissions from the U.S. transportation sector have been on the rise since the early 1980s. On a global scale, the potential is enormous for increased automobile pollution as demand rises. Certainly few could call this trend "optimal."

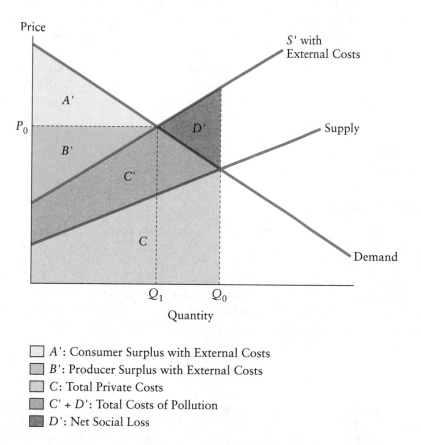

A': Consumer Surplus with External Costs
B': Producer Surplus with External Costs
C: Total Private Costs
$C' + D'$: Total Costs of Pollution
D': Net Social Loss

FIGURE 3-6 *Welfare Analysis of the Automobile Market with Pollution Costs*

Property Rights and the Coase Theorem

The theory of externalities also raises another fundamental issue, that of rights. Do I have a right to drive my automobile even though it pollutes? Do others have a right to be protected from the effects of my vehicle's waste products? When we talk about prices, values, and costs, our discussion is actually about underlying rights. Patterns of resource allocation are determined by the underlying assignment of rights.

Pigovian Tax

Let's consider a simple case of **property rights.** A factory operating in a rural area emits pollutants from its stacks. The pollutants damage the crops of the neighboring farm. The externality might be remedied by imposing a tax on the factory equal to the value of the damage caused to the farmer's crops. This method of responding to externalities is known as a **Pigovian tax,** after Arthur Pigou, a well-known British economist who published his *Economics of Welfare* in 1920. It has come to be known as the **polluter pays principle,** which sounds like a reasonable solution to many people.

However, the Pigovian approach has been much criticized by economic theorists. Suppose we take a different, less clear-cut case. A farmer drains a swamp on his property to create a field suitable for growing crops. His downstream neighbor complains that without the swamp to absorb heavy rainfalls, her land now floods—damaging her crops. Should the first farmer have the right to do what he wants on his own land, or should he be obliged to pay the second farmer the value of crop damages?

This issue involves not just externalities but also the nature of property rights. Does the ownership of land include a right to drain swamps on that land? Or is this right separate, subject to control by the community or other property owners?

The Coase Theorem

We could resolve the problem in two ways. Suppose we say that the first farmer (we'll call him Albert) *does* have the right to drain the swamp. But let's also suppose that the net value of crops grown on the former swampland would be only $2,000, and the net value of crops damaged on the second farmer's land would be $6,000. The two farmers might reach an agreement. The second farmer (call her Betty) can offer an amount between $2,000 and $6,000—say, $4,000—to Albert in return for an agreement *not* to drain the swamp. Betty will not be happy about this, but she's better off giving up $4,000 than losing her $6,000 crop. Albert will also be better off taking the $4,000 than making a mere $2,000 growing crops on drained land. In effect, Betty purchases the right to say how the swampland will be used (without having to purchase the land itself).

We can also assign the relevant right to Betty, by passing a law stating that no one can drain swampland without the agreement of any affected parties downstream. In that case, Albert must reach an agreement with Betty before draining the swamp. With the crop values we have assumed, the same result would occur—the swamp would not be drained, because the value of doing so to Albert ($2,000) would not compensate Betty for her loss. Betty would demand at least $6,000 to grant her permission, a price too high for Albert.

Now suppose a new gourmet crop item becomes popular, a crop that grows well on former swampland and would bring Albert $10,000 in revenues. A deal is now possible—Albert would pay Betty $8,000 for the right to drain the swamp and earn $10,000 for the new crop, netting $2,000 profit for himself and leaving Betty $2,000 better off as well.

The principle at issue in this simple example has come to be known as the **Coase theorem,** after Ronald Coase, a Nobel Prize–winning economist who discussed similar examples of property rights and externalities in his famous article "The Problem of Social Cost."[5] The Coase theorem states that if property rights are well defined, and no significant **transactions costs** exist, an efficient allocation of resources will result even with externalities. Transactions costs are the costs of conducting negotiations—in the case of Albert and Betty, these costs should be low because they need only talk the issue over, although some legal costs may be involved in formalizing an agreement.

Through negotiations, the two parties will balance the external costs against the economic benefits of a given action (in this case, draining the swamp). In the example above, the external costs were $6,000. An economic benefit of $2,000 would not justify incurring these costs, but an economic benefit of $10,000 would. Regardless of which farmer holds the property right, this "efficient" result will occur through negotiation.

The principle of the Coase theorem can also be expressed in terms of a **right to pollute.** This sounds strange, but it is similar to the principle embodied in, for example, the U.S. Clean Air Act of 1990. This act creates a system of permits to emit such pollutants as sulfur oxides and nitrogen oxides; these permits can be traded among polluting industries. Individual firms can acquire rights to increase their own pollution—provided they purchase them from other firms that reduce pollution by an equal amount. By controlling the total number of permits issued, the government can gradually reduce overall pollution.

It is also possible for public interest groups to buy up pollution permits and retire them, permanently reducing pollution totals. In effect, this system turns pollution, and pollution reduction, into marketable goods. From the economist's point of view, it has the advantage of efficiency and can be a practical application of the "right to pollute" principle.

Applying the Coase Theorem

We can illustrate the Coase theorem by showing the marginal benefits and marginal costs of an economic activity that generates an externality. Suppose, for example, a factory emits effluent into a river, polluting the water supply of a downstream community. The factory is currently emitting one hundred units of effluent. If forced to reduce effluent to zero, the company operating the factory would have to abandon a

---

[5]Coase, 1960, reprinted in Stavins, 2000.

valuable production line. Thus we can say that the company gains marginal benefits from emitting pollution, and the community incurs marginal costs through damage to the water supply. We might form a reasonable quantitative estimate of these external costs by estimating the costs of water treatment. Figure 3-7 shows both marginal costs and marginal benefits.

What is the optimal solution? The emission of 100 units of pollution clearly imposes high marginal costs on the community and brings the company lower marginal benefits. This is "too much" pollution. But suppose emissions were limited to 60 units. Marginal benefits to the company would then equal marginal costs to the community. A further limitation to, say, 20 units, would result in high additional loss to the company and bring only low additional benefit to the community. The efficient or "optimal" solution, therefore, is at 60 units of pollution. At this level the extra benefit to the company from production just balances the extra cost imposed on the community through pollution.

This solution can be achieved by assigning the pollution rights either to the company *or* to the community. Suppose the community has the right to say how much pollution can be emitted. The company can offer them up to $200 per unit for pollution permits to allow 60 units of pollution. The company can afford to pay this much; their marginal benefits from producing 60 units exceed $200 up to the sixtieth unit. It will also be to the community's advantage to accept this offer, granting permits for 60 units of pollution at $200 each. The first 60 units of pollution impose less than $200 per unit of costs on the community.

Costs and Benefits per Unit

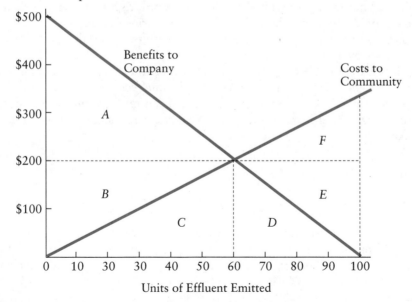

FIGURE 3-7 *Application of the Coase Theorem*

We can measure the total cost of pollution at this level as the area C on the graph, or $6,000. But the amount the company pays to the community will be $B + C$ or $60 \times $200 = $12,000$. The community can then pay $6,000 to treat the water and still come out $6,000 ahead. The company gains $A + B + C = $21,000$ in benefits, pays $12,000, and has a net profit of $9,000 (area A).

We can also assign the right to pollute to the company. Would they then emit the full one hundred units of pollution? If they did so their gain would be areas $A + B + C + D = $25,000$. They can do better by negotiating with the community. The community will pay them up to $200 per unit, or areas $D + E = $8,000$, to cut back their pollution to only 60 units. This saves the community $D + E + F = $10,667$ in environmental damage or water treatment costs. They still suffer environmental costs equal to C, or $6,000. The company's net gain will now be $A + B + C + D + E = $29,000$, better for them than the maximum pollution option. This approach may seem unfair to the community, but it leads to the same equilibrium solution—60 units of pollution emitted—as when the community held the right to control pollution levels.

This more formal demonstration of the Coase theorem shows that the participants reach the efficient solution regardless of who holds the property right governing pollution. Provided that right is clearly defined, the party who values it most highly will acquire it, with the result that the external costs of pollution and the economic benefits of production are balanced through the marketplace.

Note, however, that the assignment of the right makes a big difference in distribution of gains and losses between the two parties (see Table 3-1). The net social benefit from production is the same in both cases: area $A + B = $15,000$. In one case, however, this benefit is divided between the community and the company. In the other case, the community has a net loss of $14,000 and the company a net gain of $29,000 (for an overall social net benefit of $29,000 − $14,000 = $15,000$).

The value of the right to pollute, or to control pollution, is $20,000 in this case. By redistributing that right, we make one party $20,000 better off and the other $20,000 worse off. The different assignments of rights are equivalent in terms of efficiency because the final result balances marginal benefits and marginal costs, but they clearly differ in terms of **equity**, or social justice.

TABLE 3-1 *Different Assignments of Pollution Rights*

	If Community Holds Rights	*If Company Holds Rights*
Net Gain/Loss to Community	$12,000 payment	−$8,000 payment
	−$6,000 environ. cost	−$6,000 environ. cost
	$6,000	−$14,000
Net Gain/Loss to Company	$21,000 benefits	$21,000 benefits
	−$12,000 payment	$8,000 payment
	$9,000	$29,000
Net Social Gain	$15,000	$15,000

Limitations of the Coase Theorem

According to the Coase theorem, the clear assignment of property rights appears to promise fully efficient solutions to problems involving externalities. In theory, if we could clearly assign property rights to *all* environmental externalities, no further government intervention would be required. Individuals and business firms would negotiate all pollution control and other environmental issues among themselves once it was clear who had the "right to pollute," or the "right to be free from pollution."

This is the basis for the approach known as **free market environmentalism.** In effect, this approach seeks to bring the environment into the marketplace by setting up a system of property rights in the environment and allowing the free market to handle issues of resource use and pollution regulation.

As we will see in dealing with specific examples in future chapters, this approach has significant potential, especially in areas such as water rights. New markets may evolve, such as a market in tradable permits for airborne pollutants. But there are also significant problems with this approach, in terms of both efficiency and equity. The use of market mechanisms to solve environmental problems turns out to have crucial limitations.

Community protest against pollution from a gasoline tank farm in Texas. Both economic and political power affect the ability of communities to defend their environment.

The Free Rider Effect

One important limitation derives from the assumption of no transactions costs, stated in the Coase theorem. Our previous examples have had only two parties in the negotiation. In more typical cases, environmental issues affect many parties. If, for example, fifty downstream communities are affected by pollution from a factory's effluent, negotiating effluent limits becomes very cumbersome and perhaps impossible.

Suppose we assign the factory the right to pollute. The communities can then offer compensation for reducing pollution. But which community will pay what share? Unless all fifty can agree, making a specific offer to the company will be impossible. No single community, or group of communities, is likely to step forward to pay the whole bill. In fact, many may hang back, waiting for other communities to "buy off" the factory—and supply the rest with free pollution control benefits. This barrier to successful negotiations is known as the **free rider effect.**

The Holdout Effect

A similar problem arises if the communities have the right to be free from pollution, and the factory must compensate them for any pollution emitted. Who will determine how much compensation each community receives? With all the communities situated on the same river, any single community can exercise a kind of veto power—a problem known as the **holdout effect.** Suppose forty-nine communities have hammered out an agreement with the company on permissible pollution levels and compensation. The fiftieth community can demand a much higher rate of compensation, for if they withhold their consent the whole agreement will fail and the company will be restricted to zero pollution (that is, forced to shut down).

Public Choice Versus Private Choice

In general, the Coase theorem is inapplicable where large numbers of parties are affected. Such cases require regulation, a Pigovian tax, or some other form of government intervention. The state or federal government might set a standard for waterborne effluent or a tax per unit of effluent. Although taxation has its impact through market processes, this would not be a pure market solution because government officials determine the degree of regulation or taxation. Economists call this a process of **public choice** rather than the process of **private choice** characteristic of the market solutions.[6]

---

[6]For further discussion of private property rights and the environment, see Schmid, 1995.

3-2   Property Rights and Environmental Regulation

Governments can apply the principle of eminent domain to appropriate private property for public purposes. However, the Fifth Amendment of the U.S. Constitution requires that the property owner be fairly compensated. Specifically, the Fifth Amendment concludes with the statement—"nor shall private property be taken for public use, without just compensation."

A government action that deprives someone of their property rights is referred to as a "takings." When the takings removes all property rights, the U.S. Constitution clearly orders full compensation. For example, if a state government decides to build a highway through a parcel of private property, the landowner must receive the property's fair market value.

A more ambiguous situation arises when a government action limits property use and, consequently, reduces property value. Instances of government regulations reducing the value of private property are often called "regulatory takings." Suppose, for example, a new law regulates timber harvesting and reduces the value of private forests. Are the landowners entitled to compensation under the Fifth Amendment?

The most notable case concerning a regulatory takings is *Lucas* v. *South Carolina Coastal Council.* David Lucas, a real estate developer, purchased two oceanfront lots in 1986 and planned to construct vacation homes. However, in 1988 the South Carolina state legislature enacted the Beachfront Management Act, which prohibited Lucas from building any permanent structures on the property. Lucas filed suit claiming that the legislation had deprived him of all "economically viable use" of his property.

A trial court ruled in Lucas's favor, concluding that the legislation had rendered his property "valueless," and awarded him $1.2 million in damages. When the South Carolina Supreme Court reversed this decision, the court ruled that further construction in the area posed a significant threat to a public resource and in cases where a regulation is intended to prevent "harmful or noxious uses" of private property no compensation is required.

The case was appealed to the U.S. Supreme Court. Although the Supreme Court overturned the state court ruling, it delineated a distinction between total and partial takings. Compensation is necessary only in cases of total takings— when a regulation deprives a property owner of "all economically beneficial uses." A regulation that merely reduces a property's value requires no compensation.

In essence, this ruling represented a victory for environmentalists because cases of total takings are rare. Partial takings as a result of government regulations, on the other hand, are common. A requirement of compensation for partial takings would have created a legal and technical morass that would effectively render

(continued on following page)

many environmental laws ineffective. Still, partial takings can incur significant costs to individuals, and the debate continues over equity when private costs are necessary to achieve the public good.

SOURCES

Ausness, Richard C. "Regulatory Takings and Wetland Protection in the Post-Lucas Era." *Land and Water Law Review* 30, no. 2 (1995): 349–414.
Johnson, Stephen M. "Defining the Property Interest: A Vital Issue in Wetlands Takings Analysis After Lucas." *Journal of Energy, Natural Resources & Environmental Law* 14, no. 1 (1994): 41–82.
Hollingsworth, Lorraine. "*Lucas* v. *South Carolina Coastal Commission:* A New Approach to the Takings Issue." *Natural Resources Journal* 34, no. 2 (1994): 479–496.

The Coase Theorem and Equity

Other criticisms of the Coase theorem concern its effects on equity. Suppose that in our original example the community suffering from pollution is a low-income community. Even if the water pollution is causing serious health problems with medical costs of millions of dollars, the community may simply be unable to "buy off" the polluter. In this case, the market solution clearly is not independent of the assignment of property rights. Pollution levels will be significantly higher if the right to pollute is assigned to the company.

It is also possible that, even if the right is assigned to the community, poor communities will accept location of toxic waste dumps and other polluting facilities out of a desperate need for compensatory funds.[7] Although this appears consistent with the Coase theorem—it is a voluntary transaction—many people would say that no community should be forced to trade the health of its residents for needed funds. An important criticism of free market environmentalism is that under a pure market system poorer communities and individuals will generally bear the heaviest burden of environmental costs.

A similar example would be preservation of open space. Wealthy communities can afford to buy up open space for preservation, and poor communities cannot. If communities can use zoning to preserve wetlands and natural areas, poor communities too will be able to protect their environment. Zoning, a form of government regulation, allows communities to achieve significant environmental protection while incurring only relatively low enforcement costs.

Another point to note in considering the limitations of the Coase theorem is the issue of environmental effects on nonhuman life forms and ecological systems. Our

---

[7]Bullard, 1994, provides practical examples of the differential impact of environmental pollution on rich and poor communities.

examples so far have assumed that environmental damage affects specific individuals or businesses. Certain environmental damages, however, may affect no individual directly but threaten plant or animal species with extinction. A pesticide may be harmless to humans but lethal to birds. Who will step into the marketplace to defend the preservation of nonhuman species? No individual or business firm is likely to do so, except on a relatively small scale.

Consider, for example, the activities of a group such as The Nature Conservancy, which buys up ecologically valuable tracts of land in order to preserve them. Here is an organization that *is* prepared to pay to save the environment. Their purchases, however, reach only a tiny proportion of the natural areas threatened with destruction through development, intensive farming, and other economic activities. In the "dollar vote" marketplace, purely ecological interests will almost always lose out to economic interests.

We should also note that property rights and regulating capabilities are limited to the current generation. What about the rights of the next generation? Many environmental issues have long-term implications. Rights to nonrenewable resources can be assigned today, but those resources may also be needed in the future. This important issue of resource allocation over time is the subject of Chapter 4.

In some cases, property rights are simply inappropriate tools to deal with environmental problems. It may be impossible, for example, to establish property rights to the atmosphere, or to the open ocean. When we confront problems such as global warming, ocean pollution, the decline of fish stocks, or endangered species, we find that the system of private property rights, which has evolved as a basis for economic systems, cannot be fully extended to ecosystems. It may be possible to use market transactions such as tradable permits for air emissions or fishing rights, but these apply to only a limited subset of ecosystem functions. In such cases, other techniques of economic analysis will be helpful in considering the interaction between human economic activity and aspects of the broader ecosystem. We will consider some of these analyses in Chapter 5.

SUMMARY

Many economic activities have significant external effects—impacts on people not directly involved in the activity. Pollution from automobile use is an example. Market price usually fails to reflect the costs of these external impacts, leading to excessive production of goods with negative externalities.

One approach to pollution control is to internalize external costs by a tax or other instrument that requires producers and consumers of the polluting good to take these costs into account. In general, such a tax will raise the product price and reduce the quantity produced, thereby also reducing pollution. Market equilibrium then shifts toward a socially more desirable result. In theory, a tax that exactly reflects external costs could achieve a social optimum—but it is often difficult to establish a proper valuation for externalities.

Not all externalities are negative. Positive externalities result when economic activities bring benefits to others not directly involved in the transaction. Preservation of open land directly benefits those who live nearby, often raising their property values. In addition, it brings greater satisfaction to hikers, tourists, and passers-by. A positive externality can create an economic case for a subsidy to increase the market provision of the good.

The analysis of externalities implies that seeking to reduce pollution to zero is usually not appropriate. Rather, the social costs of pollution-creating goods should be balanced against their social benefits. This usually means reducing, not eliminating, pollution. In other words, some optimal level of pollution usually exists. This formulation arouses the criticism that "optimal" pollution levels may become unacceptable with increased demand and greater production of pollution-creating goods.

An alternative to taxation is the assignment of property rights to externalities. A clear legal right either to emit a certain amount of pollution or to prevent others from emitting pollution can create a market in "rights to pollute." However, this solution depends on the ability of firms and individuals to trade these pollution rights with relatively low transactions costs. Where large numbers of people are affected, or where the environmental damages are not easy to define in monetary terms, this approach is not effective. It also raises significant questions of equity, because under a market system the poor will generally bear a heavier burden of pollution.

KEY TERMS AND CONCEPTS

Coase theorem
complementary goods
consumer surplus
economic efficiency
environmental externalities
environmental valuation
equity
external benefit
external cost
free market environmentalism
free rider effect
government regulation
holdout effect
internalizing externalities
marginal benefit
marginal cost
market demand schedule
market equilibrium
market supply schedule
net social benefit

net social loss
optimal pollution
Pigovian tax
polluter pays principle
pollution tax
private choice
private optimum
producer surplus
property rights
public choice
right to pollute
social benefits
social cost
social optimum
subsidies
total cost of pollution
transactions costs
utility
welfare analysis

DISCUSSION QUESTIONS

1. Discuss your reaction to the following statement: "Solving the problems of environmental economics is simple. It is just a matter of internalizing the externalities." Does the theory of externalities apply to most or all environmental issues? What are some practical problems involved in internalizing externalities? Describe some examples where the principle works well, and some where it is more problematical.

2. A pollution tax is one policy instrument for internalizing externalities. Discuss the economic policy implications of a tax on automobiles, a tax on gasoline, or a tax on tailpipe emission levels as measured at an auto inspection. Which tax would be the most efficient? Which do you think would be most effective in reducing pollution levels? How do these taxes compare as policy instruments to a measure such as the requirement for oxygenated (less-polluting) fuels introduced by the Environmental Protection Agency in 1995? Bear in mind that oxygenated fuels are more expensive than standard fuels.

3. Does it make sense to speak of "the right to pollute"? How can anyone have a right to pollute? What do you think of the concept of "optimal pollution"? Can we really combine the economic concept of efficiency with the idea of protecting the environment? What are the strengths and the weaknesses of such an approach?

PROBLEMS

1. Consider the following supply and demand schedule for steel:

Price per ton ($)	20	40	60	80	100	120	140	160	180
Q_D (million tons)	200	180	160	140	120	100	80	60	40
Q_S (million tons)	20	60	100	140	180	220	260	300	340

Pollution from steel production is estimated to create an external cost of sixty dollars per ton.

Show the external cost, market equilibrium, and social optimum on a graph.

What kinds of policies might help to achieve the social optimum? What effects would these policies have on the behavior of consumers and producers? What effect would they have on market equilibrium price and quantity?

2. A chemical factory is situated next to a farm. Airborne emissions from the chemical factory damage crops on the farm. The marginal benefits of emissions to the factory and the marginal costs of damage to the farmer are as follows:

Quantity of Emissions	100	200	300	400	500	600	700	800	900
Marginal Benefit to factory ($000)	320	280	240	200	160	120	80	40	0
Marginal Cost to farmer ($000)	110	130	150	170	190	210	230	250	270

From an economic point of view, what is the best solution to this environmental conflict of interest? How might this solution be achieved? How should considerations of efficiency and equity be balanced in this case?

REFERENCES

Baumol, William J., and Wallace E. Oates. "The Use of Standards and Prices for Protection of the Environment." Chapter 18 in *Environmental Economics: A Reader,* edited by Anil Markandya and Julie Richardson. New York: St. Martin's Press, 1993.

Bromley, Daniel W., ed. *Handbook of Environmental Economics.* Cambridge, Mass. and Oxford, England: Basil Blackwell, 1995.

Bullard, Robert D. *Dumping in Dixie: Race, Class, and Environmental Quality.* Boulder, Colo.: Westview Press, 1994.

Coase, Ronald. "The Problem of Social Cost." *Journal of Law and Economics,* vol. 3, 1960. Reprinted in Stavins, ed., 2000.

Cobb, Clifford W. *The Roads Aren't Free: Estimating the Full Social Costs of Driving and the Effects of Accurate Pricing.* San Francisco: Redefining Progress. Resource Incentives Program Working Paper No. 3, 1998.

Hodge, Ian. "Public Policies for Land Conservation." Chapter 5 in Bromley, ed., 1995.

Stavins, Robert N., ed. *Economics of the Environment: Selected Readings.* 4th ed. New York: Norton, 2000.

Schmid, A. Allan. "The Environment and Property Rights Issues." Chapter 3 in Bromley, ed., 1995.

Tietenberg, Tom H. "Economic Instruments for Environmental Regulation." Chapter 16 in Stavins, ed., 2000.

WEB SITES

1. **http://www.rprogress.org/** Home page for Redefining Progress, "a nonprofit organization that develops policies and tools that reorient the economy to value people and nature first." Their site includes many publications on integrating environmental externalities into market prices.
2. **http://www.eia.doe.gov/cneaf/electricity/external/external_sum.html** A report published by the U.S. Department of Energy that estimates the magnitude of the externalities associated with electricity generation.
3. **http://www.aere.org/news/** Web site for the most recent copy of a newsletter published by the Association of Environmental and Resource Economists, an organization "established as a means of exchanging ideas, stimulating research, and promoting graduate training in resource and environmental economics." The newsletter includes a few short articles on resource issues.
4. **http://iisd1.iisd.ca/susprod/browse.asp** A compendium of case studies of economic regulation, information, and planning instruments designed to promote sustainable production and consumption.
5. **http://www.sustainableeconomy.org/** The home page for the Center for a Sustainable Economy, whose researchers "use economic modeling and policy analysis to determine the impact of environmental taxes, tax incentives, auctioned permits, and similar market-based tools on the economy, the environment, and society." The site includes several papers on environmental tax reform.

CHAPTER FOCUS QUESTIONS

■ How should we decide whether to use or conserve nonrenewable resources?
■ How can we value resource consumption that will take place in the future?
■ What will happen to prices and consumption if resources start to run out?

CHAPTER

4

Resource Allocation over Time

Allocation of Nonrenewable Resources

Resources can be **renewable** or **nonrenewable.** Renewable resources, if properly managed, can last indefinitely. We might reasonably expect that a well-managed farm, forest, or fishery could remain productive for centuries. Nonrenewable resources, on the other hand, cannot last forever. Some may be in relatively short supply. Examples would be high-grade deposits of copper ore or crude oil supplies. This raises questions of how much of these nonrenewable resources we use today and how much we save for future use, or for future generations.

A common concern is that we are using up earth's resources too fast. Another point of view is that technological progress and adaptation will avoid resource shortages. What does economic theory have to say about this issue?

A simple version of nonrenewable resource analysis begins by assuming that we have a known, limited quantity of a resource that we can use during two different time periods. The supply of high-grade copper, for example, is relatively fixed in amount. How should we allocate this limited resource between current and future time periods?

If we consider all possible future periods, the problem becomes more complex (though not theoretically insoluble, as we will see). A simple initial model of nonrenewable resource allocation deals with only two time periods. Our economic analysis will weigh the economic value of copper in the present as compared with copper in the future. Owners of copper deposits will decide whether to exploit them immediately, or

Offfshore oil drilling has increased as domestic supplies of oil become more difficult to obtain. The allocation of oil resources between present and future consumption depends on prices and on government policy.

to hold them for a future period, based on an estimate of probable future prices. We can formulate the problem as a simple extension of standard supply and demand theory.[1]

Equilibrium in the Current Time Period

First, let us consider only the current time period. Figure 4-1a shows a hypothetical supply and demand for copper. From this we can derive the **marginal net benefit** curve for copper, which shows the difference between value to the consumer and cost of supply for each unit of copper. (For example, if we can extract a unit of copper for $50 and its value to the purchaser is $150, its marginal net benefit is $100.)

Graphically, marginal net benefit is the vertical difference between the supply curve and the demand curve. Marginal net benefit is generally largest for the first units extracted, then declines to zero at equilibrium (where the supply and demand curves meet). If we were to produce more than the equilibrium quantity, marginal net benefit would become negative as supply costs rise above the value to the purchaser.

---

[1]This analysis assumes no copper recycling; we'll consider the economics of recycling in Chapter 12.

The marginal net benefit concept is a handy way of compressing into one curve information about both supply and demand in one period. The marginal net benefit of copper in the present period is shown by curve MNB in Figure 4-1b.

Algebraically, if the demand and supply schedules are given by

$$P_d = 150 - 0.25Q_1$$

and

$$P_s = 50 + 0.25Q_1$$

marginal net benefit is given by

$$MNB = P_d - P_s = 100 - 0.5Q_1$$

At the supply and demand equilibrium of $Q_1 = 200$, marginal net benefit is zero, indicating that producing and consuming more than 200 units of copper will provide no additional net benefit. The area under the marginal net benefit curve shows **total net benefit** (just as the area under a demand curve shows total benefit and the area under a supply curve shows total cost).

When marginal net benefit is just equal to zero, total net benefit is maximized (as shown by the area under the marginal net benefit curve in Figure 4-1b). This corresponds to the ordinary supply and demand equilibrium for the first period, at a quantity of 200 and a price of 100. We will call this the **static equilibrium**—the market equilibrium that will prevail if only present costs and benefits are considered.

Balancing Present and Future Periods

Now let's consider the marginal net benefit of copper in the second time period. We cannot know this value for sure, of course, because no one can foretell the future, but we *do* know that a fixed quantity of copper must be divided between the two periods. Let's make a simplifying assumption that the marginal net benefit of copper in Period 2 will be *exactly the same* as in Period 1. (This assumption is not necessary for the analysis, but it will make our first example simpler.)

A graphical trick will allow us to compare the two periods. We use the horizontal axis to measure the total available quantity of copper—say, 250 units—and put the marginal net benefit curve for the first period, MNB_1 on this graph in the usual way. Then we put the marginal net benefit curve for the second period, MNB_2, as on the graph in mirror-image fashion, going from right to left. Thus we have two horizontal scales, with the quantity used in period 1 shown left to right, and the quantity used in period 2 shown right to left (Figure 4-2).

One more step will complete our analysis. Because we want to compare two different time periods, we must translate future values into their equivalent in present values. The economic concept of **present value** relies on use of a **discount rate** to convert future to present monetary values. Suppose, for example, I promise to give you $1,000—ten years from now. What is the value of this promise today?

(a) Supply and Demand for Copper

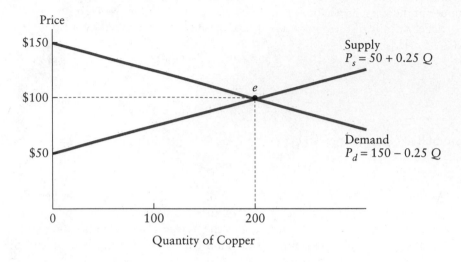

(b) Marginal Net Benefit for Copper

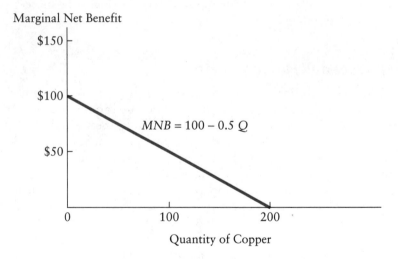

FIGURE 4-1 *Supply, Demand, and Marginal Net Benefit for Copper*

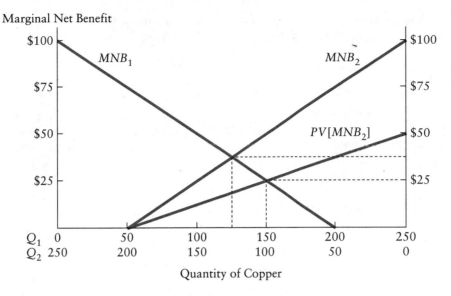

FIGURE 4-2 *Allocation of Copper over Two Time Periods*

Assuming I am trustworthy and you will definitely receive the money, the answer depends on the discount rate, reflected in financial terms as a rate of interest on deposits. Let us assume a 7.25 percent interest rate.[2] Five hundred dollars put in the bank today at compound interest would be worth almost exactly $1,000 in ten years. We can say that the present value of $1,000 to be received ten years from now is equal to $500 in cash today. In other words, you would be equally well off with $500 today or $1,000 ten years from now.[3]

Using this present value method, we can convert the marginal net benefit of copper in Period 2 into Period 1 values. We do this using the formula:

$$PV[MNB_2] = MNB_2/(1+r)^n$$

where r is the annual discount rate and n is the number of years between periods. If $r = 0.0725$ or 7.25%, and $n = 10$, we can closely approximate $PV[MNB_2]$ as

$$MNB_2/(1.0725)^{10} = MNB_2/2.$$

---

[2]For this example, we will assume this is a real interest rate, corrected for expected inflation.

[3]You might object that you would prefer to have an actual $500 to spend today. You can do so by borrowing $500 at 7.25 percent interest, and paying off the loan plus accumulated interest, totaling $1,000, in ten years' time.

This present value of marginal net benefit schedule for Period 2 is shown in Figure 4-2 as a line exactly half the height of the undiscounted MNB_2.

Dynamic Equilibrium for Two Periods

The reason for the special graphical format now becomes apparent. Consider the point where the two curves MNB_1 and $PV[MNB_2]$ cross. At this point the present value of the marginal net benefit of one unit of copper is *the same* in both time periods. This is the optimum economic allocation between periods since at this point no additional net benefit can be obtained by shifting consumption from one period to another. As you can see from the graph, this optimal allocation is 150 units in Period 1 and 100 units in Period 2. Algebraically, we obtain this solution by solving two equations:

$$MNB_1 = PV[MNB_2]$$

and

$$Q_1 + Q_2 = 250$$

The second equation is the **supply constraint,** which tells us that the quantities used in the two periods must sum to exactly 250, the total quantity available.

We can solve the equations as follows:

$$MNB_1 = 100 - 0.5Q_1 = MNB_2 = (100 - 0.5Q_2)/2$$

$$100 - 0.5Q_1 = 50 - 0.25Q_2$$

Because $Q_1 + Q_2 = 250$, $Q_1 = 250 - Q_2$. Substituting this in we have:

$$100 - 0.5(250 - Q_2) = 50 - 0.25Q_2$$

$$0.75Q_2 = 75$$

$$Q_1 = 150; Q_2 = 100$$

We can check the assertion that this solution is economically optimal by using the kind of welfare analysis introduced in Chapter 3 (see Figure 4-3). By choosing the equilibrium point where $Q_1 = 150$ and $Q_2 = 100$, we have achieved maximum total net benefit, shown by the shaded area $A + B$ in Figure 4-3a. (Area A is the net benefit in the first period, area B the net benefit in the second period).

Compare this result with the welfare effects of any other allocation, for example, the allocation $Q_1 = 200$, $Q_2 = 50$. As shown in Figure 4-3b, total welfare for the two periods is less with this new allocation (by the area B_2). By shifting fifty units from Period 2 use to Period 1 use, we have gained a first-period benefit equal to A_2, but lost a

(a) Optimal Intertemporal Resource Allocation

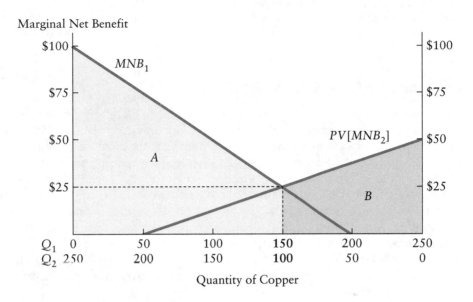

(b) Suboptimal Intertemporal Resource Allocation

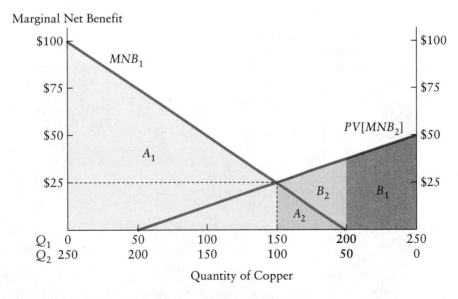

FIGURE 4-3 *Different Intertemporal Resource Allocations*

second-period benefit equal to $A_2 + B_2$, for a net loss of B_2. Total welfare is now $A_1 + A_2 + B_1$, less than the area $A + B$ in Figure 4-3a. Similarly, any other allocation we try will prove inferior to the optimal solution of $Q_1 = 150$, $Q_2 = 100$. (Try, for example, $Q_1 = 100$, $Q_2 = 150$. Show the effect of this allocation on total net benefit.)

User Costs and Resource Depletion

Let's translate what we have learned from this algebraic and graphical analysis into more common-sense terms. We know that we can increase our benefit today by using more copper (in this example up to 200 units, which is the most we would use today if we took no account of future needs). If we chose to use only fifty units today, two hundred would be left for the next period—enough to fulfill the maximum demand in that period. At any use level greater than 50 units, we start to cut into the amount of copper available for future use.

Another way of putting this would be to say that we start *imposing costs on future consumers of copper* by using up copper today. On our graph, those **user costs** show up as the steadily rising curve $PV[MNB_2]$. The more we use today, the higher these costs become. User costs are in fact a different kind of third-party cost or externality—*externalities in time.*

We can justify using up copper today so long as the benefits from doing so outweigh user costs imposed on future citizens. But once the user costs become higher than the benefits from consumption today—in our example, at any level of present consumption above 150 units—we reduce total economic welfare by our excessive present consumption.

Going back to our algebraic and graphical analysis, we define an exact value for the user cost at the Period 1 consumption level we have defined as is optimal. The vertical distance to the intersection point of MNB_1 and $PV[MNB_2]$ shows the user cost at equilibrium. We can calculate this easily by evaluating either MNB_1 or $PV[MNB_2]$ at the intersection point where $Q_1 = 150$ and $Q_2 = 100$:

$$\text{user cost} = MNB_1 = 100 - 0.5(150) = 25$$

or

$$= PV[MNB_2] = 50 - 0.25(100) = 25$$

The user cost at equilibrium is thus $25.

What does this mean? Suppose we go back to the original supply and demand schedules for Period 1 (redrawn in Figure 4-4a). If we don't consider Period 2 at all, the market equilibrium in Period 1 will be 200 units of copper at a price of $100. Now suppose we add to the ordinary supply costs the user cost derived from Figure 4-2—just as we added an environmental external cost to the ordinary supply costs in the previous section. The result is shown in Figure 4-4a as the **social cost** schedule S'.

(a) Market for Copper with User Costs (First Period)

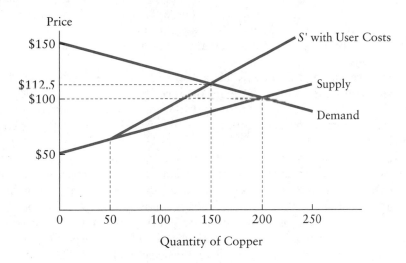

(b) Market for Copper (Second Period)

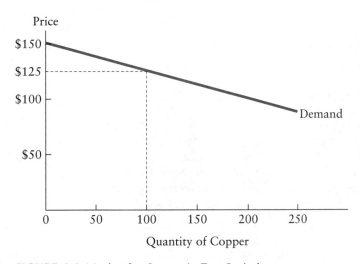

FIGURE 4-4 *Market for Copper in Two Periods*

A new equilibrium appears at 150 units of copper consumption, with a price of $112.50. The user cost at this new equilibrium is $25—the vertical distance between the old supply curve S and the new social cost curve S'. With a first-period consumption of 150 units, 100 units will remain for consumption in the second period, at a second-period price of $125 (assuming demand conditions are unchanged).[4] This is shown in Figure 4-4b.

If user costs are internalized in this fashion, the new market equilibrium, known as **dynamic equilibrium**, reflects *both* the needs of the present and of the future. The higher price will send a signal to producers and consumers of the resource to produce and use less today, thereby conserving more for the future. But how will user costs be reflected in the market?

One possibility is a **resource depletion tax** imposed on copper ore production and sales. Like a pollution tax, this tax will raise the effective supply schedule to the real social cost S'. Other policy mechanisms could include direct government control of resource exploitation, setting aside resource deposits or maintaining stockpiles.

In some cases, however, government intervention may not be necessary for user costs to be internalized into the market. This would be true especially if the time period until expected resource exhaustion is relatively short. In this case, private owners of the resource will anticipate the second-period situation and act accordingly.

If resource shortages are foreseen, profit-seeking resource owners will hold some copper stocks off the market or leave copper ores in the ground and wait for the higher prices likely to prevail in a shortage. This supply limitation will have exactly the same effect (a leftward and upward shift of the supply curve to S') as the imposition of a resource depletion tax. In this case no tax is necessary—the market process will automatically adjust for anticipated future limits on copper resources.

Hotelling's Rule and Time Discounting

What if we want to consider the real world, which presents not two periods but an infinite number of future periods? How much copper should we be prepared to set aside for 50 years from now? One hundred years? Extending our two-period analysis to a more general theory offers perspective on these issues. Such questions test the limits of our economic model and also address the interrelationship between social values and the more specific market values we deal with in economic theory.

---

[4]We can calculate the new first- and second-period prices using the original equations for the supply and demand schedules, with $25 added to the first-period supply schedule to reflect the user cost. For the first period this gives us

$$P_d = 150 - 0.25Q_1 \text{ and } P_s = 75 + 0.25Q_1$$

Setting these equal and solving, the first-period equilibrium is

$$Q_1 = 150, P_1 = 112.5$$

Because we know only 100 units remain for the second period, we can use the demand curve for the second period (which we assumed to be the same) to solve for the second-period price:

$$P_2 = 150 - 0.25(100) = 150 - 25 = 125$$

Our simple two-period example makes clear that the discount rate is a critical variable. At different discount rates, the optimal allocation of copper between the two periods will vary significantly. Let's start at one extreme—a discount rate of zero. In the example, the equilibrium allocation of copper would be 125 units consumed in each period. At a discount rate of zero, future net benefits receive *exactly the same value* as if they were current net benefits. The available copper is therefore divided evenly between the periods.

At any discount rate above zero, we favor present consumption over future consumption to some degree. At a very high discount rate—say 50 percent per annum—the first-period allocation of copper is 198 units, close to the 200 units that are consumed in the static equilibrium case, and user costs fall nearly to zero. In general, at high discount rates we weight present benefits much more heavily than future benefits (see Figure 4-5 and Table 4-1).

We can extend this logic from one period to many periods, and even to an infinite future. The principle involved is known as **Hotelling's rule.** This rule states that in equilibrium the resource **net price** (defined as the price minus extraction costs) must rise at a rate equal to the rate of interest.

Consider an example from the perspective of a copper ore deposit owner. The owner's profit per unit extracted is equal to the net price. In deciding whether or not to produce and sell the copper, the owner will weigh the net price available today against a possible higher future net price. She will compare the two using a discount rate equal to the commercial rate of interest. If the present net price, plus interest, exceeds the probable future net price, she will profit more by extracting the resource today and investing the proceeds, rather than waiting. If the expected future net price is higher than the net price today plus interest, she will wait and sell at the future date.

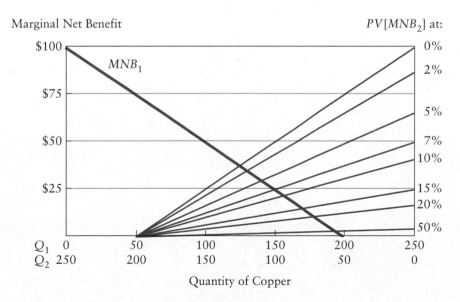

FIGURE 4-5 *Intertemporal Resource Allocation*

TABLE 4-1 *Different Discount Rates for Intertemporal Resource Allocation*

Discount Rate (%)	$(1 + r)^{10}$	Q_1	Q_2
0	1.0	125	125
2	1.2	132	118
5	1.6	143	107
7.5	2.0	150	100
10	2.6	158	92
15	4.0	170	80
20	6.2	179	71
50	57.7	198	52

If all resource owners follow this logic, the quantity of copper supplied today will increase until today's copper price falls low enough to encourage resource owners to conserve, hoping for a better future price. At this point Hotelling's rule will hold: the expectations of future price increases will exactly follow an exponential curve $P_1(1+r)^n$, where P_1 is today's price, r is the discount rate, and n is the number of years from the present (see Figure 4-6).

If this sounds confusing, consider this simpler, common-sense formulation: high discount rates create an incentive to use resources quickly; low discount rates create greater incentive to conserve. More generally, we can say that economic theory implies

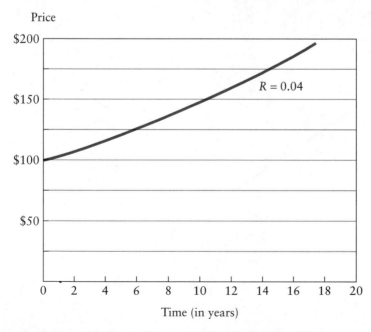

FIGURE 4-6 *Hotelling's Rule on Equilibrium Resource Price*

the existence of an **optimal depletion rate.** Under market conditions, a nonrenewable resource will be used up at a certain "optimal" rate, and this rate will be faster at higher discount rates.[5]

Interestingly, according to this theory it is optimal to deplete certain resources to complete exhaustion over a period of time—the higher the discount rate, the shorter the time. Like the theory of optimal pollution, this sounds wrong to many people. What about the ethical imperative to leave something for future generations?

The answer in economic terms is that a discount rate based on standard commercial rates of interest will give a low weight to the well-being of future generations.[6] This leads some people to question whether we can justifiably apply present value analysis, based on a discount rate, over long periods of time. This issue will be important in our discussion of valuation and cost/benefit analysis in Chapter 6 and of long-term sustainability in Chapter 7.

SUMMARY

Nonrenewable resources can be used in the present or conserved for future use. Economic theory offers some guidance concerning the principles of nonrenewable resource allocation over time. In essence, the net value gained from using a resource today must be balanced against the net value of its potential future use. To compare values across time periods, we use a discount rate to measure the present value of future consumption.

The concept of user costs captures the idea that, by using resources today, we impose some cost on future potential consumers. User cost is a kind of externality in time, and like other externalities should be reflected in market price to internalize all social costs. Including user costs in market price will reduce consumption today, leaving more for future use.

If resource owners foresee future resource shortages, current prices will reflect user costs. The expectation that prices will rise creates an incentive to hold resources off the market today in order to sell them at a higher price in the future. According to Hotelling's rule, in equilibrium the net price of a resource (market price minus extraction costs) must rise at a rate equal to the rate of interest. The higher the interest rate, the more likely the owner is to profit from extracting and selling a nonrenewable resource today rather than waiting for future higher prices.

Especially in figuring for long time periods, discounting reduces the significance of user costs almost to zero and creates little market incentive for conserving nonrenewable resources. If governments wish to ensure a long-term supply of certain resources, they can internalize user costs through a resource depletion tax—much as a pollution tax can internalize current externalities.

---

[5]We will examine the relationship of resource prices and resource extraction patterns in more detail in Chapter 12.

[6]See, for example, Howarth and Norgaard, 1995.

The alternative may be to exploit nonrenewable resources to exhaustion, leaving no reserves for future use. A major question is whether it is appropriate to use current discount rates to determine the allocation of resources over the long term, or whether we have a social obligation to conserve resources for future generations.

KEY TERMS AND CONCEPTS

discount rate
dynamic equilibrium
Hotelling's rule
marginal net benefit
net price
nonrenewable resources
optimal depletion rate
present value

renewable resources
resource depletion tax
social cost
static equilibrium
supply constraint
total net benefit
user costs

DISCUSSION QUESTIONS

1. It has been argued that any government policy aimed at nonrenewable resource conservation is an unwarranted interference with the free market. According to this point of view, if a resource is likely to become scarce, the people most likely to realize this are the private investors and traders who deal in the resource. If they anticipate scarcity, they will hold stocks of the resource for future profit, driving up its price and leading to conservation. Any action by government bureaucrats is likely to be less well informed than that of profit-motivated private firms. Evaluate this argument. Do you think that in some cases government should step in to conserve specific resources? If so, what policy tools should government use?

2. How could the principle of resource allocation over time be applied to environmental resources such as groundwater supplies or species diversity? Would the same kind of conclusions about optimal depletion apply or not?

PROBLEM

We can modify the interperiod allocation model to deal with the issue of intergenerational allocation of resources. Suppose a generation is thirty-five years and we are concerned with two generations only. Demand and supply functions for oil in the present generation are given by

$$\text{Demand: } Q_d = 200 - 5P \text{ or } P = 40 - 0.2Q_d$$

$$\text{Supply: } Q_s = 5P \text{ or } P = 0.2Q_s$$

1. Draw a demand and supply graph showing the equilibrium price and quantity consumed in this generation in the absence of any consideration of the future. Now draw a graph showing the marginal net benefits from consumption in this period at all levels of consumption up to the equilibrium level. Express the net benefit (benefit minus cost) algebraically.

2. Suppose the net benefit function is expected to be the same for the next generation, but a discount rate (interest rate) of 4 percent per annum for 35 years works out to $(1.04)^{35}$, approximately equal to 4. Total oil supply for both generations is limited to 100 units. Calculate the efficient allocation of resources between the two generations and show this graphically. (Set marginal benefits equal for the two periods, remembering to include the discount rate.)

3. What is marginal user cost for this efficient allocation? If you include this user cost in your original supply and demand graph, what is the new equilibrium? If the demand curve is the same in the second generation, what will be the price and quantity consumed in that period?

4. How would the answers differ if we used a zero discount rate? What can you conclude from this example about the general problem of allocation of resources over long time periods?

REFERENCES

Hartwick, J. M. "Intergenerational Equity and the Investing of Rents from Exhaustible Resources." *American Economic Review* 66 (1977): 972–974.

Hotelling, Harold. "The Economics of Exhaustible Resources," *Journal of Political Economy,* 39 (April 1931): 137–175.

Howarth, Richard B., and Richard B. Norgaard. "Intergenerational Choices under Global Environmental Change," in *Handbook of Environmental Economics,* edited by Daniel W. Bromley. Cambridge, Mass. and Oxford, England: Basil Blackwell, 1995.

Solow, R. M. "On the Intertemporal Allocation of Natural Resources." *Scandinavian Journal of Economics* 88 (1986): 141–149.

WEB SITES

1. **http://members.iinet.net.au/~tommy/essays/essay19.html** A paper on the application of Hotelling's rule to the issue of natural resource depletion.
2. **http://hadm.sph.sc.edu/Courses/Econ/Dis/Dis.html** A web site with an interactive tutorial about discounting and present values.
3. **http://dieoff.org/page87.htm** A paper by Robert Costanza titled "Three General Policies to Achieve Sustainability." The paper also includes a discussion of a natural capital depletion tax.

CHAPTER FOCUS QUESTIONS

- Why are resources such as fisheries often damaged through excessive use?
- What policies are effective for managing public-access resources?
- How should we preserve national parks, forests, oceans, and the atmosphere?

CHAPTER

5

Common Property Resources and Public Goods

Common Property, Open-Access, and Property Rights

Property rights lie at the heart of economic analysis. In market economies, private property rights are central. This has not always been the case. In traditional or tribal societies, private property rights over resources are rare. Resources important to the life of the tribe are either held in common (as with a common grazing ground), or are not owned at all (as with animals hunted for food). Economically developed societies—we like to think of ourselves as "advanced" societies—have generally evolved elaborate systems of property rights covering most resources as well as most goods and services. But even modern industrialized nations have resources, goods, and services difficult to categorize as property.

A free-flowing river is an example. If we think of the river simply as a quantity of water flowing past people's land, we can devise rules for "ownership" of the water that allow a certain amount of water withdrawal per landowner. But what about the aquatic life of the river? What about the use of the river for recreation: canoeing, swimming, and fishing? What about the scenic beauty of the riverside?

Some of these aspects of the river might also become specific types of property. For example, in Scotland trout fishing rights on certain rivers are jealously guarded property. Still, it is difficult to parcel up every function of the river and define it as somebody's property. To some degree the river is a **common property resource.** What rules apply to the use of common property?

The Economics of a Fishery

A classic example of a common property resource is a fishery. Inland and coastal fisheries often are governed by private, traditional, or government management systems. Fisheries in the open ocean are typically **open-access resources.**[1] Anyone can fish in nonterritorial waters, which means that no one owns the basic resource, the wild stock of fish. We will use this example to apply some of the basic concepts of production theory to an open-access resource.

How can we apply economic theory to a fishery? Let's start with common sense. If just a few fishing boats start operations in a rich fishing ground, their catch will certainly be good. This is likely to attract other fishers, and as more boats join the fishing fleet the total catch will increase.

As the number of fishing boats becomes large, the fishery's capacity will be strained and the catch of individual boats will diminish. We know from experience that if this process is taken too far, the output of the whole fishery can be badly damaged. At what point does it become counterproductive to put in more effort, in the shape of more boat trips? What forces may drive us past that point? Economic theory can give us some insights into these critical questions of common property resource management.

We can envision the fishery's **total product** as shown in Figure 5-1. The horizontal axis shows fishing effort, measured in numbers of boat trips. The vertical axis shows the total catch of all the boats. As the number of boat trips increases, the total product curve shown in Figure 5-1 goes through three distinct phases.

The first is a period of **constant returns to scale** (here shown from 0 to 400 boats). In this range, each extra boat finds an ample supply of fish, and returns to port with a catch of 10 tons. The second is a period of **diminishing returns** to effort, shown from 400 to 850 boats. It is now becoming more difficult to catch a limited number of fish. When an extra boat puts out to sea, it increases the total catch, but it also reduces by a small amount the catch of all the other boats. The natural resource is no longer ample for all; intense competition for fish stocks makes the job tougher for all fishers.

Finally there is a period of **absolutely diminishing returns,** above 850 boats, where more boats actually *decrease* the total catch. **Overfishing** is taking place, and stocks of

---

[1]There is sometimes confusion between the concepts of common property and open access. In essence, an open-access resource is a common property resource that lacks any system of rules governing its use.

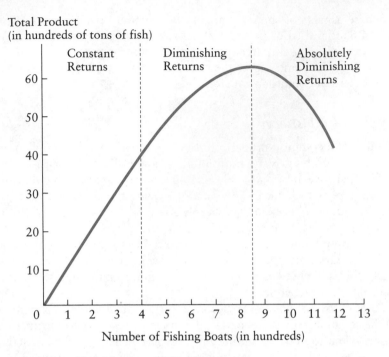

Total Product
(in hundreds of tons of fish)

FIGURE 5-1 *Total Product of the Fishery*

fish are being depleted. The fish population's ability to replenish itself is damaged, and we have the makings of both an economic and an ecological collapse.

To understand the economic forces motivating the fishers, we must convert the quantitative measure of tons of fish landed into a money figure showing total revenue earned. We simply multiply the quantity of fish by the price per ton ($TR = PQ$). Let us assume a stable price of $1,000 per ton. (We are implicitly assuming that this fishery is small enough relative to the total market that its output does not significantly affect the market price. If this fishery were the market's only source of fish we would have to consider price changes also.)

We can now calculate the **total revenue** from the fishery, the **average revenue** (revenue per boat), and the **marginal revenue** (revenue added to the total by an extra boat), as shown in Table 5-1. To complete our financial data, we will also need to know the costs of operating a fishing boat. Here we will assume that the **marginal cost** of operating a boat is constant at $4,000 per boat trip. This gives us a simplified, but complete, picture of the economic forces confronting the individual fishers in this industry (Figure 5-2).

Suppose that only 400 boats are operating. What is the position of the individual boat operator? We can see from Figure 5-2 that revenues per boat are $10,000 per trip. Costs per boat are $4,000 per trip. That leaves $6,000 as net revenue, or profit.

TABLE 5-1 *Revenues and Costs for the Fishery*

Number of boats (Q in hundreds)	1	2	3	4	5	6	7	8	9	10	11	12	13
Total fish catch (hundred tons)	10	20	30	40	48	54	58	60	60	58	54	48	40
Total value of catch (TR in million $)	1.0	2.0	3.0	4.0	4.8	5.4	5.8	6.0	6.0	5.8	5.4	4.8	4.0
Total costs (TC in million $)	0.4	0.8	1.2	1.6	2.0	2.4	2.8	3.2	3.6	4.0	4.4	4.8	5.2
Total net revenue (TR–TC in million $)	0.6	1.2	1.8	2.4	2.8	3.0	3.0	2.8	2.4	1.8	1.0	0	-0.8
Marginal revenue (MR in thousand $)		10	10	10	8	6	4	2	0	-2	-4	-6	-8
Revenue per boat (AR in thousand $)	10	10	10	10	9.6	9	8.2	7.5	6.6	5-8	4.9	4	3.1
Cost per boat (MC, AC in thousand $)	4	4	4	4	4	4	4	4	4	4	4	4	4
Net revenue per boat (AR–MC)	6	6	6	6	5-6	5	4.2	3.5	2.6	1.8	0.9	0	-0.9

Marginal revenue is defined as $MR = \Delta TR/\Delta Q$
Average revenue is defined as $AR = TR/Q$
Marginal cost is defined as $MC = \Delta TC/\Delta Q$

This obviously profitable business will attract new entrants. So long as fishers have free entry into the industry, the number of boats operating will increase.

Incentives for Overfishing

Figure 5-2 also shows, however, that as more boats join the fishing fleet, the extra or marginal revenue will rapidly decline. By the time we have reached 800 boats, the marginal revenue brought in by the last 100 entrants is less than the marginal cost of operating the boats. Does this mean that operations will become unprofitable, inducing some owners to leave the industry? No, because the lower average revenues are spread throughout the fishing fleet. The average revenue, or revenue per boat, is now about $7,500, which still covers costs of $4,000, with $3,500 profit. Rather than fishers leaving the industry, considerable incentive remains for more to enter.

This process of entry will continue until average revenue falls below the marginal cost of operating a boat—in our example, when 1,200 boats are operating. Only then do individual operators find the business unprofitable, causing some to leave the industry. The market sends a "signal"—through unprofitability—that the industry is overcrowded.

But this economic signal comes far too late—too late for economic efficiency, and too late for ecological sustainability. The economically efficient number of boats would have been 650. At this point the extra benefits of adding one more boat are just

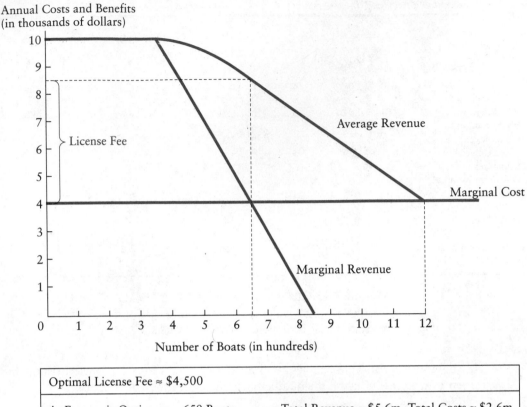

Annual Costs and Benefits
(in thousands of dollars)

FIGURE 5-2 *Economic Conditions in the Fishery*

Optimal License Fee ≈ $4,500	
At Economic Optimum ≈ 650 Boats	Total Revenue ≈ $5.6m, Total Costs ≈ $2.6m Total Social Benefit ≈ $3m
At Open-access Equilibrium = 1,200 Boats	Total Revenue = Total Costs = $4.8m Total Social Benefit = 0

balanced by the extra costs of operating that boat. The problem is that individual operators fail to "notice" that the industry as a whole is becoming less profitable above 650 boats.

So long as each boat is profitable, fishers have an incentive to continue fishing, and others see incentive to enter the fishing business. The forces of free entry and competition, which usually work to promote economic efficiency, have exactly the opposite effect in this case. They encourage overfishing that ultimately destroys both the fish stocks and the profitability of all operators. The economic explanation is that fishers have free access to a crucial resource—fish stocks. Economic logic tells us that an underpriced resource will be overused, and a resource priced at zero will be squandered.

This phenomenon is sometimes referred to as the **tragedy of the commons.**[2] Because common property resources belong to no one in particular, no one has an incentive to conserve them. On the contrary, the incentive is toward using as much as you can before someone else gets it. When resources are ample, problems are few, as in precolonial America when fish stocks were far beyond the needs or fishing abilities of the small population. When population, demand, and fishing technologies expand enough, the economic logic that we have sketched out leads to critical danger of overfishing and even complete collapse of the fishery.

Is there a better solution? From the point of view of formal economic analysis, the **economic optimum** for this fishing industry would be at 650 boats, where marginal revenue = marginal cost. At this point the **net social benefit** from the fishing industry is maximized. Net social benefit, as we saw in Chapter 3, can be defined as total benefits (in this case equal to the total value of the catch) minus total costs. Table 5-1 shows that this is indeed maximized between 600 and 700 boats. In this example, the straight-line pattern of marginal revenue decline means that the economic optimum will be 650 boats.[3]

From an ecological point of view, this equilibrium is probably also sustainable. The **maximum sustainable yield** from this fishery occurs when 850 boats are operating and the total catch is just over 6,000 tons.[4] The economic optimum output of 650 boats is somewhat below maximum sustainable yield, which implies that the fishery can maintain ecological health at this level of output. When fishing efforts push beyond the point of maximum sustainable yield, long-term damage to the fishery—even species extinction—can occur. The **open-access equilibrium** at 1,200 boats clearly threatens such an ecological collapse, in addition to being economically inefficient.

Policies for Fishery Management

What policies might achieve a more efficient equilibrium, protect the fishery ecosystem, and improve social net benefit? A simple answer suggests itself: impose a fee. If fishers must pay a **license fee,** this will reduce the economic incentive for excessive entry into the industry. Figure 5-2 illustrates the optimal level for such a fee. At the optimal equilibrium of 650 boats, the difference between marginal cost and average revenue is approximately $4,500. If fishers must pay a per-boat license fee of $4,500, entry into the industry will be profitable up to 650 boats. After this, profits fall below zero, and there is no further incentive for entry.

---

[2]This concept was first introduced by Hardin, 1968. Feeny et al., 1999, give a recent assessment of the issue.

[3]The best placement of marginal values on a graph is halfway between the total values from which they are derived. Between 600 and 700 boats, the total revenue changes from $5.4 million to $5.8 million, and the marginal revenue value (equal to $0.4 million/100 = $4,000) is best placed at 650 boats.

[4]Assuming the Total Product curve is smooth, its maximum will occur at 6,025 tons when 850 boats are operating.

Each fisher will now be in the position of a perfect competitor, making minimal or "normal" profit. In this case, however, the logic of competition will work to protect the ecosystem, not to destroy it. In effect, fishers must pay a fee to use a previously free resource—access to fish stocks. This policy might be politically unpopular in fishing communities, but it will prevent the industry from destroying the means of its own livelihood.

Another policy to achieve the same goal would be the use of a **quota**, or catch limit. Government officials may determine a quota for the entire fishery, but deciding who receives the rights to a limited fish catch can become controversial. If the right is allocated to current fishers, new entrants will be barred from the industry. Alternatively, fishers might receive **individual transferable quotas (ITQs)**, which could be sold to someone entering the business. In some cases, limited rights to hunt or fish certain species are allocated to indigenous peoples (Aleut people, for example, have the right to hunt a limited number of endangered bowhead whales).

Yet another possibility is to sell fishing quotas at auction, which will lead to an economic result similar to the license fee. Any such method requires a consciously planned government intervention. Although economists often argue that markets operate more efficiently without government intervention, here is a case that *requires* government intervention to achieve an economically efficient (and ecologically sustainable) solution.

The need for social regulation of common-property resources has been well recognized throughout history. The longest place name in America is that of Lake Chargoggagoggmanchauggagoggchaubunagungamaug, located near the town of Webster, Massachusetts. The name, a Native American phrase meaning "I fish on my side, you fish on your side, and nobody fishes in the middle," reflects a long-standing principle of limited catch and conservation of resources.[5]

Population growth, high demand, and advanced technology have complicated the implementation of such sound principles. Even so, both economic theory and ecological principles tell us that we must find ways to do so or risk having our common property resources destroyed through overuse.[6]

The Environment as a Public Good

Economists have long recognized the concept of **public goods.** Ordinary goods, such as automobiles, are generally purchased by one household, and only the purchaser enjoys their benefits. Public goods, in contrast, benefit a large number of people, often the whole society. Public goods are said to be **nonexclusive**—that is, they are available

---

[5]See Feeny et al., 1999, for a discussion of institutions for common property management.

[6]For an extensive treatment of the economic analysis of fisheries and other natural resources, see Clark, 1990.

North American birds such as this warbler winter in South American rainforests. Preserving rainforests protects species diversity on both continents.

to all for consumption—and **nonrival,** because their use by one person does not reduce their availability to others.[7]

An example is the national park system of the United States. National parks are open to all, and (except where overcrowding becomes a significant problem) their use by some people does not reduce others' ability to enjoy them. Public goods are not necessarily environmental in character: the highway system and the national defense are often cited as examples of public goods. Many aspects of environmental preservation do, however, fit easily into the public goods category, because virtually everyone has an interest in a sound and healthy environment.[8]

---

[7]The formal definition of a public good is "a commodity or service which if supplied to one person can be made available to others at no extra cost" (Pearce, 1992). A "pure" public good is one that the producer cannot exclude anyone from consuming. Thus a pure public good demonstrates both nonrival consumption and nonexcludability.

[8]Technically, national parks are not a "pure" public good because they may charge entry fees, thereby excluding nonpayers. Even so, the parks remain a public good so long as national policy allows free or low-fee entry.

How can we best understand the logic of demand and supply for public goods? These goods cannot be bought and sold in the same way as ordinary goods, yet their adequate supply is of crucial interest to the whole society. We begin by noting that the provision of such goods must be decided in the political arena. This is generally true of, for example, national defense. We cannot resolve the issue of national defense by having everyone buy his or her own tank. The resolution requires a political decision that takes into account some citizens' wish for more defense spending, others' for less. Once the decision is made, we all pay a share of the cost through taxes.

Similarly, decisions regarding environmental public goods must be made through the political system. Congress, for example, must decide on funding for national parks. Will more land be acquired for parks? Might some existing park areas be sold or leased for development? Such decisions require some understanding of public demand for environmental amenities.

The problem, however, cannot be solved through the ordinary market process of supply and demand. In the fishery example discussed above, the problem lay on the production side—the ordinary market logic led to overexpansion of production and excessive pressure on resources. With public goods, the problem is on the demand side. The ordinary market process will lead to a low **effective demand**[9] for public goods (possibly a zero demand), despite the fact that the public needs these goods. Thus without specific government policies in this area, **undersupply of public goods** will occur.

The Economics of Rainforest Conservation

An example may help illustrate the point. Rainforest conservation in Central and South America can be considered a public good. Such conservation certainly benefits people who tour the area and see unspoiled rainforest, whether they are local residents or foreign tourists. Many more people also gain from spin-off benefits such as preservation of species diversity and the pharmaceutical products derived from rainforest species. Bird-watchers in North America see warblers and thrushes that depend on winter habitat in rainforests. Cutting and burning of rainforest adds to atmospheric carbon dioxide, which contributes to the problem of global climate change.

Many people derive what economists call a **psychic benefit** simply from knowing that forests and species have been preserved, even if they never see the forests personally. For all these reasons, we can state with confidence that rainforest preservation yields considerable benefit. But how can we reflect this benefit in actual demand for preserved rainforest acres? The question is critical; market demands for timber, minerals, and agricultural land all create pressure to cut down rainforest for development. Can the preservation interest compete with this market demand?

Let's examine whether we can represent the benefits of preservation in market demand. Some private conservation groups have exactly that goal—to create demand

---

[9]Effective demand is defined as demand backed up by purchasing power.

for rainforest preservation. One particularly effective campaign mounted by these groups offers people the opportunity to "buy" a rainforest acre for $50. If a conservation-minded citizen chooses to respond to such an appeal, the organization promises to use her $50 contribution to purchase one acre of rainforest for preservation. This kind of appeal is popular because it offers direct results. In effect it sets up a new kind of market for a public good. Just as I can purchase a refrigerator, I can now "purchase" rainforest preservation.

Unfortunately, this fails to solve the problem of undersupply of public goods. To see why, we can graph the supply and demand for rainforest preservation in standard economic terms, as shown in Figure 5-3. Interpreting this graph is a little tricky, but it is fully consistent both with economic theory and, as we will see, with real-world experience.

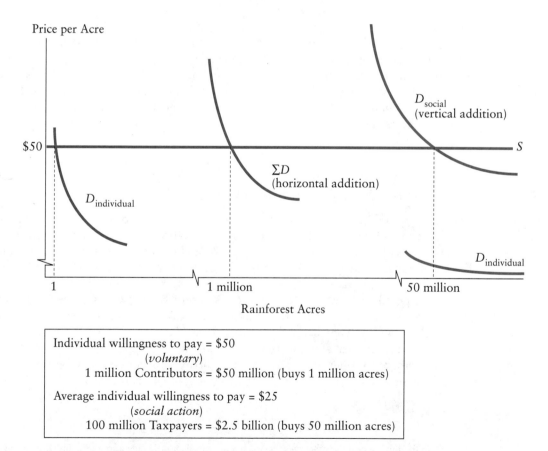

FIGURE 5-3 *Public Good Example: How (Not) to Save the Rainforest*

The supply function for rainforest acres preserved is simple. We assume that the going price is $50 per acre, giving us a horizontal or **perfectly elastic supply.** On the demand side, let's look first at the **individual demand schedule** of Ms. Mary Ecosmith, who sends in $50 to the appeal. We don't know the exact shape of her individual demand curve, but we do know that at the price of $50 she has demanded exactly one acre, and an approximate demand curve reflects this in Figure 5-3.

Now let's consider the **market demand schedule** for rainforest preservation. Just as individual demands for automobiles or refrigerators can be *added horizontally*[10] to obtain market demand, we can add the quantities of rainforest preservation demanded by different individuals to obtain the market demand. Let's suppose this appeal enjoys great success, and 1 million people respond, each buying one acre. The market demand is then shown by the curve ΣD, representing the *horizontal addition* of 1 million individual demand curves like Ms. Ecosmith's. One million acres of rainforest are successfully preserved, at a total cost of $50 million. (In real life, this result would be an extraordinary success, and it is unlikely that conservation organizations would do this well.)

Such a result would certainly represent some progress in promoting supply of a public good, but does it represent adequate supply? No. Estimates of the global loss rate of tropical forest indicate as much as *50 million acres* destroyed per year. Even such an extraordinarily successful conservation effort would fall far short of what is needed. Despite the creative work of conservation groups in creating a new market for this public good, it remains woefully undersupplied. In the meantime, the market demands for timber, minerals, and agricultural land continue to increase the pressure on remaining forests.

Social Demand for Rainforest Preservation

The problem is that response to the conservation group's appeal fails to adequately reflect the true public demand for rainforest preservation. Concern about rainforest destruction is widespread; most people would probably like to see it stopped. But only a limited number of people will actually send $50. Such behavior typifies the **free-rider effect,** which we discussed in Chapter 3.

Many people will wait for someone else to contribute to a cause, even though they themselves will benefit. They are happy to see some rainforest preservation; they either neglect to write a check or they can't afford $50. Even if offered the opportunity to contribute a smaller amount, they may fear that the appeal will fail and they will have contributed money for nothing. Some people, of course, may be unconcerned about the problem—their willingness to contribute is zero. Most likely, however,

---

[10]Horizontal addition of demand curves means that at any given price, we add all the individual quantities demanded to obtain market demand.

many more people do care at least a little and might contribute something, but they miss the appeal or for any of the above reasons fail to respond.

In terms of economic theory, what we need is not a horizontal addition, but a *vertical addition of demand curves*. We need to add the actual benefit to each individual from rainforest preservation to find the **social benefit.** Look at the right side of Figure 5-3. Here a vertical addition shows the **social demand** for actually stopping rainforest destruction by purchasing not 1 million but 50 million acres for preservation.

The benefit to each individual is small—a tiny fraction of a cent per acre. But when we consider that practically everyone derives some benefit, it adds up to a considerable social benefit. For $2.5 billion, we could purchase the entire 50 million acres at risk. If government policy mandated such a purchase, how much would it cost taxpayers? If we consider only U.S. taxpayers, it would come to about $25 per family. This is, for comparison, about 1 percent of the U.S. defense budget, to which each family contributes about $2,500 in taxes. Might the provision of this public good be worth the cost?

Opinions might differ on the appropriate amount, especially in a climate of budgetary cutbacks. Our point is this: effective provision of a public good requires a public decision. The efforts of private conservation groups, while commendable, are only a drop in the bucket.

Of course, our example is oversimplified. The supply cost of rainforest land is undoubtedly not perfectly elastic, and large-scale preservation could probably not be purchased. But $1.5 billion could go a long way—much further than $50 million. Offered as debt relief, it could be a massive inducement for governments such as Brazil's to institute effective rainforest preservation plans. If Europe and Japan joined the United States in a worldwide rainforest conservation program, we could make much progress, offering developing nations significant incentive for rainforest conservation at relatively low cost. The lack of such a public effort leaves only the much smaller efforts of private conservation groups standing against the widespread market demand forces promoting rainforest conversion. Clearly, the result will be continued rapid loss of forests.[11]

Many environmental issues, such as clean air and clean water, have a similar public good nature. All land preservation policies, including wetlands, forests, wilderness, and rural area protection require government action to succeed. As we have seen, markets can help provide some of these environmental public goods, but their essential public good character places practical limits on our ability to "marketize" them. As our rainforest example shows, attempts at private provision of public goods fail to reflect many of the true public benefits of environmental preservation. Only a social decision to act together—and pay the necessary costs—will gain these public benefits for all.

---

[11]The initiation of some public funding for forest preservation through the Global Environmental Facility (GEF) is discussed in Chapter 20.

The Global Commons

Examining these examples of common property resources and public goods extends the scope of our resource and environmental analysis. In addition, these cases relate closely to the theory of externalities, which we discussed in Chapter 3. Here we are in a sense dealing with special cases of externalities. The fisher who adds an extra boat to the fishing grounds imposes an external cost on all the other fishers by slightly lowering the average catch. The conservation group that preserves rainforest confers an external benefit on the rest of us who, whether or not we contributed to the effort, gain a slightly improved global environment.

Extending the analysis to these examples, however, seems to raise another question. Can we really continue to define all these environmental issues as "externalities"? The use of the term seems to imply a secondary role in economic theory—external costs are added to economic analysis after the rest of the theory is essentially complete. But are these so-called externalities actually symptoms of something more fundamental?

As we consider the multitude of environmental problems that have gained increased attention in recent years, we see the rising importance of cases involving common property resources and public goods. Global warming, ozone layer depletion, ocean pollution, freshwater pollution, groundwater overdraft, species loss—all have clear similarities to the cases we have discussed above. The increasing prevalence of such examples has led to a new focus on the concept of the **global commons.** If so many of the earth's resources and environmental systems show the characteristics of common-property resources or public goods, perhaps we should revise our thinking about the global economy.[12]

Rather than focusing on the goals of economic growth, and dealing with the "externalities" as an afterthought, we need to recognize that the global economic system is strongly dependent on the health of global ecosystems. Evaluation of the state of these systems, and an assessment of how economic development can best be adapted to planetary limits, is essential.[13] This implies the need for new approaches to economic policy, and new or reformed institutions at the national and international level. Clearly this raises issues which go beyond the management of individual fisheries or national parks.

Proper management of the global commons poses special challenges in securing agreement among many different nations. Despite the many possibilities for conflicting views and free-rider temptations, important international agreements such as the Montreal Protocol on ozone layer depletion have been put into place to deal with

[12]See Heal, 1999, and Johnson and Duchin, 2000.

[13]For a recent assessment of the state of planetary ecosystems, see World Resources Institute 2000.

threats to the global atmosphere, oceans, and ecosystems. Effective agreement on implementation has been harder to achieve in other cases, such as the Kyoto Protocol on global climate change.

We will examine some of the implications of this broader perspective on common property issues in Chapter 7 and consider some issues of managing the global commons in later chapters.

SUMMARY

Common-property resources are those that are owned by a community, without specific assignment of private property rights to individuals or firms. Various possible systems for managing such resources include traditional use customs and government management. No rules limit use of open-access resources, which leads to overuse and sometimes to the collapse of the resource's ecological functions.

A classic case of resource overuse is overfishing of the oceans. Because no restrictions limit access to fisheries in the open ocean, economic incentives result in an excessive number of boats operating. Depletion of the fish stocks results, with declining revenues for all fishers. Until net revenue (revenue minus costs) reaches zero, however, incentive continues for new participants to enter the fishery. This open-access equilibrium is both economically inefficient and ecologically damaging.

Possible policy responses to overuse of open-access resources include imposing licenses or quotas. Quotas can be assigned to individual fishing boats and can be transferable (salable). Smaller traditional societies often follow social principles of resource management, but large industrialized societies, with advanced technology for fishing and other resource extraction, require government management of open-access resources.

A similar need for active government policy arises in public goods provision. Public goods, once provided, benefit the general public rather than selected individuals. They include goods and services such as parks, highways, public health facilities, and national defense. No individual or group of individuals is likely to have sufficient incentive or funds to provide public goods, yet their benefits are great and often essential to social well-being. Many environmental public goods, such as forest and wetlands preservation, cannot be adequately supplied through the market. Government intervention and public funds are needed to achieve the social benefits that flow from providing these public goods.

The global scope of many common-property resources and public goods, including the atmosphere and oceans, raises issues regarding proper management of the global commons. New and reformed institutions are needed to manage common property resources at the global level. The difficulty often has been to establish effective international authority to regulate activities that threaten global ecosystems.

KEY TERMS AND CONCEPTS

absolutely diminishing returns
average revenue
common property resource
constant returns to scale
diminishing returns
economic optimum
effective demand
free-rider effect
global commons
individual transferable quotas (ITQs)
individual demand schedule
license fee
marginal cost
marginal revenue
market demand schedule
maximum sustainable yield

net social benefit
nonexclusive good
nonrival good
open-access equilibrium
open-access resource
overfishing
perfectly elastic supply
psychic benefit
public goods
quota
social benefit
social demand
total product
total revenue
tragedy of the commons
undersupply of public goods

DISCUSSION QUESTIONS

1. Would a good policy for fishery management aim at obtaining the maximum sustainable yield? Why or why not? When we speak of an optimal equilibrium from an economic point of view, will this equilibrium also be generally ecologically sound? What might cause economic and ecological principles to conflict in fisheries management?

2. Suppose that the fishery example discussed in the chapter was *not* a common-property resource, but was a lake fishery owned by an individual or a single firm. The owner could choose to allow fishing and charge a fee for access to the lake. How would the economic logic differ from the common-property resource case? Would a greater net social benefit accrue? Who would receive this net social benefit?

3. Discuss the effects of technological improvement in an industry that uses a common-property resource. For example, consider a technological improvement in fishing equipment that cuts the costs of a fishing boat trip in half. Technological progress usually increases net social benefit. Does it do so in this case? How would government policies relating to this industry affect your answer?

4. Do you think it is possible to draw a clear distinction between private and public goods? Which of the following might be considered public goods: farmland, forest land, beachfront property, highways, a city park, a parking lot, a sports arena? What market or public policy rules should apply to providing these goods?

PROBLEMS

1. Farmers in an arid region of Mexico draw their irrigation water from an underground aquifer. The aquifer has a natural maximum recharge rate of 340,000 gallons per day (that is, 340,000 gal/day filter into the underground reservoir from natural sources). The total product schedule for well operations looks like this:

Wells Operating	10	20	30	40	50	60	70	80	90
Total Water Output (Thousand Gals./Day)	100	200	280	340	380	400	400	380	340

a. The cost of operating a well is 600 pesos per day; the value of water to the farmer is 0.1 peso per gallon. Calculate total revenue ($TR = PQ$) for each level of output.

b. If each well is privately owned by a different farmer, how many wells will operate? (To calculate this you will need to calculate average revenue, which is TR/Q. Note that the quantity of wells is given in units of ten.) Analyze this result in terms of economic efficiency and long-term sustainability.

c. What would be the economically efficient number of wells? (To calculate this you will need marginal revenue, which is $MR = \Delta TR/\Delta Q$, best shown *between* two levels of output.) Show that net social benefit is maximized at this level of output.

d. How could the socially efficient equilibrium be achieved? In this case, is the socially efficient equilibrium also ecologically sustainable?

e. How would the answers change if the cost of well operation was 400 pesos per day?

2. Four towns share a common water source. By buying open land along the watershed (area from which the water flows) the towns can preserve its purity from sewage, road runoff, and such. The land demand schedule for each town based on water treatment costs saved can be expressed as:

$$P = \$34,000 - 10Q_d$$

where Q_d is acres purchased and P is the price the town would be willing to pay.

a. If the cost of land is $30,000 per acre, how much land will be purchased if each town operates independently? How much if they form a joint commission for land purchases? Graph the different possibilities. (If the economic theory is not clear, imagine representatives of the four towns sitting around a table, discussing the costs and benefits of purchasing different amounts of land.)

b. Which is the socially efficient solution and why? How would the answers change if the price of land was $36,000 per acre?

c. Discuss this in terms of the demand for clean water. Is clean water a public good in this case? Can water generally be considered a public good?

REFERENCES

Clark, Colin W. *Mathematical Bioeconomics: The Optimal Management of Renewable Resources.* New York: Wiley, 1990.

Feeny, David, Fikret Berkes, Bonnie J. McCay, and James M. Acheson. "The Tragedy of the Commons: Twenty-Two Years Later." Chapter 8 in *Environmental Economics and Development,* edited by J. B. (Hans) Opschoor, Kenneth Button, and Peter Nijkamp. Cheltenham, England: Edward Elgar, 1999.

Hardin, Garrett. "The Tragedy of the Commons." *Science* 162 (1968).

Heal, Geoffrey. "New Strategies for the Provision of Public Goods: Learning for International Environmental Challenges." In *Global Public Goods: International Cooperation in the 21st Century,* edited by Inge Kaul et al. New York: Oxford University Press, 1999.

Johnson, Baylor, and Faye Duchin. "The Case for the Global Commons," in *Rethinking Sustainability,* edited by Jonathan M. Harris. Ann Arbor, Mich.: University of Michigan Press, 2000.

Pearce, David W., ed. *The MIT Dictionary of Modern Economics,* 4th ed. Cambridge, Mass.: MIT Press, 1992.

World Resources Institute, United Nations Development Programme, United Nations Environment Programme, and World Bank. *World Resources 2000–2001: People and Ecosystems: the Fraying Web of Life.* Washington, D.C.: World Resources Institute, 2000.

WEB SITES

1. **http://www.indiana.edu/~iascp/articles.html** Links to articles related to management of common pool resources. The site is managed by the International Association for the Study of Common Property, "a nonprofit Association devoted to understanding and improving institutions for the management of environmental resources that are (or could be) held or used collectively by communities in developing or developed countries."

2. **http://www.gci.org.uk/** Home page for the Global Commons Institute, a British organization comprised of "an independent group of people whose aim is the protection of the Global Commons." The institute mainly focuses on global climate change issues.

CHAPTER FOCUS QUESTIONS

- How can we calculate the costs and benefits of environmental outcomes?
- Can we put a value on ecological systems, or on human health and life?
- How can we weigh the interests of future generations?

CHAPTER **6**

Valuing the Environment

Cost-Benefit Analysis

One advantage of using environmental policy tools that work through market mechanisms—for example, taxes, subsidies, and transferable permits—is that the final decisions on resource use and goods production lie with firms and individuals. The government acts to modify market outcomes, but not to determine the exact result. In some cases, however, governments must make specific decisions that have both economic and environmental implications. In such cases, decision-makers often use **cost-benefit analysis (CBA)**[1] to balance the positive and negative consequences of a proposed action.

Take the example of a proposed government project: the construction of a large dam. The project will have some major economic benefits: hydroelectric power, a stable water supply for irrigation, and flood control. It will also have negative effects: Farmland and wildlife habitat will be flooded, some communities will have to relocate, and some fish species may become extinct. The project may create new recreational

---

[1]The terms "cost-benefit analysis" and "benefit-cost analysis" have the same meaning. "Cost-benefit analysis," the more common term, will be used here.

opportunities for lake boating and fishing, but it will reduce scenic whitewater rafting and hiking.

How can we evaluate whether or not to build the dam? Some costs and benefits are relatively easy to assess. We can probably obtain good estimates of the construction costs of the dam, and of the value of hydroelectric power and irrigation water, for example. But how can we put a dollar value on the social and ecological losses that will result?

Estimating Value

Economists use various techniques to estimate different kinds of values. The most obvious kind of value is **use value.** In this example, the value of farmland used for raising crops is a **direct use value,** which can be measured by its market price. Certainly farmers whose land is submerged by the dam waters will suffer losses at least equal to the value of their farms. These should be included in our estimates of costs associated with dam construction. Rafting on a river or hiking through the woods are also direct uses that bring benefits to those who enjoy these activities, although the benefits may be more difficult to measure in monetary terms.

Indirect use values include ways in which forested lands and wetlands benefit nearby communities by filtering rainfall, preventing flooding, and absorbing potential pollution. These are real economic values that we certainly should consider, but they may be less evident than something like crop values.

In addition to use values, we must consider important kinds of **non-use values.** One of these is **option value.** If we decide to go ahead and build the dam, the flooded farms and forests will be lost forever—the decision is characterized by **irreversibility.** On the other hand, if we decide not to build the dam today, we could still decide to build it 10 or 20 years from now. Thus we can preserve the option of building or not building the dam by simply doing nothing.

Option values are important because economies change over time, and so do the values of different goods, services, and environmental assets. Farmland or undeveloped natural areas might become much more valuable in the future; on the other hand, the need for hydroelectric power or irrigation water might become much greater. In either case, the decision on the dam might be made with better information at a later date[2].

Another non-use value is **existence value.** Consider the fish species that might be made extinct by building the dam. Even if these species have no commercial value, many people might believe they should be preserved. Some might argue that other species have their own rights to exist, independent of human valuations, or that the existence of many different species means that we ourselves live in a richer world— richer in a spiritual rather than a monetary sense. In addition, we may be unaware of ways that maintaining biological diversity may improve the health of ecosystems.

---

[2]If we take this logic to its extreme, of course, we would never make any decisions on resource use—which is why we weigh option values against other values.

TABLE 6-1 *Categories of Value*

	Present	*Future*
Direct use	direct use value	option value (direct use)
Indirect use	indirect use value	option value (indirect use)
Non-use	existence value	bequest value (option existence value)

Source: Adapted from V. & E. Ostrom, 1977.

It is also important to consider the value of leaving an undamaged world to future generations, something that economists identify as **bequest value.** Clearly existence and bequest values will be difficult to put in monetary terms—but may nonetheless be important. These different categories of value are summarized in Table 6-1.

Techniques of Valuation

How can we obtain an economic measure of these different kinds of value? Economists use a variety of techniques to put **nonmarket values** such as whitewater rafting or the pollution-absorption services of a wetland into dollar terms.

Contingent Valuation

One such approach is called **contingent valuation.** This is essentially a survey method, in which people are asked how much they would be willing to pay to preserve rafting or hiking opportunities or other environmental functions. The resulting estimate of **willingness to pay (WTP)** can be included in a cost-benefit analysis—although its reliability may be subject to challenge.

Questions arise concerning the accuracy of such survey answers. Their hypothetical nature—with no actual money involved—might lead some respondents to give unrealistically high valuations. Also, respondents might have limited knowledge of functions like wetland pollution-absorption, leading them to underestimate the real benefits of wetland preservation.

Sometimes economists try to estimate **willingness to accept (WTA)** rather than willingness to pay. In the dam example, people might be asked how large a payment would adequately compensate them for the loss of hiking and rafting opportunities. WTA estimates are often much higher in dollar value than WTP estimates for the same items. This has led some critics to question the usefulness of the contingent valuation approach.

Consider an example. Suppose you were asked, as part of a contingent valuation survey, how much you would be prepared to pay to prevent the extinction of the blue whale, the largest animal on earth (and one of the most endangered). Depending on your level of concern, you might be willing to contribute, say, $100 to a preservation effort that you thought would be effective. Unless you were very wealthy, a significantly larger amount such as $1,000 would almost certainly be too high.[3]

But now suppose the question was phrased in WTA terms. Would you accept $1,000 to give the go-ahead for the extinction of the blue whale? Most likely you would regard such a proposal as ethically unacceptable. People who are concerned about the growing problem of species extinction might well refuse *any* amount offered.

This disparity between WTP and WTA indicates an inherent problem with the economic valuation of environmental issues. Unlike a more ordinary economic transaction such as the purchase of a house, placing a pricetag on the environment involves serious ethical and philosophical considerations. Economic values are clearly important in decision making, but can the true value of environmental preservation really be expressed in dollar terms?

Although one response would be that some things are indeed priceless, many actual decisions on environmental issues do depend on dollar values. Land preservation organizations such as The Nature Conservancy are familiar with this dilemma. Often, the reality is that if the money can be raised to preserve a natural area, it will be saved; otherwise, it will be lost to other, economically profitable uses. So even those who resent economists' efforts to put a money value on everything cannot avoid dealing with the issue of economic valuation.[4]

Demand-Side Methods

Some other techniques of valuation more closely relate to people's actual market decisions. **Hedonic pricing** attempts to value environmental services as they relate to the value of marketed goods. For example, the value of a house situated next to a conservation area is likely to be higher than that of a comparable house situated next to the town dump. By an econometric analysis of the various attributes that determine housing values (size, location, access to schools, and so forth), we may isolate the effect of specific environmental factors.[5] This gives the basis for an estimate of the benefits and costs associated with various environmental and land-use policies.

Another market-related technique is the **travel cost method.** This can be used to value the recreational attributes of environmental resources such as parks and scenic

---

[3]In a survey, not an actual contribution, you might of course claim that you were willing to pay $1,000 or more. Unless you would be prepared to back that up with real money, your inflated estimate is an example of **strategic bias**—you are attempting to bias the survey upward by stating an amount that exceeds your actual willingness to pay.

[4]See the Symposium on Contingent Valuation in *Journal of Economic Perspectives* 8, no. 4 (1994) for a debate between proponents (Portney, 1994; Hanemann, 1994) and critics (Diamond and Hausman, 1994) of the use of survey techniques for valuation.

[5]Econometric analysis uses statistical techniques to estimate economic relationships.

areas. A survey of visitors to a national park can show how far they have traveled to reach the park, giving an estimate of the amount they have spent (gas, tolls, fares, entry fees, and the value of time spent traveling) to enjoy the park's amenities. Such data can be used to simulate a demand curve, indicating how many people are willing to visit the park at different total costs for the trip. The area under the demand curve indicates the total value of the park to its visitors (using the welfare analysis outlined in Chapter 3). Note that this approach cannot represent the full ecological value of the park, nor does it capture option, existence, or bequest values.

Supply-Side Methods

Whereas hedonic and travel cost methods derive value estimates from the demand side of the market, **production function** and **engineering cost** methods are based on the supply side. Here the goal is to evaluate how much it would cost to duplicate or replace environmental services. For example, a pollution treatment plant might replace wetland pollution-absorption capabilities. We can obtain engineering estimates of the size and nature of the facility required, then calculate the cost of building and operating such a plant. If the wetland is preserved, building and operating the treatment plant is unnecessary, and this **avoided cost** can be used as an estimate of the value of wetland pollution control services.

A combination of these techniques can be used to derive an estimated dollar value for environmental services.[6] How valid are these estimates? The answer may depend on how broad a view we wish to take of the concept of value. We may often obtain a fairly good approximation of the purely **economic value** involved. However, the broader concept of **ecological value** is less easy to define.

Note that all the measures we have discussed refer to value to humans, and are defined in terms of people's ability or willingness to pay, or the capacity to provide substitutes through human productive activity. Some environmental issues, such as the preservation of endangered species, are difficult to define in such terms. We cannot recreate a species once it is extinct; we do not usually think of whole species as commodities with a market value (though individual members of a species can be bought and sold); and we may not even understand the relationships between species and their complex interactions in ecosystems. Thus although economic estimates may capture part of the value of a species (as food or as a source of medicinal products, for example), the total value may transcend economic analysis.[7]

There is an extensive and ongoing debate about the potential and the limits of economic valuation of environmental costs and benefits. We will consider this controversy in more depth later in this chapter. First, however, we need to address a specific issue of considerable importance to economic valuation: the question of time. How do

---

[6]For an extensive overview of valuation methods, see Smith, 1996; Hanley and Spash, 1998; and Markandya and Richardson, 1993. The application of valuation techniques to specific projects is discussed, with case studies, in Dixon et al., 1997.

[7]For differing approaches to this issue, see Pearce and Moran, 1997; Daily, 1997.

6-1   Valuing Human Health and Life

How do economists value human lives? Shouldn't life be beyond monetary value? Such questions are sometimes unavoidable in performing environmental cost-benefit analyses. For example, policies for tighter control of pesticide residues may reduce the amount of cancer-causing chemicals to which children and adults are exposed (children's exposure can be a more serious concern since growing bodies may be more vulnerable to damaging effects). Such tighter regulation might cause increased production costs in the agricultural sector—say, increased labor costs to implement integrated pest management, which limits chemical use. But to measure the benefits we must place some kind of money value on reduced incidence of cancer.

One obvious measure would be the avoided cost of health care for cancer patients. To estimate this, we need a reliable scientific estimate of the probable reduction in cancer cases, which we would multiply by the average cost of hospital care to obtain a measure of total medical costs. But what about avoided cancer deaths? Suppose our evidence indicates that several deaths per year will be avoided. How can we balance that with the increased production costs involved?

We might base a simple economic estimate on what an individual contributes in terms of production of goods and services to society. This, however, would assign the life of a CEO a dollar value 20 to 30 times the life value of a manual worker, a valuation many would consider unjustified. Alternatively, if we consider what people spend on life insurance and safety precautions, we can derive an estimated value, usually in the range of several million dollars, for a human life. If, for example, someone is willing to accept a hazardous job with a one in one hundred chance of death in return for an extra $20,000 in income, this implies a life valuation of $(100)(\$20,000) = \$2$ million. Or if someone is willing to spend an extra $500 for car safety features that reduce the chances of a fatal accident by one in ten thousand, he or she is setting an implicit value of $(\$500)(10,000) = \$5$ million on his or her life.

Clearly, this kind of estimate cannot capture the full value of life. Few of us would be prepared to die for $5 million. Rather, it indicates the value of what economists call a "statistical life," based on demonstrated willingness to pay to avoid risks to life.

Many of us might object to having the value of our lives expressed in economic terms. Yet if we reject monetary valuation, we must either set the value of life at zero, which is clearly wrong, or make it infinite—meaning that *no* risks of any sort could be tolerated, which is impossible. This dilemma cannot be resolved by economists alone—it involves political and ethical judgments as well.

we value the future? How can we balance costs and benefits today with costs and benefits at some other time? Will our evaluation change depending on whether we are considering a period a few years from now, or several generations in the future? Many environmental issues have long-term consequences, so the question of time is a critical aspect of valuation.

Balancing Present and Future: The Discount Rate

Economists evaluate future costs and benefits with a technique called discounting. In Chapter 4, we discussed the use of discounting for resource allocation over time. More generally, discounting, applied to *any* cost or benefit expected in the future, provides an estimate of its **present value**.

The theory behind discounting is that a dollar today is worth more than a dollar tomorrow—even correcting for inflation. The **discount rate** is the annual rate at which dollar values are considered to increase over time. Thus at an 8 percent discount rate, $1.00 today becomes $1.08 next year and $(\$1.00)(1.08^{10}) = \$2.16$ 10 years from now. Similarly, $1.00 to be received 10 years from now is worth $(\$1.00)/(1.08^{10}) = \$0.46$ today. Use of a discount rate makes sense for most financial calculations. However, its application to environmental costs and benefits is more complicated.

For longer time periods, the discount factor becomes much more dramatic. The present value of $1,000 to be received 50 years from now is only $87.20 at a 5 percent discount rate. And the present value of $1,000 to be received in 100 years is only $7.60 today (see Figure 6-1). This would mean that, according to present value theory, it is not worth spending more than $7.60 today to avoid $1,000 worth of damages 100 years from now. This has led to another serious criticism of the economic perspective. How can we justify a technique that may evaluate serious damages to future generations as less important than moderate costs today?

Discounting is essential if we consider the economics of, for example, taking a mortgage to buy a house or a loan to finance a business investment. The benefits of being able to own and live in the house starting today may well outweigh the future costs of paying interest on the mortgage over the next twenty years. Similarly, the income generated by the business investment can be compared to the annual payments on the loan.

In this case it makes sense to use the commercial discount rate, determined in current markets, to compare present benefits and future costs. Even so, can we say that a GNP gain today, or in the near future, outweighs major damage in the next generation? How should we evaluate broader environmental impacts that will continue over long periods of time?

Applying the Discount Rate

In the case of cost-benefit evaluation of a dam project, the choice of discount rate may play a crucial role in the relative weighting of costs and benefits. Three time periods must be considered: the dam construction period (say, three years); the

(a) Present Value of $1,000 at 1% and 2% Discount Rates

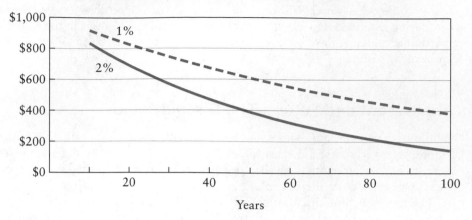

(b) Present Value of $1,000 at 5% and 10% Discount Rates

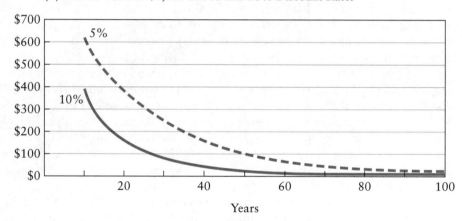

FIGURE 6-1   *Present Value of $1,000 at Different Discount Rates*

period of active dam operation (say, fifty years); and, in the case of dams prone to silting up over time, the period after the dam ceases to provide benefits (see Figure 6-2).

During the construction period we experience only costs, no benefits. Once the dam starts to operate in the fourth year, there are benefits such as hydroelectric power, irrigation water, and flood control. But there are also two types of costs: operating costs and external environmental and social costs (some of the external costs might begin before dam operation starts, but for simplicity we have assumed here that they start simultaneously with dam operation). During the 50-year expected lifetime of the dam, both benefits and costs must be reckoned. After the dam ceases to operate, the

6-2	The Discount Rate

If r is the discount rate, the present value $PV[B]$ of a future benefit B expected n years from now is given by: $PV[B] = B / (1+r)^n$

Consider two extreme cases:

Case 1: $r = 0$

In this case the future is not discounted at all. Future costs and benefits are weighted as if they took place in the present. This is almost never the case for individuals. We are all mortals and therefore tend to always favor the present more than the future. But families or whole societies may choose to put a higher value on the future. Parents may weigh future gains or losses to their children at least as much as consumption today. Societies that set aside land for preservation as national parks and wildlife refuges willingly give up the possibilities of commercial exploitation today in order to guarantee recreational and wilderness areas to future generations.

Case 2: r is Extremely High

In this case the future is totally neglected in favor of the short term. This situation can occur in poor societies where the struggle for survival today makes it impossible to devote any resources to future needs. But something like it can also occur in more affluent democratic societies where the vision of decision-makers extends no further than the next election, so that costs that will occur in 10, 20, or 50 years are neglected in favor of present benefits.

environmental and social costs may continue indefinitely. Thus the evaluation of net present value includes four components: a benefit sum from years 4–53, a construction cost sum from years 1–3, an operating cost sum from years 4–53, and an external cost sum from year 4 to infinity. All of these must be discounted back to year 0, using the formula shown in Figure 6-2. Let's look at some of the implications of different discount rates for this evaluation.

A *high* discount rate will mean that the benefits of the dam, which start after three years, will have a lower present value. This may make it less likely that the dam can be justified on economic grounds. On the other hand, environmental damages resulting from the dam, which may extend far into the future, will also be discounted to a relatively low present value. This might make it more likely that an environmentally destructive project will be approved.

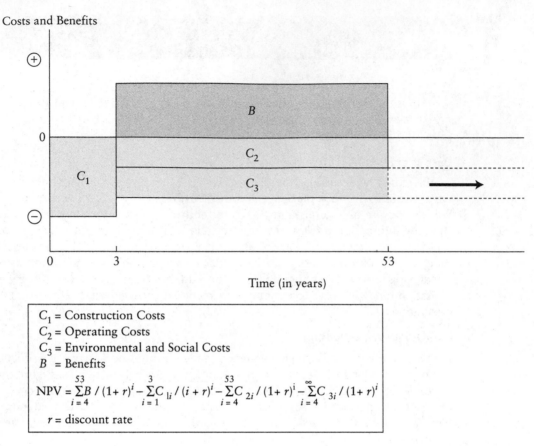

Costs and Benefits

C_1 = Construction Costs
C_2 = Operating Costs
C_3 = Environmental and Social Costs
B = Benefits

$$\text{NPV} = \sum_{i=4}^{53} B / (1+r)^i - \sum_{i=1}^{3} C_{1i} / (i+r)^i - \sum_{i=4}^{53} C_{2i} / (1+r)^i - \sum_{i=4}^{\infty} C_{3i} / (1+r)^i$$

r = discount rate

FIGURE 6-2 *Costs and Benefits of a Dam Project over Time*

A *low* discount rate will raise the present value of the dam's economic benefits relative to construction costs. At the same time, it will weight long-term environmental damages more heavily. Especially if these damages extend well beyond the useful life of the dam, environmental costs could become a decisive factor in a decision to cancel the project.

This means that neither a high nor a low discount rate is inherently better for environmental valuation. However, for some issues a low rate has been advocated on the grounds that it better reflects future interests, including those of future generations. In the case of global climate change, for example, potential damages rise significantly over a period of decades, or even centuries (assuming that emission levels remain high). Some analysts believe that a low discount rate is justified in evaluating these long-term effects. The same argument can be applied to other cumulative environmental problems such as soil erosion, caused by current farming practices but whose most damaging impacts may occur decades later.

The Social Discount Rate

We can try to resolve the problem by defining a **social discount rate** or **social rate of time preference (SRTP)**—a rate that attempts to reflect the appropriate social valuation of the future. We can define:

$$\text{SRTP} = p + \epsilon c$$

where SRTP is the social rate of time preference;

> p is the "pure" rate of time preference, representing the human tendency to prefer the present over the future;
> c is the growth rate of consumption per capita;
> ϵ is a measure of the rate at which our extra satisfaction from increased consumption declines as consumption increases (in economic terms, the elasticity of the marginal utility of consumption).

From a social point of view, setting p at zero makes sense. Our well being today is not inherently any more important than that of our children or grandchildren. This means that a positive discount rate must be based on the ϵc term in the equation.

The principle behind the ϵc term is that extra consumption will be of greater relative value to a poor person than to a rich one. The implication for discounting is that if we expect to be richer in the future, it is reasonable to place a higher value on consumption today (when our unfilled needs are greater) relative to the future.

If our children and grandchildren will be richer than we are, favoring consumption today over consumption tomorrow may be somewhat justified.

Long-term rates of growth in per capita consumption over the past several decades have been about 2 percent. Economic studies based on consumption patterns indicate that plausible values for ϵ are around 1.5. If we set p at zero, this implies a long-term discount rate of no more than 3 percent, perhaps less if we are cautious about the prospects for future growth.[8]

A different method of estimating SRTP is based on the **opportunity cost of capital.** This refers to the rate of return available on alternative investment projects. If society can obtain an 8 percent rate of return on investment, it makes no sense to settle for a project that returns only 3 percent. Estimates based on the opportunity costs of capital tend to be higher than those based on long term consumption.

From an environmental point of view, however, this method has serious drawbacks. Human-made capital typically lasts 10 to 20 years, or 20 to 50 years for infrastructure investment such as roads and bridges. Thus current rates of return on investment may overestimate long-term benefits.

Consider, for example, a nuclear power plant. After its productive lifetime of about 40 years, nothing is left for future generations except long-lived radioactive

---

[8]In a study of global climate change, Cline (1992) suggests the use of a 1.5 percent SRTP to evaluate long-term impacts of climate change.

wastes. Even if the plant is profitable in current financial terms, its long-term social impact may be negative. The discount rate used in cost-benefit analysis should give adequate weight to these long-term costs.

The choice of a discount rate is clearly a controversial issue, and it is not possible to select a single rate that satisfies all the criteria of commercial viability, environmental sustainability, and social responsibility. One way of dealing with this is to use several different discount rates for cost-benefit analysis, which permits a **sensitivity analysis,** showing the relationship of the results to the choice of discount rate.

The dam project, for example, may look good at a moderate discount rate, but at a low rate the long-term environmental costs may outweigh the benefits. Therefore, decision-makers could reach different conclusions regarding net benefits of a project, depending on the relative weighting of present and future values.

Any discount rate selected may be subject to challenge. Some argue that the issue of resource and environmental considerations for the future are a matter of **intergenerational equity,** and that our obligation to leave a healthy environment for future generations is one that cannot be measured in economic terms. If we take this approach, we must distinguish between issues that can reasonably be dealt with through the economic system, and issues where moral imperatives for environmental protection must take precedence.[9]

Dealing with Risk and Uncertainty

The evaluation of future costs and benefits may also involve issues of risk or uncertainty. For example, operating a nuclear power plant involves some risk of a serious accident and major release of radiation. How great is this risk? The nuclear industry calls it small, but some critics call it substantial. Any cost-benefit analysis of a nuclear power plant would have to take this issue into account.

Defining Risk and Uncertainty

Risk and uncertainty are not the same thing. In some cases, *risk* can be estimated with a high degree of confidence. For example, statistical studies can define the risks associated with smoking. While no one can tell whether a particular smoker will suffer an early onset of serious disease or live to a ripe old age, it is clear that smoking increases the chances of disease and death, and for a large population these risks can be calculated fairly precisely. Similarly, emissions of certain toxic atmospheric pollutants are likely to increase cancer risks, and epidemiological studies can link pollution levels to increases in cancer incidence and death rates.

Uncertainty, in contrast, implies a much less clearly defined understanding of the possible outcomes. The issue of global climate change, discussed in depth in Chapter

---

[9]See Toman, 1994, and Page, 1997; these articles are summarized and the issue is discussed further in Harris et al., 2001, Part 1.

Earthquake damage in Watsonville, California. Added insurance costs are required to cover earthquake risks.

18, demonstrates this. The full effects of global climate change resulting from emissions of greenhouse gases are not predictable. Although scientists have generally agreed on a range of possible temperature increases likely to result over the next century, the global weather system is so complex that dramatic and unpredictable events are possible.

For example, it is possible that positive **feedback effects** such as the release of CO_2 from melting of the Arctic tundra could add huge additional volumes of greenhouse gases to the atmosphere, greatly accelerating warming. Climate change could also lead to changes in ocean currents such as the Gulf Stream, changing the climate of Northern Europe to something like that of Alaska, and alterations in tropical weather patterns leading to much more violent hurricanes. But no one can determine the likelihood of these events.

Calculating Expected Value

Well-defined risks are easier to incorporate into economic analysis than uncertain future possibilities. If we can estimate both the risk and the cost of a potential outcome, we can express its **expected value** as

$$EV[X] = p[X] \, C[X]$$

where EV is expected value, p is the probability of event X, and C is its cost.

This expected value can then be used for economic analysis just like any other estimate. Suppose, for example, that building a house in an earthquake-prone area involves an annual risk of about 1 in 100 of significant earthquake damage. (This reflects the likelihood that an earthquake will occur about once every 100 years.) An insurance company will insist on a higher premium to insure such a house.

The homeowner will pay an extra amount (above the cost of ordinary insurance) equal to the expected value of annual damages. The costs of a catastrophic event—which may or may not occur—can thus be internalized, allowing a normal housing market to operate, with somewhat higher costs reflecting earthquake risks. Expected value estimates can be used in cost-benefit analysis in a similar way, assuming that the probability of the event can be predicted with reasonable confidence.

The formula for expected value does not take into account **risk aversion**—the common tendency to prefer a certain outcome to a risky one. For example, suppose you were offered the choice of gaining $100,000 versus a 50-50 chance of gaining either $200,000 or nothing. You might well prefer to take the certain $100,000, even though the expected value of the two options is the same. If risk aversion is significant, the expected value method will overestimate the value of options where some risk is involved.

How about when we do not know the probability of the event? In the dam project case, suppose that some chance exists of a major earthquake that could break the dam, causing massive flooding and the loss of many lives. The chance of a major quake is considered small—say, less than 1 in 1,000—but is not known with any degree of certainty.

In this case the **precautionary principle** may apply. People in the area may be unwilling to take even a remote chance of such a huge catastrophe. A similar logic applies to the unpredictable possibilities of extreme global warming effects. We can't tell whether they will occur, but the unknown risk of such major planetary disruptions makes us properly nervous and lends urgency to efforts to reduce greenhouse gas emissions.

The precautionary principle is especially appropriate when irreversibility is involved. Some types of pollution and environmental damage can be remedied by reducing emissions or allowing time for natural systems to regenerate. Others, like species loss, are irreversible. In cases where we can adjust for mistakes or change our policies to adapt to new circumstances, an economic balancing of costs and benefits may be appropriate. But when essential natural systems could suffer irreversible damage, it is better to apply a **safe minimum standard** of environmental protection.

Damage to the atmospheric ozone layer, for example, could threaten all life on earth by removing an essential barrier to destructive radiation. As a result, international treaties have sought to impose a complete ban on ozone-depleting substances, regardless of any economic benefits they offer.[10]

---

[10]Loopholes in these treaties, allowing limited production in developing nations for economic reasons, constitute one major threat to their effectiveness. Another major threat is illegal production and trade.

Dealing with issues involving risk and uncertainty requires good judgment regarding which risks can reasonably be estimated and given an expected monetary value. Inability to know outcomes with certainty does not render economic analysis of environmental impacts inappropriate. Still, we must exercise caution in order to recognize cases where economic valuation of possible outcomes may fail to capture the full impact of potential outcomes on human health or ecosystems.[11]

Comparing Costs and Benefits

We have seen that cost-benefit analysis necessarily involves controversy as well as difficult questions of valuation and discounting. Suppose that, having grappled with these issues, we are satisfied that we have done the best job possible of measuring all the costs and benefits associated with the dam project discussed above. If the benefits outweigh the costs, should we proceed with dam construction? Not necessarily—even if we are fully confident of our valuation techniques, important issues remain regarding how we evaluate the results.

On the benefit side, we can sum up the present value of total benefits over time as:

$$PV[B] = B_0 + B_1/(1+r) + B_2/(1+r)^2 + B_3/(1+r)^3 \ldots B_n/(1+r)^n$$

while the total present value of costs is:

$$PV[C] = C_0 + C_1/(1+r) + C_2/(1+r)^2 + C_3/(1+r)^3 \ldots C_n/(1+r)^n$$

where period 0 is the current year, r is the discount rate, and our analysis extends n years into the future. To calculate the value of an infinite stream of benefits or costs, we can use the formula $PV[B] = B_i/(1+r)^i = B/r$.

The **net present value** of the project is then:

$$NPV = PV[B] - PV[C]$$

while the **benefit/cost ratio** for the project is:

$$PV[B]/PV[C]$$

If we are prepared to give the green light to a project whose benefits exceed its costs, we are using the **positive net present value criterion**:

$$NPV = PV[B] - PV[C] > 0$$

---

[11]See Toman, 1994, and O'Brien, 2000 for discussion of the limitations of economic valuation.

6-3   Cost-Benefit Analysis of Arsenic in Drinking Water

The case of arsenic standards for drinking water illustrates some practical difficulties and ambiguities of applying cost-benefit analysis (CBA). The maximum arsenic concentration allowed in U.S. public drinking water was established at 50 parts per billion (ppb) in 1942. A 1999 report by the National Academy of Sciences concluded that the 50 ppb standard "does not achieve EPA's goal for public-health protection and, therefore, requires downward revision as promptly as possible" (National Research Council, 1999).

In 2001, the U.S. Environmental Protection Agency published the results of a CBA that estimated the costs and benefits of four new standards: 20, 10, 5, and 3 ppb (U.S. EPA, 2001). The costs of complying with each standard are relatively certain. However, the benefits of each standard are much more difficult to estimate for several reasons. First, incomplete toxicological data prevents accurately determining the health benefits of lowering the arsenic standard, measured in terms of reduced illnesses and deaths. Second, the economic methods used to value these benefits are imprecise and controversial. Third, some benefits associated with lower arsenic standards can not be estimated at all.

The arsenic CBA estimates the number of lung and bladder cancer cases that would be avoided at each standard. About half of these cases would result in death. Considerable uncertainty exists over how many cancer cases would be avoided, particularly when the standard drops below 10 ppb. The CBA estimates the benefit of an avoided cancer death by placing a $6.1 million value on a statistical life. The benefit of an avoided nonfatal cancer case is valued at $607,000 based on a study of willingness to pay to avoid a case of chronic bronchitis.

The exact values chosen for these benefits fail to reflect the considerable uncertainty associated with such estimates. For example, the CBA's $6.1 million value of a statistical life is the average of 26 estimates ranging from $0.9 million to $20.8 million in 1999 dollars (Abt Associates, 2000).

The quantified costs and benefits indicated that the arsenic standards of 10 and 20 ppb may provide positive net benefits. The arsenic standards of 3 and 5 ppb apparently fail to provide positive net benefits. However, the CBA notes that several categories of benefits could not be quantified. Arsenic exposure has been associated with other health effects including skin cancer, kidney cancer, pulmonary effects, cardiovascular effects, and neurological effects. Treatment of water supplies to reduce arsenic levels may also reduce the levels of other contaminants. A reduction in arsenic levels may also provide psychic benefits to users because of

(continued on following page)

reduced anxiety over health effects. In light of these unquantified potential benefits, the CBA cannot conclude that the lower arsenic standards do not provide positive net benefits.

Based on this CBA, the U.S. EPA recommended a new arsenic standard of 10 ppb. However, in March 2001 the Bush administration announced it was withdrawing plans to proceed with the new standard. The administration ordered a review of the proposed standard, stating that the "scientific indicators are unclear." EPA administrator Christie Whitman said that the "standard should be less than 50 ppb" but not necessarily as low as 10 ppb. She also vowed, "When we make a decision on arsenic, it will be based on sound science and solid analysis." This set the stage for vigorous public criticism of the administration's environmental policies. In July 2001 the U.S. House of Representatives voted to direct the EPA to implement the 10 ppb standard. Clearly, the issue of arsenic standards is one that involves political and social debate as well as economic analysis.

Estimated Costs and Benefits of Different Arsenic Standards

Arsenic Standard (ppb)	Compliance Costs ($ millions 1999)	Health Benefits ($ millions 1999)	Bladder and Lung Cancer Cases Avoided
3	$698–$792	$214–$491	57–138
5	$415–$472	$191–$356	51–100
10	$180–$206	$140–$198	37–56
20	$67–$77	$66–$75	19–20

Source: Table III.E-7 of U.S. EPA (2001).

SOURCES

Abt Associates, Inc. *Arsenic in Drinking Water Rule Economic Analysis.* U.S. EPA report number EPA-815-R-00-026, 2000.

National Research Council. *Arsenic in Drinking Water.* Washington, D.C.: National Academy Press, 1999.

United States Environmental Protection Agency. "National Primary Drinking Water Regulations; Arsenic and Clarifications to Compliance and New Source Contaminants Monitoring; Final Rule." *Federal Register* 40 CFR Parts 9, 141, and 142, vol. 66 (January 22, 2001): 6975–7066.

(a) Total Costs and Benefits of Various Dam Projects

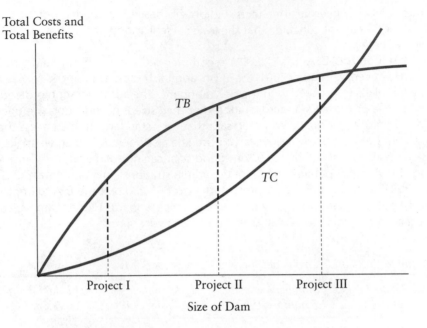

(b) Marginal Costs and Benefits of Various Dam Projects

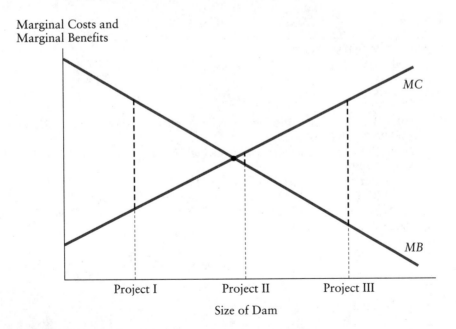

FIGURE 6-3 *Costs and Benefits of Various Dam Projects*

Unfortunately, this criterion only ensures that the project is of some positive value, not that it is the best choice available. Suppose that the power and irrigation benefits we seek could be obtained by dams of various sizes, as shown in Figure 6-3.

If we conduct a cost-benefit analysis for the largest dam, Project III, we will find that the positive net present value criterion is satisfied: total benefits exceed total costs. Yet, to go ahead with this dam would clearly be a mistake. The two smaller projects have better benefit/cost ratios. The smaller dams may offer less total hydroelectric power and irrigation benefits, but their costs, including environmental costs, are significantly lower.

We can see the logic behind this by looking at the marginal benefit and marginal cost curves, shown in the lower part of Figure 6-3, corresponding to the total benefit and total cost curves shown in the upper part. From an economic point of view, as we saw in Chapter 3, the best principle is to equate marginal benefit and marginal cost. The intersection point of the MB and MC curves satisfies **maximum net present value criterion.** Of the three projects in this example, Project II offers the maximum net present value. Although both Project I and Project III bring some net benefits, neither have net benefits as high as Project II.

Unfortunately, in applying this criterion in real-world situations we generally cannot "see" the marginal benefit and cost curves. Nor can we see the whole total benefit and total cost curves. We can only evaluate the costs and benefits of particular projects using the techniques we have discussed. Unless we consider a range of possible projects, we may be misled into approving a project that is not economically optimal. In this example, the fact that the benefit/cost ratio for the large dam is only slightly greater than one (total benefits only slightly exceed total costs) should serve as a warning sign that we need to investigate other possibilities.

Conclusion: How Useful Is Cost-Benefit Analysis?

Valuing the environment is necessarily a troublesome endeavor. Some argue that what nature gives us is priceless and reject reducing these "services" to mere monetary values; others maintain that putting a value on ecological functions is essential because the alternative is to allow the economic system to value them at zero.

Critics of cost-benefit analysis point to the many difficulties involved in obtaining reliable estimates, and the fact that some elements, such as spiritual value or the value of community, are essentially impossible to estimate in dollar terms. Economists generally maintain that cost-benefit analysis is a useful tool, provided it is used with proper caution. It would be unreasonable to assume that we can place a precise dollar value on everything—but in many cases economic valuations can assist decisionmakers by providing specific estimates of policy impacts.

The most significant difficulty with the use of cost-benefit analysis is the requirement that we evaluate *all* costs and benefits in monetary terms to arrive at a single "bottom-line" result. One way of bypassing this problem is to use **cost-effectiveness analysis.** In this approach, economists do not attempt to decide which policy is best, but rather to analyze different means of achieving a given end.

6-4   Valuing the Global Ecosystem

Economists have devised various techniques to estimate nonmarket values for ecological services. These values allow us to incorporate ecosystem services into cost-benefit analyses. Most nonmarket applications estimate the value of a particular ecosystem or service, such as the value of a wetland or the value of clean air. A much more ambitious approach is to consider the value of the entire global ecosystem.

Although many would argue that the global ecosystem's value is priceless, large-scale application of nonmarket techniques is feasible. In fact, a group of researchers estimated the global value of ecosystem services in a 1997 article in the journal *Nature* (Costanza et al., 1997). The researchers considered the value of 17 ecosystem services including climate regulation, erosion control, waste treatment, food production, and recreation. They extensively reviewed nonmarket valuation studies to obtain estimates for the value of these services for each of 16 ecosystems, or biomes.

The Global Value of Ecosystem Services

Biome (ecosystem)	Area (millions of hectares)	Annual Value (millions of 1994 dollars)
Open ocean	33,220	8,381
Estuaries	180	4,110
Seagrass/algae beds	200	3,801
Coral reefs	62	375
Shelf	2,660	4,283
Tropical forest	1,900	3,813
Temperate/boreal forest	2,955	894
Grass/rangelands	3,898	906
Tidal marsh/mangroves	165	1,648
Swamps/floodplains	165	3,231
Lakes/rivers	200	1,700
Desert	1,925	NA[1]
Tundra	743	NA[1]
Ice/rock	1,640	NA[1]
Cropland	1,400	128
Urban	332	NA[1]
TOTAL	51,645	33,268

[1]No estimate provided.

(continued on following page)

The researchers estimated total annual value of the global ecosystem at $33 trillion, with a range of $16 to $54 trillion (for comparison, global GNP is currently about $30 trillion). Slightly more than half of the total is for nutrient cycling services. The biomes with the highest total values are open oceans, continental shelves, and estuaries. The highest per-hectare ecosystem values are for estuaries, swamps/floodplains, and seagrass/algae beds.

The Costanza et al. research has been criticized for its attempt to use fairly simple economic methods to reduce all ecological functions to money values (Turner et al, 1998; El Serafy, 1998). Still, even the critics acknowledge "the article's potential to influence environmental discourse" and generate "rich methodological discussions" (Norgaard et al., 1998). Although any specific dollar value estimate is necessarily controversial, attempts to value the global ecosystem certainly demonstrate the significant value of ecological services and their importance in policy decisions.

SOURCES

Costanza, Robert Ralph d'Arge, Rudolf de Groot, Stephen Farber, Monica Grasso, Bruce Hannon, Karin Limburg, Shahid Naeem, Robert V. O'Neill, Jose Paruelo, Robert G. Raskin, Paul Sutton, and Marjan van den Belt. "The Value of the World's Ecosystem Services and Natural Capital." *Nature* 387 (May 15, 1997): 253–260.
El Serafy, Salah. "Pricing the Invaluable: The Value of the World's Ecosystem Services and Natural Capital." *Ecological Economics* 25, no. 1 (1998): 25–27.
Norgaard, Richard B., Collin Bode, and Values Reading Group. "Next, the Value of God, and Other Reactions." *Ecological Economics* 25, no. 1 (1998): 37–39.
Turner, R. K., W. N. Adger, and R. Brouwer. "Ecosystem Services Value, Research Needs, and Policy Relevance: A Commentary," *Ecological Economics* 25, no. 1 (1998): 61–65.

Suppose, for example, that we have established a goal of cutting sulfur dioxide pollution, a major cause of acid rain, by 50 percent.[12] This might be done by requiring high-polluting plants to install scrubbers; by imposing taxes or fines based on emission levels; or by issuing tradable permits for certain levels of emissions, with the total number of permits not to exceed 50 percent of current levels. As we will see in more detail in Chapter 16, economic analysis can give a good estimate of the costs arising from each of these policies.

Clearly, there is a good case for adopting the least-cost method of reaching a given goal. In this approach, we do not rely on economic analysis to tell us *how much* we ought to reduce pollution—that decision is made based on other factors including

---

[12]This was in fact the goal set by the U.S. Environmental Protection Agency under the Clean Air Act Amendment of 1990.

scientific evidence, political discussion, and ordinary common sense. Instead, we use economic analysis to choose the most efficient policies to achieve a desired result.

The Positional Analysis Alternative

Another alternative to cost-benefit analysis, **positional analysis,** involves consideration of broader social and political factors. Here the estimation of economic costs of a particular policy is combined with an evaluation of the effects on different groups of people, possible alternative policies, goals and objectives other than economic gain, social priorities, and individual rights. No single "bottom line" emerges, and particular outcomes may favor some groups over others.[13]

For example, the construction of a major dam may require relocation of large numbers of people. Even if the dam's economics appear favorable, these people's rights to remain in their homes may be given a greater social priority. Such judgments cannot be made on a purely economic basis. However, some of the valuation techniques we have discussed may be useful in defining economic aspects of what must ultimately be a social and political decision.[14]

If we do decide to use cost-benefit analysis, we will often encounter factors that are difficult to measure in economic terms. These unknown or immeasurable factors can be represented in our summation of costs and benefits by Xs and Ys—indicating an acknowledgment of the limits of valuation techniques. (See, for example, the cost-benefit analysis of global climate change discussed in Chapter 18.)

In the chapters that follow, we will be discussing some of the broader perspectives on environmental issues that we have referred to as ecological economics. Here we will see some examples of both the use and the limitations of economic valuation of the environment. Then, when we return to specific resource and environmental topics in Parts 4–6, we will see examples of how the economic analysis techniques presented in Chapters 3–6 can be applied to environmental policy issues.

SUMMARY

Cost-benefit (also known as benefit-cost) analysis helps evaluate proposed projects and government actions. The kinds of value relevant to cost-benefit analysis include direct and indirect use values as well as non-use values such as option, existence, and bequest value. Environmental factors are often involved in cost-benefit analysis, and can be some of the most controversial to value.

Valuation techniques include contingent valuation, based on a survey that asks respondents to value environmental or other amenities in terms of their willingness to

---

[13]Söderbaum, 1999, discusses the basis of positional analysis.

[14]For a discussion of the interaction between estimation techniques and underlying values, see Gouldner and Kennedy, 1997.

pay for them, or to accept compensation for their loss. Contingent valuation is controversial, partly because "willingness to pay" and "willingness to accept" values tend to differ substantially and partly because the survey technique is vulnerable to bias and inaccurate or inflated responses.

Other techniques more closely related to market pricing include hedonic valuation and travel cost methods. Production function and engineering values are based on the costs of replacing environmental functions such as pollution absorption by wetlands with treatment plants or other human-made facilities.

Although these techniques can approximate some environmental values, they cannot capture the full ecological value of, for example, the preservation of endangered species. Some have argued that pricing the environment is inherently wrong, because dollar values are an inadequate metric for ecological systems. Others maintain that some valuation is essential for comparing policy options, and if done with caution will not misrepresent environmental values.

Economists use the technique of discounting to balance present and future costs and benefits. Selecting an appropriate discount rate is important and can significantly affect the results of cost-benefit studies. The socially appropriate discount rate may be different from the commercial discount rate used to evaluate investment returns.

Special issues arise when attempting to value human life and health, risk and uncertainty, and impacts on the future. While economic techniques exist that can be used in all these areas, they have often aroused further controversy. An alternative to economic valuation of risk is the precautionary principle, which states that we should avoid even a small possibility of a damaging outcome, especially when such an outcome may be irreversible. In such cases, a safe minimum standard of environmental protection may replace economic calculation.

KEY TERMS AND CONCEPTS

avoided cost	indirect use values	present value
benefit/cost ratio	intergenerational equity	production function
bequest value	irreversibility	method
contingent valuation	maximum net present	risk aversion
cost-benefit analysis (CBA)	value criterion	safe minimum standard
cost-effectiveness analysis	net present value	sensitivity analysis
direct use value	nonmarket values	social discount rate
discount rate	non-use values	social rate of time
ecological value	opportunity cost of	preference (SRTP)
economic value	capital	strategic bias
engineering cost method	option value	travel cost method
existence value	positional analysis	use value
expected value	positive net present	willingness to
feedback effects	value criterion	accept (WTA)
hedonic pricing	precautionary principle	willingness to pay (WTP)

DISCUSSION QUESTIONS

1. Suppose that you are asked to conduct a cost-benefit study of a proposed coal-fired power plant. The plant will be built on the outskirts of a residential area and will emit a certain volume of pollutants. It will require a substantial amount of water for its cooling system. Industries in the region argue that the additional power is urgently needed, but local residents oppose construction. How would you evaluate social and environmental costs and weigh them against economic benefits?

2. It has been proposed that a cost-benefit analysis should be required before formulating government pollution control regulations. This would involve weighing the costs to industry of conforming to the regulations versus health and environmental benefits accrued from regulation. Do you believe this proposal makes sense? Discuss how economic, health, and environmental criteria should be balanced in formulating regulations.

3. Suppose the government of a developing nation is considering establishing a national park in a scenic forested area. Local opposition arises from those who wish to use the forestland for timbering and agriculture. On the other hand, the national park would draw both local and foreign visitors as tourists. Could cost-benefit analysis aid the decision on whether or not to establish the park? What factors would you consider and how would you measure their economic value?

PROBLEM

1. The World Bank is considering an application from the country of Equatoria for a large dam project. Some project costs and benefits (dollar values) are as follows:

Construction costs: $500 million/year for 3 years
Operating Costs: $50 million/year
Hydropower to be generated: 3 billion kilowatt hours/year
Price of electricity: $0.05/kilowatt hour
Irrigation water available from dam: 5 billion gallons/year
Price of water: $0.015/gallon
Agricultural product lost from flooded lands: $45 million/year
Forest products lost from flooded lands: $20 million/year

Additional losses are less easily quantifiable: human costs to villagers who will be forced to move, watershed damage, and ecological costs of habitat destruction. It is also possible that the new lake area may contribute to the spread of waterborne diseases.

a. Do a formal cost-benefit analysis using the quantifiable factors listed above. Remember to distinguish between one-time costs and annual costs extending into the future. Discount all future costs and benefits to find present value. The simplest technique is to calculate costs and benefits as of dam start up in year 4.

Compound construction costs forward using the formula $C_t(1+r)^{(4-t)}$ for years 1–3, which gives the value of the total construction costs, plus interest, as of start up.

For costs C_i or benefits B_i extending into the indefinite future, use the formulae $PV[C] = C_i/r$ or $PV[B] = B_i/r$ to obtain the value of the (infinite) stream of benefits. You may assume that the dam will operate for the foreseeable future.

Do a complete cost/benefit analysis for *two* possible interest rates: 10 percent and 5 percent. In each case do your figures indicate a definite "yes," definite "no," or uncertain result?

b. Now consider an alternative project: a number of smaller dams constructed so as not to flood significant agricultural areas or forestlands. For this project, total construction costs are exactly half the costs of the big dam project, and power/irrigation benefits are also half as much. No damages affect farmland or forest, and the project incurs no ecological or resettlement costs. Evaluate this project and compare to the larger project at the two interest rates.

REFERENCES

Cline, William R. *The Economics of Global Warming*. Washington, D.C.: Institute for International Economics, 1992.

Daily, Gretchen C., ed. *Nature's Services: Societal Dependence on Natural Ecosystems*. Washington, D.C.: Island Press, 1997.

Diamond, Peter A., and Jerry A. Hausman. "Contingent Valuation: Is Some Number Better Than No Number?" *Journal of Economic Perspectives* 8, no. 4 (fall 1994): 45–64.

Dixon, John A., et al., eds. *Economic Analysis of Environmental Impacts*. London: Earthscan Publications, 1997.

Gouldner, Lawrence H., and Donald Kennedy. "Valuing Ecosystem Services: Philosophical Bases and Empirical Methods." In Gretchen C. Daily, ed., op. cit.

Hanley, Nick, and Clive L. Spash, eds. *Cost-Benefit Analysis and the Environment*. Cheltenham, England: Edward Elgar, 1998.

Hanneman, W. Michael. "Valuing the Environment through Contingent Valuation." *Journal of Economic Perspectives* 8, no. 4 (fall 1994): 19–43.

Harris, Jonathan M., Timothy A. Wise, Kevin P. Gallagher, and Neva R. Goodwin, eds. *A Survey of Sustainability: Social and Economic Dimensions*. Washington, D.C.: Island Press, 2001.

Markandya, Anil, and Julie Richardson. *Environmental Economics: A Reader*. Part II: Valuation Methods and Applications. New York: St. Martin's Press, 1993.

O'Brien, Mary. *Making Better Environmental Decisions: An Alternative to Risk Assessment*. Cambridge, Mass.: MIT Press, 2000.

Ostrom, Vincent, and Elinor. "Public Goods and Public Choices." In *Alternatives for Delivering Public Services: Toward Improved Performance,* edited by Emanuel S. Savas. Boulder, Colo.: Westview Press, 1977.

Page, Talbot. "On the Problem of Achieving Efficiency and Equity, Intergenerationally," *Land Economics* 73, (November 1997): 580–596.

Pearce, David, and Dominic Moran. *The Economic Value of Biodiversity.* London: Earthscan Publications, 1997.

Portney, Paul. "The Contingent Valuation Debate: Why Economists Should Care." *Journal of Economic Perspectives* 8 (fall 1994): 3–17.

Smith, V. Kerry, ed. *Estimating Economic Values for Nature: Methods for Non-Market Valuation.* Cheltenham, England: Edward Elgar, 1996.

Söderbaum, Peter. "Valuation as Part of a Microeconomics for Ecological Sustainability." In *Valuation and the Environment: Theory, Method, and Practice,* edited by Martin O'Connor and Clive Spash. Cheltenham, England: Edward Elgar, 1999.

Toman, Michael A. "Economics and 'Sustainability': Balancing Trade-offs and Imperatives," *Land Economics* 70 (November 1994): 399–413.

WEB SITES

1. http://www.rff.org/ Home page for Resources for the Future, a nonprofit organization that conducts policy and economic research on natural resource issues. Many RFF publications available on their web site use nonmarket techniques to value environmental services.
2. http://www.cnie.org/nle/rsk-4.html A paper by John Moore discussing the use of cost-benefit analysis as a basis for government regulations.
3. http://www.epa. gov/ogwdw/regs.html The EPA's 2001 cost-benefit analysis of the arsenic drinking water standard for public water supplies in the United States.

THREE

Ecological Economics and Environmental Accounting

CHAPTER FOCUS QUESTIONS

- Are natural resources a form of capital?
- How can we account for and conserve resources and environmental systems?
- Are there limits to the scale of economic systems?
- How can we sustain economic well-being and ecosystem health in the long term?

CHAPTER **7**

Ecological Economics: Some Basic Concepts

Natural Capital

The relationships between economic and environmental issues can be viewed from a variety of perspectives. In Chapters 3–6 we applied concepts derived from standard economic analysis to environmental issues. The school of thought known as ecological economics, however, takes a different approach. Ecological economics redefines some basic economic concepts to make them better applicable to environmental problems. One such fundamental concept is **natural capital.**

Most economic models of the production process focus on two factors of production: capital and labor. A third factor, usually referred to as "land," is acknowledged but usually has no prominent function in economic models. Some of the classical economists, especially David Ricardo, author of *The Principles of Political Economy and Taxation* (1817), were concerned with land and its productivity as a fundamental determinant of economic production. Modern economics, however, generally assumes that technological progress will overcome any limits on the productive capacity of land.

121

Ecological economists have reintroduced and broadened the classical concept of land, renaming it *natural capital*. Natural capital is defined as the whole endowment of land and resources available to us, including air, water, fertile soil, forests, fisheries, mineral resources, and the ecological life-support systems that make economic activity, and indeed life itself, possible.[1]

In an ecological economics perspective, natural capital should be considered at least as important as humanmade capital as a basis for production. Further, a careful accounting should be made of the state of natural capital and of its improvement or deterioration, and this should be reflected in national income accounting.

Accounting for Changes in Natural Capital

Defining natural resources as capital raises an important economic implication. A central principle of prudent economic management is to preserve the value of capital. It is generally desirable to add to productive capital over time, a process economists call **net investment.** A nation whose productive capital decreases over time (net disinvestment) is a nation in economic decline.

Sir John Hicks, Nobel laureate in economics and author of *Value and Capital* (1939), defined income as the amount of goods and services an individual or nation can consume over a period of time and remain at least as well off at the end of the period as at the beginning. In other words, you cannot increase your income by reducing your capital.

To see what this means in practice, imagine that you receive an inheritance of $1 million (few of us will ever be so lucky, but we can dream). Suppose that the million dollars is invested in bonds yielding a real return[2] of 5 percent. This will give an annual income of $50,000. However, if you decide to spend $100,000 per year from the inheritance, you will be spending $50,000 of capital in addition to the $50,000 income. This means that in future years the income will be reduced, and eventually the capital will be gone entirely. Clearly, this is different from a prudent policy of living only on income, which would allow you (and your heirs) to receive $50,000 per year indefinitely.

This principle is generally accepted insofar as humanmade capital is concerned. National income accounting includes a calculation of the wearing-out of humanmade capital over time. This **capital depreciation** is estimated annually and subtracted from gross national product to obtain net national product. To maintain national wealth requires at least enough investment to replace the capital that wears out each year. We recognize this also by distinguishing between gross and net investment. Net investment is gross investment minus depreciation, and can be zero or below zero if insufficient replacement investment occurs. A negative net investment implies a decline in national wealth.

---

[1]For a more detailed account of the development of ecological economics and its relation to economic theory, see Costanza et al., eds., 1997, and Krishnan et al., eds., 1995.

[2]Real return is return in excess of inflation.

But no similar provision is made for **natural capital depreciation.** If a nation cuts down its forests and converts them to timber for domestic consumption or export, this enters the national income accounts only as a positive contribution to income, equal to the value of the timber. No accounting is made of the loss of standing forest, either as an economic resource or in terms of its ecological value. From the standpoint of ecological economics, this is a serious omission that must be corrected.

The Dynamics of Natural Capital

The natural capital concept further implies that a purely economic analysis cannot fully capture the stock and flow dynamics of natural resources. As we saw in Chapter 6, economists have been at some pains to devise ways of expressing natural resource and environmental factors in money terms suitable for standard economic analysis. But this only captures one dimension of natural capital.

The basic laws that govern behaviors of natural capital elements such as energy resources, water, chemical elements, and life forms are physical laws described in the sciences of chemistry, physics, biology, and ecology. Without specific consideration of these laws, we cannot gain a full understanding of natural capital.

For example, in agriculture soil fertility is determined by complex interactions among chemical nutrients, microorganisms, water flows, and plant and animal waste recycling. Measuring soil fertility in terms of, say, grain output, will be valid for short-term economic calculations, but may mislead over the long term as subtler ecological processes come into play. A purely economic analysis could result in insufficient attention to long-term maintenance of soil fertility.

Thus it is necessary to combine insights from economic analysis with ecological principles when dealing with issues of the maintenance of natural capital. This does not render the economic techniques of Chapters 3–6 irrelevant; rather they must be complemented with ecological perspectives on natural systems to avoid misleading results. Some of the techniques advocated by ecological economists for natural capital accounting and conservation include the following:

- **Physical accounting** for natural capital. In addition to the familiar national income accounts, **satellite accounts** can be constructed to show the abundance or scarcity of natural resources and to estimate their variations from year to year. These accounts can also show pollutant build-up, water quality, soil fertility variations, and other important physical indicators of environmental conditions. Accounts that indicate significant resource depletion or environmental degradation, call for measures to conserve or restore natural capital.
- Determination of **sustainable yield** levels. As we saw in Chapters 4 and 5, economic exploitation of natural resources often exceeds ecologically sustainable levels. An ecological analysis of a natural system harvested for human use can help to determine the sustainable yield level at which the system can continue to operate indefinitely. If the economic equilibrium yield exceeds the sustainable yield, the resource is threatened, and specific protective policies are necessary. This has happened with many fisheries and forests, a topic dealt with in Chapters 14 and 15.

- Determination of the **absorptive capacity of the environment** for human-generated wastes, including household, agricultural, and industrial wastes. Natural processes can break down many waste products over time and reabsorb them into the environment without damage. Other wastes and pollutants, such as chlorinated pesticides, chlorofluorocarbons (CFCs), and radioactive wastes are difficult or impossible for the environment to absorb. Scientific analysis can offer a baseline estimate of acceptable levels of waste emissions. This will not necessarily coincide with the economic concept of "optimal pollution levels" introduced in Chapter 3.

All these measures point toward a general principle of **natural capital sustainability.** According to this principle, nations should aim to conserve their natural capital by limiting its depletion or degradation and investing in its renewal (for example, through soil conservation or reforestation programs). The difficult and controversial process of translating this general principle into specific policy rules brings into focus the differences between economic and ecological analyses. We will deal with some of these questions in more detail in Chapter 8.

Issues of Macroeconomic Scale

Standard macroeconomic theory recognizes no limitation on an economy's scale. Keynesian, classical, and other economic theories deal with the conditions for equilibrium among the macroeconomic aggregates of consumption, savings, investment, government spending, taxes, and money supply. But with economic growth, the equilibrium level can rise indefinitely, so that a country's GNP can multiply tenfold or a hundredfold over time.

With a 5 percent growth rate, for example, GNP would double every 14 years, becoming more than 100 times as large within a century. From the point of view of mathematical computation of economic equilibrium, such growth poses no problem. But ecological economists, in particular Robert Goodland and Herman Daly, have argued that resource and environmental factors impose practical limits on feasible levels of economic activity, and that economic theory must include some concept of optimal **macroeconomic scale.**[3]

This concept is relevant both for individual economies dependent on limited resource bases, and for the global economy. Its implications for the global economy are especially important, because national economies can overcome resource limitations through international trade. The situation is illustrated in Figure 7-1. Although reminiscent of our original schematic showing the relationship between economic and ecological systems (see Figure 1-2, p. 8), Figure 7-1 also shows the economy growing within the supporting ecosystem to the point where it applies significant physical and life cycle stress.

In Figure 7-1, we see that the economic system (shown as a rectangle) uses both energy and resources as inputs, and releases waste energy and other wastes into the

---

[3]See Daly, 1991 and Goodland et al., 1992.

(a) Economic Subsystem at Small Scale

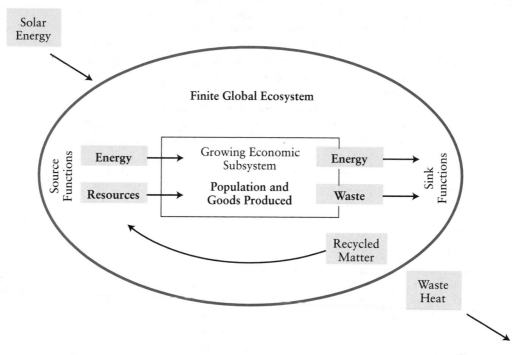

(b) Economic Subsystem at Large Scale

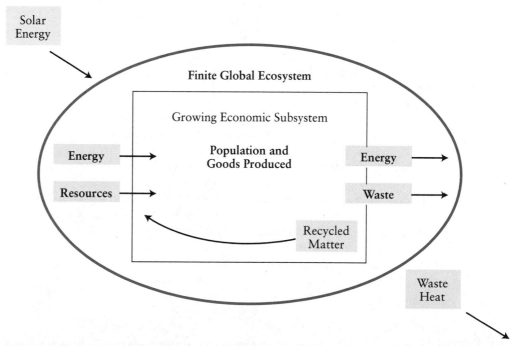

FIGURE 7-1 *The Finite Global Ecosystem Relative to the Growing Economic Subsystem*

Source: Adapted from Robert Goodland, Herman Daly, and Salah El-Serafy, eds., *Population, Technology, and Lifestyle: The Transition to Sustainability.* UNESCO, 1992. Courtesy of UNESCO.

ecosystem (shown as a circle). The combined input and waste flows can be called **throughput.**[4] The economic system shown here is an **open system,** exchanging energy and resources with the global ecosystem within which it is located. The global ecosystem has an inflow of solar energy and an outflow of waste heat, but is otherwise a **closed system.**

As the open economic subsystem grows within the closed planetary ecosystem, (shown by the enlarged rectangle in Figure 7-1b), its resource needs and waste flows are more difficult to accommodate. The fixed size of the planetary ecosystem places a scale limit on economic system growth.

We should note that this diagram refers to the *physical* growth of the economic system, measured in terms of its resource and energy demands and waste flows. It is possible for GNP to grow without higher resource requirements, especially if growth is concentrated in the service sector. Expanded automobile production, for example, requires more steel, glass, rubber, and other material inputs, as well as gasoline to operate the vehicles. But more opera productions or child-care services require few physical resources. Energy and physical resource use may also become more efficient, thus requiring less throughput of resources per unit of output. In general, though, growing GNP is associated with higher throughput of energy and resources.

Economic activity undoubtedly faces *some* scale limits. How can we determine whether the economic subsystem is in fact straining the limits of the ecosystem? One way is simply by noting the increased prevalence of large-scale or global environmental problems such as global climate change, ozone layer destruction, ocean pollution, soil degradation, and species loss. In common sense terms as well as in ecological analysis, these pervasive problems suggest that important environmental thresholds had been reached by the late twentieth century.[5]

Measuring the Relationship Between Economic and Ecological Systems

Ecological economists have also suggested a specific measure by which to link ecological and economic systems theoretically. Both systems have the function of *using energy* to support and expand the functions of life. We can thus identify energy as in some sense fundamental to all economic activity: human labor, capital investment, and natural resource exploitation all require energy.

Living systems obtain solar energy through plant photosynthesis. As the human economic system grows, we directly or indirectly use a larger proportion of this **net primary product of photosynthesis (NPP)** to support economic activity. This appropriation of photosynthetic energy takes place through agriculture, forestry, fisheries, and fuel use. In addition, human activities convert land from natural or agricultural func-

---

[4]See Daly, 1993.

[5]See, for example, Goodland et al., 1992, Chapters 1 and 2; Meadows, 1992. For a recent assessment of global ecosystem stresses, see UNEP, 1999 and World Resources Institute, 2000.

Urban and residential sprawl requires increasing amounts of land for highways.

tions for urban and industrial uses, transportation systems, and housing construction. Humans currently appropriate about 40 percent of terrestrial (land) photosynthetic capacity and about 25 percent of the global total, including ocean ecosystems.[6]

This NPP figure implies that a doubling of economic activity will bring us close to absolute limits. As we saw in Chapter 2, such a doubling is virtually certain unless population growth or economic growth rates alter dramatically. We must, therefore take the question of scale limits, seriously. We will look at some of the specific implication of this issue for agriculture, energy use, and other resources in Chapters 10–17, but some general implications for economic theory also emerge.

Herman Daly has argued that the rapid economic growth of the twentieth century has brought us from **empty-world economics** to **full-world economics.**[7] In the "empty-world" phase, when the economic system is small relative to the ecosystem, resource and environmental limits are unimportant and the main economic activity is the exploitation of natural resources to build up humanmade capital stocks and to expand consumption. In this stage economic activity faces only the main constraint of limited quantities of humanmade capital.

---

[6]Vitousek et al., 1986.
[7]Daly, 1992.

In the "full-world" phase, however, when the dramatically expanded human economic system presses against ecosystem limits, the conservation of natural capital becomes far more important. If we do not implement adequate measures to conserve resources and protect the "full-world" environment, environmental degradation will undermine economic activity no matter how large stocks of humanmade capital may become.

This perspective differs in significant respects from standard economic theory, which generally assumes **substitutability** between resources. For example, industrially produced fertilizer might compensate for loss of fertile soil. The ecological perspective tells us that substitution is not so easy—the natural resource base for economic activity is in some sense irreplaceable, unlike humanmade factories or machinery. If this is true, we need to modify standard theories of economic growth to take into account issues of long-term sustainability.[8]

Long-Term Sustainability

We have already mentioned sustainability in terms of natural capital, but how can we define this term more precisely? We want to limit the loss or degradation of natural capital, and to invest in its conservation and renewal. Taken in its strictest sense, this would mean that we could neither use any depletable resource, nor conduct any economic activity that would substantially alter natural systems. In a world of more than 6 billion people, largely either industrialized or rapidly industrializing, this is clearly impossible. On the other hand, unrestrained resource use and ever-increasing waste generation is also unacceptable. How can we strike the balance?

We have already examined elements of the standard economic answer to this question. The theories of external economies, resource allocation over time, and common-property resource management, which we outlined in Chapters 3–5, offer some economic principles on when to use and when to conserve resources, and on "optimal" pollution levels. In the long-term global context, however, these theories may be insufficient. Oriented toward individual markets, they may fail to guarantee environmental sustainability at the macroeconomic level. We need some guidelines for overall conservation of the national and global resource bases. Within these guidelines, market solutions to specific resource and environmental management problems will become relevant.

We can distinguish between the concepts of **strong sustainability and weak sustainability.** ("Strong" and "weak" in this context express how demanding our assumptions are, and do not imply that one is necessarily better or worse than the other.) Strong sustainability assumes limited substitutability between natural and humanmade

---

[8]An assessment of the ecological economics of sustainability is found in Wackernagel and Long, 1999.

capital. Weak sustainability assumes that natural and humanmade capital are generally substitutable.[9]

Taking the *strong sustainability* approach, we would keep separate accounts for humanmade and natural capital and ensure against depleting overall natural capital stocks. It would be acceptable, for example, to cut down forests in one area only if similar forests were being expanded elsewhere so that the overall forest stock remained constant. Petroleum stocks could be depleted only if alternative energy sources of equal capacity were simultaneously developed. Implementing strong sustainability would require extensive government intervention in markets and a radical change in the nature of economic activity.

Weak sustainability is easier to achieve. This principle allows for substitutability between natural and humanmade capital, provided that the total value of capital does not decline. This may allow us, for example, to cut down forests in order to expand agriculture or industry. It does require, however, an adequate accounting for the *value* of the cleared forest. The forest clearing activity would be an economic loss unless the value generated in new humanmade capital equaled or exceeded the economic and ecological value of the cleared forests.

This principle is closer to standard economic theory. A private owner presumably would make such a calculation and would not willingly exchange a higher-valued resource for a lower-valued one. Government intervention would, however, be required to maintain even weak sustainability when:

- Private owners fail to consider the full ecological value of natural capital (say, a forest products company that considers timber values but is indifferent to endangered species).
- Property rights in natural resources are poorly defined, as is often true in developing nations. Short-term concession holders or illegal users can rapidly plunder a natural resource base.
- Private property owners with short-term perspectives fail to consider long-term effects such as cumulative soil erosion.
- Common property resources or public goods are involved.
- Truly irreplaceable resources are at issue, as in the case of species extinction or limited water supplies in arid areas.

Policy Choices and Discounting the Future

The choice between strong and weak sustainability may be difficult. In managing forest resources, for example, strong sustainability may be too restrictive, requiring a

---

[9]A discussion of the principles of strong and weak sustainability can be found in Daly, 1994. The concept of sustainability is criticized by Beckerman (1994) and defended by Daly (1995) and El Serafy (1996). Application of the weak sustainability concept is discussed by Gowdy and O'Hara (1997), while Common (1996) argues that the distinction between strong and weak sustainability is invalid.

country to maintain the same area of forest cover under all circumstances. Weak sustainability, however, places no inherent limits on the amount of forest that can be cut, requiring only a sound economic accounting of its value. Although some middle ground must be defined, this cannot happen simply through the market process. It must be a conscious social choice.

One crucial factor in defining this middle ground is the issue of discounting the future. Our discussion of resource allocation over time (Chapter 4) highlighted the importance of the discount rate in market choices regarding resource use. In general, the higher the discount rate, the greater the incentive to exploit resources in the present. By Hotelling's rule, private owners must expect a resource's net price to rise at a rate at least equal to the interest rate before they will conserve that resource for the future. This rarely occurs for most depletable natural resources.

Consider that at a 5 percent discount rate, owners would have to expect net resource prices to double every 14 years before they would pursue conservation rather than extract the resource immediately and invest the proceeds at 5 percent. For renewable resources such as forests, the annual yield must at least equal the market interest rate for private owners to practice sustainable management (see Chapter 15 for a full treatment of this issue). At lower yields, economic incentives favor logging the forest for immediate monetary gains. In effect, this means treating the renewable resource as a depletable resource and "mining" it out as fast as possible.

The logic of discounting imposes a stiff test on natural resource systems. Unless they can meet a certain yield level, immediate exploitation will take precedence over sustainable management. If major ecological systems and important natural resources fail this test, the resulting rush to exploit resources as fast as possible will make little provision for the future.

Here the strong sustainability principle becomes relevant: can we trust that a world with much more humanmade capital but a severely depleted resource base will meet the needs of the future? Or should we impose a stronger principle of resource conservation to guard our own and future generations' interests?

This is not a philosophical debate about the long-term future. Critical resources such as petroleum could be largely used up within 30 to 40 years; tropical forests could be virtually eliminated in the same period; soil erosion could destroy the fertility of hundreds of millions of acres of cropland within a generation. Applying a strict commercial discounting principle, all this destruction could be seen as quite "rational" and even "optimal."

Norgaard and Howarth have argued against using market-based discount rates to guide decisions on long-term resource use.[10] They recommend using a sustainability criterion, to promote **intergenerational equity.** In this view it is wrong to decide issues of long-term investment and conservation in the present simply by applying profit-maximizing criteria. Some social judgment on conservation of resources for the future is required.

---

[10]Norgaard and Howarth, 1991; Howarth and Norgaard, 1994.

Complexity, Irreversibility, and the Precautionary Principle

Another major justification for a sustainability criterion relates to **ecological complexity** and **irreversibility.** Current ecological systems have evolved over many centuries to achieve a balance involving interactions among thousands of species of plants and animals (the total number of species is unknown, but is in the millions), as well as delicately balanced physical and chemical relationships in the atmosphere, oceans, and in freshwater and terrestrial ecosystems.

Extensive exploitation of natural resources permanently alters these ecological balances, with effects that are not fully predictable. In some cases, upsetting the ecological balance can lead to disaster—desertification, collapse of ocean food systems, destruction of the ozone layer, pollution of aquifers, outbreaks of super-pests resistant to insecticides, and the like.

Ecological economists therefore argue for a **precautionary principle**—we should strive for minimum interference with the operation of natural systems, especially where we cannot predict long-term effects. This principle obviously defies easy definition in economic calculations of resource value and use. Such calculations, therefore, are of value only if we can place them in the broader ecological context, whose priorities should sometimes override market equilibrium logic.[11]

As we explore resource and environment topic areas in Chapters 10–18, we will bear in mind the tension between the standard economic techniques outlined in Chapters 3–6 and the general principles of ecological economics set forth in this chapter. In addition, before addressing specific topic areas, we will examine some new analytical techniques developed by ecological economists.

One important issue is adding an environmental dimension to the measurement of economic output or GNP—or perhaps replacing GNP with a more inclusive measure of human well-being and ecosystem health. We will deal with this topic in Chapter 8. Another approach is to model the interrelationship between economic and environmental systems, focusing on flows of energy, resources, and wastes. These new approaches to economic/ecological modeling are the topic of Chapter 9.

SUMMARY

Ecological economics gives special emphasis to the concept of natural capital. Although much of standard economics concerns the accumulation and productivity of humanmade capital, ecological economics focuses on maintaining the natural capital systems that support life and economic activity. Natural capital includes all planetary natural resources, oceans, atmosphere, and ecosystems. These must be accounted for and should be managed according to sustainable principles so that their functions do not degrade over time.

In this perspective, economic systems cannot grow without limit, but must achieve some sustainable scale for economic activity at which the planet's ecosystems

---

[11]Application of the precautionary principle is discussed in Raffensperger and Tickner, 1999.

are not subjected to undue stress. Significant evidence indicates that current economic activity exceeds these limits or badly strains them. One measure of this is the proportion of photosynthetic energy appropriated for human use, now about 40 percent of terrestrial photosynthesis. Significant further growth in human demand would thus leave little room for other living systems of the earth.

The concept of sustainability, although important to managing natural capital, is difficult to define. A "weak" definition relies on the possibility of replacing natural ecosystem functions with humanmade substitutes. To the extent that this is possible, natural capital can be used up without diminishing net wealth. A "strong" definition assumes that humans have limited ability to replace natural system functions and that a sustainable society must therefore maintain most of its natural systems without significant depletion or degradation.

Long-term sustainability involves issues of discounting the future, and the question of our responsibility to provide for future generations. Economic incentives and property rights systems affect decisions regarding resource use, as does public policy on resource management. A precautionary principle is appropriate in cases where irreversible effects may result from damage to complex ecosystems. Resource conservation for future generations requires social judgment in addition to economic calculation.

The principles of ecological and of standard economics are both relevant to resource management issues. Sometimes the principles will conflict, but it is important to consider how best to apply both to specific resource and environmental issues, as well as to the measurement of economic output, human well-being, and ecosystem health.

KEY TERMS AND CONCEPTS

absorptive capacity of the environment
capital depreciation
closed system
ecological complexity
empty-world and full-world economics
intergenerational equity
irreversibility
macroeconomic scale
natural capital
natural capital depreciation
natural capital sustainability

net investment
net primary product of photosynthesis (NPP)
open system
physical accounting
precautionary principle
satellite accounts
strong and weak sustainability
substitutability
sustainable yield
throughput

DISCUSSION QUESTIONS

1. In what respects is natural capital similar to humanmade capital and in what respects does it differ? We often speak of a "return to capital," meaning the stream of income generated by a capital investment. Can we speak of a return to natural cap-

ital? What might be some examples of investment in natural capital? Who would be motivated to make such investments? Who would suffer in the absence of such investments or if resource depletion or environmental degradation lead to "disinvestment"?

2. How can we apply the concept of optimal scale for an economy? Have the economies of the United States, Europe, and Japan reached optimal scale? Exceeded it? How about the economies of Latin America? of Africa? of other Asian economies? How would you relate the concept of optimal scale at the global level to economic growth in national economies at different levels of development?

3. Distinguish between the concepts of strong and weak sustainability and give some practical examples, other than those cited in the text, for their application. Where would each concept be most appropriate? What economic policy measures would be relevant to achieving sustainability?

REFERENCES

Beckerman, Wilfred. "Sustainable Development: Is It a Useful Concept?" *Environmental Values* 3 (1994), 191–209.

Common, Mick. "Beckerman and His Critics on Strong and Weak Sustainability: Confusing Concepts and Conditions." *Environmental Values* 5 (1996), 83–88.

Costanza, Robert. *Ecological Economics*. New York: Columbia University Press, 1991.

Costanza, Robert, John Cumberland, Herman Daly, Robert Goodland, and Richard Norgaard, eds. *An Introduction to Ecological Economics*. Boca Raton, Florida: St. Lucie Press, 1997.

Daly, Herman E. "Elements of Environmental Macroeconomics." Chapter 3 in Costanza, ed., op. cit., 1991.

Daly, Herman E. "From Empty-world Economics to Full-world Economics: Recognizing an Historical Turning Point in Economic Development." Chapter 2 in Goodland, Daly, and El Serafy, op. cit., 1992.

Daly, Herman E. "On Wilfred Beckerman's Critique of Sustainable Development." *Environmental Values* 4 (1995), 49–95.

Daly, Herman E. "The Steady-State Economy: Toward a Political Economy of Biophysical Equilibrium and Moral Growth," Chapter 19 in *Valuing the Earth: Economics, Ecology, Ethics,* edited by Herman E. Daly and Kenneth N. Townsend. Cambridge, Mass.: MIT Press, 1993.

Daly, Herman E. "Operationalizing Sustainable Development by Investing in Natural Capital," in *Investing in Natural Capital: The Ecological Economics Approach to Sustainability,* edited by AnnMari Jansson et al. Washington, D.C.: Island Press, 1994.

Daly, Herman E., and John B. Cobb. *For the Common Good: Redirecting the Economy Toward Community, the Environment, and a Sustainable Future,* 2nd ed. Boston: Beacon Press, 1994.

El Serafy, Salah. "In Defense of Weak Sustainability: A Response to Beckerman." *Environmental Values* 5 (1996), 75–81.

Goodland, Robert, Herman Daly, and Salah El Serafy, eds. *Population, Technology, and Lifestyle: The Transition to Sustainability.* United Nations Educational, Scientific and Cultural Organization (UNESCO), 1992.

Gowdy, John and Sabine O'Hara. "Weak Sustainability and Viable Technologies." *Ecological Economics* 22 (1997): 239–247.

Hicks, Sir John R. *Value and Capital.* Oxford, England: Oxford University Press, 1939.

Howarth, Richard B., and Richard B. Norgaard. "Intergenerational Transfers and the Social Discount Rate." *Environmental and Resource Economics* 3 (August 1993), 337–358.

Krishnan, Rajaram, Jonathan M. Harris, and Neva R. Goodwin, eds. *A Survey of Ecological Economics.* Washington, D.C.: Island Press, 1995.

Meadows, Donnella, et al. *Beyond the Limits: Confronting Global Collapse, Envisioning a Sustainable Future.* White River Junction, Vermont: Chelsea Green, 1992.

Norgaard, Richard B., and Richard B. Howarth. "Sustainability and Discounting the Future," in Costanza, op. cit.

Raffensperger, Carolyn, and Joel Tickner. *Protecting Public Health and the Environment: Implementing the Precautionary Principle.* Washington, D.C.: Island Press, 1999.

Ricardo, David. *On the Principles of Political Economy and Taxation* in *The Works and Correspondence of David Ricardo,* edited by Piero Sraffa. Cambridge, England: Cambridge University Press, 1951.

Vitousek, P. M., P. R. Ehrlich, A. H. Ehrlich, and P. A. Matson. "Human Appropriation of the Products of Photosynthesis." *BioScience* 36, no. 6: 368–373.

Wackernagel, Mathis, and Alex Long, eds. "Ecological Economics Forum." *Ecological Economics* 29 (1999), 13–60.

World Resources Institute, United Nations Development Programme, United Nations Environment Programme, and World Bank. *World Resources 2000–2001: People and Ecosystems: The Fraying Web of Life.* Washington, D.C.: World Resources Institute, 2000.

United Nations Environment Programme. *Global Environmental Outlook 2000: UNEP's Millennium Report on the Environment.* London, U.K.: Earthscan Publications, 1999.

WEB SITES

1. **http://www.ecoeco.org/** The web site for the International Society for Ecological Economics, a nonprofit organization "dedicated to advancing understanding of the relationships among ecological, social, and economic systems for the mutual well-being of nature and people." Their site includes links to research and educational opportunities in ecological economics.

2. **http://csf.colorado.edu/ecolecon/** An ecological economics discussion board managed by Communications for a Sustainable Future. The site includes an extensive collection of archived articles.

3. **http://kabir.cbl.cees.edu/** Web site for the Institute for Ecological Economics at the University of Maryland, "established to fill the growing need to integrate the study and management of 'nature's household' (ecology) and 'humankind's household' (economics)."

4. **http://www.psrast.org/precaut.htm** A web site with information about the precautionary principle, including a consensus statement written by a group of "scientists, government officials, lawyers, and labor and grassroots environmental activists."

CHAPTER FOCUS QUESTIONS

- Do measures of GNP or GDP give a distorted picture of development?
- Can these measures be adjusted to better reflect environmental and resource factors?
- Are new, "greener" measures of national well-being needed?

CHAPTER

8

National Income and Environmental Accounting

Greening the National Income Accounts

Taking the environment seriously affects how we view measures of national income and well-being. Can we say that a nation with a higher per-capita national income is necessarily better off than another country with a lower per-capita income? Before making this judgment, we should compare factors such as the state of the environment and natural resources in the two countries.

Standard measures of gross national product (GNP), or gross domestic product (GDP), are commonly used to measure a country's level of economic activity and progress in development.[1] Almost all statistics used in macroeconomic analysis are

---

[1]GNP and GDP are distinguished by whether or not the foreign earnings of individuals and corporations are included in the total. U.S. GNP, for example, includes the foreign earnings of U.S. residents and corporations but excludes the earnings of foreign individuals and corporations from activities in the United States. U.S. GDP includes all income earned within the United States, regardless of the nationality of the resident, but excludes earnings of U.S. residents and corporations from foreign sources.

based on these measures, and most economists, as well as the general public, recognize them as standards of economic progress.

However, some critics have argued that these measures can give a highly misleading impression of economic development. Inconsistencies have long been noted in GNP measurement, such as the failure to account for unpaid work, production for domestic use, and the value of leisure time. We must add another major criticism of the standard GNP measure—it fails to account for environmental degradation and resource depletion.

This issue can be important especially in developing nations, which depend heavily on natural resources. If a nation cuts down its forests, depletes its soil fertility, and pollutes its water supplies, this surely makes the nation poorer. Even so, national income accounts will merely record the value of the timber, agricultural produce, and industrial output as positive contributions to GNP. This may lead economic policymakers to view the nation's development in an unrealistically rosy light—at least until the effects of the environmental damage become apparent, which in some cases may be decades.

If we are measuring economic activity with, so to speak, the wrong ruler, we can hardly expect the rest of our economic analysis to be reliable. Economic growth alone does not necessarily represent true economic development, and may even lower human well-being if it is accompanied by growing inequity and environmental degradation. The attempt to define better measures of development has led to several new formulations of national income analysis that attempt to take into account resource and environmental factors.[2]

One approach to revising national income accounts is to estimate an economic value for **natural capital depreciation**, and subtract this estimate from the standard measure of GNP. In standard national income accounting, the **net national product (NNP)** or **net domestic product (NDP)** is calculated by subtracting the depreciation of humanmade capital such as buildings and machinery.[3] A measure of **adjusted net national product (NNP*)** or **adjusted net domestic product (NDP*)** extends this logic by calculating a value for natural resource depreciation and subtracting this also from GNP. Some early efforts at calculating adjusted net domestic product showed significant variations from the standard measure (see Figure 8-1).

In the case of Indonesia, the revised measure of NDP shows significantly slower growth than the standard measure. (The 1974 temporary spike in NDP* results from discovery of new oil reserves and high world oil prices.) Costa Rica's agricultural product is generally rising over a 20-year period by standard measures, but is lower for the whole period and falls in the later years according to the revised measure.

---

[2]For an overview of natural resource accounting methods, see National Research Council, 1994.

[3]Depreciation is simply a measure of the loss of capital value through wear and tear. For accounting purposes, it can be calculated using a "straight-line" formula according to which, for example, a new machine is estimated to lose 10 percent of its original value each year over a 10-year period, or using more complex valuation methods.

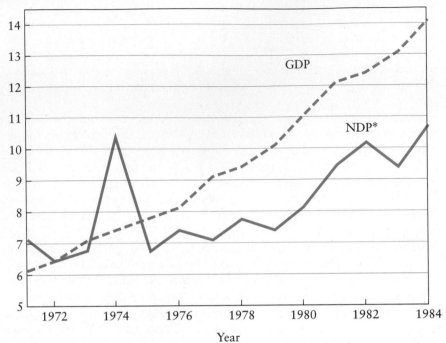

(a) Indonesian GDP and NDP* Adjusted for Resource Depreciation

Billion Rupiah
(in thousands)

14

13   GDP

12

11   NDP*

10

9

8

7

6

5

1972   1974   1976   1978   1980   1982   1984

Year

(b) Costa Rica's Agricultural Product Before and After Resource Depreciation

Product (in billions of
1984 colones)

40

35

Gross Agricultural Product

30

25

20   Net Agricultural Product

15

10

5

0

1970   1975   1980   1985

Year

FIGURE 8-1 *Adjusting GDP for Natural Resource Depreciation*
Sources: (a) Adapted from Robert Repetto et al., *Wasting Assets: Natural Resources in the National In-come Accounts*. Washington, D.C.: World Resources Institute, 1989. Reprinted by permission of World Resources Institute. (b) Adapted from Robert Repetto et al., *Accounts Overdue: Natural Resource Depre-ciation in Costa Rica*. Washington, D.C.: World Resources Institute, 1991. Reprinted by permission of World Resources Institute.

Even more striking than the altered pattern of GDP is the impact on **net invest-ment**. The standard measure of net investment adjusts gross investment[4] by subtract-ing depreciation of manufactured capital. If we include natural capital depreciation, numerous developing nations show much smaller, or even negative net investment (see Figure 8-2). This has significant implications for development strategy, because invest-ment is the most crucial economic determinant of long-term growth. These studies in-dicate that by failing to take into account resource and environmental depreciation we systematically overestimate the true value of investment.[5]

As a step toward integrating economic, environmental, and social policy analysis, the World Bank's Environment Department has developed a **genuine saving (S*)** mea-sure that includes natural capital depreciation as well as foreign borrowing.[6] This measure seeks to determine how much of national income is being saved for the fu-ture, taking into account both depletion of natural resources and additions to capital stock. A genuine-saving analysis, particularly appropriate for developing countries, indicates that what may appear a development "success story" can conceal serious natural capital depletion and in some cases even a net negative genuine saving rate.

Figure 8-3 shows estimates of genuine national saving for several major regions. For Latin America, Sub-Saharan Africa, and the Middle East/North Africa the results are striking—genuine saving is low, and often significantly negative, indicating that environmental and resource degradation frequently outweigh humanmade capital ac-cumulation. This can create a pattern of "reverse development" in which countries grow poorer over time when we account for both humanmade and natural capital. In-troducing natural capital depreciation into accounting may have significant trade and macroeconomic policy implications, especially for countries that depend heavily on natural resource exports (see Box 8-1).[7]

Estimating Sustainable Economic Welfare

Estimating resource depreciation is only one approach to incorporating environmen-tal considerations into national income accounts. Another way in which standard national income accounts may overestimate a nation's economic success involves

---

[4]Gross investment is total spending by businesses on capital formation.

[5]See Repetto, 1994 on the significance of natural resource accounting.

[6]Hamilton and Clemens, 1997.

[7]See El Serafy, 1997. Neumayer, 2000, critiques the World Bank methodology.

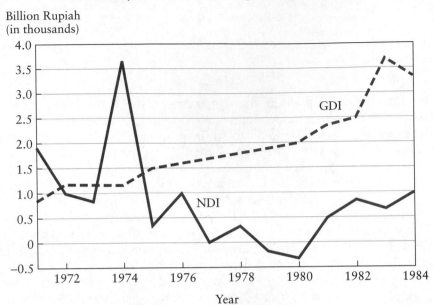

(a) Indonesia's Gross Domestic Investment and Net Domestic Investment Adjusted for Resource Depreciation

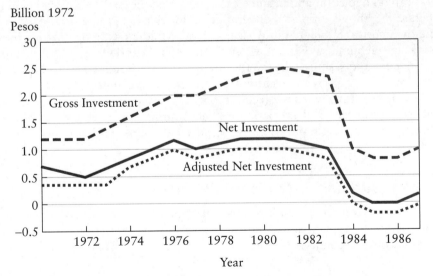

(b) Philippines' Investment Adjusted for Resource Depreciation

FIGURE 8-2 *Adjusting Investment for Natural Resource Depreciation.*
Sources: (a) Adapted from Robert Repetto et al., *Wasting Assets: Natural Resources in the National Income Accounts.* Washington, D.C.: World Resources Institute, 1989. Reprinted by permission of World Resources Institute. (b) Adapted from Wilfredo Cruz and Robert Repetto, *The Environmental Effects of Stabilization and Structural Adjustment Programs: The Philippines Case.* Washington, D.C.: World Resources Institute, 1992. Reprinted by permission of World Resources Institute.

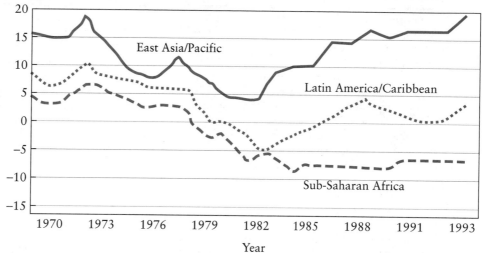

(a) Genuine Saving Rates by Region, 1970–1993: East Asia/Pacific, Latin America/Caribbean, Sub-Saharan Africa

Percentage of GNP

East Asia/Pacific

Latin America/Caribbean

Sub-Saharan Africa

Year

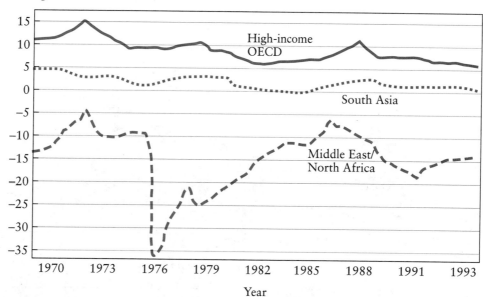

(b) Genuine Saving Rates by Region, 1970–1993: High-Income OECD South Asia, Middle East/North Africa

Percentage of GNP

High-income OECD

South Asia

Middle East/North Africa

Year

FIGURE 8-3 *Genuine National Saving*

Source: Adapted from World Bank, *Expanding the Measure of Wealth: Indicators of Environmentally Sustainable Development.* Copyright 1997 by World Bank. Reproduced with permission of World Bank in the format textbook via Copyright Clearance Center.

TABLE 8-1 *Index of Sustainable Economic Welfare (United States, 1990)*

Constant 1972 dollars (in billions)

Personal consumption adjusted for income distribution	**$1,164**
+ services for household labor	+520
+ services of consumer durable goods	+225
+ services of highways and streets	+18
+ consumption portion of public spending on health and education	+45
− consumer spending on durable goods	−235
− defensive private spending on health and education	−63
− cost of commuting and auto accidents	−67
− cost of personal pollution control	−5
− cost of air, water, and noise pollution	−39
− loss of wetlands and farmland	−58
− depletion of renewable resources	−313
− long-term damage from nuclear wastes, greenhouse gases, and ozone depletion	−371
+ net capital growth	+29
+/− change in net international investment position	−34
Index of Sustainable Economic Welfare	**$818**

Note: Total differs from sum of items due to rounding.
Source: Daly and Cobb, 1994, Table A.1.

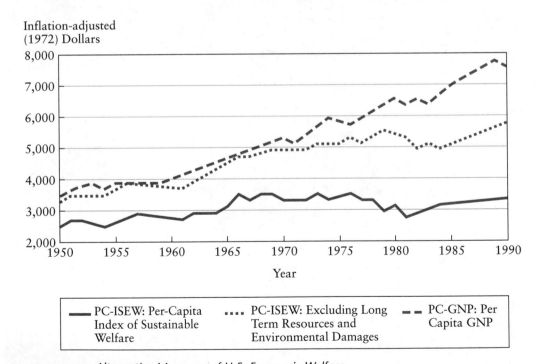

Inflation-adjusted (1972) Dollars

Year

PC-ISEW: Per-Capita Index of Sustainable Welfare   •••• PC-ISEW: Excluding Long Term Resources and Environmental Damages   ▬ ▬ PC-GNP: Per Capita GNP

FIGURE 8-4 *Alternative Measures of U.S. Economic Welfare*
Source: Adapted from Cobb and Cobb, *The Green National Product: A Proposed Index of Sustainable Economic Welfare.* Lanham, MD.: University Press of America, 1994. Reprinted by permission of University Press of America, Inc.

defensive expenditures. These are expenses associated with cleaning up pollution or attempting to repair or compensate for other environmental damage. In standard accounting, all such expenditures simply add to GNP.

For example, all expenditures by the U.S. government Superfund for cleaning up toxic waste sites count as contributions to GNP. The medical costs of treating diseases caused by air or water pollution similarly add to GNP. If coastal homeowners or businesses suffer property damage from an oil spill and sue for damages, the legal expenditures involved and the cleanup costs also contribute to GNP. By this logic, the more pollution damage and resulting cleanup expense a nation experiences, the better off it is—a clearly irrational position.

Herman Daly and John Cobb have calculated an **Index of Sustainable Economic Welfare (ISEW)** for the United States. ISEW adjusts economic output by subtracting out estimates of all such defensive expenditures.[8] Together with adjustments for natural resource depletion and for inequality of income distribution, ISEW indicates a much slower improvement in U.S. welfare—compared to the steadily rising GNP indicator (see Table 8-1 and Figure 8-4). Long-term resource and environmental damage account for much of the difference between GNP and ISEW. If we exclude long-term and cumulative environmental effects, the resulting measure, ISEW*, is closer to GNP but still shows much less gain since 1970.

Henry Peskin and Roefie Hueting have put forward a third approach to correcting national income accounts for environmental damage.[9] They suggest defining the environment as a productive sector that contributes services to the economy, many of which remain unaccounted for because they are apparently free. Examples include provision of clean air and water, removal of carbon dioxide from the atmosphere by trees, health and recreational benefits provided by natural areas).

If these **environmental services** are impaired—say, for example, by draining a wetland—an estimate of the cost of duplicating the service must be subtracted from national output. Because wetlands perform important functions that include water purification, nutrient recycling, flood control, and provision of wildlife habitat, this estimated value could be quite high. According to current accounting methods, the wetland makes no contribution to output, but a shopping mall built on drained wetland would add to output, both through construction of the mall and through its annual sales.

All of these approaches to modifying GNP/GDP accounts have merit, but arriving at a single, uniform measure has proved difficult. Some analysts reject attempts to derive a single figure for "greened" GNP/GDP. Instead, they suggest the use of **satellite accounts,** which measure environmental stocks and functions in physical terms, without necessarily attempting valuation.[10]

---

[8]Daly and Cobb, 1994.

[9]See Peskin, 1991 and 1994; Hueting, 1991.

[10]See Lange and Duchin, 1993.

8-1   Green Accounting in the Philippines

Satellite accounts do not reduce environmental accounting to a single value, as do measures such as NNP* or ISEW. The satellite account's advantage of greater detail is offset by a difficulty in interpreting and assessing data measured in different units. The system of environmental accounting adopted by the Philippines illustrates these issues well.

A 1999 article in the journal *Ecological Economics* (Bartelmus, 1999) summarizes environmental accounting data for the Philippines. One satellite account estimates the stock value of various natural resources. As seen in the table, the value of natural capital is generally on the rise in the Philippines. Still, we cannot conclude that natural capital is increasing in the Philippines. The value of natural capital may increase because of an increase in prices rather than an increase in the physical stock.

Looking further at the data, we find that between 1988 and 1994 the stock volume of forests in the Philippines decreased by 30 percent even though total forest value increased by nearly 25 percent. Thus, economic data alone may fail to identify declining natural resource stocks. This illustrates the need for "alternative or supplementary indicators linked to quantifiable standards or targets" (Bartelmus, 155).

The Value of Natural Capital in the Philippines (in billions of Pesos)

	Natural Capital Category			
Year	Forests	Minerals	Groundwater	Agricultural Land
1988	594	39	538	389
1989	521	45	473	434
1990	569	48	522	492
1991	557	54	542	580
1992	605	39	649	635
1993	690	MD[1]	719	688
1994	739	MD[1]	757	MD[1]

[1]Missing data.

(continued on following page)

Deducting environmental costs from net domestic product for the Philippines lowers NDP by 2 percent to 13 percent. The magnitude of the environmental deduction has been decreasing, "indicating a relative reduction in environmental costs generated by the economy" (Bartelmus, 160). A logging ban instituted in 1992 dramatically reduced the annual value of forest capital depletion. Other data indicate that the quantity of air pollutants released from electricity generators in the Philippines has remained relatively constant. The annual economic loss from groundwater depletion increased more than 40 percent between 1988 and 1994.

Although conflicting environmental data may impede an overall assessment of sustainability, a system of satellite accounts can identify problems with particular resources. Linking physical measures with economic data helps integrate environmental concerns into standard macroeconomic accounting. However, green accounting reaches "its limits when attempting to value welfare effects on human health" (Bartelmus, 169). Thus, forcing environmental accounting to accord with standard economic analysis may fail to provide the details necessary for a full environmental assessment of the country's sustainability.

SOURCE

Bartelmus, Peter. "Green Accounting for a Sustainable Economy, Policy Use and Analysis of Environmental Accounts in the Philippines." *Ecological Economics* 29, no. 1 (1999):155–170.

Satellite accounts can give a detailed picture of the natural resource base and the state of the environment by measuring such variables as forest cover, mineral resources, and water supplies and noting their changes over time. Such data are useful for different kinds of analysis. Input-output analysis can show the probable effects on resource stocks of various economic policies (see Chapter 9 for more on this approach). Economic valuation methods can also convert these physical measures to money measures for estimates of adjusted NNP/NDP. The United Nations has published a guide to integrated environmental and economic accounting using the satellite approach.[11]

---

[11]United Nations, 1993.

No single system for revising national income accounts for environment and resource impacts has won general acceptance. This means that most economic analysis still relies on standard GNP or NNP measures. If the advocates of revised measures are right, we need to adjust our broader economic theories to reflect new measurements of national product and income. Even though there is no consensus on new measurement techniques, we can explore the implications of environmental or **green accounting** approaches such as those discussed above. In the next section, we discuss their application in more analytical detail.

Application of Environment and Resource Accounting

How can revised measures of national income guide development policy? We can identify a sustainable development path as one in which the stock of overall capital assets remains constant or rises over time. These capital stocks include manufactured capital, human capital (skills and education), and natural capital. As we discussed in Chapter 7, these different types of capital may share some degree of substitutability, but we should also take special note of **critical natural capital**—resources such as essential water supplies, for which no good substitutes exist.[12]

Thus the total capital stock of an economy can be presented as:

$$K = K_m + K_h + K_n + K_n^*$$

where

K_m is manufactured capital
K_h is human capital
K_n is noncritical natural capital
K_n^* is critical natural capital

National income accounting must consider any changes in these categories of capital. Investment in capital is a component of standard GNP or GDP. Depreciation of manufactured capital (D_m) is subtracted from GNP to get NNP (net national product). Human capital is assumed not to depreciate (although this is only true if educational expenditures are adequate).[13] The main issue in environmental and resource accounting is to estimate and subtract depreciation of natural capital (D_n) to obtain adjusted net national product, NNP*.

---

[12]Pearce and Warford (1993) discuss the concept of critical natural capital. The analytical presentation here uses the categories they propose for the definition of different kinds of capital.

[13]To take this factor into account, World Bank researchers have calculated a measure of "expanded net investment" that includes educational expenditures. See World Bank, 1997, and Harris et al., 2001.

Safety-suited workers fill bags with contaminated sand after an oil spill off Huntington Beach, California. The costs of cleanup will be a positive, not a negative, in standard GDP accounts.

Thus:

$$NNP = GNP - D_m$$

$$NNP^* = GNP - D_m - D_n \text{ (or } NNP^* = NNP - D_n)$$

The first issue, therefore, is to obtain an estimate of D_n. The pioneering study of Indonesia by Repetto et al. (1989) employed two methods: value of **end-of-year stocks** (for oil and timber) and **productivity loss estimates** (for soil). The end-of-year stocks method compares the value of standing timber or estimated oil reserves at the end of the year as compared to their value at the beginning of the year, using current prices. This method can show an increase in natural resource value if new resource discoveries are made or if prices increase during a given year (this accounts for the 1974 spike in NDP* in Figure 8-1a and NDI in Figure 8-2a). It also takes no account of forests' ecological and service values other than timber production.

Productivity loss estimates require the use of a discount rate to obtain a present value of a stream of future losses:

$$PV[\text{Loss}] = L_0 + L_1/(1+r) + L_2/(1+r)^2 + \ldots L_n/(1+r)^n$$

where L_i is the loss in year i, r is the discount rate, and n is the number of years. If annual losses are the same in each future year, this can be simplified to:

$$PV[\text{Loss}] = L/r$$

where L is the annual loss and r is the interest rate.[14]

In Indonesia, severe highland erosion has led to soil productivity losses. If projected into the future, the present value of future losses from Indonesia's erosive agricultural production may be greater than the value of current crops.

The estimates of changes in end-of-year resource stocks and productivity loss estimates combined to give the total value of resource depreciation for a given year. This total is subtracted from standard NNP to derive an adjusted NNP, and from net investment to obtain adjusted net investment. It is also possible to subtract estimates of defensive expenditures and short-term pollution damages from GDP. These estimates, however, should not be subtracted from net investment, since they affect only one year's national well being. Long-term pollution damages, which lower the value of natural capital, can appropriately be subtracted from net investment.

Measures of True Income

El Serafy, a critic of the end-of-year stocks method, prefers the **user cost** method.[15] This method estimates **true income** by subtracting the portion of total income that theoretically must be invested at current long-term interest rates to guarantee a continued flow of income at the same level.

The principle here is similar to an individual's investing in a retirement account. By the time the wage-earner reaches age 65, she or he hopes to have a substantial enough retirement account to provide an adequate income. In the same way, a nation with a nonrenewable resource base should invest a sufficient amount from the proceeds of selling that resource to guarantee a continued flow of income once the resource is exhausted.

The relationship of this true income *(X)* to **net receipts** *(R)* from resource sales is given by the following formula:

$$X/R = 1 - 1/(1 + r)^n$$

where r is the discount rate and n is the expected lifetime of the resource. For example, if $r = .04$ and $n = 20$, $X/R = 0.55$. Including depreciation of natural capital in In-

---

[14]Mathematically, the value of the sum of an infinite series L is equal to L/r where r is the discount rate.

[15]El Serafy, 1993.

donesia's GDP accounts gives an estimate of NNP* about 5 percent to 15 percent lower than standard GDP.[16]

The impact of proper natural resource accounting is more dramatic if we look only at the saving/investment component of GDP. Together with standard manufactured capital depreciation, the effect can be to lower adjusted net investment (I_n^*) close to zero or below zero. A measure of genuine saving (S^*) for developing nations should subtract both types of depreciation and also **net foreign borrowing (NFB)** from gross investment (I_g). Thus:

$$S^* = I_g - D_m - D_n - \text{NFB}$$

As shown in Figure 8-3, this adjusted saving figure gives a startling picture of low or negative saving rates in many developing nations.

What policy implications arise from using these revised measures of national income? One obvious lesson would be the need for environmental policies to conserve natural capital. Rather than simply striving to maximize economic growth as it is conventionally defined, policymakers need an integrated plan for economic and environmental goals. El Serafy has analyzed trade and macroeconomic policy effects that arise from the failure to account adequately for resource depletion (see Box 8-2).

Measuring Well-Being: Social and Ecological Dimensions

The field of environmental and natural resource accounting continues to develop. Policy conclusions vary, depending on the analytical approaches chosen. Many developing countries experience significant problems with obtaining adequate data.[17] Some of the following underlying issues, also reviewed in Chapters 6 and 7, have important implication for green accounting:

- **Weak versus strong sustainability.** Note that the analysis of natural capital depreciation implicitly assumes **substitutability** of different types of capital, as measured in money value. For example, the loss of $1 million in timber (natural capital) can be fully compensated for by acquiring $1 million in machinery (manufactured capital). From an accounting point of view, the value of total capital in this case is unchanged. **Weak sustainability** accepts this view of different types of capital as substitutable.

---

[16]This revised estimate of Indonesian natural resource depreciation is calculated in El Serafy, 1993. Crowards, 1996, estimates natural resource depreciation for Zimbabwe at 1–3 percent, but believes that data problems and distorted prices resulting from government subsidies and price controls make this a significant underestimate.

[17]See, for example, Crowards, 1996. For a recent discussion of green accounting practices, see Vincent, 2000.

8.2   Incorrect Accounting Leads to Incorrect Policies

If economists accept conventional GDP estimates, their policy recommendations are likely to be wrong regarding natural-resource–dependent economies. Output estimates may be exaggerated by 20 percent or more, and true estimates of capital formation may turn out to be nil or negative. Factor productivity estimates are thrown into question when neither the products nor the inputs are measured correctly. Capital/output ratios will be incorrect if they ignore rapid liquidation of natural capital. Sophisticated macroeconomic models based on such data will give highly questionable results for guiding long-term development.

International trade will tend to align domestic and international prices, but international prices are often distorted by agricultural subsidies, political and military interventions, and the failure to internalize externalities. As a result, natural resources are likely to be sold below full environmental cost.

The impact of natural capital depletion will be especially large in estimates of national saving and investment. Estimates of "genuine saving" by the World Bank indicate that many countries' net saving and capital formation may in fact be negative, which clearly indicates lack of sustainability.

The export of natural capital also distorts exchange rates, and creates a bias against non–resource-exporting sectors, including manufacturing. Methods used to estimate exchange rate overvaluation become unreliable when proceeds from the unsustainable export of natural assets finance an import surplus. In this case, an apparently stable domestic price level is illusory, masking significant damage to non–resource-exporting sectors that must compete with artificially cheap imports. A trade deficit may be concealed or appear to be a surplus in the balance of payments accounts because the proceeds of natural capital exports are recorded incorrectly in the current account.

"Greening the national accounts is more important for economic than for environmental policy . . . especially for those countries whose natural resources are rapidly eroding, and the erosion is counted misleadingly in GDP as value added. Once the accounts are greened, macroeconomic policies need to be reexamined."

SOURCE

El Serafy, Salah. "Green Accounting and Economic Policy." Summarized in *A Survey of Sustainable Development,* edited by Harris et al., 2001.

Strong sustainability identifies types of natural capital for which this type of substitution is considered unacceptable. This involves the concept of critical natural capital ($K_n{}^*$), which must be preserved and whose destruction would not be compensated for by acquisition of other forms of capital. Another interpretation of strong sustainability would suggest that if a specific resource (for example, fossil fuels) is depleted, it must be replaced by capital with a comparable function (for example, solar energy installations that produce hydrogen fuel).[18]

- **Valuation of environmental damages.** The loss-of-productivity calculation referred to above provides one measure of soil erosion damage. An alternative method might be to examine the **replacement cost** of restoring fertility to eroded lands, for example by applying fertilizer. This method was used in the World Resources Institute study of Costa Rica and has also been used in United Nations studies. This approach is weakened by the fact that applying fertilizer may not fully restore the functions of eroded soil (such as soil structure, tilth, water-retention capability, and micronutrient supplies).

- **Valuation of environmental services.** The value of environmental assets is often more than is indicated by a simple economic measure. Forests, for example, provide more than timber value. They also provide watershed stabilization, runoff control and filtration, carbon sequestration, and maintenance of biodiversity, as well as having aesthetic and recreational value. As we saw in Chapter 6, some methods can be used to estimate these nonmarket values, but they have rarely been applied to natural resource and environmental accounting. In addition, it is questionable whether any economic valuation technique can capture the full **ecological value** of these varied ecosystem services.

- **Contribution to global environmental damages.** Economic activity in one country may cause environmental damage to the atmosphere or oceans that leads to **transboundary pollution** or **global pollution.** The polluting country's national product may be unaffected, but some account should be made of the environmental damage done to other countries or to the world as a whole. Often this involves **cumulative pollutants.** Daly and Cobb attempt to estimate the effects of such cumulative damage on sustainable welfare, and include this in one version of their ISEW measure.

- **Equity and basic needs.** In some cases increases in GNP are unequally distributed, with most of the benefits going to the already rich. Standard measures take no account of inequity, or of its practical effects on health, education, literacy, availability of clean water, and access to basic needs including food and housing. In addition to being important in themselves, these issues interrelate with environmental degradation—poverty often forces people to use resources in an unsustainable manner, and resource degradation in turn worsens poverty.

---

[18]For an extensive discussion of weak versus strong sustainability, see Neumayer, 1999.

TABLE 8-2 *Human Development Index Scores for Selected Developing Nations*

Nation	Life Expectancy (Years)	Adult Literacy (%)	School Enrollment Ratio (%)	Real Per Capita GDP (PPP$)*	HDI Score
Costa Rica	76.0	95.1	66	6,650	0.801
Brazil	66.8	84.0	80	6,480	0.739
Turkey	69.0	83.2	61	6,350	0.728
Sri Lanka	73.1	90.7	66	2,490	0.721
Congo	50.8	70.7	39	880	0.479
Pakistan	64.0	40.9	43	1,560	0.508

*PPP = purchasing power parity. PPP measures domestic income in terms of goods-purchasing power rather than converting domestic currency into dollars based on currency exchange rates. Levels of income in Sri Lanka, Congo, and Pakistan are similar when mentioned in conventional terms, but vary considerably when converted to a PPP measure.

Source: UNDP, *Human Development Report,* 1999.

The United Nations Development Programme's **Human Development Index (HDI)** combines equity and basic needs measures with standard GDP. The HDI uses an adjusted measure of real per capita GDP as one component of an index that also includes life expectancy and access to education. Often countries with similar conventional GDP levels can vary quite dramatically in human welfare as measured by these multivariate development indicators (Table 8-2).

To take account of education, the World Bank has also introduced an expanded measure of national investment, which counts all educational expenditures as an integral part of national investment.[19] The combination of this with natural capital depreciation gives a revised measure that indicates the importance of public investment in education in improving the genuine saving picture in many developing nations (Figure 8-5). For low-income nations, including a full measure of education spending approximately doubles genuine saving.

What can we conclude from this variety of approaches to revising or supplementing GNP/GDP measures? No single clear alternative to GNP/GDP emerges. Yet the environmental and social factors omitted in standard accounting have important implications both for policy and for our understanding of the meaning of economic development.

Environmental accounting efforts by international institutions such as the World Bank and the United Nations have led to more extensive reporting of social and environmental data.[20] These data will provide a basis for ongoing efforts to rethink standard measures of economic development.

---

[19]Hamilton and Clemens, 1997.

[20]See World Bank, 2000; UNDP, 2000.

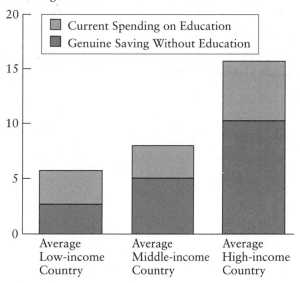

FIGURE 8-5 *Genuine Saving Including Education*

Source: Adapted from World Bank, *Expanding the Measure of Wealth: Indicators of Environmentally Sustainable Development.* Copyright 1997 by World Bank. Reprinted with permission of World Bank in the format textbook via Copyright Clearance Center.

SUMMARY

Standard measures of national income such as gross national product (GNP) and gross domestic product (GDP) fail to capture important environmental and social factors. This can result in misleading measurements of national well being, potentially ignoring important environmental problems. A variety of methods can be used to correct the GNP/GDP measure, or to provide alternatives.

Estimates of natural capital depreciation measure the depletion of natural resources such as oil, timber, minerals, and agricultural soils. Figures for these losses are subtracted from the standard measures of national income and investment. The results for many developing nations indicate substantial effects from natural resource depletion and environmental degradation.

For developed nations, expenditures on pollution control and cleanup, as well as the cumulative effects of long-lived pollutants, are significant factors. It is also possible to estimate the value of environmental services such as water purification, nutrient recycling, flood control, and provision of wildlife habitat. Systematic calculation of such factors can give a measure of sustainable economic welfare, which often differs significantly from GNP/GDP.

The application of modified national income accounting has wide-ranging policy implications. Nations that gain a large proportion of their export earnings from resource exports may be overestimating their economic progress. Natural resources may be sold below their true costs, leading to a net loss for the nation despite an apparent trade surplus.

Social as well as environmental conditions affect calculations of national income. Questions of human development including educational expenditures and measures of equity are often interrelated with issues of environmental degradation. Despite the evident importance of these factors, there is no consensus on how to include them in national accounts. An alternative approach is to maintain satellite accounts, measuring social and environmental indicators separately from GNP/GDP. International institutions have moved toward more extensive reporting of such data, giving a basis for more accurate assessments of true national well-being.

KEY TERMS AND CONCEPTS

adjusted net domestic product (NDP*)
adjusted net national product (NNP*)
critical natural capital
cumulative pollutants
defensive expenditures
ecological value
end-of-year stocks
environmental services
genuine saving (S*)
global pollution
green accounting
Human Development Index (HDI)
Index of Sustainable Economic Welfare (ISEW)
natural capital depreciation
net domestic product (NDP)

net foreign borrowing (NFB)
net investment
net national product (NNP)
net receipts
productivity loss estimates
replacement cost
satellite accounts
strong sustainability
substitutability (of natural and
    manufactured capital)
transboundary pollution
true income
user cost
weak sustainability

DISCUSSION QUESTIONS

1. What kinds of problems arise from the focus on standard GNP/GDP measures in discussing economic policy? How do these problems differ for highly industrialized nations such as the United States and developing nations such as Indonesia?

2. What main approaches can be used to correct GNP/GDP for natural resource depletion and environmental damage? What are some difficulties and controversies that arise in calculating these adjustments to GDP?

3. Would you consider a revised national income measure an improvement over current GNP concepts, or would you think it better to keep GNP and resource/environmental considerations separate by using satellite accounts?

4. What are some policy implications of using a revised measure that takes into account environmental and resource depreciation? How might using revised measures affect such policy areas as macroeconomic policy, trade policy, and resource pricing policy?

PROBLEMS

1. The following is macroeconomic information for the developing nation of Equatoria (expressed in international $ values). The Equatorian economy is composed of three sectors: agriculture, mining, and industrial.

Value of Agricultural Sector Output	$800 million
Value of Mining Sector Output	$450 million
Value of Industrial Sector Output	$750 million
Gross Investment (I_g)	$550 million
Net Foreign Borrowing (NFB)	$110 million
Depreciation of Manufactured Capital (D_m)	$150 million

Use these statistics to compute a standard measure of gross domestic product (GDP), net domestic product (NDP), and net investment (NI = $I_g - D_m$), for this three-sector economy.

Now consider the following information about natural resources and environment in Equatoria:

Agricultural Area (million Ha)	8
Soil Erosion (tons/Ha/year)	200
Yield Loss Factor per 100 tons/Ha erosion	0.75%
Copper Reserves (million tons)	150
Copper Extraction Per Year (million tons)	6.0
Net Price (Price—extraction costs) of Copper Per Ton	$75
Industrial Pollution (SO_2) Per Year (thousand tons)	750
Damage Estimate Per Ton of SO_2 Emitted	$120

Use these data to compute an environmentally adjusted measure of net domestic product (NDP*) and net investment (NI*).

$$NI^* = I_g - D_m - D_n$$

where D_n is depreciation of natural capital. Remember that soil erosion damage will continue to affect yields in future years.

To calculate the present value of future losses, use a discount rate (r). Experiment with 10 percent, 5 percent, and 2 percent discount rates and compare the results (round to the nearest million).

For nonrenewable resource depletion, you will need a measure of user costs. This can be derived from the formula relating true income (X) from extraction of a depletable resource to net receipts (R):

$$X/R = 1 - 1/(1+r)^n$$

where n is the expected resource lifetime.

$$\text{User Cost} = R - X = R/(1+r)^n$$

2. Using the same figures for Equatoria, compute a measure of genuine national savings (S^*), defined as gross investment minus depreciation of manufactured capital (D_m) minus depreciation of natural capital (D_n) minus net foreign borrowing (NFB):

$$S^* = I_g - D_m - D_n - \text{NFB} = \text{NI}^* - \text{NFB}$$

Suppose we have some further information related to environmental policies for Equatoria:

- An effective soil conservation program can be put in place at a cost of $20/Ha.
- SO_2 emissions can be cut by up to 50 percent for a cost of $50 per ton of pollution reduced.

Using this information, discuss some of the implications of your adjusted national income, investment, and savings calculations for policy in Equatoria. Be specific in your policy recommendations, remembering that Equatoria is a low-income developing nation.

REFERENCES

Cobb, Clifford W., and John B. Cobb Jr., *The Green National Product: A Proposed Index of Sustainable Economic Welfare*. Lanham, Md.: University Press of America, 1994.

Crowards, Tom M. "Natural Resource Accounting: A Case Study of Zimbabwe." *Environmental and Resource Economics* 7 (1996): 213–241.

Cruz, Wilfredo, and Robert Repetto, *The Environmental Effects of Stabilization and Structural Adjustment Programs: The Philippines Case*. Washington, D.C.: World Resources Institute, 1992.

Daly, Herman, and John B. Cobb Jr., *For the Common Good: Redirecting the Economy Toward Community, the Environment, and a Sustainable Future*. Boston: Beacon Press, 1994.

El Serafy, Salah. *Country Macroeconomic Work and Natural Resources*. World Bank Environment Department Working Paper No. 58, March 1993.

El Serafy, Salah. "Green Accounting and Economic Policy," *Ecological Economics* 21 (1997): 217–229. Summarized in *A Survey of Sustainable Development: Social and Economic Dimensions*, edited by Harris et al. Washington, D.C.: Island Press, 2001.

Hamilton, Kirk, and Michael Clemens. "Are We Saving Enough for the Future?" Chapter 2 in *Expanding the Measure of Wealth: Indicators of Environmentally Sustainable Development*, World Bank (1997). Summarized in *A Survey of Sustainable Development: Social and Economic Dimensions*, edited by Harris et al. Washington, D.C.: Island Press, 2001.

Harris, Jonathan M., Timothy A. Wise, Kevin P. Gallagher, and Neva R. Goodwin, eds. *A Survey of Sustainable Development: Social and Economic Dimensions.* Washington, D.C.: Island Press, 2001.

Hueting, Roefie. "Correcting National Income for Environmental Losses: A Practical Solution for a Theoretical Dilemma." In *Ecological Economics,* edited by Robert Costanza. New York: Columbia University Press, 1991.

Krishnan, Rajaram et al., eds. *A Survey of Ecological Economics.* Washington, D.C.: Island Press, 1995.

Lange, Glenn-Marie, and Faye Duchin. *Integrated Environmental-Economic Accounting: Natural Resource Accounts, and Natural Resource Management in Africa.* Winrock International Institute Technical Report No. 13; also summarized in *A Survey of Ecological Economics,* edited by Krishnan et al. Washington, D.C.: Island Press, 1995.

Lutz, Ernst, ed. *Toward Improved Accounting for the Environment.* Washington, D.C.: World Bank, 1993.

National Research Council. *Assigning Economic Value to Natural Resources.* Washington, D.C.: National Academy Press, 1994.

Neumayer, Eric. "Resource Accounting in Measures of Unsustainability: Challenging the World Bank's Conclusions." *Environmental and Resource Economics* 15 (2000): 257–278.

Pearce, David W., and Jeremy J. Warford. *World Without End: Economics, Environment, and Sustainable Development.* New York and Oxford, England: Oxford University Press, 1993.

Peskin, Henry M. "Alternative Environmental and Resource Accounting Approaches," Chapter 13 in *Ecological Economics: The Science and Management of Sustainability,* edited by Robert Costanza. New York: Columbia University Press, 1991.

Peskin, Henry M. "Sustainable Resource Accounting," Chapter 4 in *Assigning Economic Value to Natural Resources.* National Research Council. Washington, D.C.: National Academy Press, 1994.

Repetto, Robert, ct al. *Wasting Assets: Natural Resources in the National Income Accounts.* Washington, D.C.: World Resources Institute, 1989.

Repetto, Robert, et al. *Accounts Overdue: Natural Resource Depreciation in Costa Rica.* Washington, D.C.: World Resources Institute, 1991.

Repetto, Robert. "What Can Policymakers Learn from Natural Resource Accounting?" Chapter 2 in *Assigning Economic Value to Natural Resources.* National Research Council. Washington, D.C.: National Academy Press, 1994.

United Nations Department for Economic and Social Information and Policy Analysis. *Integrated Environmental and Economic Accounting.* New York: United Nations, 1993.

United Nations Development Programme. Human Development Report 2000. Oxford, England: Oxford University Press.

Vincent, Jeffrey R. "Green Accounting: From Theory to Practice," *Environment and Development Economics* 5 (Feb–May 2000): 13–24.

World Bank. *Expanding the Measure of Wealth: Indicators of Environmentally Sustainable Development*. Washington, D.C.: The World Bank, 1997.

World Bank. *Entering the 21st Century: World Development Report 1999/2000*. New York and Oxford, England: Oxford University Press, 2000.

WEB SITES

1. **http://www.bea.doc.gov/bea/an/0494od/maintext.htm** and **http://www.bea.doc.gov/bea/an/0494od2/maintext.htm** These 1994 articles published by the U.S. Bureau of Economic Analysis discuss the concepts and estimation of natural resource satellite accounts for the United States.

2. **http://www.rprogress.org/progsum/nip/gpi/gpi_main.html** A web site from Redefining Progress on the Genuine Progress Indicator. The site includes information on how the GPI is calculated and presents trend data on the GPI.

3. **http://www-esd.worldbank.org/eei/** The World Bank's Environmental Economics and Indicators web site. The site includes links to theoretical and empirical reports on green accounting.

CHAPTER FOCUS QUESTIONS

■ What principles explain the flow of energy and resources through the economic system?
■ How do we analyze economic inputs and outputs of materials, energy, and wastes?
■ What models best describe the interactions of economic and environmental systems?

CHAPTER

9

Modeling Economic and Ecological Systems

Energy and Resource Flow Analysis

Economic analysis of environmental issues focuses on markets, prices, internalization of externalities, and valuation of the environment. In Chapters 3–6, we applied concepts from economic theory to resource and environmental issues. Suppose we wish to reverse the perspective and apply the logic of physical and biological systems to the human economy, as suggested by the ecological economics perspective discussed in Chapter 7. What measure might we employ that possesses scope and explanatory power comparable to market price as a measure of value?

Ecological economics has arrived at no such single alternative measure. A prominent exponent, Richard Norgaard, has argued that the use of various analytical perspectives is essential in dealing with environmental topics, as well as other controversial issues. Norgaard maintains that "multiple insights guard against mistaken action based on one perspective."[1] He identifies this approach as **methodological pluralism:**

---

[1]Norgaard, 1989.

Through a combination of perspectives we can achieve a more comprehensive picture of the problems we study.

In the environmental area, one of the most important alternative perspectives incorporates principles drawn from the laws of thermodynamics, as applied to economic processes. The **first law of thermodynamics** states that matter and energy can be neither created nor destroyed (although matter can be transmuted into energy through nuclear processes). This means that any physical processes, including all economic processes can be seen as a transformation of matter and energy from one form to another. The **second law of thermodynamics** tells us something more about the nature of this transformation. It states that in all physical processes energy is degraded from an *available* to an *unavailable* state.

The formal measure of this process is called **entropy.** Entropy is a measure of the *unavailable* energy in a system; according to the second law, *entropy increases* as natural processes proceed. The concept of entropy also applies to resources other than energy. An easily usable resource, for example a high-grade metal ore, has low entropy. A poorer grade of ore has higher entropy; it requires the application of external energy to refine it for use.

The best way to understand this rather slippery concept is to think in terms of a specific example such as burning a lump of coal. In its original state, coal has **low entropy**—that is, it contains available energy. This energy can be obtained by burning the coal. Once burned, the coal is transformed into ashes and waste heat. The energy is no longer useful, and the system has moved to a high entropy state.

Nicholas Georgescu-Roegen, a pioneer of ecological economic thought, has argued that we should see this law of entropy as the fundamental governing principle of economics. All economic processes require energy, and all transform energy from a usable to an unusable form. The physical outputs of any economic process thus can be said to contain **embodied energy.**

For example, an automobile embodies energy used to produce steel and to shape the steel into auto parts, as well as the energy workers used to assemble it (or the energy used to run assembly-line robots). It also, of course, will require additional fuel energy to run. But eventually all this energy ends up in an unusable form. The fuel energy dissipates in waste heat and pollution. The car is eventually scrapped and itself becomes waste. In the process it has provided transportation services to its users, but the net result is the degradation of usable energy and resources into an unusable form.

If we think about the economic process from this perspective, two points become clear. One is that the economic process requires a continual stream of usable energy and resources (low entropy). The other is that it produces a continual stream of waste energy and other waste products (high entropy). Thus the input and output flows of resources and energy to and from the economic system become the fundamental governing mechanisms of production.

This perspective differs dramatically from standard economic theory, in which labor and capital usually rank as the fundamental productive factors. Energy and resource inputs are often not specifically considered, and sometimes omitted altogether. Energy and resources prices have no special significance over other input prices, and waste flow effects, as we have seen, are generally defined as "externalities" rather than as a central reality of production.

The standard approach works well enough when energy and resources are abundant and cheap, and when the environment easily absorbs waste and pollution damage. But as energy and resource demands grow, along with waste and pollution, the entropy perspective emerges as an important factor in understanding the relationship between the economic and ecological systems.

Energy Flows and the Economic Production System

Existing ecological systems are precisely organized for the efficient capture of energy. Millennia of evolution have developed complex and interdependent life systems that draw energy from the environment, using the **solar flux** (flow of sunlight). The fundamental process in all ecosystems is photosynthesis, by which green plants use the sun's energy to produce the organic compounds necessary for life. Because animals lack the ability to utilize the solar flux directly, all animal life depends completely on plant photosynthesis.

Viewed from the perspective of the entropy law, the economic process is essentially an extension of the biological process of using low entropy to support life activity, and at the same time increasing overall entropy. Industrial systems greatly increase the use rate of entropy. Low-entropy mineral deposits and stored low entropy in the form of fossil fuels are mined to support the industrial process. Intensive agriculture also "mines" the stored resources of the soil. At the same time, the industrial system greatly increases the emission of high-entropy waste products into the environment. Standard economic theory recognizes no inherent limits to growth, but the entropy theory implies that economic systems must operate subject to the constraints of:

- Limited stocks of low-entropy resources, in particular high-grade ores and easily available fossil fuels;
- Limited capacity of soils and biological systems to capture low-entropy to produce food and other biological resources;
- Limited capacity of the ecosystem to absorb high-entropy waste products.

In some cases we might evade specific constraints. For example, we can increase soil productivity by adding artificial fertilizers. We cannot evade the entropy law, however; since fertilizer production itself requires energy. In effect, we can expand the limits of the agricultural system by "borrowing" low entropy from somewhere else, but only with a more rapid use of energy resources (and faster generation of wastes and pollution). The one truly "free" source of low entropy is solar energy. Even in the case of solar energy, there are usually material and labor costs involved in capturing and using the available energy.

We can apply the entropy perspective to many different sectors of production: the energy sector itself, agriculture, mining, forestry, fishing, as well as other industrial sectors. This often gives a different picture of how these economic activities operate. A mining industry, for example, may show increasing productivity over time, measured

(a) Total Metal Mining

Output/BTU

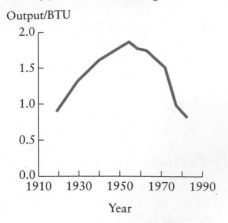

Year

(b) Total Petroleum Production

Energy output/energy input

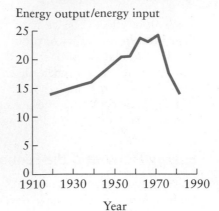

Year

(c) Total Coal Production

Energy output/energy input

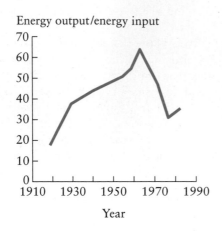

Year

(d) Farm Output Index per BTU of Total Energy Use (1977 = 100)

Output index/BTU

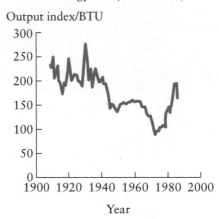

Year

(e) Output per Energy Input in the New Bedford Fisheries

Energy output/energy input

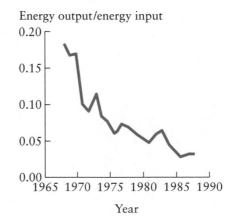

Year

BTU = British
Thermal Units

162

FIGURE 9-1 *Energy Use in Mining, Agriculture, and Fisheries*

Source: Cleveland, 1991, pp. 300–306. Adapted from *Ecological Economics: The Science and Management of Sustainability,* edited by Robert Costanza. Columbia University Press, © 1991. Reprinted with the permission of the publisher.

in standard terms relative to output of labor or capital inputs. But if we concentrate on output of energy inputs per unit, we may well see declining productivity. In other words, we need increasing amounts of energy to achieve the same output, as the quality of the mined ore declines.

In this case, we are *substituting* energy for labor and capital, an economically advantageous choice so long as energy is cheap. However, it means that our economic system becomes more dependent on fossil fuels, which as we will see in Chapter 13, provide 85 percent of our commercial energy. Pollution problems associated with fossil fuels also increase.

Analysis of trends in energy use in agriculture, fisheries, metal mining, and fossil fuel extraction show varying patterns, but in many cases output per unit of energy input decreases over time (Figure 9-1). This has significant implications for future industrial and energy use patterns, especially as growing populations in developing economies seek to follow the industrial growth path.

Ecological economic analysis thus emphasizes the *physical* basis of production, as opposed to the economic costs of production. This provides a direct link to the physical realities of planetary ecosystems. If we focus only on economic costs, even though we attempt to internalize resource depletion and environmental costs, we may miss the full scope of resource and environmental impacts of economic activity. As we examine the specific areas of agriculture, energy, resources, and pollution in Chapters 10–18, we will find value in both the standard economic approach and the ecological perspective.

Input-Output Analysis

Another economic technique that focuses on the physical basis of production is **input-output analysis.** Input-output analysis, based on a model of relationships between productive sectors in the economy, can easily be extended to apply to resource and environmental issues.

The basic input-output model describes quantitative flows between economic sectors, showing, for example, that producing an automobile might require one ton of steel, 20 square feet of glass, 100 pounds of plastic, and so on. A matrix A can be constructed for the entire economy showing the inputs from each sector to every other sector (see Figure 9-2).

Each cell in the matrix shows a coefficient a_{ij} indicating the amount of input from sector i used in the production of one unit of output from sector j. This matrix can show what levels of production in each sector are required to satisfy a given total demand from consumers, investors, government, and foreign purchasers.

It is a simple task to add a matrix B showing resource inputs to each sector of the economy and a matrix C showing waste outputs from each sector (see Figure 9-3). We can then use these matrices to calculate the resource requirements and waste outputs generated for any given level of demand. For example, if automobiles are sector 1, a projected increase of one unit in automobile production will require industrial inputs

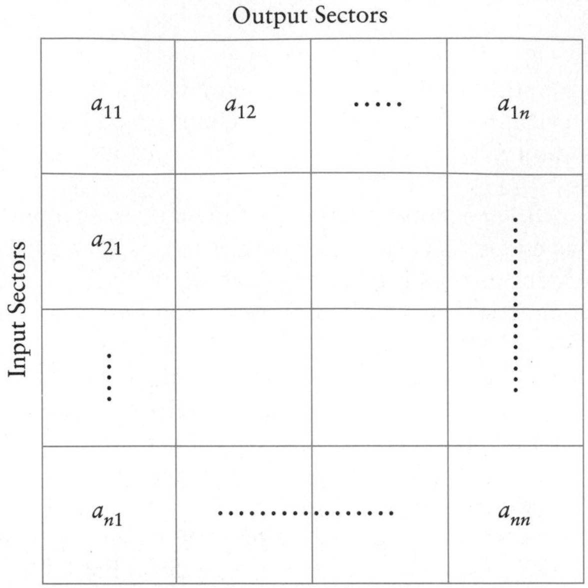

Output Sectors

FIGURE 9-2 *Basic Inter-Industry Input-Output Matrix*

$a_{11} - a_{n1}$ and resource inputs $b_{11} - b_{m1}$. If steel is sector 2, an increase of one unit of steel production will generate wastes $c_{21} - c_{2q}$.

The values of the parameters in the matrix cells depend on the production technologies employed. It is possible to extend this **static input-output analysis** to take account of changes in technology and capital stock, transforming it to a **dynamic input-output analysis.** Alternatively, we can compare different static analysis scenarios embodying different technologies. Thus we can consider possibilities of resource-conserving or pollution-reducing technologies, or add specific pollution-cleanup sectors to the model.

Modeling National and Global Systems

Rather than focusing on resource use and environmental impacts in only one industry, input-output analysis allows us to examine national, regional, or global effects of entire economic systems. For example, input-output models of the world economy have helped project global levels of carbon dioxide, sulfur and nitrogen oxides, and other pollutant emissions well into the twenty-first century given specific assumptions about economic growth rates in industrialized and developing nations.[2]

Input-output models are particularly useful for dealing with environmental problems, especially those that increase over time with economic growth. They allow us to combine analysis of the internal flows in the economy with measurement of the stocks

---

[2]Duchin and Lange, 1994.

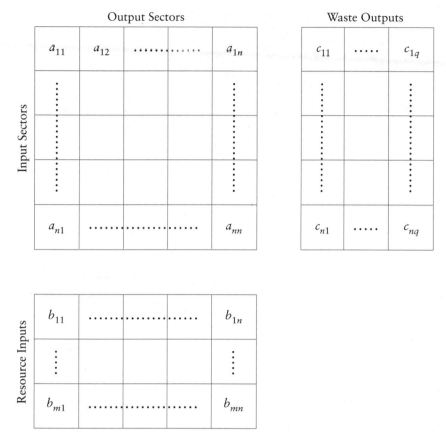

FIGURE 9-3 *Expanded Input-Output Matrix with Resources and Wastes*

and flows of resources and pollutants. However, the input-output technique also has some drawbacks.

A comprehensive input-output model requires large amounts of data input and computation, which may limit its feasibility for many specific problems. Also, some economists question the ability of such models to reflect changes in technology and production patterns. But from the ecological economist's point of view, the focus on the physical realities of production may be easier to integrate with "real world" issues of resource depletion and pollution impacts than are more abstract price-centered models.

Taking this logic a step further, the emerging theory of **industrial ecology** attempts to apply the analysis of resources, energy, and waste flows to the management of industrial activity. Industrial ecology, discussed at greater length in Chapter 17, requires the use of new analytical tools in addition to those ordinarily used by economists.[3]

---

[3]For a comprehensive overview of the principles of industrial ecology, see Socolow et al., eds., 1994.

Daewoo Motors assembly line, South Korea. Industrial production of automobiles requires inputs of metal, plastic, and glass as well as energy.

Input-output analysis, one way of approaching this problem, can be applied to individual industries, economic sectors, or to national or global systems.

Economic and Ecological Modeling

More complex dynamic models of economic/ecological systems are sometimes needed to capture changes and interactions among different system components. The construction of such models must consider such factors as demographics (of human and other species), resource depletion and regeneration, stocks and flows of wastes and pollutants, as well as natural physical and biological cycles.

It boggles the imagination to think of constructing a single model that will adequately represent all these factors. We cannot safely afford to leave out any of these elements, however, in a world in which population is still growing, in which economic pressures on the environment are ubiquitous, and in which the interactions and cumulative effects of pollutants affect whole ecosystems. How can we resolve this dilemma?

Some ecological/economic modelers have chosen to approach the problem by defining areas of study in terms of systems and processes. The first step is to establish a **system boundary.** For example, we might choose to study the economy and ecology of an estuary (the wide tidal mouth of a river). Within this system boundary are numerous species of land and water plants and animals, wetlands, human settlements, factories, and a fishing industry. Numerous processes support life and economic activity within the system boundary.

Natural processes include photosynthesis by plants, consumption of plants by animals, predation by some animal species on others, and decay and regeneration of organic matter. Economic processes include water use by households and industry, pollutant and sewage discharge, factory goods production, fishing industry exploitation of marine resources, and filling of wetlands for construction. We can model each of these processes, accounting for what it draws from the environment, what products it produces, and what it returns to the environment.

The model will show significant input and output flows between processes; for example, industrial discharge of pollutants may reduce yields in the fishing industry and adversely affect other plant and animal species. Filling in wetlands may increase economic output but decrease ecological activity.

We must also consider **cross-boundary flows.** The system as a whole receives solar energy, water from upstream, and goods and energy sources imported by humans. It discharges water to the ocean, waste heat and carbon dioxide to the atmosphere, and outputs of goods to other communities (for example, some of the fish caught may be shipped out and sold in cities). The first step in modeling is to note as carefully as possible all these internal processes and cross-border flows.

Of course, we can never completely describe all these flows; some will escape our attention or be impossible to measure. Even so, this view of the system is much more comprehensive than a purely economic model to which we attempt to add estimates of external costs and benefits. Our measurements of system activities will be primarily in physical terms, but we may also be able to convert some of them to dollar value estimates.

Modeling Individual Processes

We can choose to focus on a single process, noting carefully its inputs and outputs to other processes. Some of these we may ignore as insignificant to the problem under consideration. Those that we wish to analyze we must carefully measure in physical and/or value terms. For example, we could measure physical quantities of factory-emitted pollutants, or the value of damage to the fishing industry from these pollutants.

If the process we are examining is primarily economic, we may choose to express most flows in value terms, and our process model might resemble the kinds of analysis covered in Chapters 3–5 (externalities, common property resources, and public goods). If the process is primarily ecological, we will measure the impacts of economic activity in physical terms. If a process such as the fishing industry involves both economic and ecological components, we must integrate analysis of economic incentives to fishers and demographics of fish stocks (discussed further in Chapter 14).

Figure 9-4 focuses on a single process within a system. Inputs to this process come both from other processes in the system and from outside the system. Some of the process outputs become inputs for other processes within the system, and others are exported out of the system. As a result, the product stock within the system changes over time.

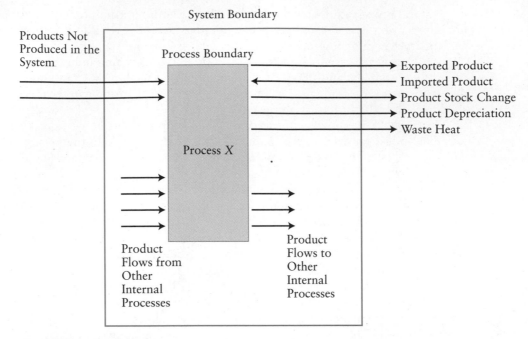

FIGURE 9-4 *Process Flows in an Ecosystem*

Source: Hannon, 1991, p. 239. Adapted from *Ecological Economics: The Source and Management of Sustainability,* edited by Robert Costanza. Columbia University Press, © 1991. Reprinted with the permission of the publisher.

This general framework applies both to economic and to ecological processes and can show the patterns of changes over time. For example, we might use it to track carbon storage in a forest ecosystem, taking into account inputs of carbon from the atmosphere and outputs through decay or through human exploitation of the forest.

Modeling Complete Systems

Integrating the analysis of different processes can give a comprehensive picture of economic and ecological activity within the system boundary. Such an integrated analysis is depicted in Figure 9-5.

This example shows a schematic of economic and ecological flows in the city of Brabant, The Netherlands. Local natural resource systems provide inputs to the farms and industries of Brabant. Other inputs, including fossil fuels, are imported, and the products of industry are exported. Agricultural production in Brabant provides products both for local consumption and for export. Industry, agriculture, and households all draw on local water systems, which suffer some pollution from nitrate and pesticides runoff. Forests provide outdoor recreation, as well as inputs for wood-processing industries. Agricultural runoff also affects forests as well as heathlands.

A model of this sort offers insight into patterns of economic production, land use, and environmental change. Although some of the system flows follow economic rules,

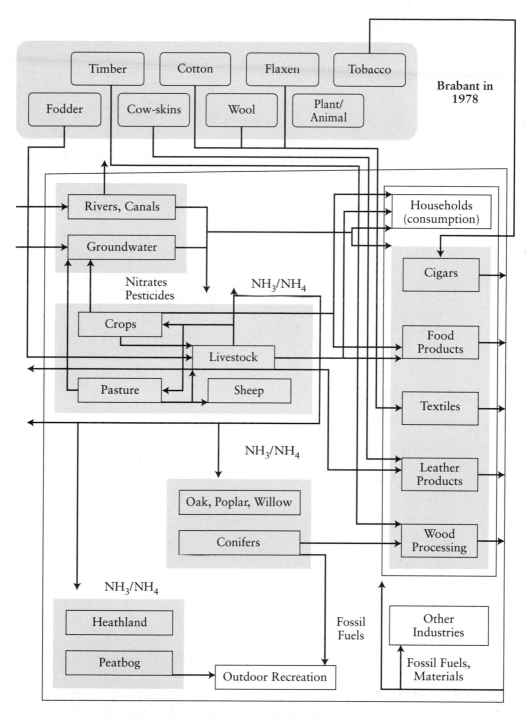

FIGURE 9-5 *Ecological-Economic Model of Brabant, The Netherlands*

Source: Braat and Steetskamp, 1991, p. 283. Adapted from *Ecological Economics: The Science and Management of Sustainability,* edited by Robert Costanza. Columbia University Press, ©1991. Reprinted with the permission of the publisher.

others are biophysical in nature. The model attempts to capture the interactions between the two systems as well as their changes over time.

Computer analysis can model the changes in such a system as economic growth creates greater demands on resources and environment. The model can indicate the scale and severity of environmental pressures. In turn, we can project economic effects of environmental changes and note whether cross-border flows, such as dependence on imported energy sources, will increase.[4]

As we discuss issues of population, agriculture, energy, natural resources, and pollution in the following chapters we will use both standard economic and ecological-economic forms of analysis. We will employ the logic of systems modeling as well as economic analysis of market prices and consumer or producer incentives. We will also, of course, draw on examples of current research in ecological economics as well as in mainstream environmental economics.

In covering both environmental and ecological perspectives, we have reviewed a formidable toolbox of analytical methods. Because different approaches give different insights, we will take an eclectic approach (meaning we'll select useful elements from varied sources). We will focus first on population, a fundamental issue in the analysis of ecological systems. We will discuss different approaches to population analysis in Chapter 10, giving a basis for the evaluation of food supply in Chapter 11, resources and energy in Chapters 12–15, and wastes and pollution in Chapters 16–18.

SUMMARY

Ecological perspectives on the relationship between the economic system and the environment complement standard, market-based analysis. The differing approaches are not mutually exclusive, but offer a broader picture of economy/ecosystem interactions.

Analysis of energy and resource flows demonstrates the importance of energy supplies and high-quality resources to the economic process. Important issues concerning the use of energy and resources include possible constraints on energy and resource supply, as well as the inevitable problems created by wastes and pollution. We must also consider the complex life-supporting functions of existing ecosystems. From this perspective, the potential for substituting humanmade production systems for natural functions is subject to clear ecological limits.

Input-output analysis shows resource flows through complex economic systems. It can be adapted to include resource supply and environmental impact sectors and to take account of changes in technology and capital stock. Expanded input-output models help project the resource and environmental impacts of different economic growth patterns.

Other types of modeling can also apply to economic/ecological systems. Such models attempt to capture numerous flows of materials and energy between sectors of

---

[4]For an in-depth treatment of dynamic computer modeling of economic-ecological systems, see Hannon and Ruth, 1994.

the economy and elements of the ecosystem. These flows are measured either in physical or in value terms, and can be related to geographical data to show regional patterns. Computer analysis provides a sophisticated representation of the interaction of economic development and ecosystem modification in specific industries or for whole economies.

A combination of these techniques and of standard economic analysis offers varied insights into issues of population, agriculture, natural resources, energy, and pollution. An eclectic approach based on methodological pluralism can escape the problem of narrow theoretical models, giving a more comprehensive picture of environmental issues.

KEY TERMS AND CONCEPTS

cross-boundary flows
embodied energy
entropy
first law of thermodynamics
industrial ecology

input-output analysis (static and dynamic)
methodological pluralism
second law of thermodynamics
solar flux
system boundary

DISCUSSION QUESTIONS

1. How is the thermodynamic concept of entropy relevant to economics? Is energy simply one factor of production among others, or does something about energy merit the special attention it receives from ecological economists? Consider how the principle applies to specific areas of economic production such as agriculture, industry, and transportation.

2. Construct a simple schematic model of an economic/ecological system. Choose a relatively simple subject, such as a rural village rather than a large city. Define a system boundary and note as many process flows as you can within the system and across boundaries. How might your model be used? What kind of data would you need to complete it?

REFERENCES

Braat, Leon C., and Ineke Steetskamp. "Ecological Economic Analysis for Regional Sustainable Development." Chapter 18 in Costanza, ed., 1991.

Cleveland, Cutler. "Natural Resource Scarcity and Economic Growth Revisited: Economic and Biophysical Perspectives." Chapter 19 in Costanza, ed., 1991.

Costanza, Robert, ed. *Ecological Economics: The Science and Management of Sustainability.* New York: Columbia University Press, 1991.

Duchin, Faye, and Glenn-Marie Lange. *The Future of the Environment: Ecological Economics and Technological Change.* New York: Oxford University Press, 1994.

Georgescu-Roegen, Nicholas. "The Entropy Law and the Economic Problem," in *Valuing the Earth: Economics, Ecology, Ethics,* edited by Herman E. Daly and Kenneth N. Townsend. Cambridge, Mass.: MIT Press, 1993.

Hannon, Bruce. "Accounting in Ecological Systems," Chapter 16 in Costanza, ed., 1991.

Hannon, Bruce, and Matthias Ruth. *Dynamic Modeling.* New York: Springer-Verlag, 1994.

Norgaard, Richard B. "The Case for Methodological Pluralism." *Ecological Economics,* 1 (February 1989): 37–57.

Socolow, Robert, et al., eds. *Industrial Ecology and Global Change.* Cambridge, England: Cambridge University Press, 1994.

WEB SITES

1. **http://esa.sdsc.edu/issues.htm** Several online reports published by the Ecological Society of America that apply ecological concepts to current environmental issues.
2. **http://www.riles.org/** Home page for the ReSource Institute for Low Entropy Systems, a "nonprofit organization that works in partnership with communities in English- and Spanish-speaking countries to protect public health and the environment." The site includes information about the projects they sponsor across the world, focusing on ecological waste management and low-entropy technology transfer.
3. **http://www.geocities.com/RainForest/3621/DALY.HTM** An article by Herman Daly with links to other material by him. Daly is a proponent of intergrating economic and ecological systems.

FOUR

Population, Agriculture, and the Environment

CHAPTER FOCUS QUESTIONS

- How fast is world population growing?
- What are the prospects for future population growth?
- What relationship exists between population and economic growth?
- How does population growth affect the global environment?

CHAPTER

10

Population and the Environment

The Dynamics of Population Growth

Human population has grown slowly throughout most of our history. Only within the past 200 years has more rapid global population growth become a reality. Figure 10-1 shows the history of global population increase during the nineteenth and twentieth centuries, with a baseline projection for the twenty-first century. As the diagram shows, in the past 100 years population growth has accelerated at a pace unprecedented in global history.

In 1800, global population had reached about 1 billion after many centuries of very slow growth. In a century and a half more, the figure reached 2.5 billion. A rapid post–World War II acceleration in growth doubled population to 5 billion in less than 40 years. By the year 2000, world population had passed 6 billion.

Extraordinarily rapid population growth—about 2 percent per year—took place from 1950 to 1975. At first consideration, 2 percent may not sound remarkable—but at this rate of growth population doubles in about 35 years. After 1975, the growth rate slowed, but the much larger total population meant that the absolute number of people added each year continued to increase until the 1990s (Figure 10-2).

Population (in billions)

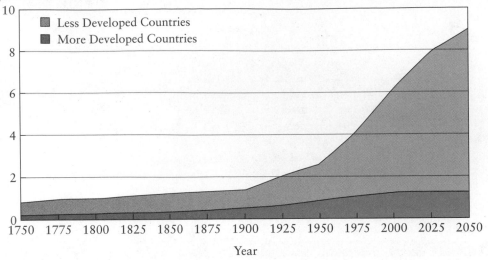

FIGURE 10-1 *Global Population Growth and Projections, 1750–2050*
Source: United Nations Department of Economic and Social Affairs, Population Division, 2001.

Population (in millions)

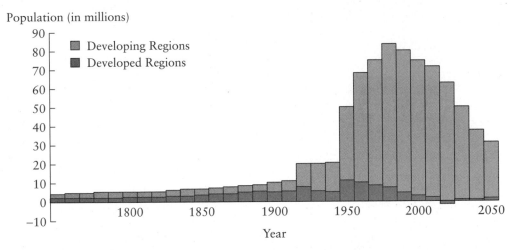

FIGURE 10-2 *Net Annual Increase in Population Per Decade, 1750–2050*
Source: United Nations Department of Economic and Social Affairs, Population Division, 2001; Repetto, 1991.

During this extremely rapid growth, various authors sounded the alarm regarding the dangers of **exponential growth.** A population of 5 billion that continued to grow at 2 percent per year, for example, would reach 20 billion in 70 years and 40 billion in a little over a century. Finding food, water, and living space for such a vastly increased population would be impossible; the grim Malthusian controls of famine and disease would take over.

Authors such as Paul and Anne Ehrlich warned in *The Population Bomb* (1968) and later in *The Population Explosion* (1990) that runaway population growth could overcome all the benefits of modern science and economic growth, leaving a devastated and miserable planet. This **neo-Malthusian** perspective has gained much attention, and provides the starting point for the modern debate on population growth.

Those who find the Ehrlichs' perspective overly negative often point out that **population growth rates** have been declining since the 1970s; as of the year 2000 the overall global rate was down to 1.3 percent and continuing to fall. Does this mean that population will soon stabilize, and fears of rapid growth are mere alarmism? Unfortunately not.

First, the declining growth rate is occurring at a time when total population is much higher than ever before. The global **gross annual population increase** as of 2001 was 77 million (1.3 percent of 6 billion). This annual addition to the planet's human numbers is greater than the entire population of France. Each year, we now add more people than we added annually during the 1960s, when the growth *rate* was at its highest (see Table 10-1 and Figure 10-2). The equivalent of a new New York City every 6 weeks, a new France every 10 months, a new India in about 13 years—this is hardly cause for complacency. The global demographic picture is far from stabilized, and this reality will continue to underlie environmental issues for many more decades.

The second reason why population is a crucial concern relates to regional patterns of population growth. It is precisely in the poorest and most hard-pressed nations that continuing population growth will be most rapid. More than 90 percent of the projected growth will come in the currently developing nations of Asia, Africa, and Latin America (Table 10-2). Many of these nations, especially in Africa, currently have trouble providing adequate food supplies and basic goods to their present populations.

TABLE 10-1 *Global Population Growth Rates and Average Gross Annual Increase by Decade*

	1960s	1970s	1980s	1990s (est.)	2000s (est.)
Population Growth Rate	2.0 percent	1.8 percent	1.7 percent	1.4 percent	1.2 percent
Average Annual Increase (millions)	67	75	83	80	74

Source: U. S. Census Bureau web site, www.census.gov/ipc/www/worldpop.html, *Total Midyear Population for the World: 1950–2050.*

TABLE 10-2 *2050 Population Projections Under Three Fertility Scenarios*

Region	2000 population (millions)	2050 population projections (millions)		
		Low Fertility	Medium Fertility	High Fertility
Africa	794	1,694	2,000	2,320
Asia	3,672	4,527	5,428	6,430
Latin America and Caribbean	519	657	806	975
Europe	727	556	603	654
Northern America	314	389	438	502
Oceania	31	42	47	53
More-developed regions	1,191	1,075	1,181	1,309
Less-developed regions	4,865	6,791	8,141	9,625
World total	6,057	7,866	9,322	10,934

Source: United Nations Department of Economic and Social Affairs, Population Division, 2001.

Developed nations currently create the greatest environmental impact through their high per capita demand on resources, as well as pollution generation. If the developing nations succeed in raising living standards for their expanding populations—as China and other East Asian nations are—their per capita demands for food and resources, as well as their pollution generation, will also increase. The combined effects of population and economic growth will significantly increase environmental pressures.

Predicting Future Population Growth

How well can we predict future population growth? The projected population shown in Figure 10-1 is a baseline prediction. Could the actual figures go much higher or much lower? As Table 10-2 and Figure 10-3 show, assumptions about changes in fertility, rates significantly influence projections. The three scenarios shown cover a range of possibilities for global population in the year 2050, ranging from 7.8 to 10.9 billion people. Within this range, the major factor lending credibility to projections of continued population growth is the phenomenon of **population momentum.**

To understand population momentum, let's consider a hypothetical country, Equatoria, which has been experiencing rapid population growth for several generations. For simplicity, we'll define a generation as equal to 25 years, and divide the population of Equatoria into three age categories: under 25, 25 to 50, and over 50 years old. Suppose the population growth rate averages 3 percent per annum (this is a high but not unprecedented rate in developing nations—the current population growth rate for Nigeria, for example, is close to 3 percent). At this rate, each generation will be roughly twice as numerous as the preceding generation. This will give a **population age profile** shaped like a pyramid (Figure 10-4).

Population (in billions)

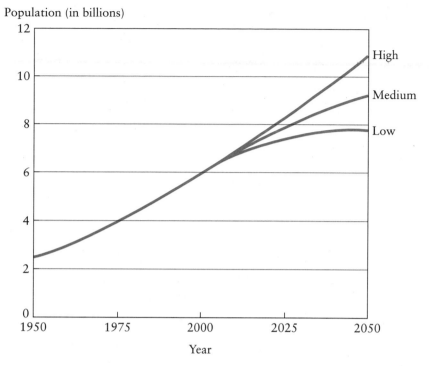

FIGURE 10-3 *Population Projections Under Three Fertility Scenarios*
Source: Adapted from United Nations Department of Economic and Social Affairs, Population Division, *World Population Prospects: The 2000 Revision.* United Nations, 2001. The United Nations is the author of the original material.

Now consider the future demographics of Equatoria. If this growth rate continues, the population will double every 25 years. If it is 7 million in 2000, as shown in the first part of Figure 10-4, it will be 14 million by 2025, 28 million by 2050, and 56 million by 2075. No nation can long withstand the environmental and social pressures of such growth. Sooner or later, the growth rate must decline.

For this to happen, the average **fertility rate** must fall. The fertility rate is defined as the number of children borne by the average woman during her lifetime. The fertility rate in Equatoria must be over 4 children per woman to account for such rapid rates of growth. Again, this is not unusual in the developing world. The average fertility rate for Sub-Saharan Africa in 2000 was 5.8, for Nigeria 6.0, for Pakistan 5.6, for Syria 4.7, and for Nicaragua 4.4.[1]

Population policies usually seek to achieve a **replacement fertility level,** which is just over 2 children per woman (the precise number depends on the rate of infant and child mortality). At replacement fertility, each new generation will be exactly the size of the preceding one. Achieving such a lowered fertility rate usually takes many years

---

[1]Population Reference Bureau, 2000.

Hypothetical Population Age Structure for "Equatoria"

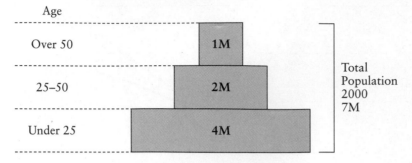

Projected Population Age Structure for "Equatoria"

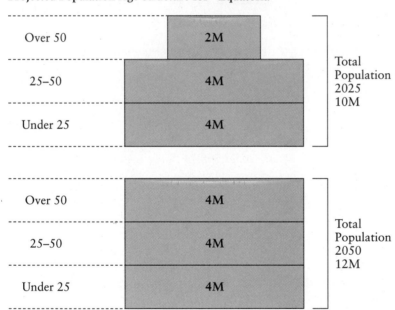

FIGURE 10-4 *Projected Population Age Structure for "Equatoria"*

in a country such as Equatoria. Suppose Equatoria reaches this goal. Is the population growth problem over? Absolutely not!

Imagine a fantastically effective population policy that would lower fertility to replacement level *immediately*. Equatoria's demographic future would be as shown in the second and third parts of Figure 10-4. Each new generation would be exactly the size of the last. The current generation of under-25s, however, is Equatoria's largest

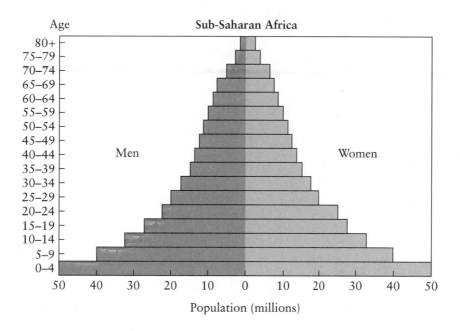

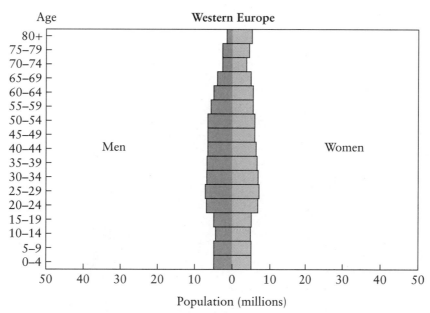

FIGURE 10-5 *Population Age Structures for Sub-Saharan Africa and Western Europe, 1990*

Source: Adapted from Wolfgang Lutz, *The Future of World Population*. Washington, D.C.: Population Reference Bureau, 1994. Reprinted by permission of the Population Reference Bureau.

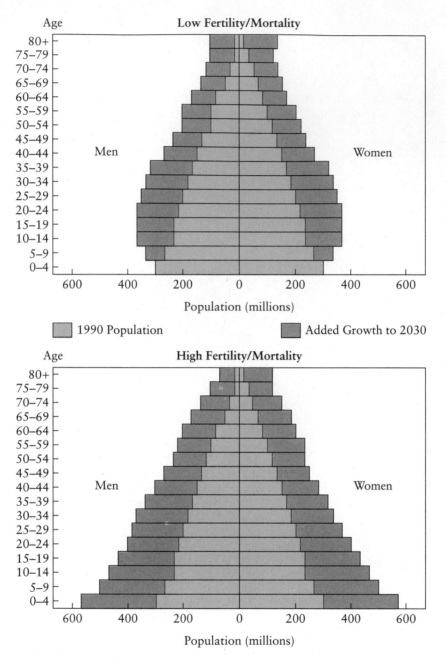

FIGURE 10-6 *Alternative Futures for World Population*

Source: Adapted from Wolfgang Lutz, *The Future of World Population*. Washington, D.C.: Population Reference Bureau, 1994. Reprinted by permission of Population Reference Bureau.

ever. Even if they only replace themselves in numbers, the population will continue to grow for two more generations.

The next generation of children will be four times as large as the current over-50 generation, meaning that the birth rate will be several times as high as the death rate for another 25 years. During the 25 years after that, the birth rate will still be about double the death rate. The population growth rate, which is the difference between the birth and death rates, will remain positive. Only when the current generation of children reach the end of their lifespan will *their* grandchildren no longer outnumber them. Thus Equatoria's population will continue to grow for 50 years before it stabilizes, reaching a total of 12 million, 71 percent more than its current level.

This is the meaning of population momentum. When a nation has a history of rapid population growth, continued growth for the next several generations is virtually guaranteed, short of some massive Malthusian catastrophe that dramatically raises death rates. A more realistic projection for Equatoria might be that fertility rates, rather than falling instantaneously as in our hypothetical case, would take about a generation to reach replacement level. In this case, population would continue to grow for 75 years, finally stabilizing at well over double the 2000 level.

The case of Equatoria is not merely an abstract example. As Figure 10-5 shows, the simplified population pyramid we have described is close to reality for much of Africa. (Use Figure 10-4, frame 3, to visualize a future Africa where all **population cohorts** or age groups are at least as large as the current cohorts of young children.)

Population momentum is also considerable throughout Asia and Latin America. Projections of population growth for these regions are therefore well founded. The inexorable logic of population momentum guarantees growing human numbers well into the twenty-first century. The stable age structure of Western Europe shown in the second frame of Figure 10-5 is the exception, not the rule. This is why the lowest global population projections for 2030 are about 7.5 billion.

Population momentum makes substantial increase inevitable, but a huge difference remains between relatively low and high forecasts for the years 2030, 2050, and beyond (see Figure 10-3 and 10-6). The critical variable in these differing projections is the rate of future fertility decline. If fertility falls rapidly throughout the developing world, the global population age pyramid could approach a more stable pattern within the next 35 years. (Compare the global low fertility scenario for 2030 in Figure 10-5 with the West European population age structure in Figure 10-4.) On the other hand, a slow decline would leave the world with both a higher population and considerable remaining momentum in 2030 (as shown in the second frame of Figure 10-6).

The Theory of Demographic Transition

The third United Nations International Conference on Population and Development, meeting in Cairo in September 1994, grappled with the issue of an appropriate response to growing world population. The conference adopted the ambitious goal of stabilizing world population at about 7.27 billion by the year 2015—an increase of roughly 30 percent over 1994 levels.

If this stabilization effort fails, the conference projected population rising to 12.5 billion by 2050, more than doubling the 1994 figure. We have seen why the alternatives differ so starkly. A failure to lower fertility levels in the next two decades yields both higher population and continuing momentum. This suggests that we stand at a crucial juncture for population policy.

Current Population Reference Bureau projections indicate a world population of 7.8 billion by 2025, a net addition of 1.8 billion people over 2000 levels, with growth continuing after that toward a possible 9 billion in 2050. Thus the goal of the Cairo conference may not be achievable—but the most pessimistic projections may not occur either. Certainly the task of supplying the needs of an extra 1.8 to 3 billion people is a daunting one. The course of population growth and fertility levels over the next 20 years will profoundly affect food production, resource use, and pollution generation, issues that we consider in upcoming chapters. What, then, can an environmental or ecological economics analysis tell us about population policy?

Much thinking about the relationship between population and economic growth rests on western European experience. Western Europe's situation is considered the final stage of the **demographic transition** from high to low birth and death rates. Figure 10-7 shows the pattern of this demographic transition.

In the first stage, corresponding to preindustrial Europe, both birth and death rates are high. Large families are common, but medical care is poor and many children die young. On average, a family produces only two surviving children. Thus the population remains about the same from generation to generation. These social conditions resemble in many ways the state of nature, where birds and animals typically produce

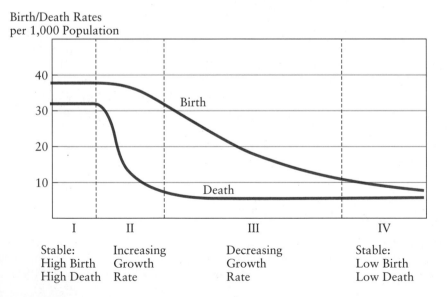

FIGURE 10-7 *The Demographic Transition*

numerous progeny to offset high rates of predation and disease. It is a harsh but ecologically stable regime.

In the second stage, industrialization takes off, as in nineteenth-century Europe. Death rates fall rapidly as standards of living, public health, and medical care improve. Birth rates remain high, however, because families still view numerous children as valuable, both to work on the farm or in the factory, and as a form of old-age insurance. If more children now survive, so much the better from the individual family's point of view. Because net population growth rate is equal to the birth rate minus the death rate (the distance between the two lines in Figure 10-7), the result is a rapidly growing population.

Population Growth Impact

Is growing population a good or bad thing for the country as a whole? If resources are abundant, the nation's leaders may welcome it. A large labor force promotes rapid economic growth and helps in taking advantage of unexploited resources and new technology. However, this period of rapid population and economic growth probably contains some self-limiting factors.

One such factor is the improvement in social conditions likely to accompany economic growth. This development, by no means automatic, often requires hard-fought battles for social and economic reform. Eventually, however, the nation may achieve social changes characteristic of economically developed nations, including child labor laws, unemployment compensation, social security systems, private pension plans, and greater educational opportunity.

In this changed atmosphere, people's attitude toward family size changes. Smaller families now seem more desirable—a large family becomes an economic burden rather than a benefit, and greater opportunities arise, especially for women, as family size shrinks. Contraceptive techniques become more available. For all these reasons, fertility rates fall—often quite rapidly. We enter the third stage, of declining birth rates and declining net population growth rates.

Here we must remember that Figure 10-7 shows only the *rate* of population growth (the difference between birth and death rates). The total population, of course, is considerably larger at this stage, so that a lower *rate* of growth may still mean a higher net addition to population (gross annual increase) each year. Population, as we have seen, could double or triple during this period of declining birth rates. If birth rates continue to decline, however, the country will eventually reach the final stage of stabilized population with low birth rates and low death rates (stage 4).

As a retrospective view of European history, this process appears relatively benign. Despite the great hardships involved in the early stages, overall it appears that population growth, economic growth, and social progress went hand in hand, and that population growth was eventually self-limiting. The Malthusian vision failed to develop—on the contrary, larger populations typically led to better living conditions.

Does this picture fit the present global population reality? Certainly the first two stages of the demographic transition theory apply well to the developing world's experience in the second half of the twentieth century. Death rates have fallen much faster than birth rates; fertility and population growth rates rose to historic highs in the

W hen we think of population problems, we tend to focus on rapid population growth rates in developing nations. But population is far from stable in the United States as well. Although Europe has completed the demographic transition to stable population levels, both natural increase and immigration keep the U.S. population growing. U.S. fertility rates are at replacement levels, but population growth since 1950 has generated large cohorts of people still in their reproductive years, creating significant continuing population momentum.

The 1990s saw a larger increase in U.S. population than any other 10-year period in the nation's history, surpassing even the 1950s baby boom decade. Population grew from 248.7 million to 281.4 million during the 1990s, an increase of 32.7 million, or 13 percent. All 50 states increased their populations, ranging from a half percent in North Dakota to 66 percent in Nevada. Metropolitan areas sprawled out into formerly rural regions. Immigration accounted for at least one-third of the population increase, with the fastest growth in the South and West (U.S. Census Bureau, *New York Times* and *Boston Globe,* April 3, 2001).

U.S. population will likely grow for at least the next three decades. The Population Reference Bureau projects U.S. population for 2025 at 337.8 million, an increase of 56.4 million, or 20 percent, over 2000 levels. Projected population for 2050 is more than 400 million. The longer-term figures, may be somewhat uncertain, but these numbers indicate the continuing power of population momentum combined with immigration.

Because U.S. residents have the highest resource consumption and waste generation rates on the planet, they will have much greater environmental impact than a comparable number of consumers in a low-income nation. Thus the projected U.S. population increase, although only about 3 percent of likely global population growth, has considerable significance for global environmental issues such as greenhouse gas emissions.

The increasing U.S. population will also put growing pressure on domestic land and resources. Urban and suburban sprawl, overdraft of water supplies, and air and automobile traffic congestion, will all become more difficult to manage. Population policy is clearly as relevant for the United States as it is for developing nations in considering these various environmental issues.

SOURCES

Population Reference Bureau. *2000 World Population Data Sheet.* Washington, D.C.: Population Reference Bureau, 2000.

U.S. Census Bureau. "Largest Census-to-Census Population Increase in U.S. History As Every State Gains." http://www.census.gov/Press-Release/www/2001/cb01cn64. html.

"U.S. Population Has Biggest 10-Year Rise Ever." *New York Times,* April 3, 2001.

"Census Gain Largest Ever." *Boston Globe,* April 3, 2001.

period 1950–1975. Since then, strong evidence indicates that most nations have entered the third phase, with overall growth rates falling. In many respects, however, currently developing nations' experiences differ significantly from Europe's:

- The total population numbers at issue are much larger, unprecedented in planetary history. Every decade the developing nations add population equal to the *entire* population of Europe and Russia.

- In their expansion, Europe and the United States drew on the rest of the world for natural resource supplies. The currently developed nations also have disproportionately exploited the global environment's waste absorption capacities (contributing by far the greatest proportion of greenhouse gas emissions, ozone depleting chemicals, and such). The developing world obviously will not have these options.

- There is significant uncertainty concerning the role of fertility decline. Factors that contribute to fertility decline may be present in some nations but absent in others. Projections of population stabilization depend strongly on rapid fertility decline, which may or may not occur.

- The rapid economic growth that accompanied population growth in Europe has occurred in some parts of the developing world but not in others. Africa in particular has experienced high population growth and stagnant or declining output and food production per capita. In some places where economic growth has been strong, its benefits have not filtered down to the poor, resulting in increased inequality and a greater absolute number of extremely poor people. In the "dual economies" of many Latin American countries, modern urban development coexists with extreme rural poverty and huge slums surrounding major cities. Many people have not yet achieved the improved living standards that contribute to fertility decline.

All these arguments suggest that looking back to the history of population and economic growth offers insufficient insight into the population-related issues of the next 40 or 50 years. Social, economic, and environmental factors intertwine with demographics. We cannot simply wait for the second, global process of demographic transition to play itself out. Rather, we must apply the best analysis and policy response possible to what is likely to be the most important issue determining the economic and environmental parameters of the twenty-first century.

Population Growth and Economic Growth

What does economic theory say about population? A typical economic model, the Cobb-Douglas production function, shows economic output as a function of labor input, capital input, and technological parameters:

$$Q_t = A_t \, K^{\alpha}_t \, L^{\beta}_t$$

where Q is total output, K is the capital stock, L is the labor force, α and β are parameters related to the productivity of capital and of labor respectively, A reflects a given state of technology, and t indicates a particular time period. The values of α and β are assumed to be fractions between zero and one; if $\alpha + \beta = 1$, the function shows **constant returns to scale.** This means that if labor and capital inputs were both doubled, output would also double.

Suppose that we increase only one factor, labor. Output will also increase, but by a smaller proportion than the increase in labor input.[2] If labor is roughly proportional to total population, **per capita output** will decline. As more and more labor is added, the **law of diminishing returns** comes into play, giving smaller output boosts for each additional unit of labor input. Thus in a simple economic model, population increase alone would yield falling living standards. This is a result of **capital shallowing,** which means that each worker has less capital to work with and is thus less productive.

However, few economists would view this simple logic as an accurate representation of the effects of population growth. They would point to the capital stock variable K, noting that if K grows at a rate at least equal to L, output per capita will remain constant or rise. In addition, **technological innovation** will tend to increase the variable A over time, leading to greater output for each unit of labor or capital input. Provided capital formation and technological progress are adequate, a rising standard of living can accompany population and labor force growth.

Economic theory, then, sees population growth as inherently neither good nor bad. Its effects depend on its context. If economic institutions are strong, markets work well, and environmental externalities are not great, population growth can be positive. Indeed, Ester Boserup[3] has argued that population growth may act as a spur to technological development, especially in agriculture. She finds evidence that increased population pressure forces the adoption of more efficient agricultural techniques. At least in the early stages of development, **economies of scale** may prevail; increasing population density may make possible larger-scale, more productive agriculture and industry.

Does Population Growth Promote or Retard Economic Growth?

Some analysts generalize this argument to present a positive view of population growth both as a proof of successful advance in human technological skill and as a spur to further progress. One of the strongest proponents of this point of view, Julian Simon, suggested that we should welcome further population growth because human ingenuity will always overcome resource limitations and environmental problems.[4] Most economists and ecologists, however, reject this unqualified optimism. While acknowledging the importance of technological progress, most analyses of the overall impact of population growth present the issue as significantly more complex.

---

[2]This is because the exponent β is less than one. If, for example, $\alpha = \beta = 0.5$, a doubling of labor alone would increase output by a factor of 1.414. A doubling of both labor and capital would increase output by a factor of 2.

[3]Boserup, 1981.

[4]Simon, 1996.

Economic theory recognizes several ways in which population growth may negatively affect economic growth:

- Increased **dependency ratios.** We have seen that a growing population typically includes a high proportion of children. Families must spend more on supporting dependent children, and thus have less to save, lowering the national savings rate. Higher spending on health and education is required, reducing funds available for capital investment. These effects tend to slow capital accumulation and economic growth.

- Increased income inequality. A rapidly growing population creates excess labor supplies, which draw down wage rates. High rates of unemployment and underemployment are likely, and a large class of extremely poor people receives no benefits from economic growth. This situation prevails in many Latin American countries as well as in India, where unemployed rural laborers migrate to large cities in search of jobs, creating vast slums surrounding city centers.

- Natural resource limitations. Note that natural resources do not appear as a variable in the production function used above. In theory, capital, labor, and output in this function could grow without limit. But what about resource and environmental limitations? The presence of **fixed factors,** such as a limited supply of land, will lead to diminishing returns to labor and capital. In general, economists have tended to assume that technological progress can overcome these limitations.[5] But as resource and environmental problems become more pervasive and complex, this assumption may not hold.

- In cases of **market failure,** like the open-access fishery discussed in Chapter 5, increased population accelerates excessive depletion of the resource. Where private or social property rights are poorly defined, as in the African Sahel or the Brazilian Amazon, population pressure contributes to desertification and deforestation. Also, where externalities such as air and water pollution are uncontrolled, population growth will worsen existing pollution problems.

In an article summarizing the economic research on economic and population growth, Nancy Birdsall suggested that "the long debate over population growth and development is entering a new phase. The emphasis is now on the interaction of rapid population growth with market failures."[6] Similarly, an extensive review of the economic literature in this area concluded that

Economic growth (as measured by per capita output) in many developing countries would have been more rapid in an environment of slower population growth, although in a number of countries the impact of population was probably negligible, and in some it may have been positive. Population's adverse impact has most likely occurred where arable land and water are particularly scarce or costly to acquire, where property rights to land and natural resources are poorly defined, and where government policies are biased against the most

---

[5]See, for example, Solow, 1986.
[6]Birdsall, 1989.

abundant factor of production—labor. Population's positive impact most likely occurred where natural resources are abundant, where the possibilities for scale economies are substantial, and where markets and other institutions (especially government) allocate resources in a reasonably efficient way over time and space.[7]

This statement summarizes much economic research on population growth impact. If we consider this generalization in the light of a broader ecological perspective, however, another question arises. Are the "positive" effects of population growth mainly characteristic of an earlier period in world history—what Herman Daly has referred to as the "empty world" stage in which resources and environmental absorptive capacities are abundant relative to the scale of the human economy?[8] As global population rises toward 8 billion or more, will the negative impact become dominant? To answer these questions requires a consideration of a broader, more ecologically oriented perspective on population growth.

Ecological Perspectives on Population Growth

Whereas the standard economic perspective sees no inherent limitations on population or output growth, the ecological approach is based on the concept of **carrying capacity,** which implies some practical limits to the population that can occupy a certain region. This certainly applies to animal populations in nature.

If, for example, a herd of grazing animals exceeds the land's carrying capacity, food will run short, many individuals will starve, and the population will drop to more sustainable levels. Predator species are even more tightly constrained in numbers, based on the available prey populations. Because animals live by consuming either other animals or plants, all life on earth is dependent on the ability of green plants to capture solar energy. The available **solar flux,** or flow of sunlight to the earth's surface, thus ultimately determines carrying capacity.

Can human populations escape the logic of carrying capacity? Certainly we have successfully stretched its limits. We have used artificial fertilizers to increase agricultural outputs. Fossil fuel and nuclear energy provide far more power for our industrialization than any solar flux we currently capture either directly through solar energy systems or indirectly through hydroelectric and wind power. Through these means more than 6 billion people can live on a planet that a century ago supported only slightly more than 1 billion.

However, this expansion of carrying capacity carries significant ecological cost. The extraction of large quantities of fossil fuels and mineral stocks causes environmental degradation both in production and through the waste products generated. Some of the wastes and pollutants are cumulative—their negative environmental effects build up over time.

---

[7]Kelley, 1988.

[8]Daly, 1992 (as discussed in Chapter 7).

Vietnamese family planning posters contrast a large family in poverty with a prosperous small family.

A prime example is global warming caused by burning fossil fuels, known as the **greenhouse effect.** While increasing earth's carrying capacity today, we build up problems for the future. Soil erosion, depletion of aquifers, and buildup of long-lived toxic and nuclear wastes are all cumulative processes. Many of these issues already pose major problems—how much worse will they become if a significantly larger population is consuming at higher per capita levels than today?

Ecologists Paul and Anne Ehrlich identify three major areas in which current economic activities are systematically undermining the planet's long-term carrying capacity. One is erosion and degradation of topsoil; topsoil losses worldwide are currently estimated at 24 billion tons annually. A second is overuse and pollution of fresh water supplies—a problem in virtually every country, reaching critical levels in China, India, and parts of the former Soviet Union. The third, and perhaps most serious, is the loss of biodiversity, with more species driven to extinction every year than at any time in the preceding 65 million years of planetary history.[9]

The Impact of Population, Affluence, and Technology

We can conceptualize the interrelationship of population, economic growth, and environment in an equation linking all three, known as *IPAT*:

$$I = P \times A \times T$$

where

I = Environmental impact (units of pollution)
P = Population
A = Affluence measured as output/person
T = Technology variable measuring pollution per unit of output

This equation is an identity, a mathematical statement that is true by definition. The right side of the equation can be mathematically stated as follows:

$$(\text{Population}) \times (\text{Output/Population}) \times (\text{Pollution/Output})$$

"Population" and "Output" cancel out because they occur both in numerator and denominator, leaving only "Pollution"—which is the same as the left variable I (units of pollution).

Thus we cannot argue with the equation itself. The only questions are the levels of the variables and what determines them. What do we know about these questions?

We have seen that global population is projected to increase by 30–50 percent over the next 50 years, according to the United Nations low and medium-variant projection (see Table 10-2 and Figure 10-5). We also know that average per capita consumption, the A variable, is steadily increasing throughout the world. If per capita consumption grows at 2 percent per year, which most development economists would view as a minimally satisfactory rate, it will increase by a factor of 2.7 in 50 years. The combined impact of A and P will therefore multiply the right side of the equation by a factor of three to four.

What about the technology variable T? Improved technology could lower the pollution per unit GNP—let us say by a factor of two. This would still leave us with a significantly increased level of overall pollution. Given the current level of concern about environmental problems, this seems unacceptable. In order to project lower overall

---

[9]Ehrlich and Ehrlich, 1991.

environmental impact, we will need technological improvements that would lower environmental impact by a factor of four or more.

Of course, a mathematical abstraction such as *IPAT* gives little insight into the specifics behind these broad concepts. *IPAT* has faced strong criticism on the grounds that it covers up some basic issues concerning causes of population growth, consumption distribution, and the workings of markets. One obvious concern is highly unequal consumption per capita throughout the world.

The one-quarter of the world's population living in developed countries accounts for roughly three-quarters of global consumption and global pollution. Poverty, lack of basic health services, and poor education in many developing nations contribute to high population growth rates. This suggests a crucial need to focus on issues of inequality, rather than only on total population or economic output.[10]

Some economists criticize *IPAT* as a highly abstracted view that ignores the capacity of markets to improve efficiency, delivering more goods while using fewer resources and creating less pollution. This perspective was summarized in the World Bank's 1992 report *Development and the Environment*:

> Under present productivity trends, and given projected population increases, developing country output would rise by 4–5 percent a year between 1990 and 2030 and by the end of the period would be about five times what it is today. Industrial country output would rise more slowly but would still triple over the period. World output by 2030 would be 3.5 times what it is today, or roughly $69 trillion (in 1990 prices).
>
> If environmental pollution and degradation were to rise in step with such a rise in output, the result would be appalling environmental pollution and damage. Tens of millions more people would become sick or die each year from environmental causes. Water shortages would be intolerable, and tropical forests and other natural habitats would decline to a fraction of their current size. Fortunately, such an outcome need not occur, nor will it if sound policies and strong institutional arrangements are put in place.[11]

This puts the focus on "sound policies and strong institutional arrangements" rather than on absolute limits on population or economic growth. Nonetheless, the World Bank's presentation makes it clear that the pressures of population and growing output increase the urgency of environmental threats.

Perhaps the economic and ecological perspectives can converge. Even if we cannot identify a fixed carrying capacity for the planet, population growth at the levels we are now experiencing clearly increases virtually all resource and environmental stresses. This makes progress on all fronts vital—reducing population growth, moderating the growth of consumption, improving social equity, and introducing environmentally friendly technologies.[12]

---

[10]Hynes, 1993.

[11]World Bank, 1992.

[12]For an overview of different perspectives and projections on population, see Cohen, 1995; Baudot and Moomaw, 1999; and Harris et al, eds., 2001, Part 4: Population and Urbanization.

10-2   Humanity's Ecological Footprint

Substantial research has focused on measuring human impact on the environment. Humans affect the environment in multi-dimensional ways. From a policy perspective, an ideal measurement approach should convert all these effects to a single index. Further, this index should be measured in units that we can easily understand and interpret.

One such index calculates environmental impacts using "ecological footprints." Originally developed by Wackernagel and Rees (1996), the ecological footprint (EF) concept attempts to convert human impact into equivalent units of biologically productive land area. In other words, a person's ecological footprint is the amount of land required to support his or her lifestyle.

Some effects convert easily to land area footprints. For example, demand for meat converts to pasture area needed to raise livestock. For others, such as carbon dioxide emissions from burning fossil fuels, for example, the EF approach estimates the area of vegetation required to absorb the carbon.

Calculation of a country's ecological footprint requires data on more than 100 factors, including demand for food products, timber, energy, industrial machinery, office supplies, and vehicles. A demonstration of the detailed calculations involved in obtaining a county's ecological footprint, using Italy as an example, is available at http://www.iclei.org/iclei/efcalcs.htm.

Comparing a region's ecological footprint to its available land helps determine whether the region creates a sustainable environmental impact. The following table presents per capita ecological footprints and available productive land for 20 selected countries and the world. The per capita ecological footprints are much higher in developed countries, such as the United States, Australia, and Canada, than in developing countries such as India, Bangladesh, and Ethiopia.

Most countries, developed or developing, currently run at an ecological deficit. The global per capita impact of 2.8 hectares per person exceeds the available biologically productive land on earth (2.0 hectares per capita). In other words, the EF approach indicates that current global environmental impact is not sustainable, implying a depletion of natural capital.

The concept and methodology of ecological footprints remains controversial. The March 2000 *Ecological Economics* journal presented a forum of 12 articles related to the ecological footprint concept. Some of the articles are particularly critical of the approach. For example, Ayres (2000) claims that the EF concept "is too aggregated (and too limited in other respects) to be an adequate guide for policy purposes at the national level." Other researchers, while recognizing that the EF approach requires further refinement, believe it is a valuable analytical tool with

(continued on following page)

policy relevance. Herendeen (2000) notes that the "EF, as modified and improved, is an excellent tool to illustrate the larger picture, and the details." At the least, the debate over the EF methodology has raised awareness of the need to go beyond the rhetoric of sustainability toward quantifiable results.

Ecological Footprints of Nations

Country	Ecological Footprint (ha/cap)	Available Productive Land (ha/cap)	Ecological Surplus or Deficit (ha/cap)
Australia	9.0	14.0	5.0
Bangladesh	0.5	0.3	−0.2
Canada	7.7	9.7	1.9
China	1.2	0.8	−0.4
Denmark	5.9	5.2	−0.7
Ethiopia	0.8	0.5	−0.3
France	4.1	4.2	0.1
Iceland	7.4	21.7	14.3
India	0.8	0.5	−0.3
Italy	4.2	1.3	−2.9
Japan	4.3	0.9	−3.4
Mexico	2.6	1.4	−1.2
Nigeria	1.5	0.6	−0.9
Norway	6.2	6.3	0.1
Peru	1.6	7.7	6.1
Russian Federation	6.0	3.7	−2.3
Singapore	6.9	0.1	−6.8
Spain	3.8	2.2	−1.6
United States	10.3	6.7	−3.6
Venezuela	3.8	2.7	−1.1
WORLD	2.8	2.0	−0.8

Source: Wackernagel et al., 1999.

SOURCES

Ayres, Robert U. "Commentary on the Utility of the Ecological Footprint Concept." *Ecological Economics* 32, no. 3(2000): 347–349.

Herendeen, Robert A. "Ecological Footprint Is a Vivid Indicator of Indirect Effects." *Ecological Economics* 32 no. 3(2000): 357–358.

Wackernagel, Mathis, et al. "National Natural Capital Accounting with the Ecological Footprint Concept," *Ecological Economics* 29 no. 3(1999): 375–390.

Wackernagel, Mathis, and William Rees. *Our Ecological Footprint: Reducing Human Impact on Earth.* Stony Creek, Conn.: New Society Publishers, 1996.

Population Policies for the Twenty-First Century

In recent years, the population policy discussion has shifted. Past debate was dominated by the conflict between "optimists" who saw no problem in increasing population and "pessimists" who predicted catastrophe. Now elements of consensus are emerging. Most analysts accept that increasing population places extra stress on the environment and resources, and there is broad agreement that slower population growth in the future is essential. How will we accomplish this?

Nations have sometimes attempted to control population growth by government compulsion. The most prominent example of this is China's draconian "one-child family" policy. Although effective in a strongly controlled economy such as communist China's, such policies have also been discredited in most other nations both on human rights grounds and because they fail to alter basic incentives regarding fertility.

Birthrates can fall rapidly, however, when people—especially women—reach higher levels of education and literacy, and enjoy better employment opportunities. Significant voluntary reduction of birthrates in many East Asian countries as well as in the state of Kerala in India has resulted from higher levels of basic education, health care, and job security.[13]

In analyzing which population policies are most effective, Nancy Birdsall focuses on the link between high fertility and poverty and the resulting vicious circle of negative social and environmental outcomes. She identifies a significant range of policies that can help both to slow population growth and to improve economic efficiency and output. Prominent among these are promotion of education and other social programs, improvement in the status of women, and improved nutrition and health care, including contraceptive availability.[14]

All these policies tend to lower fertility rates, and Birdsall identifies them as win-win policies that benefit both the economy and the environment through voluntary moderation of population growth. Sound macroeconomic policies, improved credit markets, and improved conditions for agriculture are also important in promoting broad-based growth and poverty reduction, which in turn is essential to population–environment balance.

Such policies are essential to avert serious environmental and social breakdowns in many developing nations. As people struggle to respond to higher demands on the land, slower population growth allows crucial breathing space—time to innovate and adapt. Higher population growth rates can lead to serious environmental degradation—not because of an absolute limit on carrying capacity, but because the means and incentives to adopt new techniques were not forthcoming in time.

Urban areas, where population growth is most rapid, often experience major social and infrastructure problems. Inadequate housing and sanitation, congestion, air and water pollution, disruption of water cycles, solid waste problems and soil contamination are typical of large cities in the developing world. Attempts to respond to

---

[13]The cases of China and Kerala are reviewed in Sen, 1999, pp. 219–224.

[14]See Birdsall, 1994.

massive social and environmental problems in cities are frustrated by continuing rapid and unplanned growth. Moderation of overall population growth must be an essential component of efforts to achieve urban sustainability.[15]

Population growth has been a major factor in shaping development patterns during the second half of the twentieth century and will continue to play a central role during the first half of the twenty-first century. The differing perspectives of economists, ecologists, demographers, and other social theorists all contribute toward developing effective policies that can promote population stabilization and population–environment balance.

In future chapters, we will use this overview of population as our basis for examining some specific stresses associated with growing population and higher consumption levels—in agriculture, energy use, demands on natural resources, and pollution generation. In Chapter 20 we will return to the issue of sustainable global futures for a growing human population.

SUMMARY

Global population grew rapidly during the second half of the twentieth century. Although population growth rates are now slowing, total annual additions to global population remain high. With a global population of 6 billion in the year 2000, growth is projected to continue for at least the next three decades, reaching a level of 8 to 10 billion by 2050. Over 90 percent of the projected growth will be in the developing nations of Asia, Africa, and Latin America.

Population projections offer no certainty about actual future numbers, but the population momentum phenomenon guarantees significant further growth. Currently, average fertility rates (number of children per woman) remain high throughout the developing world. Although fertility rates are generally falling, decades will pass before population growth stabilizes.

Europe has accomplished the demographic transition from rapid population growth to a relatively stable population. In the United States, growth continues both due to population momentum and annual immigration. In the developing world, the demographic transition is far from finished, and significant uncertainty remains about future birth rates. Economic growth, social equity, access to contraception, and cultural factors all play a role.

The economic analysis of population growth emphasizes the potential of other factors such as technological progress to offset the effects of population growth. Under favorable conditions for economic and technological progress, population growth may be accompanied by rising living standards. However, rapid population growth accompanied by social inequity and significant environmental externalities may lead to a decline in living standards.

---

[15]See Harris et al., 2001, Part 4: Population and Urbanization.

An ecological perspective recognizes more stringent limits to the population carrying capacity of regional and global ecosystems. Greater population increases the demand for materials, energy, and natural resources, which in turn increases pressures on the environment. Given the extent of existing environmental damage, especially where this damage is cumulative or irreversible, the challenge of providing for significantly larger populations poses severe challenges to the earth's ecosystems.

Compulsory population control policies generally fail to alter basic incentives regarding fertility. More effective population policy measures include improved nutrition and health care, greater social equity, women's education, and contraceptive availability.

KEY TERMS AND CONCEPTS

capital shallowing
carrying capacity
constant returns to scale
demographic transition
dependency ratios
economies of scale
exponential growth
fertility rate
fixed factors
greenhouse effect
gross annual population increase

law of diminishing returns
market failure
neo-Malthusianism
per capita output
population age profile
population cohort
population growth rate
population momentum
replacement fertility level
solar flux
technological innovation

DISCUSSION QUESTIONS

1. What criteria would you use to evaluate the argument between the neo-Malthusians, who see population growth as the major problem facing humanity, and those who argue that population growth is a neutral, or even positive factor for economic development? How would you assess the relative urgency of population concerns in the United States (population growth rate 0.7 percent per annum), India (1.9 percent per annum), and Kenya (3.3 percent per annum)?

2. "Every extra mouth brings with it an extra pair of hands. Therefore we do not have to worry about growing population." Relate this statement to the more formal economic analysis of labor force and production. To what extent is the statement true? To what extent is it misleading?

3. The concept of carrying capacity is a useful one for ecological analysis of animal and plant populations. Is it also useful for analyzing human population growth? Why or why not?

REFERENCES

Birdsall, Nancy. "Economic Analyses of Rapid Population Growth." *World Bank Research Observer* 4 (January 1989).

Birdsall, Nancy. "Government, Population, and Poverty: A Win-Win Tale." In *Population, Economic Development, and the Environment,* edited by Kerstin Lindahl-Kiessling and Hans Landberg. New York and Oxford: Oxford University Press, 1994.

Baudot, Barbara, and William Moomaw, eds. *People and Their Planet: Searching for Balance.* New York: St. Martin's Press, 1999.

Boserup, Ester. *Population Growth and Technological Change: A Study of Long-Term Trends.* Chicago: University of Chicago Press, 1981.

Cohen, Joel E. *How Many People Can the Earth Support?* New York: Norton, 1995.

Daly, Herman E. "From Empty World Economics to Full-World Economics: Recognizing an Historical Turning Point in Economic Development." In *Population, Technology and Lifestyle: The Transition to Sustainability,* edited by Goodland, Daly, and El Serafy. Washington, D.C.: Island Press, 1992.

Ehrlich, Paul R., and Anne H. "Population Growth and Economic Security." *Georgia Review* 45, Summer 1991.

Ehrlich, Paul R. *The Population Bomb.* New York: Ballantine Books, 1968.

Ehrlich, Paul R., and Anne H. *The Population Explosion.* New York: Simon and Schuster, 1990.

Harris, Jonathan M., Timothy A. Wise, Kevin Gallagher, and Neva R. Goodwin, eds. *A Survey of Sustainable Development: Social and Economic Perspectives.* Washington, D.C.: Island Press, 2001.

Hynes, H. Patricia. *Taking Population out of the Equation: Reformulating I=PAT.* North Amherst, Mass.: Institute on Women and Technology, 1993.

Kelley, Allen C. "Economic Consequences of Population Change in the Third World." *Journal of Economic Literature* 26 (December 1988): 1685–1728.

Lutz, Wolfgang. *The Future of World Population.* Washington, D.C.: Population Reference Bureau, 1994.

Population Reference Bureau. *2000 World Population Data Sheet.* Washington, D.C.: Population Reference Bureau, 2000.

Repetto, Robert. *Population, Resources, Environment: An Uncertain Future.* Washington, D.C.: Population Reference Bureau, 1991.

Sen, Amartya. *Development as Freedom.* New York: Knopf, 2000.

Simon, Julian L. *The Ultimate Resource 2.* Princeton, N.J.: Princeton University Press, 1996. (Original publication as *The Ultimate Resource*, 1981.)

Solow, Robert. "On the Intertemporal Allocation of Natural Resources," *Scandinavian Journal of Economics* 88 (1986): 141–149.

United Nations Department of Economic and Social Affairs, World Population Division. *World Population Prospects: The 2000 Revision*. United Nations, 2001.

World Bank. *World Development Report 1992: Development and the Environment*. New York and Oxford, England: Oxford University Press, 1992.

WEB SITES

1. **http://www.prb.org/** Home page for the Population Reference Bureau, an organization that provides data and policy analysis on U.S. and international population issues. Their World Data Sheet provides demographic data for every country in the world.
2. **http://www.un.org/esa/population/unpop.htm** Web site for the United Nations Population Division, which provides international information on population issues including population projections.
3. **http://www.zpg.org/** Home page for Zero Population Growth, a nonprofit environmental organization "working to slow population growth and achieve a sustainable balance between the Earth's people and its resources."

CHAPTER **11**

CHAPTER

CHAPTER FOCUS QUESTIONS

- Can we produce enough food for a growing global population?
- Are agricultural production systems degrading the environment?
- What are the effects of new agricultural technologies?
- How can we develop a sustainable agricultural system for the future?

Agriculture, Food, and Environment

Feeding the World: Population and Food Supply

Food supply constitutes a fundamental relationship between any human society and its environment. In the wild, animal populations wax and wane based largely on food availability. For many centuries, human numbers were also linked closely to food abundance or scarcity. In the past two centuries, increasingly productive agricultural technology has spurred a significant increase in human population.

Despite unprecedented population growth, average world per capita food production has risen, not fallen. Figure 11-1 shows this trend for the important category of cereal crops. Many economic theorists have asserted, based on this trend, that history has disproved the Malthusian argument that population would outrun food supply. Before we dismiss concerns over food limitations, however, we must consider several factors that cast a different light on the issues of population, agriculture, and the environment.

- *Land Use.* Since World War II agricultural land use has expanded considerably, but the expansion has slowed (see Figure 11-2a). The land most suitable for agriculture is already being farmed, and most remaining lands are marginal in

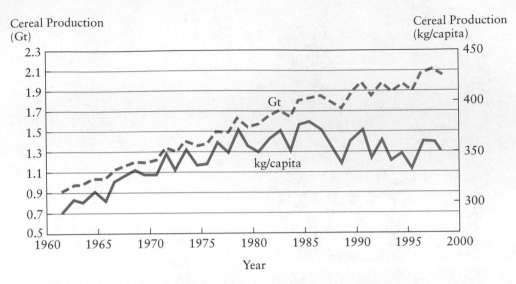

FIGURE 11-1 *World Cereal Production and Cereal Production Per Capita*

Source: Adapted from Vaclav Smil, *Feeding the World: A Challenge for the Twenty-First Century.*
MIT Press, © 2000. Reprinted by permission of MIT Press.

quality. Also, urban and industrial encroachment is cutting into agricultural land and available farmland per person is steadily decreasing (Figure 11-2b). To feed the world better, we must continually increase productivity on this shrinking per capita acreage.

- *Consumption patterns.* Existing food supplies are distributed according to market demand, which strongly favors upper-income consumers. Per capita grain consumption in the United States, for example, is more than three times that in the developing world. This is not because U.S. citizens eat more grains, but because three-quarters of U.S. domestic grain use goes to animal feed. The meat-centered U.S. diet thus requires nearly four times as much agricultural output per person as a typical diet for, say, a citizen of Mexico.

- *Inequalities in food distribution.* On average enough food is produced to provide an adequate diet for everyone on earth. In practice, however, many low-income areas suffer from a **nutritional deficit,** meaning that between 500 million and 1 billion people receive inadequate nutrition.

- *Environmental impact of agriculture.* As agricultural land use has expanded, more marginal and fragile lands have come under the plow. The result is increased erosion, deforestation, and loss of wildlife habitat. Erosion and depletion of nutrients in the soil mean that a **renewable resource** is being turned into a **depletable resource,** and soil fertility is being "mined" over time. Increased irrigation, crucial to modern agriculture, also brings many environmental problems in its wake, including salinization, alkalinization, and waterlogging, as well as overdraft of ground water and pollution of surface water.

Runoff from chemical fertilizer and pesticide use pollutes land and water and contributes to atmospheric problems such as global warming and ozone depletion. Depletion of **biodiversity** and the creation of "super-pests" resistant to pesticides are also

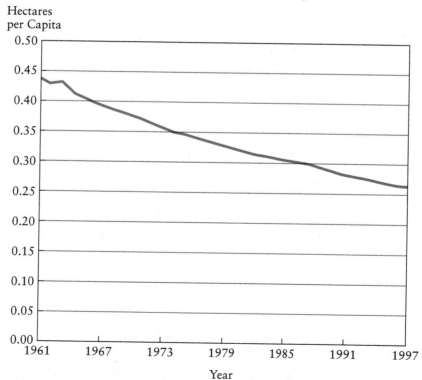

(a) Total World Arable and Permanent Cropland

Cropland
(in millions of hectares)

(b) World Arable and Permanent Cropland Per Capita

Hectares
per Capita

Year

FIGURE 11-2 *World Cropland and Cropland Per Capita, 1961–1997*
Source: FAO, 1998.

results of intensive agriculture. At a minimum, management of these problems is an important issue in the economics of agriculture. More broadly, this complex of environmental issues raises questions about the global agricultural system's capacity to sustain growing populations without unacceptable environmental damage.

These factors contribute to a more sophisticated perception of the problems involved in feeding an expanded world population. Rather than focusing on the simple dichotomy of population and food, we must examine interactions between population, per capita food consumption, and the environment.

If growing population does not necessarily mean famine, it may nonetheless create irresistible pressures on available agricultural land that increase environmental degradation and leave future generations with a depleted agricultural base. This is occurring in developing nations such as Haiti and Ethiopia that have permanently lost much productive land to erosion and soil degradation. We must, therefore, examine more carefully the realities behind the macroeconomic statistics showing increasing agricultural output.

Trends in Global Food Production

First, let us take a more careful look at the trends in global food production shown in Figure 11-1. The total output of grains appears to rise over the whole period from 1961.[1] The per capita production figures, however, tell a slightly different story. From 1961 to 1985, we see a slow but steady increase in output per capita. This increase—about 0.5 percent per year—is of crucial importance. It means that people throughout the world are experiencing gradually improving average nutritional levels. Of course, as we have noted, not all benefit equally, but to some extent "a rising tide lifts all ships."

During the later years, however, we notice a change. Per capita output no longer increases, and appears to decline slightly after 1985. Does this represent some fundamental change in the dynamics of world agriculture?

Some analysts, such as Lester Brown of Worldwatch Institute, have suggested that it does. Citing many of the environmental problems mentioned above, Brown argues that ecological limits already reached will prevent further rapid expansion in agricultural output. In this view, the 1980s represent a major turning point. Agricultural yields leveled off worldwide and total grain production no longer outpaced population growth: " . . . the next four decades could be a mirror image of the last four, with grain availability levels in 2030 returning to those of 1950."[2] This, of course, would have enormous implications for economic development and for the nutritional status of the worlds' poorest people.

---

[1]Grain, or cereal, output is easily measured and is a fairly good proxy for total food output. Grain consumption accounts for about 50 percent of food consumption worldwide and up to 70 percent in many developing nations.

[2]Brown and Kane, 1994. See also Brown, 2001.

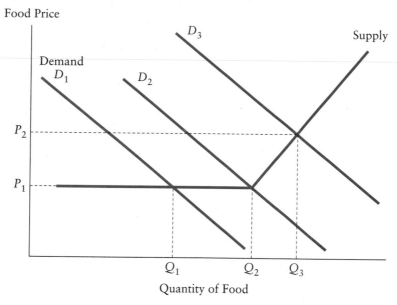

FIGURE 11-3 *Elastic and Inelastic Food Supply*

How can we evaluate Brown's hypothesis? From the point of view of economic analysis, the main question is one of price. If indeed agriculture experienced supply limitations, we would expect to see rising food prices as demand grows. The simple supply and demand analysis in Figure 11-3 shows this principle. Where **elasticity of supply** is high, as in the left half of the graph, demand increases from D_1 to D_2 with no significant upward pressure on price. With inelastic supply, in the right portion of the graph, rising demand (D_2 to D_3) causes a sharp upward move in price.

As Figure 11.4 shows, there has been no sustained increase in prices for cereal crops. What then explains the change in per capita production trends during the 1980s? Economists such as Amartya Sen have argued that it is a demand-side rather than a supply-side phenomenon. In this view, a general slowdown in economic growth during the 1980s, a result of world recession and debt problems in many developing nations, lowered people's purchasing power for food as well as for other goods. Thus "food output [was] held back by a lack of effective demand in the marketplace"[3] rather than by environmental constraints on production. In addition, Smil points out that much of the global slowdown in cereal production can be attributed to lower farm subsidies in the U.S. and Europe, as well as the economic breakdown in the former U.S.S.R.[4] If this is the case, vigorous growth in output should resume when demand increases.

---

[3]Sen, 2000.

[4]Smil, 2000.

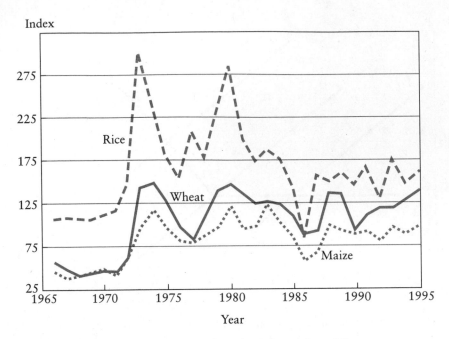

FIGURE 11-4 *U.S. Producer Price Indices for Selected Cereal Crops*
Source: FAO, 1998.

The fact that prices are generally stable or declining, however, does not preclude significant environmental impact on food production. In many developing nations, the poor bear the greatest burden of economic recession, increasing the problem of inequality of distribution. At the same time, the marginal lands farmed by the poor suffer the greatest damage from erosion and other environmental problems.

Loss of food-buying power for the poor, combined with a decline in the productive capacity of marginal farmlands, would clearly impair nutrition with little impact on world prices. Stagnation or decline in per capita production of grain in South America and Sub-Saharan Africa (see Figure 11-5) may result primarily from weakening demand, but in these areas environmental damage to marginal lands is also widespread.

Land Use and Equity Issues

The issue of unequal distribution is linked to that of land use. We have already noted that most good agricultural land is currently in production. In a market economy, land will generally be used for the highest valued crop, as shown in Figure 11-6.

Here land is rated by quality on the horizontal axis, with the highest quality land on the left side, and quality declining as we move to the right. The vertical axis shows the value of crops grown on the land. This **crop value index** will differ depending on

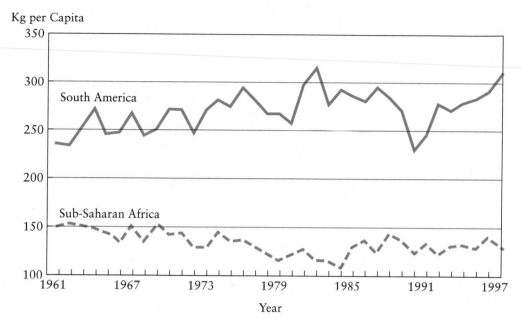

FIGURE 11-5 *Cereal Production Per Capita for South America and Sub-Saharan Africa, 1961–1997*
Source: FAO, 1998.

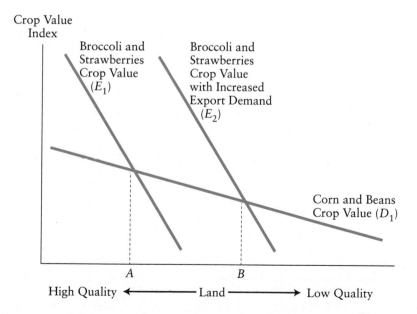

FIGURE 11-6 *Land Quality, Crop Value, and Land Use*

how the land is used. Some crops require higher quality land, and produce higher value per acre. Other crops grow on land of varying quality, but produce less market value per acre. In economic terms, the crop value index represents the **marginal revenue product** of the land, which is equal to the **marginal physical product** (quantity of a particular crop) times the price of the crop.

For example, in Mexico much land is devoted to growing corn and beans for local consumption. But growing broccoli and strawberries for export produces higher revenues. The intersection of the two crop value lines D_1 and E_1 shows how the land will be divided between production for export and production for domestic use. On the high quality land to the left of point A, the most valuable product is the export crop, and the land will be used for this. Corn and beans will be grown on the lower quality land to the right of point A.

Now suppose that demand for export crops increases, as shown by crop value line E_2, while demand for domestic foods remains the same. The crop value line for export products rises, reflecting higher prices for broccoli and strawberries. As a result, the land use pattern changes, with export production expanding up to point B and domestic production squeezed onto lower-quality land to the right of point B. In Mexico today, this land use trend is accelerating as a result of the North American Free Trade Agreement (NAFTA).

What does this imply for the environment and for the nutritional status of the population? One likely result is that larger commercial farms will displace smaller farmers who lack good access to export markets. This will increase pressure on the

TABLE 11-1 *Population and Cereal Consumption Projections for 2025*

Region	1. Population 1998	2. Cereal Production in MMT 1997–1999 Average	3. Per Capita Cereal Consumption in Kg 1995–1997 Average	4. Land Area in Cereals in MHa 1997	5. Cereal Yields in Kg/Ha 1995–1997
World	5,901	2,053	348	692	2,968
Developed Nations	1,188	839	616	229	3,669
Developing Nations	4,713	1,244	285	463	2,687
Developing Nations (excluding China)	3,450	791	258	371	2,134

Developed and developing nations are defined according to the UN classification: Europe, North America, Australia, Japan, and New Zealand are classified as developed, all others as developing. FAO figures are adjusted accordingly. MMT = million metric tons, MHa = million hectares. One metric ton = 1,000 kilograms(Kg).

Sources: Harris, 1996; FAO 1997–2000; FAOSTAT Agriculture Database http://apps.fao.org; Population Reference Bureau, *2000 World Population Data Sheet.*

marginal farmlands (to the right on the graph). Hill slopes, forest margins, and arid lands all are especially vulnerable to the kind of environmental degradation that results when displaced people move onto whatever land is available. We see the effects of this throughout much of Africa, Latin America, and Asia.

If revenues from export crops are unequally distributed, poorer peoples' diets will worsen as less corn and beans are produced for domestic consumption. Small farmers who share in export revenues can buy imported foods with the proceeds from cash crops, but more frequently they will lose out to larger producers in export markets.

Projections for the Future

Population projections for the first half of the twenty-first century show total world population reaching a level close to 8 billion by 2025. What new stresses will the additional demand for food place on the environment? Will we exceed agricultural **carrying capacity?** Will we experience food shortages? The grain production figures shown in Table 11-1 illustrate some implications of projected increases in global population. Table 11-2 gives these increases by region.

As of 1998, the world produced about 2 billion metric tons of grain (column 2). If evenly distributed, this would provide each person with 348 kilograms of grain (cereals) per year—approximately one kilogram, or 2.2 pounds, per day (column 3). This grain crop required about half of the world's cropland. The other half was devoted to vegetables, fruits, oilseeds, root crops, and nonfood crops such as cotton.

TABLE 11-1 *(continued)*

6. Projected Population for 2025	7. Projected Total Cereal Requirements in MMT for 2025	8. Projected Per Capita Cereal Consumption in Kg for 2025	9. Projected Land Area in Cereals in MHa for 2025	10. Projected Yield Requirements for Self-Sufficiency in Kg/Ha for 2025
7,810	2,867	367	739	3,879
1,236	761	616	229	3,323
6,575	2,106	320	510	4,129
5,144	1,515	295	424	3,573

TABLE 11-2 *Population and Consumption Projections by Region*

Region	1. Population 1998	2. Cereal Production in MMT 1997–1999 Average	3. Per Capita Cereal Consumption in Kg 1995–1997 Average	4. Land Area in Cereals in MHa 1997	5. Cereal Yields in Kg/Ha 1995–1997
Africa	749	112	194	92	1,220
Latin America and Caribbean	503	132	287	47	2,785
Asia	3,585	1,012	305	325	3,111
Asia (excluding China)	2,322	559	274	233	2,399
China	1,263	453	361	92	4,909
U.S. and Canada	305	392	968	80	4,930
Europe (excluding Russia)	582	339	546	82	4,150
Russia	147	63	443	49	1,265
Oceania	30	33	399	16	2,036
India, Pakistan, and Bangladesh	1,255	286	230	125	2,299
Japan	126	12	313	2	5,957

MMT = million metric tons, MHa = million hectares. One metric ton = 1,000 kilograms.

The yield requirement for self-sufficiency in 2025 shown for Japan is hypothetical; Japan imports two-thirds of its cereals and could not achieve self-sufficiency.

Sources: Harris, 1996; FAO 1997–2000; FAOSTAT Agriculture Database http://apps.fao.org; Population Reference Bureau, *2000 World Population Data Sheet.*

This level of output, evenly distributed, would be adequate to provide each person with a mostly vegetarian diet, supplemented with a little meat, fish, or eggs—the kind of diet characteristic of much of the developing world. The largely meat-centered diet characteristic of most of the developed world, however, requires much larger amounts of grain per person—not consumed directly, of course, but used for livestock feed. About three-quarters of the U.S. domestic consumption of cereal, for example, goes to feed cattle, pigs, and poultry.

TABLE 11-2 *(continued)*

6. Projected Population for 2025	7. Projected Total Cereal Requirements in MMT for 2025	8. Projected Per Capita Cereal Consumption in Kg for 2025	9. Projected Land Area in Cereals in MHa for 2025	10. Projected Yield Requirements for Self-Sufficiency in Kg/Ha for 2025
1,258	277	220	107	2,590
703	229	325	52	4,395
4,723	1,630	345	322	5,062
3,292	1,022	311	236	4,332
1,431	585	409	86	6,799
374	362	968	85	4,257
577	315	546	82	3,843
137	61	443	49	1,238
39	16	399	13	1,197
1,767	460	260	124	3,709
121	38	313	2.5	15,161

Globally, therefore, distribution of the existing output is significantly unequal. This is shown in column 3 of Table 11-1 by the disparity between the per capita consumption levels for developed and developing nations. Consumption levels throughout much of the developing world are just sufficient for an adequate non-meat-centered diet, but inequality of distribution within countries leaves many of the poorest with inadequate levels of food consumption.

As economic development proceeds, per capita demand for food rises. This is partly because poorer people can afford to buy more basic foods, and partly because middle-class consumers shift toward a meat-based diet. Between 1950 and 1985, per capita grain consumption rose slowly but steadily throughout the world, at a rate of about 0.5 percent per year. Assuming that the slowdown in consumption growth after the mid-1980s was primarily due to limited purchasing power, we can expect this trend of increasing per capita consumption to continue. As we look ahead to the future, we must prepare to provide for both an increased total population, and a higher average consumption per person.

Future Yield Requirements

The population projections in Table 11-1 for the year 2025 (column 6) are in the middle range of published estimates. Note that over 95 percent of the population growth will take place in developing nations. When we combine this population growth with a modest projected increase in per capita consumption (column 8), it is clear that grain consumption will nearly double in the developing world (column 7).[5] On the other hand, agricultural land area will increase little (compare columns 4 and 9). Output per hectare of land in developing nations must therefore rise by at least 50 percent (compare columns 5 and 10).[6]

Column 10 of Table 11-1 shows the increases in agricultural yields required for self-sufficiency in grain production (supplying domestic demand without imports) in developed and developing nations. Table 11-2 shows the same data for major regions. Average yields in the developing world must rise from the present 2.7 metric tons per hectare to about 4 metric tons per hectare.[7] For the developing world excluding China, yields must increase by 67 percent over present levels. Yields in Asia as a whole must rise from three to five metric tons per hectare. Yields in Africa would need to more than double for self-sufficiency in 2025.

Of course, not every region must achieve self-sufficiency; grain can be imported from countries with surplus capacity. The possibilities for meeting demand through increased trade, however, are limited. If we assume that most nations can achieve, but not exceed, yield levels similar to those now reached in the developed nations, both Asia and Africa will significantly increase their import demands.

According to recent studies, net cereal imports by developing countries will nearly double by 2020, from 104 to 201 million metrics tons.[8] Where will this extra export production come from? Current world cereal exports are predominantly from North America and Europe. Both of these areas already have very high yields, suggesting that future yield increases may be difficult to achieve. In addition, current Census Bureau projections show U.S. population rising from 281 to 338 million by 2025. If this larger U.S. population consumes the same kind of meat-centered diet Americans now favor, there will be a significant added grain demand for animal feed. These combined demand pressures could lead to rising grain prices, confronting the world's poorest countries with the problem of purchasing a larger volume of more expensive food imports.

---

[5]The rate of increase in per capita consumption assumed here is 0.5 percent per annum. Faster economic growth could significantly increase this if diets shift toward meat products as incomes rise.

[6]1 hectare = 2.477 acres.

[7]1 metric ton = 1,000 kilograms.

[8]Pinstrup-Andersen and Pandya-Lorch, 2001.

Analysts who offer a more optimistic view of the future rely on two factors. One is reduced population growth. As we have seen, population growth estimates show significant variation. If we accept the low-range projections, pressures on the global agricultural system are significantly less.[9] The other factor is yield increases. Some regions have achieved grain yields of six to nine metric tons per hectare (6,000 to 9,000 kilograms per hectare). If this success could be extended worldwide, grain production would be more than ample.[10]

However, these population and yield variables may move in the opposite direction. Population may rise higher than medium projections. Environmental problems, including water shortages and global climate change, might endanger even present levels of yields in major regions. It seems prudent to prepare for unpleasant as well as pleasant surprises. If we take this approach, the critical question becomes the **environmental sustainability** of agricultural production. To assess the likelihood of an adequate solution to the food problem, we must consider in more detail the environmental stresses associated with pushing our agricultural systems toward their limits.

Agriculture's Impact on the Environment

Soil Erosion and Degradation

With the exception of some hydroponics and aquaculture, almost all agriculture depends on soil. Soil, as we have noted, can be either a renewable or a depletable resource. Ideally, agricultural techniques would not degrade soils and would replenish soil productivity over time through **nutrient recycling** from crop residues. If this were the case, agricultural output would be truly sustainable and could continue at present levels indefinitely.

Unfortunately, the situation in almost all the world's major agricultural areas is quite different: soil erosion and degradation is widespread. From 30 to 50 percent of the earth's surface is affected by erosion and soil degradation. Erosion damages crop productivity by reducing the availability of water, nutrients, and organic matter; water resources are also degraded by sediments and pollutants associated with erosion. Soil loss rates are typically highest in developing countries:

> Severe soil erosion is occurring in most of the world's agricultural regions, and the problem is growing as more marginal land is brought into production and less crop residues are returned to the soil. Soil loss rates in Europe range between 10 and 20 tons/hectare/year. In the United States, soil erosion on cropland averages 16 t/ha/yr. In Asia, Africa, and South America, soil erosion rates on cropland range between 20 and 40 t/ha/yr.[11]

[9]See, for example, Seckler, 1994.

[10]Waggoner, 1994, provides a good example of optimism on yields.

[11]Pimentel, 1993.

The United Nations Environmental Programme's Global Assessment of Soil Degradation (GLASOD) estimates that erosion severely degrades an additional 5 to 6 million hectares of land each year.[12] As well as soil loss from erosion, further soil degradation occurs from over-irrigation, overgrazing, and destruction of trees and ground cover.

The Economics of Erosion and Erosion Control

In many cases, farmers can greatly reduce erosion and soil degradation by **crop rotation and fallowing**—alternating grain and legume crops and taking the land out of production every several years. The farmer's costs include foregoing revenues in any year when the land is out of production and possibly settling for lower revenues in years when the land produces other than highest value crops. Farmers must make an economic calculation as to whether the immediate costs of erosion control are worth the long-term benefits.

Consider a simple example. Suppose a farmer can obtain $100,000 in annual revenues by continually growing the highest value crops with no provision for rebuilding soils or erosion control. Under these conditions, erosion will cause an annual decline of about 1 percent in yield. An effective erosion control program will reduce revenues by $15,000 per year. Is the program worth it to the farmer?

The answer depends on the **discount rate** used to balance present versus future costs. One percent yield loss means a monetary loss of $1,000. But this is not just a one-time loss; it will continue into the future. How do we evaluate this stream of losses resulting from one year's erosion? In economic terms, we apply a discount rate as discussed in Chapters 4 and 6. Suppose we select a 10 percent discount rate. The **present value** of the stream of losses extending indefinitely into the future is equal to

$$PV = (-\$1,000)(1/0.10) = -\$10,000$$

The benefits of erosion control are thus $10,000—not enough, in this example, to justify $15,000 lost revenue. Under these conditions, it is economically optimal to continue the erosive practices—but it is certainly not ecologically sustainable. Following this economic logic, the farmer will leave severely degraded land for the next generation.

Unfortunately, many farmers face exactly this kind of economic pressure to maximize short-term revenues. Note that if we used a lower interest rate—say 5 percent—the benefits of erosion control, calculated at $20,000, would exceed the costs and in theory make erosion control economically beneficial. Even so, the short-term losses might still be difficult to accept. An ecologically sound soil management policy thus

---

[12]Oldeman et al., eds., 1990.

depends on the farmer's foresight, relatively low interest rates, and the financial flexibility to invest in erosion control today for long-term benefits.

Off-farm effects of erosion are an additional problem. In many areas, major dams have silted up with eroded soil, ultimately destroying their potential for power generation and wasting billions in investments. Heavy siltation also causes extensive damage to river ecology. Because these costs are **externalities** from the farmer's point of view, some social decision is required to respond to this aspect of erosion damage.

Fertilizer Use

The steady increase in average yields characteristic of modern agriculture depends strongly on increased fertilizer use. Figure 11-7 shows this pattern for major world regions over the past 30 years. Increased fertilizer use is clearly associated with higher yields. Over time, nations tend to shift from traditional agriculture with low fertilizer input to modernized agriculture's heavy fertilizer use and high yields. Following this trend, food output has generally outpaced population growth over the long term.

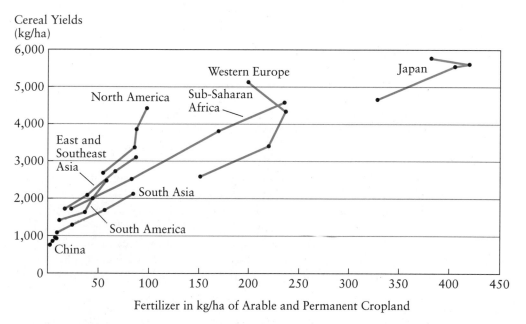

FIGURE 11-7 *Yield/Fertilizer Relationship for Major Regions Using Averaged Data for the Periods 1961–1970, 1971–1980, 1981–1990, 1991–1997*
Source: FAO, 1998.

Environmental Effects of Fertilizer Use

What are the environmental applications of this "modernizing" process in agriculture? In general, modern agricultural techniques rely on a "package" of inputs including fertilizer, pesticides, irrigation, mechanization, and high-yielding crop varieties. In Figure 11-7, fertilizer per hectare serves as what economists call a **proxy variable** for this whole package: higher use of fertilizer correlates so strongly with higher use of the other inputs that measuring fertilizer use alone gives us a good idea of the degree of agricultural modernization. Each of these inputs, however, relates to specific environmental problems, and as high-yield input use has increased, so has the seriousness of these environmental problems.

Fertilizer supplies nutrients to the soil, and thence to crops. Most fertilizers supply the three major nutrients of nitrate, phosphate, and potassium. But a significant portion of the nutrients applied do not reach the crops as intended. Instead, they leach into ground and surface water, where they become serious pollutants.

Excessive nitrate in water is damaging to human health. Nitrates and phosphates also promote unwanted algae growth that chokes out other life in rivers, lakes, and even oceans. Most agricultural areas in the U.S. Midwest and West suffer from these problems. In the Mediterranean, large portions of the sea have suffered severe ecological damage from agricultural runoff pollution, with giant mats of algae blanketing coastlines in the Aegean Sea and elsewhere. Inefficient and excessive fertilizer use have created especially severe agricultural problems in the formerly communist economies of Russia and East Europe. Inland seas such as the Black and Caspian Seas have experienced extinctions of numerous local species as a result.

Another damaging effect of excessive fertilizer use is more subtle. As large amounts of nitrate, phosphate, and potassium are added to the soil year after year, other nutrients present in smaller quantities—called **micronutrients**—become depleted.[13] This gradually reduces both yields and nutritional values of the crops. Like erosion, these can be long-term effects, which leaves little incentive for farmers to respond to them so long as short-term yields are high.

Fertilizer production is energy intensive. In effect, modern agriculture replaces solar energy and human labor with energy extracted primarily from fossil fuels.[14] Agricultural energy consumption thus contributes to all of the environmental problems associated with fossil fuel energy consumption discussed in Chapters 13 and 18. Agriculture accounts for about 3–5 percent of total energy use; although not the major component of energy-related issues, this percentage is significant, particularly for developing countries with growing populations who must buy imported energy.[15]

---

[13]Micronutrients include boron, copper, cobalt, and molybdenum. Although some of these substances can be damaging in large amounts, trace amounts are important for plant growth and human nutrition.

[14]For a detailed analysis of this process, see Martinez-Alier, 1993; Cleveland, 1994.

[15]See, for example, Hall, 1993.

Fertilizer use also contributes directly to various global atmospheric problems including global warming and ozone depletion.

Some analysts find it significant that artificial nitrogen applied to crops now exceeds the amount supplied through natural nitrogen fixation by soil microorganisms. Such a large intervention in the earth's **nitrogen cycle** must have ecological consequences. Furthermore, the use of fertilizer is projected to increase steadily to provide the yields needed for the twenty-first century.

Pesticide Use

Like fertilizer use, pesticide use has risen rapidly with the spread of modern agriculture (see Figure 11-8). Numerous health and environmental problems have accompanied this increase. Pesticides may affect agricultural workers directly—pesticide poisoning is a serious and widespread problem throughout much of the developing world. Residues in food affect consumers: measurable levels of chlorinated pesticides can be found in breast milk, and the cumulative impact of many pesticides on the human body is a serious concern. The carcinogenic effects of many pesticides are well known, and a more recent focus of research has been effects on reproductive systems.

Pesticides also affect ecosystems in various ways. Groundwater pollution from pesticides is a common problem in agricultural areas. Unintended extermination of beneficial species can lead to pest outbreaks far worse than the original problem. Since World War II (when the chemistry for many pesticides emerged), rapidly expanding pesticide use has paralleled an equally rapid expansion in **resistant pest species** (Figure 11-9). Similarly, excessive use of antibiotics in animal feed has encouraged the development of antibiotic-resistant microbes.

These developments are no surprise to ecologists, who understand the dangers of upsetting a natural species balance. However, such consequences are difficult to quantify in monetary terms or to introduce into farm-level decision making. In addition, vested interests—the manufacturers of agricultural chemicals—seek to expand pesticide use.

As with other issues of technological impact on the environment, **information asymmetry** is a problem.[16] Pesticide producers generally know the most about the chemical composition and potential effects of pesticides. With thousands of different compounds on the market, mastering this information—even if it is available—would be practically impossible for pesticide consumers. Government regulators have trouble keeping up with the rapid introduction of new compounds and usually must narrow their focus to, for example, carcinogenicity. In such circumstances it is unlikely that the **external costs** of pesticide use will be fully understood and internalized.

---

[16]Economists speak of *information asymmetry* when participants in a market economy have different levels of information access. In the case of agricultural technologies, consumers of food products, and even government regulators, may be unaware of the nature and dangers of pesticide residues.

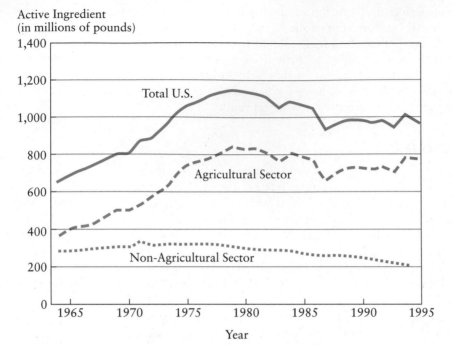

FIGURE 11-8 *U.S. Conventional Pesticide Usage 1964–1995*
Source: U.S. EPA, 1994/1995.

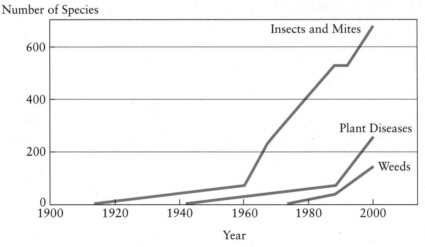

FIGURE 11-9 *Increase in Resistant Pest Species in the Twentieth Century*
Source: Adapted from Gary Gardner, "Preserving Agricultural Resources," in Brown et al., *State of the World 1996*. Washington, D.C.: Worldwatch Institute, 1996. Reprinted by permission of Worldwatch Institute.

Irrigation and Water Resources

The spread of irrigation has been just as important as increased fertilizer use in expanding agricultural output. Irrigation greatly improves yields and often permits **multiple cropping** in areas dependent on seasonal rains. The most optimistic projections of further yield increases in developing-nation agriculture rely heavily on expanded irrigation.[17] But, as with fertilizer and pesticides, the short-term benefits of irrigation often link to long-term environmental damage.

Poor drainage causes irrigation water to build up underground, eventually waterlogging fields. In tropical areas, water that reaches the surface evaporates rapidly, leaving behind a buildup of dissolved salts and leading to **salinization and alkalinization of soils.** In the Indian Punjab, for example, millions of hectares of land have been damaged by salinization. Irrigation also increases fertilizer and pesticide runoff, polluting local surface and groundwater.

The farmland most dependent on irrigation often lies in precisely those arid regions where water is in short supply. This leads to overdraft of groundwater—pumping out underground reservoirs faster than the natural water cycle can refill them—a classic example of the **common property resource** problem discussed in Chapter 5. No individual farmer has an incentive to limit water use. As a result, currently productive agriculture regions face a waterless future once the aquifers are exhausted. The Ogallala aquifer that supports much of western U.S. irrigated agriculture is as much as 50 percent depleted in some areas, and its level continues to fall. Rapid declines in groundwater levels are also taking place in India, North China, central Asia.

Withdrawals from rivers in arid areas can be equally damaging. Agricultural water demand has led to serious salinization problems in the Colorado River basin in the western U.S. as well as an international dispute over the increased salinity of the river water crossing the border into Mexico. Perhaps the worst case of excessive irrigation demand is the Aral Sea in the former Soviet Union; this entire inland sea is drying up as a result of water withdrawals (primarily for cotton production) from the rivers that feed it.[18]

Limits on water supplies may be the most significant constraint on future agricultural expansion in large areas of the world. Irrigation accounts for 65 percent of total water withdrawal worldwide and over 80 percent in developing countries.[19] Most of China and the Indian subcontinent are close to the limits of their available water supply, and urban/industrial water demand is rising steadily. Much of Africa is arid or semi-arid, as are large areas in west and central Asia, and in the western U.S. Despite clear economic incentives to expand irrigation, both externality and common property resource problems associated with irrigation mean that this expansion is likely to intensify resource and environmental problems.

---

[17]See, for example, Alexandratos, 1994.

[18]For an extensive discussion of the problems of irrigated agriculture, see Postel, 1999.

[19]Harris, 1990.

11-1   Genetically Modified Foods: A Controversial Technology

An estimated 60 million acres in the United States were cultivated with genetically modified (GM) crops in 2000. Although proponents list a variety of potential benefits from GM crops, opponents argue that widespread use of GM products creates health and environmental hazards. Opposition to introduction of genetically modified organisms and use of genetically modified ingredients in regular consumer products first started and is still strong in the European Union, but concern seems to be spreading worldwide as more countries restrict or consider restricting GM foods.

GM Foods: Concerns and Proposed Benefits

Proponents claim that the marriage of biotechnology and agriculture has great potential for providing safe, pest-resistant, adaptive, high-yielding, and nutritious food for a growing world population. They argue that certain genetic modifications would produce foods with a variety of beneficial qualities such as corn that produces a toxin that kills a corn boring beetle, a frost-resistant tomato inserted with a fish gene, and salmon that grow faster and are more resistant to cold. High-yielding GM crops could replace lower-yielding crops in developing countries, and engineering vitamins into crops such as rice could provide a more nutritious diet for poor consumers. This would not only help feed the increasing population in those countries but would also decrease the conversion rate of natural forests into agricultural land.

Opponents of GM foods claim that any social benefits are outweighed by the chance of a large-scale eco-catastrophe. Crossing the species boundaries inherent in the natural structure, according to these critics, can have disastrous implications for nature as well as for human health. Genetically modified plants could crossbreed with natural varieties to produce strains that could wreak havoc on the natural environment. A study conducted by researchers at Cornell University and reported in the journal *Nature* in 1999 described how pollen from corn genetically altered to produce its own pesticide caused significant mortality of monarch butterfly caterpillars. Also, widespread use of such pesticide-producing plants could promote the emergence of resistant "super-pests." Even a small chance of such a major disaster, critics contend, is not worth the benefits of GM crops.

Issues of Corporate Control

Formulating GM crops requires heavy investment in research and development. To earn back their investments, companies must ensure that only those who pay for

(continued on following page)

them use their products. Traditionally farmers, especially in developing countries, buy an initial consignment of seeds and subsequently save part of their crops as seeds for future cultivation. Biotechnology corporations can patent their products and ensure, through threat of legal action, that farmers buy a new consignment of seed for every season or pay royalties. Some companies have attempted to genetically modify seeds so that the subsequent crop seeds are sterile or create crops usable only with another product made by the same company. Critics claim that such developments can create monopolistic situations in which a few companies control the supply of major crop seeds. Such a market would place small-scale farmers and developing countries at a strong disadvantage.

Staunch anti–GM foods stances are causing trade conflicts between GM food producers such as the United States and importing countries. European governments, some Asian governments, and U.S. activists are calling for labeling on foods that contain GM ingredients and the right to exclude GM products from their markets. Some farmers and industry lobbyists, mainly in the United States, contend that GM and non-GM foods will have to be grown, transported, stored and processed separately, which will lead to higher prices. In addition, they claim, labeling will stigmatize products. Most countries have agreed to the need for further research on the safety of GM foods.

The debate on genetically modified foods includes powerful arguments on both sides. Decisions will have important implications for environmental sustainability, food security, and international trade and politics.[1]

---

[1]For more on both sides of this debate, see Rissler and Mellen, 1996 and Paarlberg, 2000.

Sustainable Agriculture for the Future

Many of the resource and environmental issues we discussed in Chapters 3–5 are relevant to the analysis of agricultural production. Erosion and soil degradation, as we have noted, make soil a depletable resource and impose **user costs** on future generations. Fertilizer runoff and pesticide pollution are classic examples of externalities. Excessive pumping of water from rivers and aquifers demonstrates the problem of overuse of common property resources. Problems such as resistant pest species and loss of biodiversity impose ecological costs that may be difficult to evaluate in monetary terms, as we saw in Chapter 6.

Ecological analysis offers us a somewhat different understanding of the relationship between agriculture and the environment. Rather than seeing agricultural production as a process of combining inputs (including land, water, fertilizer, and pesticides) to maximize output, the ecological economist would argue that agriculture is a process of intervention in the natural **biophysical cycles** responsible for plant growth.

A rice farmer levels his plowed field in Bali, Indonesia. Traditional techniques, such as the use of draft animals, agroforestry, and multicropping, are ecologically sustainable but have often been displaced by modernized agriculture.

These include the carbon cycle, nitrogen cycle, water cycle, and similar cycles for other plant nutrients.

In a natural state, solar energy drives these cycles. Traditional agriculture departs little from these natural cycles. Modernized agriculture relies on extra inputs of energy, water, nitrogen, and synthetic chemicals. This gives higher yields, but creates imbalances in all the natural cyclical processes. From this perspective, soil degradation, fertilizer and pesticide pollution, and water overdraft are results of disrupting natural cycles. To use another ecological concept, modern agriculture expands carrying capacity but only at the cost of increasing ecological stresses.

Both the economic and the ecological perspectives can influence our definition of **sustainable agriculture.** A sustainable agricultural system should produce a stable level of output without degrading the environmental systems that support it. In economic terms, this means no significant uninternalized externalities, user costs, or excessive use of common property resources. From an ecological point of view, a sustainable system minimizes disruption to natural cycles. This suggests some supply-side and demand-side techniques that may be appropriate for sustainable agriculture.

Production techniques such as organic fertilization from recycled plant and animal wastes, crop rotation, and **intercropping** grains and legumes help maintain the soil's nutrients balance and minimize need for artificial fertilizer. The use of reduced tillage, terracing, fallowing, and **agroforestry** (planting trees in and around fields) all help to reduce erosion. **Integrated pest management (IPM)** uses natural pest controls such as predator species, crop rotation, and labor-intensive early pest removal to minimize use of chemical pesticides.

Efficient irrigation techniques and the use of drought- and salt-tolerant crop varieties can reduce water use. Species diversity is promoted by multiple cropping (planting several different crops in the same field) rather than the **monoculture** (extensive plantings of a single crop) typical of modernized agriculture.

According to the National Research Council report *Alternative Agriculture*,[20] farms using organic techniques have been fairly successful in equaling the yields and economic record of neighboring high-input farms in Iowa, Pennsylvania, Ohio, Virginia, and California. This is a positive indication that environmentally friendly techniques may be economically feasible in larger scale agriculture. However, the barriers to implementing this kind of farming in the United States and worldwide are considerable.

One major problem is access to information. Alternative techniques tend to be both **labor intensive** and **information intensive.** In developed countries, only a minority of farmers know enough about the complex techniques of organic and low-input agriculture to make them pay. It's much easier to read the instructions on a bag of fertilizer or a canister of pesticide. In developing countries, traditional low-input farming systems have often been displaced by modernized "Green Revolution" techniques.

Policies for Sustainable Agriculture

Without strong economic incentives to alter production methods, combined with widespread information and support for alternative techniques, most farmers will stay with established methods. A shift to alternative agriculture will require a combination of government policy and market incentives.

Important market incentives include the prices of fertilizer, pesticides, irrigation water, and energy. Many governments have policies that directly or indirectly subsidize these prices. Hayami and Ruttan have shown that price ratios for agricultural inputs determine the course of **induced innovation** in agriculture.[21] If fertilizer is cheap relative to land and labor, the farm sector will develop and implement fertilizer-intensive methods. By providing low-cost fertilizer, farm chemicals, and water for irrigation, governments promote agricultural productivity—but at environmental cost.

Policies to subsidize energy development also promote the trend to more highly mechanized and input-dependent agriculture. Changing these policies would support development of a more labor- and information-intensive agriculture with less environmental impact. In developing nations with large pools of unemployed and underemployed labor, promotion of labor-intensive agricultural development might have considerable employment as well as environmental benefits.

---

[20]National Research Council, 1989.

[21]Ruttan and Hayami, 1984.

Removing energy and input subsidies would send a price signal to farmers to use less input-intensive techniques. Before they can respond effectively to these price incentives, however, farmers need information on alternative techniques—otherwise higher input prices will simply make food more expensive. Some developing nations can combine valuable knowledge of traditional agricultural techniques with some modern innovations—provided that energy-intensive monoculture does not sweep away traditional knowledge.

On the demand side, it is clear that population size is a major determinant of food demand and indirectly of agricultural pressures on the environment. The ecological concept of carrying capacity implies some maximum population that the planet's resources can sustainably support. Our discussion of agricultural futures indicates that we are close to that capacity, and may have exceeded it if we consider long-term issues of soil erosion and water overdraft. Population policy is therefore a central element in limiting the impact of agricultural production on the environment.

The other major demand-side variable is diet. As we have seen, a meat-centered diet implies much higher land, water, and fertilizer requirements per capita than a mostly vegetarian diet. Using land resources to produce meat for export also increases environmental pressures in developing nations. Thus, reduction of meat consumption in developed nations, and a slowing of the trend toward meat-centered diets in newly industrializing nations, is an important component of long-term sustainability.

Abolishing input subsidies will increase the relative price of meat as compared to more input-efficient foods; possibly health motivations may lead to some reduction in demand for meat in developed nations. To the extent that consumers shift their preferences toward more vegetables, including more organically grown produce, the incentives to producers to employ less environmentally damaging techniques will grow.

The environmental problems associated with agriculture are complex and cannot be solved by simple cost internalization policies—though these will help. It will take major changes in consumer behavior, production techniques, and government price and agricultural policies to move toward a sustainable agricultural system. The urgency of these issue will grow as population increases and cumulative soil and water impacts increase. The high-input agriculture that has been central to increasing world output during recent decades will not meet the needs of the twenty-first century without significant changes to promote sustainability.

SUMMARY

Food production has outpaced population growth during the past century, allowing for slowly rising global per capita food consumption. However, food distribution is significantly unequal, with up to 1 billion people receiving inadequate nutrition. Most suitable agricultural land is already being farmed, leaving relatively little room for further expansion. Yields have risen, and continue to rise, but greater productivity has been accompanied by rising environmental impact, including erosion, soil degradation, and fertilizer and pesticide runoff.

Rates of growth in agricultural output have slowed, but prices of basic foods are stable or declining, indicating that supply limits have not been reached. In many areas of the developing world per capita consumption has grown slowly, stagnated, or declined. Inequitable access to food means that basic food crops can be displaced by luxury or export food crops, increasing pressures on the poor and on environmentally vulnerable marginal lands.

Projections of future demand show a near doubling of food demand in the developing world over the next several decades. With little potential for land expansion, meeting this demand will require dramatic increases in yields. The challenge is to achieve this in an environmentally sustainable manner. Existing environmental effects associated with agricultural production make this a formidable task.

Erosion causes declining soil fertility as well as significant off-farm damage. Farmers facing short-term financial pressures often find investment in long-term conservation difficult. Fertilizer use has led to extensive runoff pollution and excessive nitrate release, affecting both water supplies and the atmosphere. Pesticide applications are associated with steadily increasing numbers of resistant pest species, as well as with other negative effects on ecosystems. Poorly planned irrigation systems have led to water overdraft and pollution as well as soil damage.

Future policies must promote agricultural sustainability. Practices such as crop rotation, intercropping, agroforestry, and integrated pest management can reduce input requirements and environmental impact while maintaining high yields. Efficient irrigation and land management techniques have great potential, but require appropriate economic incentives for farmers to adopt them. Removing energy and input subsidies and providing information on environmentally sound techniques must accompany more equitable and efficient distribution and consumption patterns.

KEY TERMS AND CONCEPTS

agroforestry
biodiversity
biophysical cycles
carrying capacity
common property resource
crop rotation and fallowing
crop value index
depletable resource
discount rate
elasticity of supply
environmental sustainability
external costs
externalities
induced innovation
information asymmetry
information-intensive techniques
integrated pest management

intercropping
labor-intensive techniques
marginal physical product
marginal revenue product
micronutrients
monoculture
multiple cropping
nitrogen cycle
nutrient recycling
nutritional deficit
present value
proxy variable
renewable resource
resistant pest species
salinization and alkalinization of soils
sustainable agriculture
user costs

DISCUSSION QUESTIONS

1. What evidence would you use to evaluate the proposition that the world is reaching maximum carrying capacity in terms of food supply? Some analysts believe that the world's agricultural capacity is quite adequate for a population of 10 billion people. Do you feel comfortable with this assertion? Is it useful to attempt to evaluate maximum carrying capacity, or should we just wait and see how markets adjust to increased food demand?

2. Which of agriculture's environmental effects are most amenable to market solutions? Consider the on-farm and off-farm effects of erosion, for example. What kind of incentives might induce greater erosion control? How much can private initiative accomplish and how much must rely on government policy?

3. How can we define the concept of sustainable agriculture? Can high-input agriculture be sustainable? Is organic agriculture sustainable? How is our current agricultural system not sustainable, and what kinds of policies are appropriate responses to problems of nonsustainability? How would you evaluate the economic costs and benefits of such policies?

REFERENCES

Alexandratos, Nikos. *The Outlook for World Food and Agriculture to the Year 2010.* Rome, Italy: United Nations Food and Agriculture Organization, 1994.

Brown, Lester, and Hal Kane. *Full House: Reassessing the Earth's Population Carrying Capacity.* New York: Norton, 1994.

Brown, Lester R. "Eradicating Hunger: A Growing Challenge." In Worldwatch Institute Report *State of the World 1999,* edited by Brown et al. New York: Norton, 1999.

Cleveland, Cutler J. "Reallocating Work Between Human and Natural Capital and Agriculture: Examples from India and the United States." In *Investing in Natural Capital: The Ecological Approach to Sustainability,* edited by Jannson et al. Washington, D.C.: Island Press, 1994.

Food and Agriculture Organization of the United Nations (FAO). *Production Yearbook,* 1997–2000.

Food and Agriculture Organization of the United Nations (FAO). FAOSTAT Agriculture Database, 2000.

Gardner, Gary. "Preserving Agricultural Resources." In *State of the World 1996,* edited by Brown et al. Washington, D.C.: Worldwatch Institute, 1996.

Hall, Charles A. S. "The Efficiency of Land and Energy Use in Tropical Economies and Agriculture." *Agriculture, Ecosystems and Environment* 46. Amsterdam: Elsevier, 1993: 1–30.

Harris, Jonathan M. *World Agriculture and the Environment*. New York: Garland, 1990.

Harris, Jonathan M. "World Agricultural Futures: Regional Sustainability and Ecological Limits." *Ecological Economics* 17 (May 1996): 95–115.

Martinez-Alier, Juan. "Modern Agriculture: A Source of Energy?" Chapter 2 in *Ecological Economics: Energy, Environment, and Society*. Great Britain: Blackwell, 1993.

National Research Council. *Alternative Agriculture*. Washington, D.C.: National Academy Press, 1989.

Oldeman, L. R., R. T. A. Hakkeling, and W. G. Sombroek. *Global Assessment of Soil Degradation*. Wageningen, Netherlands: ISRIC/UNEP, 1990.

Paarlberg, Robert. "The Global Food Fight." *Foreign Affairs* 79 (May/June 2000): 24–38.

Pimentel, David, ed. *World Soil Erosion and Conservation*. Cambridge, England: Cambridge University Press, 1993.

Pinstrup-Andersen, Per, and Rajul Pandya-Lorch. *The Unfinished Agenda: Perspectives on Overcoming Hunger, Poverty, and Environmental Degradation*. Washington, D.C.: International Food Policy Research Institute, 2001.

Postel, Sandra. *Pillar of Sand: Can the Irrigation Miracle Last?* Worldwatch Institute Book. New York: Norton, 1999.

Rissler, Jane, and Margaret Mellen. *The Ecological Risks of Engineered Crops*. Cambridge, Mass.: MIT Press, 1996.

Ruttan, Vernon W., and Yujiro Hayami. "Induced Innovation Model of Agricultural Development." In *International Agricultural Development* (3rd ed.), edited by Carl K. Eicher and John M. Staatz. Baltimore: Johns Hopkins University Press, 1998.

Seckler, David. *Trends in World Food Needs: Toward Zero Growth in the 21st Century*. Winrock International Institute for Agricultural Development, Center for Economic Policy Studies Discussion Paper No. 18, 1994.

Sen, Amartya. "Population: Delusion and Reality," *New York Review of Books,* September 22, 1994.

Sen, Amartya. "Population, Food and Freedom." Chapter 9 in Sen, *Development as Freedom*. New York: Knopf, 2000.

Smil, Vaclav. *Feeding the World: A Challenge for the Twenty-First Century*. Cambridge, Mass.: MIT Press, 2000.

United States Environmental Protection Agency. *Pesticides Industry Sales and Usage Report*, 1994/1995.

Waggoner, Paul E. *How Much Land Can Ten Billion People Spare for Nature?* Council for Agricultural Science and Technology, Task Force Report No. 121, February 1994.

WEB SITES

1. **http://www.ers.usda.gov/** Web site for the Economic Research Service, a division of the U.S. Department of Agriculture with a mission "to inform and enhance public and private decision making on economic and policy issues related to agriculture, food, natural resources, and rural development." Their web site provides links to a broad range of data and analysis on U.S. agricultural issues.

2. **http://www.fao.org/** Web site for the Food and Agriculture Organization of the United Nations, an organization "with a mandate to raise levels of nutrition and standards of living, to improve agricultural productivity, and to better the condition of rural populations." Their web site includes a huge amount of data on agriculture and food issues around the world.

3. **http://www.ota.com/** Home page for the Organic Trade Association, "a membership-based business association representing the organic industry in Canada, the United States, and Mexico." Their web site includes press releases and facts about the organic agriculture industry.

4. **http://www.cals.cornell.edu/extension/nabc/** Home page for the National Agricultural Biotechnology Council, a nonprofit group with membership from more than 30 research and teaching institutions designed to provide a forum for the evaluation of agricultural biotechnology. Several reports available on their web site concern the impact of agricultural biotechnology.

5. **http://www.oecd.org/agr/** Web site for the Food, Agriculture, and Fisheries division of the Organization for Economic Co-operation and Development. The site includes data, trade information, and discussions of environmental issues, including a web page on biotechnology.

FIVE

Energy and Resources

CHAPTER FOCUS QUESTIONS

- Are we running out of nonrenewable resources?
- What are the environmental costs of mining mineral resources?
- How do economic incentives affect recycling of nonrenewable resources?

CHAPTER **12**

Resources: Scarcity and Abundance

The Supply of Nonrenewable Resources

The planet holds a fixed quantity of **nonrenewable resources,** including metal and nonmetal minerals, coal, oil, and natural gas. We have extensive supplies of some resources, such as iron; others, such as mercury or helium, are in relatively limited supply. The global economy is using up these resources—often at increasing rates. Is this a cause for alarm? The authors of the original *Limits to Growth* report[1] thought so in 1972, and repeated a similar warning 20 years later in *Beyond the Limits:*

> Human use of many essential resources and generation of many kinds of pollutants have already surpassed rates that are physically sustainable. Without significant reductions in material and energy flows, there will be in the coming decades an uncontrolled decline in per capita food output, energy use, and industrial production.[2]

Limited, nonrenewable resources cannot, of course, last forever, but issues regarding their use are complex, involving changes in resource supply and demand as well as the wastes and pollution generated in their consumption. In this chapter we examine the dynamics of nonrenewable resource use; in Chapter 13 we will look more

---

[1]Meadows et al., 1972.

[2]Meadows et al., 1992, p. xv.

specifically at the use of energy resources, and in Chapters 16 and 17 we will examine analyses of pollution generation and resource recycling.

As we saw in Chapter 9, these issues are interconnected by the principle of entropy—increased use of energy and resources (low entropy) is usually associated with greater pollution and waste generation (high entropy). For purposes of economic analysis, however, we will focus on those specific aspects of the overall process that we referred to in Chapters 1 and 9 as resource **throughput**. The first part of throughput is the extraction of nonrenewable resource from available planetary supplies. What economic principles govern this process?

In our initial analysis in Chapter 4, we considered the allocation of a mineral resource over several time periods. We assumed that both the resource quantity and quality were fixed. The economic principles derived from this simple example, including the analysis of **user costs** and **Hotelling's rule** for resource pricing, are important, but a more sophisticated analysis must deal with real-world conditions. We usually see many different resource qualities (for example, different grades of copper ore), and we rarely know with complete certainty the location and total quantity of resource deposits.

Physical Supply and Economic Supply

The **economic supply** of a nonrenewable resource differs from its **physical supply.** The physical supply (in the earth's crust) is finite but generally not precisely known. The **economically recoverable reserves** provide the measure most commonly used in, for example, calculations of resource lifetime. However, this figure changes over time for three main reasons:

- The resource is extracted and used over time, diminishing reserves.
- New resource deposits are discovered over time, increasing reserves.
- Changing price and technological conditions can make more (or less) of the known reserves economically viable. These factors make predictions of resource lifetimes an inexact science.

A mineral resource such as copper is classified through a combination of geologic and economic measures (Figure 12-1).

In geological terms, resources are classified by available quantities, shown as the horizontal dimension in Figure 12-1. **Identified reserves** are those whose quantity and quality are already known. A portion of these identified reserves have been **measured** within a 20 percent margin of error; another portion are **indicated** or **inferred** based on geological principles. In addition, **hypothetical** and **speculative** amounts of the resource are as yet undiscovered, but likely to exist in certain geological situations.

Economic factors create another dimension to resource classification, shown vertically in Figure 12-1, with the most economically profitable resources toward the top. Only some identified resources are of high enough quality to be profitably produced. These are identified as **economic reserves. Subeconomic resources** are those whose costs of extraction are too high to make production worthwhile. However, if prices rise or extraction technologies improve, these deposits may become profitable.

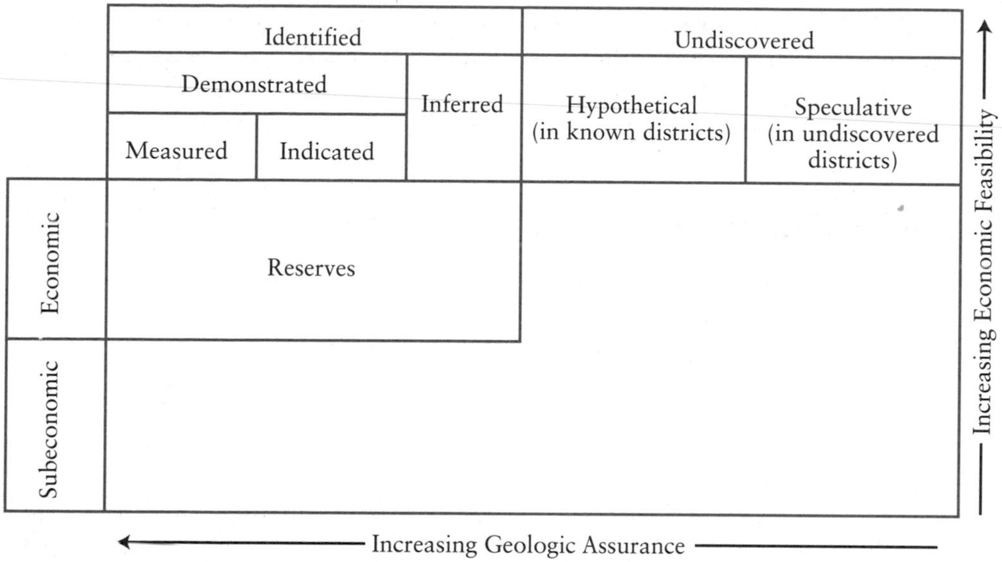

Identified				Undiscovered	
Demonstrated		Inferred	Hypothetical (in known districts)	Speculative (in undiscovered districts)	
Measured	Indicated				
Economic	Reserves				
Subeconomic					

← Increasing Geologic Assurance →

Increasing Economic Feasibility ↑

FIGURE 12-1 *Classification of Nonrenewable Resources*

Source: Adapted from U.S. Bureau of Mines and U.S. Geological Survey, *Geological Survey Bulletins 1450-A* and *1450-B*, 1976. Available at http://www.usgs.gov.

The fact that economic reserves can be expanded in both geological and economic dimensions renders projections using a **static reserve index** unreliable. A static reserve index simply divides economic reserves by the current rate of use for an estimate of **resource lifetime**:

$$\text{Expected Resource Lifetime} = \frac{\text{Economic Reserves}}{\text{Annual Consumption}}$$

Of course, current consumption is not necessarily a good indication of future use. With growing population and economic output, we can expect nonrenewable resource use to grow—although substitution and changing consumption patterns will affect rates of growth. An **exponential reserve index** assumes that consumption will grow exponentially over time, leading to more rapid resource exhaustion.

Calculations made in 1972 using both static and exponential reserve indices indicated that major mineral reserves would be exhausted within several decades—projections clearly not borne out.[3] Why not? Because reserves have grown with new discoveries and new extractive technologies. However, we cannot simply dismiss predictions of resource exhaustion. Even with reserve expansion, planetary resources are ultimately limited.

---

[3]Meadows et al., 1992.

The relevant question is how resource consumption, new technology, and discovery will interact to affect prices, which in turn will affect future patterns of resource demand and supply. To better understand these factors, we need a more sophisticated economic theory of nonrenewable resource use.

Economic Theory of Nonrenewable Resource Use

What determines the rate at which we extract and use nonrenewable resources? An individual firm operating a mine or other resource extraction operation, must be guided by the principle of maximization of **resource rents**.[4] Consider a firm operating a bauxite (aluminum ore) mine. If the firm is in a competitive industry, it is a **price taker** and sells its output at the market price, over which it has no control. It can, however, control the amount of the resource extracted in any period.

In general, as more of the resource is extracted the marginal cost of extraction will rise. Obviously, if the **marginal extraction cost** rises above the market price, producing the bauxite becomes unprofitable. Price must at least equal marginal cost to make production worthwhile. Unlike other competitive industries where price equals marginal costs in equilibrium, resource-extracting firms typically operate at an output level at which price exceeds marginal cost (Figure 12-2). Such firms must seek to maximize the value of rents not just in one period, but over an extended period of time.

The present value of a stream of rents extending into the future is given by

$$PV[R] = R_0 + R_1/(1+r) + R_2/(1+r)^2 + R_3/(1+r)^3 + \ldots + R_n/(1+r)^n$$

where R_i is the rent accruing to the firm in the ith period.

To maximize the present value of the rent stream, the firm must adjust the extraction quantity in each period until the rent rises at a rate equal to the discount rate, so that the present value of the rent in each period is the same,[5] or:

$$R_0 = R_1/(1+r) = R_2/(1+r)^2 = R_3/(1+r)^3 = \ldots = R_n/(1+r)^n$$

When all the firms in a resource-extracting industry operate on this principle, the rent, or **net price** (price minus extraction costs) must rise over time in accordance with Hotelling's rule (which we discussed in Chapter 4). The common-sense explanation for this is that if production is very profitable today, firms will produce more. The increased production will lower today's price, while the reduced reserves available for future production will raise expected future prices. This process will continue until

---

[4]*Economic rent* is the income derived from ownership of a scarce resource. In a resource-extracting industry, the usual principle of profit maximization thus becomes the maximization of resource rents.

[5]The firm seeks to equalize discounted marginal profit for each period. If a greater marginal profit is expected in a given period, it will be advantageous to increase production planned for that period until all periods yield the same discounted marginal profit.

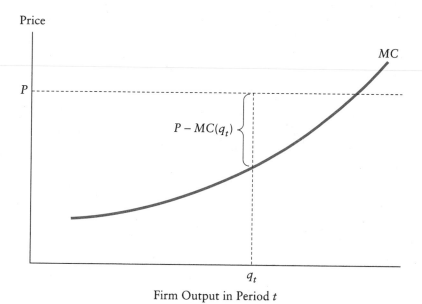

FIGURE 12-2 *Resource Rent for the Competitive Firm*[6]

Hotelling's rule is satisfied—the net price rises over time at a rate equal to the discount rate, and the discounted value of rents is equalized over time.

If marginal extraction costs fall over time, perhaps due to improved technology, net price may rise while the market price of the resource declines. However, if extraction costs are stable, we would expect the market price of the resource to rise over time. Since this has not yet occurred for most resources, the effects of Hotelling's rule may only become evident when specific resources move closer to exhaustion.

The principle of rent maximization has a more immediately relevant implication: higher-quality resources will be exploited first. Suppose, for example, that a firm owns two bauxite deposits, one high grade and one low grade. Marginal costs of production for the high-grade resource will be relatively low, so a high rent can be obtained by producing today. Costs of extracting the low-grade deposit are significantly higher. Even if extracting the low-grade deposit today would be marginally profitable, waiting until market prices rise or until better technology makes extraction less costly will be a better strategy.

This explains why resources that are subeconomic today (see Figure 12-1) can become economic in the future, possibly increasing the amount of economically recoverable reserves—at the same time that extraction has diminished the physical reserves.

---

[6]This diagram and Figure 12-3 have been adapted from Hartwick and Olewiler (1998), which provides a more advanced discussion of the economic theory of nonrenewable resource extraction.

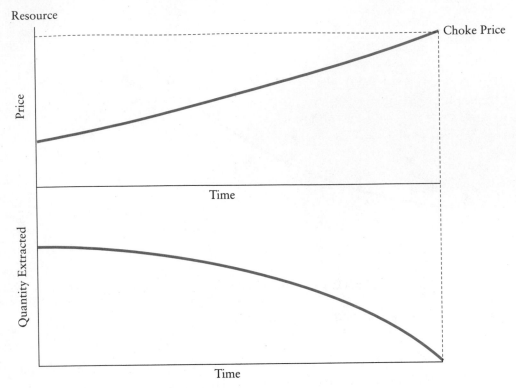

FIGURE 12-3 *Exhaustion of a Mineral Stock*

The basic theory of nonrenewable resource extraction also implies that limited resource stocks will be exploited to exhaustion. So long as the price continues to rise, delaying some production will remain profitable. But every resource has some maximum price, called the **choke price,** at which the quantity demanded falls to zero. By the time the choke price is reached, producers will have extracted and sold all economically viable reserves. Figure 12-3 shows the **price path** and **extraction path** for a resource stock being exploited to exhaustion.

Long-Term Trends in Nonrenewable Resource Use

How well does this theory of resource depletion fit with real-world experience? A classic study by Barnett and Morse[7] showed that most mineral resource prices fell from the Industrial Revolution through the mid-twentieth century. At the same time,

---

[7]Barnett and Morse, 1963.

global nonrenewable resource consumption steadily expanded. Three major factors were responsible:

- continual resource discovery
- improved resource extraction technology
- **resource substitution,** such as use of plastics in place of metals

Despite the unreliability of reserve estimates and indices of depletion, new discoveries and improved extraction technologies cannot extend nonrenewable resource lifetimes forever. In addition, the economic incentive to deplete high-quality reserves first means that over time the remaining reserves will be of lower quality, more difficult and expensive to extract. Thus we can predict a long-term **resource use profile** similar to that shown in Figure 12-4.

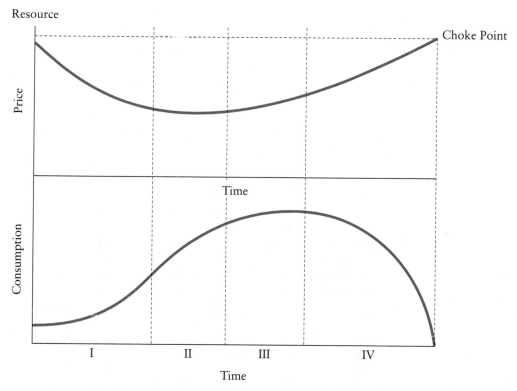

I: Falling Price, Exponentially Increasing Resource Consumption
II: Stable Price, Steadily Increasing Consumption
III: Rising Price, Slowing Rate of Increase of Consumption
IV: Price Increasing to Choke Point, Consumption Falling to Zero

FIGURE 12-4 *Hypothetical Nonrenewable Resource Use Profile*

In the early stages of resource exploitation, price falls as new discoveries and improved technology make the resource easier to obtain. In Stage II, prices are stable as increasing consumption (tending to pull prices up) balances further discovery and technological improvement (tending to pull prices down). In Stage III, demand starts to press against resource limitations, and prices begin to rise. Finally, rising price limits consumption, which eventually falls to zero as price reaches the choke point.

As we will see in Chapter 13, a profile of this kind applies to fossil fuel resources in some regions and may also apply to global use of fossil fuels. For mineral resources in general, the picture is more mixed. Considerable controversy exists as to whether a resource profile similar to Figure 12-4 applies to most minerals. Where it does apply, an interesting question is whether we are currently in Stage I, II, or III, and therefore whether we can expect falling, stable, or rising prices. We review this debate in the next section.

Global Scarcity or Increasing Abundance?

As we have noted, predictions of nonrenewable resource exhaustion have thus far not been borne out. In fact, despite growing consumption, new discoveries and improved technology have led to increased reserves of most minerals. Figure 12-5 shows this trend over time for copper, lead, and zinc.

Table 12-1 shows current estimates of reserves and of a static reserve index for major minerals. In general, the static reserve indices show expected resource lifetimes ranging from several decades to several centuries. The predictive power of a static reserve index is limited, because it does not take into account new discoveries or improved extraction technology.

The **reserve base index** reflects a broader estimate of potential reserves and therefore a longer predicted lifetime. Even with this broader index, however, we note that several important minerals have relatively short projected lifetimes, including tin, zinc, copper, lead, and mercury. Are we then likely to see increasing prices for these minerals?

Some studies indicate that a turnaround in the general pattern of declining mineral price trends may be at hand. Margaret Slade's studies of nickel and other minerals showed a possible upward trend in prices beginning in the early 1980s.[8] This could reflect the initial influence of resource limitations and the exhaustion of high-grade reserves, but whether or not this apparent price turnaround will continue remains unclear. Several key minerals have shown a downward price trend since the 1980s, and future prospects remain uncertain.[9]

One important physical consideration, not generally reflected in economic models, is the distribution of different qualities of mineral ore in the earth's crust. The bulk of

---

[8]Slade, 1982.

[9]Berck and Roberts, 1996.

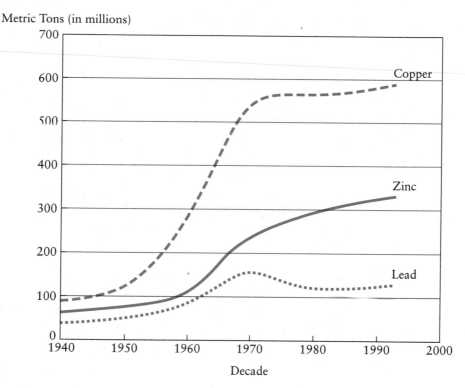

FIGURE 12-5 *Change in World Reserve Base for Selected Minerals*
Source: Hodges, 1995, p. 1306.

TABLE 12-1 *Reserve Estimates for Selected Minerals*

Mineral	Annual Consumption (thousand metric tons)	Total Reserves (thousand metric tons)	Reserve Base (thousand metric tons)	Reserve Index (years)	Reserve Base Index (years)
Aluminum	103,625*	23,000,000	28,000,000	222	270
Cadmium	20	600	1,200	30	60
Copper	10,714	340,000	650,000	32	61
Iron Ore	959,609	71,000,000	160,000,000	74	167
Lead	5,342	64,000	130,000	12	24
Mercury	6.6	120	240	18	36
Nickel	882	49,000	150,000	56	170
Tin	218	9,600	12,000	44	55
Zinc	6,993	190,000	430,000	27	62

Source: Derived from World Resources Institute, 1994; and U.S. Geological Survey, 2001.

*Annual consumption of bauxite ore.

available reserves are of considerably lower grade than those now exploited commercially. Studies of mineral abundance have often assumed a relatively smooth distribution pattern similar to that shown in Figure 12-6a. If this is accurate, the market should indicate mineral resource depletion with gradually rising prices from higher extraction costs.

However, the relative abundance of high- and low-grade ore may also be uneven, showing a pattern similar to Figure 12-6b, with a significant quality gap between ores currently being mined and lower-grade reserves. If this is the case, when the high-grade reserves are exhausted, recovering lower-grade ores will be significantly more difficult and expensive as well as more environmentally damaging. The lower the ore grade, the greater the volume of wastes generated in producing minerals of marketable quality.

Internalizing Environmental Costs of Resource Recovery

While it is unlikely that we will ever completely "run out" of a resource, we may well exhaust high-grade deposits, resulting in higher private and environmental costs of resource recovery. Figure 12-7 shows the implications of this for resource price profiles. If environmental costs are internalized, a price profile reflecting the full social costs of resource extraction will show an earlier turning point than one showing extraction costs alone.

We should consider both direct and indirect environmental costs associated with resource recovery. Typically, mining produces vast quantities of wastes, some of them extremely toxic, as well as other damage to land and water (see Tables 12-2 and 12-3). As the resource grade declines, the quantity of mining wastes per ton of product increases.

In addition, lower-grade resources typically require more energy per unit to produce.[10] Although the basic price path will reflect the higher costs of energy, energy production will also create significant environmental externalities. These could be internalized into the price of energy, but generally are not. (More on this in Chapters 13 and 18.)

If we include these indirect environmental damages, the resource price path will turn up sooner and more sharply, reaching the "choke price" at a significantly earlier time. Figure 12-8 shows the likely effects of internalizing environmental costs on the resource consumption profile.

Whereas the basic consumption profile rises until higher prices start to constrain demand and then falls fairly rapidly, including environmental costs in price leads to an earlier flattening out of virgin (primary) resource consumption.[11] Resource consumers will have an incentive to shift to backstop resources or to **recycle** the resource where possible. A **backstop resource** can substitute for the original product, but at a higher price—it will enter the market only when the price rises to a certain level. Recycling is an option for many nonrenewable resources, especially metals, and becomes more cost-effective as the price of the virgin resource rises.

---

[10]Cleveland, 1991.

[11]A *virgin resource* is one that has been newly extracted, as opposed to one being reused or recycled. These are also known as *primary resources*.

(a) Smooth Distribution

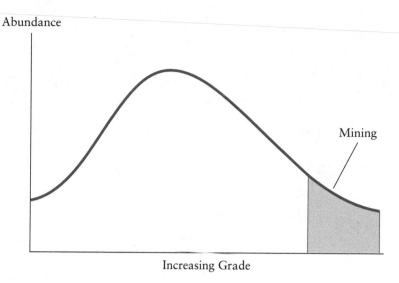

(b) Uneven Distribution

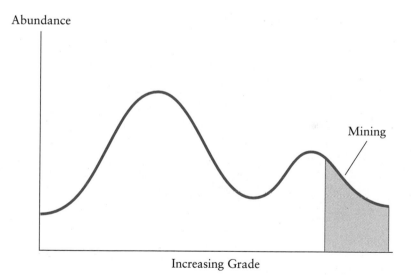

FIGURE 12-6 *Distribution of Mineral Ores in the Earth's Crust*
Source: Adapted from Skinner, 1976.

Scrap steel to be recycled for industrial use in Youngstown, Ohio. Recycled metals provide about 50% of U.S. iron and steel consumption.

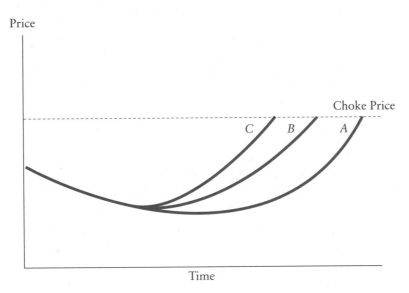

A: Basic Price Path
B: Price Path with Direct Environmental Costs
C: Price Path with Direct and Indirect Environmental Costs

FIGURE 12-7 *Resource Price Profile with Environmental Costs*

TABLE 12-2 *The Environmental Costs of Mining*

Activity	Potential Impact
Excavation and Ore Removal	Destruction of plant and animal habitat, human settlements, and other features (surface mining)
	Land subsidence (underground mining)
	Increased erosion; silting of lakes and streams
	Waste generation
	Acid drainage and metal contamination of lakes, streams, and groundwater
Ore Concentration	Waste generation (tailings)
	Organic chemical contamination
	Acid drainage and metal contamination
Smelting/Refining	Air pollution (including sulfur dioxide, arsenic, lead, cadmium, and other toxics)
	Waste generation (slag)
	Impact of producing energy (most energy used for mineral production goes into smelting and refining).

Source: Excerpted from John E. Young, *Mining the Earth*, Worldwatch Paper 109, pp. 17, 19. ©1992. Reprinted by permission of Worldwatch Institute. www.worldwatch.org.

TABLE 12-3 *Environmental Impacts of Selected Mineral Projects*

Mineral/Location	Environmental Impacts
Copper mining and smelting Ilo-Locombo area, Peru	600,000 tons of sulfur compounds emitted per year; nearly 40 million cubic meters of tailings containing copper, zinc, lead, aluminum, and traces of cyanides are dumped into the sea each year, along with 800,000 tons of slag.
Phosphate Mining Nauru, South Pacific	When mining is complete in 5–15 years, four-fifths of the 2,100-hectare South Pacific island will be uninhabitable.
Carajás Iron Ore Project Pará State, Brazil	Wood requirements for smelting iron ore will deforest 50,000 hectares of tropical forest each year.
Nickel Smelters Russia	Two nickel smelters near the Norwegian and Finnish borders pump 300,000 tons of sulfur dioxide into the atmosphere, along with lesser amounts of heavy metals. More than 200,000 hectares of local forests are dying as a result, and local residents suffer health effects.
Mamut Copper Mine Sabah Province, Malaysia	Local rivers are contaminated with high levels of chromium, copper, iron, lead, manganese, and nickel.
Gold Mining Amazon Basin, Brazil	Rivers are clogged with sediment and 100 tons of mercury are released into the ecosystem each year.

Source: Excerpted from John E. Young, *Mining the Earth*, Worldwatch Paper 109, pp. 17, 19. ©1992. Reprinted by permission of Worldwatch Institute. www.worldwatch.org.

Resource
Consumption

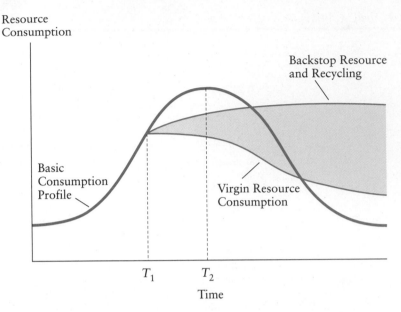

FIGURE 12-8 *Resource Consumption Profile with Backstop Resource or Recycling.* Internalization of environmental costs causes virgin resource consumption to peak at T_1 instead of T_2.

Note that with this modified consumption profile, supplies of the primary resource last longer. Consumption shows a less rapid turnaround, and technological infrastructure can adapt to the use of backstop and recycled resources. Both on these grounds and because it is generally good policy to internalize externalities, a pricing policy that encourages an earlier transition away from dependence on primary resources may be advisable.

Some assessments of global resource availability present an optimistic view of the future based on the relatively long projected lifetimes of some resources, and the possibilities for substitution in the case of those with shorter reserve indices.[12] However, this approach takes little account of the growing environmental problems resulting from recovery of lower-grade resources. In addition to environmental costs today, depleting high-grade resources also imposes user costs (discussed in Chapter 4) on future generations. Future resource users will both pay higher prices and suffer greater environmental damages from their use of low-grade resources.

Recycling resources today lessens both present and future costs resulting from primary resource use. The recycling process also has its own costs, including capital costs of recycling facilities and labor, transportation, and energy costs. It makes sense, therefore, to examine the economics of recycling and its effects on resource use.

---

[12]See, for example, Goeller and Zucker, 1984.

The Economics of Recycling

In theory, effective recycling could significantly extend the lifetimes of many nonrenewable resources. However, recycling has both economic and physical limits.

The second law of thermodynamics (the principle of increasing entropy, which we discussed in Chapter 9) implies that perfect recycling is impossible. Some loss or degradation of material will always occur during the process of fabrication, use, and recycling. In addition, recycling requires new inputs of energy. In economic terms, we must compare recycling costs to the costs of using primary materials to determine when recycling will be both physically possible and economically advantageous.

Figure 12-9 shows the economics of recycling from the manufacturer's point of view. The obvious advantage to the manufacturer is that using recycled materials saves the cost of purchasing new inputs. Reading from left to right in Figure 12-9, the total cost of virgin materials declines as the proportion of recycled inputs rises. On the other hand, the cost of recycled materials rises in a nonlinear manner, indicating that

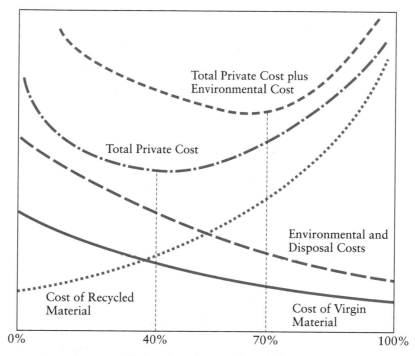

FIGURE 12-9 *Total Costs of Recycling*

Source: This graph is adapted from a simplified version of a cost analysis by Walter O. Spofford, Jr., "Solid Residual Management: Some Economic Considerations," *Natural Resources Journal.* Vol. 11, July 1971: 561–589. Reprinted by permission. Spofford analyzed paper recycling, but the economic principle illustrated here applies to recycling of any material.

as we approach a theoretical 100-percent recycling, increasing the proportion of recycled materials becomes difficult and expensive.

In this hypothetical example, the optimum mix of virgin and recycled materials, shown by the minimum point on the total private cost curve, is 40 percent recycled. This, however, neglects environmental and disposal costs. These costs are typically external—not borne by the manufacturer. Environmental costs include air and water pollution from mining and fabrication of primary materials. Disposal costs are paid by consumers or municipalities, who have no control over the proportion of virgin materials the manufacturer uses (although community decisions on recycling may eventually affect industry incentives, as discussed in Chapter 17).

If we include environmental and disposal costs associated with virgin material use, the optimum proportion of recycled materials rises to 70 percent in this example (the minimum point on the total private plus environmental cost curve). If a tax is imposed on primary resources to internalize environmental impact and disposal costs, manufacturers will find that they can minimize overall input costs, including the tax, by using 70 percent recycled material.

We can also examine recycling's private and social equilibrium levels in terms of marginal costs, as shown in Figure 12-10. Profit-maximizing producers will balance the marginal cost of recycling with the marginal cost of virgin materials. If we inter-

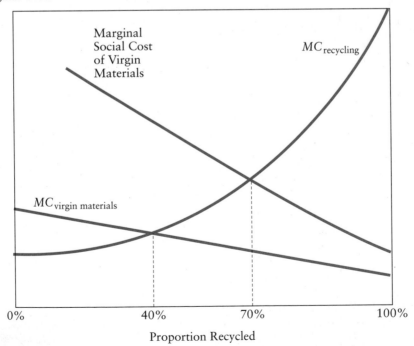

FIGURE 12-10 *Marginal Costs of Recycling*

nalize **external costs** through a tax that reflects the true social costs, their decisions will shift in favor using more recycled materials.

Policies to Promote Recycling

Even without significant policies to internalize environmental costs, metals recycling has generally been on the increase. In the United States, more than 40 percent of metals consumption now comes from recycled scrap (Figure 12-11). Among the metals with the highest annual consumption, aluminum has a 40 percent recycled content, copper about 45 percent, and iron and steel about 55 percent. Lead recycling, at about 70 percent, significantly reduces highly toxic lead residues in the environment (Figure 12-12).

These recycling rates are significant in terms of extending resource lifetimes as well as reducing economic and environmental costs. If global metal recycling rates could be boosted to 50 percent or more, resource lifetimes would be more than double those based on using only virgin materials. In addition, pollution from metal mining and fabrication, as well as problems of waste disposal, would drop significantly.

What kinds of policies would best promote increased recycling of nonrenewables? Policy options for increasing recycling include the following:

- *Altering public policies that encourage rapid resource extraction.* Governments often make mineral resources available for exploitation at extremely low cost. For instance, the U.S. General Mining Act of 1872 offers mineral exploitation rights on government land at a few dollars an acre—a price unchanged in more than a century. Despite efforts to change the law to recapture a portion of

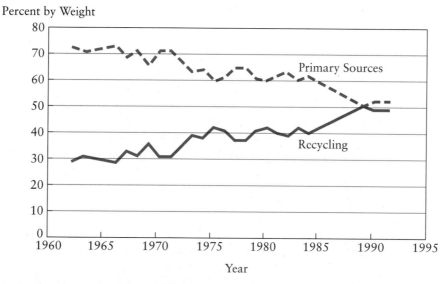

FIGURE 12-11 *U.S. Metals Consumption from Primary and Recycled Sources*
Source: Adapted from Hodges, "Mineral Resources, Environmental Issues, and Land Uses." Reprinted from *Science* 268 (June 2, 1995), p. 1307.

Scrap Metal (percent)

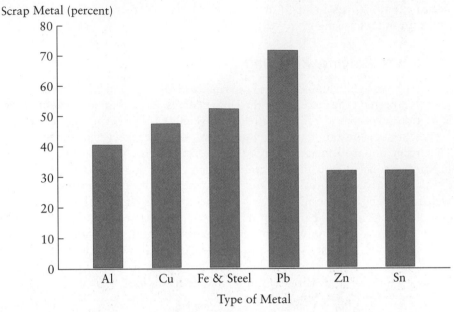

FIGURE 12-12 *Scrap Metal as a Percentage of Total U.S. Consumption*

Source: Adapted from Carol Hodges, "Mineral Resources, Environmental Issues, and Land Uses."
Reprinted from *Science* 268 (June 2, 1995), p. 1307.

resource rents through more adequate royalty payments,[13] mining interests
have been successful in preventing amendments or new rules. In addition to
lost revenues, low prices for valuable resources promote resource overuse and
excessive external and user costs.

- *Imposing taxes on the use of primary resources.* As Figure 12-10 shows, internalizing environmental costs through a tax promotes increased use of recycled
materials. However, because the cost of virgin materials usually represents only
a small portion of the final product cost, a tax alone may have little effect on
consumption patterns.[14]

- *Combining market incentives for recycling with measures to promote the technology and infrastructure needed for recycling systems.* A phenomenon known
as **technological lock-in** leads an industry that has once acquired a certain kind
of plant and machinery—in this case production technology using primary resources—to continue investing in the same kind of plant. Changing over a
whole industry from one production system to another involves heavy costs
and requires a significant amount of initial capital. Tax incentives, support for
research and development of recycling technologies, and **government procurement**—programs that guarantee a certain government demand for recycled materials—can help to jump-start this process.

---

[13]A *royalty* is a payment to the owner of a scarce resource for the use of that resource.

[14]See Ackerman, 1996, Chapter 2.

- *Municipal programs and institutions to promote recycling.* Curbside recycling pickup makes recycling waste materials much easier for consumers and businesses. Communities can often recoup the costs of curbside recycling through sale of recyclable materials, as well as through reduced disposal costs. Even if these programs require a subsidy, they can be justified on environmental grounds. Municipal recycling institutions create the basis for mining the waste stream—obtaining metals and other materials from waste rather than from mineral deposits or other primary resources. Increased supplies of recycled materials will lower their prices, making them more attractive to manufacturers as inputs.
- *Consumer incentives such as **deposit/return systems** or **pay-by-the-bag** rules for collecting nonrecyclable garbage.* These give consumers a financial incentive to recycle and impose a cost for failing to recycle. In general, these consumer incentives prove much more effective if combined with other institutional mechanisms for recycling such as curbside pickup or rules requiring manufacturers to identify different kinds of material to facilitate recycling.

Promoting recycling can be environmentally beneficial both for nonrenewable and renewable resources. Metal recycling reduces the need for ore mining, plastics recycling reduces demand for primary petroleum products, and paper recycling (as we will discuss in Chapter 15) lessens demand pressures on forests.

Energy resources, however, cannot be recycled, and energy is a requirement for both primary resource extraction and recycling. According to the second law of thermodynamics, usable energy is inevitably degraded into waste heat after use.[15]

For this reason, energy deserves special attention in our analysis of resource use. In the following chapters, we will consider the full cycle of resource use, including pollution and waste generation from resource consumption. We will focus our examination on energy resources in Chapter 13, consider the economics of renewable resources in Chapters 14 and 15, and analyze pollution control policies in Chapter 16. In Chapter 17, we will return to the overall cycle of resource use and waste management and the emerging field of **industrial ecology.**

SUMMARY

Nonrenewable resources are limited in supply, but available reserves can be expanded either by new discovery or by increasing recovery of lower-grade deposits. Concerns over exhaustion of major nonrenewable resources have so far not been borne out. Despite growing demand, new discoveries and improved technology have increased available reserves of key minerals.

The economic theory of nonrenewable resource use implies that the net price (price minus extraction costs) of a resource of given quality will rise over time. Profit-maximizing firms will exploit high-grade resources first. As lower-grade resources

---

[15]We can use captured waste energy from electricity production to heat buildings, a process called **cogeneration,** but after a single use this energy, too, escapes to the atmosphere as waste heat.

enter the market, the energy and environmental costs of recovery will tend to rise. Because technological progress and expanded resource availability can offset these price effects, resource price projections remain uncertain.

Global reserves of major minerals vary from great abundance to relatively limited stocks. A broader measure of the reserve base indicates projected lifetimes of several hundred years for some minerals, but only several decades for others.

The mining process generates many toxic wastes and has extensive negative environmental effects on land and water. Internalizing the full environmental cost of resource recovery would encourage a shift to renewable resource use or recycling, rather than increased consumption of virgin resources.

In the United States, more than 40 percent of metal production currently uses recycled scrap. Although complete recycling is impossible, recycling rates for most major metals can increase considerably. In addition to extending nonrenewable resource lifetimes, recycling significantly reduces environmental damage associated with the production of virgin materials.

Public policies to promote recycling include raising royalty payments for access to minerals on public lands, internalizing environmental costs through taxes on primary resource use, developing technology and infrastructure, and government procurement of recycled products.

Although metals, plastics, and paper can be recycled, energy resources cannot be recycled. Energy is an essential input both for primary resource extraction and for recycling, giving energy resources a special importance in the analysis of nonrenewable resource use.

KEY TERMS AND CONCEPTS

backstop resource
choke price
cogeneration
deposit/return systems
economic reserves (economically recoverable reserves)
economic supply (of a resource)
exponential reserve index
external costs
extraction path
government procurement
Hotelling's rule
hypothetical and speculative resources
identified reserves
indicated or inferred reserves
industrial ecology
marginal extraction cost

measured reserves
net price (of a resource)
nonrenewable resources
pay-by-the-bag systems
physical supply (of a resource)
price path
price taker
recycling
reserve base index
resource lifetime
resource rents
resource substitution
resource use profile
static reserve index
subeconomic resources
technological lock-in
throughput
user costs

DISCUSSION QUESTIONS

1. Is scarcity of nonrenewable resources a major problem? What kinds of physical and economic measures are relevant to understanding this issue, and in what ways can some measures be misleading? What do you think will be the main issues relating to nonrenewable use in the twenty-first century?

2. What is the significance of the distribution pattern of mineral ores in the earth's crust (Figure 12-6)? How would mineral extraction economics be affected if minerals show a nonuniform distribution pattern (Figure 12-6b) rather than a uniform pattern (Figure 12-6a)? What would this imply for government policy?

3. Some critics of municipal recycling programs have argued that they are uneconomic because they cost more than ordinary waste disposal. What economic factors would you use to evaluate this argument? What relationship exists between recycling incentives for end-users and incentives for manufacturers to use recycled materials? How can environmental costs be internalized at various stages of the production cycle?

REFERENCES

Ackerman, Frank. *Why Do We Recycle? Markets, Values, and Public Policy*. Washington, D.C.: Island Press, 1996.

Barnett, Harold J., and Chandler Morse. *Scarcity and Growth: The Economics of Natural Resource Availability*. Baltimore: Johns Hopkins Press, 1963.

Berck, Peter, and Michael Roberts. "Natural Resource Prices: Will They Ever Turn Up?" *Journal of Environmental Economics and Management* 31 (1996): 65–78.

Cleveland, Cutler J. "Natural Resource Scarcity and Economic Growth Revisited: Economic and Biophysical Perspectives," Chapter 19 in *Ecological Economics: The Science and Management of Sustainability,* edited by Robert Costanza. New York: Columbia University Press, 1991.

Goeller, H. E., and A. Zucker. "Infinite Resources: The Ultimate Strategy." *Science* 27 (1984): 456–462.

Hartwick, John M., and Nancy D. Olewiler. *The Economics of Natural Resource Use,* 2nd ed. Reading, Mass.: Addison Wesley Longman, 1998.

Hodges, Carol A. "Mineral Resources, Environmental Issues, and Land Use," *Science* 268 (June 2, 1995): 1305–1312.

Meadows, Donnella, et al. *The Limits to Growth*. New York: Universe Books, 1972.

Meadows, Donnella, et al. *Beyond the Limits: Confronting Global Collapse, Envisioning a Sustainable Future*. Post Mills, Vt.: Chelsea Green, 1992.

Skinner, B. J. "A Second Iron Age Ahead?" *American Scientist* 64 (1976): 263.

Slade, Margaret E. "Trends in Natural Resource Commodity Prices: An Analysis of the Time Domain." *Journal of Environmental Economics and Management* 9 (June 1982): 122–137.

Spofford, Walter O., Jr. "Solid Residual Management: Some Economic Considerations." *Natural Resources Journal* 11 (July 1971): 561–589.

Tietenberg, Tom. *Environmental and Natural Resource Economics*, 5th ed. Reading, Mass.: Addison Wesley Longman, 2000.

U.S. Geological Survey. *Mineral Commodity Summaries*. USGS, January 2001.

World Resources Institute. *World Resources 1994-95*. New York and Oxford, England: Oxford University Press, 1994.

Young, John E. *Mining the Earth*. Worldwatch Paper 109. Washington, D.C.: Worldwatch Institute, 1992.

WEB SITES

1. http://www.epa.gov/msw/index.htm The EPA's web site on municipal waste management. It includes information about recycling, pay-as-you-throw programs, and waste management nationally and in each state.
2. http://imcg.wr.usgs.gov/usbmak/c831.html A report detailing the U.S. government classification scheme to measure mineral reserves.
3. http://minerals.usgs.gov/ The web site for the Minerals Resources Program of the U.S. Geological Survey. The site includes links to extensive technical data as well as information about the environmental implications of mining.

CHAPTER FOCUS QUESTIONS

- What special role does energy play in economic systems?
- What are our current energy uses and future energy needs?
- Are we in danger of energy shortages?
- Can we shift from fossil-based energy systems to alternative systems?

CHAPTER **13**

Energy: The Great Transition

Energy and Economic Systems

Energy is fundamental to economic systems and indeed to all life. On deep ocean floors, far below the reach of sunlight, giant tube-worms and other strange life forms cluster around heat vents. Energy from the earth's interior drives their metabolic processes. On the earth's surface, and at shallower ocean levels, all plant life depends on sunlight, and all animal life depends directly or indirectly on plants.[1] Our own equally critical need for energy is to some degree camouflaged in a modern economy. Measured in terms of gross domestic product, energy resources represent only about 5 percent of economic output. Yet the other 95 percent depends absolutely on energy inputs.

In less developed, agrarian economies the dependence is more evident. People's basic need for food calories is, of course, a need for energy input. Traditional agriculture is essentially a method of capturing **solar energy** for human use. Solar energy captured in firewood meets other basic needs for home heating and cooking.

---

[1]The few plants that can live without direct sunlight make use of soil nutrients deposited by the decay of other plants.

As economies develop and become more complex, energy needs increase greatly. Historically, as supplies of firewood and other **biomass** proved insufficient to support growing economies, people turned to **hydropower** (also a form of stored solar energy), then to coal, and then to oil and natural gas as major energy sources. In the past half-century, nuclear power has entered the energy mix.

Each stage of economic development has been accompanied by a characteristic energy transition from one major fuel source to another. Today, fossil fuels—coal, oil and natural gas—are by far the dominant energy source in industrial economies. The twenty-first century will see a further great transition in energy sources. The nature and speed of this transition is a fundamental issue in the relationship of the economy to the environment.

From the point of view of economic analysis, the most important factor affecting the use of energy is its market price. Distortion of this price, for example by government subsidies, leads to inefficient energy use. A major goal of energy policy, in this view, should be to avoid or to correct such distortions. But we must also consider the need to internalize externalities such as the impacts of pollution and the user costs of resource depletion, as well as the environmental advantages of conservation and renewable energy sources. The existence of positive or negative externalities may justify government subsidy or tax policies directed at particular energy sectors.

We can also take a broader, more ecologically oriented, perspective on energy. Theorists of the ecological economics school see energy as fundamental to economic development, and focus on a crucial distinction between the **stock** of nonrenewable fossil fuel reserves and the renewable **flow** of solar energy.[2] In this perspective, the period of intensive fossil fuel use that began in the nineteenth century amounts to a one-time, unrepeatable bonanza—the rapid exploitation of a limited stock of high-quality resources.

Because so much of the **capital stock** and **energy infrastructure** of modern economic systems rely on fossil fuel use, any transition away from fossil-fuel dependence will involve massive restructuring and new investment. The considerable economic implications of this justify a special focus on energy use as a central economic and environmental issue.

Economic and Ecological Analyses of Energy

What makes energy special? To answer this question we turn to the physical laws of thermodynamics. The first law of thermodynamics states that matter and energy can be neither created nor destroyed. This means that all physical processes, including all life processes and all economic systems, merely move or transform matter and energy. But these processes are also subject to the second law of thermodynamics.

---

[2]For the classic assertion of energy's critical role in the economy, see Georgescu-Roegen, 1971. An overview of differing analytical perspectives on energy can be found in Krishnan et al., 1995, pp. 169–224.

The second law relates to the concept of **entropy.** Entropy is defined as a measure of *unavailable* energy—energy in a form that is not available to do work. The second law states that entropy increases in all physical processes. The best way to grasp entropy's significance is through an example.

Consider the process of burning a lump of coal. The coal in its original state contains available or free energy. In this form it is said to have low entropy. Once it is burned, the energy is dissipated. According to the first law, the energy is not destroyed, but it is now in an unavailable or bound form. In ordinary terms, the coal has been transformed into ashes and waste heat. In this form, it has high entropy—and is no longer a potential energy source.

All economic processes, as well as all life processes, transform low entropy inputs into high entropy waste products in accordance with the second law. Therefore all economic processes are limited by the availability of low entropy resources. These come in two forms: stocks of nonrenewable terrestrial resources such as fossil fuels, and a flow of renewable energy from the sun. Our current economic activities depend heavily on the use of limited stocks. Ultimately we must adapt our economic system to use the flow of solar energy, or **solar flux.**

Another way of looking at the concept of entropy offers further insights into energy use. We can consider entropy as a measure of *disorder* in a system. The coal in our previous example represents a highly ordered form of matter and energy, whereas the ashes and waste heat from its burning are a more disorderly form. Thus we see a correspondence between orderliness and available energy. As entropy and disorder increase in any environment, that environment becomes less useful to support life. Wastes and pollution represent a high-entropy state of matter and energy. According to the second law, all life processes and all economic systems must necessarily generate increasing amounts of high-entropy wastes while consuming low-entropy resources.

We can see, then, two kinds of problems associated with energy use. One is the depletion of limited stocks of energy resources. Another is the inevitable generation of wastes and pollution through energy use. Recall from Chapter 1 the expanded circular flow diagram (Figure 1-2 on p. 8), which showed cycles of resources and environmental services, but a one-way flow, or **throughput** of energy. Whereas labor, capital, renewable resources, and some recyclable resources can be regenerated through the expanded circular flow, energy cannot. In this sense energy throughput, constrained both by resource availability and by the pollution arising from its use, represents a fundamental factor determining levels of economic activity.[3]

Economic Perspectives on Energy Supply

We can also analyze energy's role in resource supply using more conventional economics theory. In Chapter 12 we noted that the **economic supply** of nonrenewable resources differs from the **physical supply.** The reserves of any given nonrenewable

---

[3]The concept of throughput, introduced by Georgescu-Roegen, is discussed extensively in Daly, 1991.

resource are fixed in physical terms, but the economically recoverable proportion of these reserves varies with changing prices and technology.

Energy reserves have a specific importance in this process because energy is essential to the recovery of other resources. For example, if we use up high-grade copper ores, recovering copper from lower-grade ore will generally require more energy per unit of copper recovered. Recalling our discussion of the economics of nonrenewable resource extraction in Chapter 12, we can see that so long as the marginal cost of extra energy does not drive the price of copper above what the market will bear, firms will keep bringing lower-grade ores into production.

The following equation links energy's price and productivity to the price of a nonrenewable resource such as copper:

$$P_E/MP_{EC} = P_C$$

where

P_E = Price of energy
P_C = Price of copper
MP_{EC} = Marginal productivity of energy in producing copper.

This relationship implies that more copper can be obtained from lower-grade ores (with lower MP_{EC}) if either the price of energy falls or the price of copper rises.[4] An abundance of low-cost energy will make it possible to obtain increasing quantities of all other resources, in essence without limit (or at least until the vast quantities of low-grade ores have been exhausted). Also, if copper prices rise, producers have an incentive to increase recycling of copper, which will extend the effective resource lifetime, using energy for recycling rather than for primary production.

However, the same logic does not hold for energy itself. For one thing, energy is by nature nonrecyclable. In addition, MP_{EE}, the productivity of energy in producing energy—sometimes called *energy return on investment* (EROI)—has an inherent limit.[5] If we replace copper output with energy output in the equation above, it simplifies to

$$P_E/MP_{EE} = P_E \qquad \text{or simply} \qquad MP_{EE} = 1$$

This is the theoretical limit for energy production: when recovering an extra barrel of oil requires a barrel of oil as energy input, net production of oil is neither economically nor physically possible—as much oil will be used up as is produced. Most current energy production is far from this margin, but the EROI or MP_{EE} is close to 1 for some forms of energy, such as ethanol produced in high-energy-input agriculture.

---

[4]The equation can be understood in more commonsense terms by noting that the left-hand side represents the cost of the additional energy required to produce one additional unit of copper.

[5]For a discussion of the EROI concept, see Cleveland, "Natural Resource Scarcity and Economic Growth Revisited: Economic and Biophysical Perspectives," 1991.

Political forces such as effective farm lobbies, or the desire for energy self-sufficiency, have led countries including the United States and Brazil to mandate ethanol use. But unless ethanol is produced from agricultural wastes, it is difficult to justify this policy on the grounds of saving energy, because producing it uses almost as much energy as it provides.

Abundant available energy reserves are essential for recovering nonrenewable resources and for economic production in general. Limitations on other resource supplies can be overcome—provided we have enough energy. Also, as we saw in Chapter 11, the output of renewable resources such as productive soils can be boosted by extra energy inputs. Agricultural and industrial system productivity depends on the continued supply of high-quality energy. Although we can seek out alternative energy sources, we cannot evade the laws of thermodynamics, which tell us that the scale of economic activity is limited by available energy supplies.

Economic and Thermodynamic Efficiency

This unique relationship between energy and economic activity can lead to significant tension between the concepts of **economic efficiency** and **thermodynamic efficiency.** As we know, economic efficiency is a central goal of economic theory and policy. But paradoxically, increased economic efficiency can lead to lower thermodynamic efficiency—more energy use to obtain a given output. The availability of cheap energy creates an economic incentive to shift toward energy-intensive production methods. Rather than conserving energy, which would be thermodynamically efficient, low prices encourage individuals and firms to substitute energy for labor and capital.

For example, it is much more energy efficient to walk or ride a bicycle for short trips. But if gas is cheap, many people will choose to drive instead, burning gallons of gas to move tons of steel in order to save a small amount of labor time. From a strictly economic point of view, nothing is wrong with this—the consumer has made the rational decision that he or she prefers paying a small price for gas to making the effort to walk or bicycle. But this kind of decision, multiplied millions of times, can significantly affect a society's energy consumption.

The same kind of logic affects the economic behavior of business. Commercial farms won't employ relatively costly labor if they can do the same job at lower cost with energy-using machinery. Over time, more firms will shift to more energy-intensive methods if these are more profitable. And as high-grade ores are used up, one strategy for keeping productivity high in resource-extracting industries is to use more energy. Some studies suggest that increased energy use per unit output is a common trend in many resource-based industries and agriculture.[6]

The dependence of modern economic systems on cheap energy was dramatically demonstrated during the 1970s, when sudden increases in oil prices caused economic crisis, inflation, and recession throughout the world economy. Prices rose in this case

---

[6]See Cleveland, 1991 and Figure 9-1, p. 162.

not because of natural shortages but through successful action by a powerful **cartel** of oil-producing nations.

By acting together to restrict supply, the OPEC[7] cartel quadrupled world oil prices. For a time, this focused much attention on the importance of energy and the need for conservation and alternative energy sources. However, as the cartel's power waned over time, oil prices fell and efforts to promote energy-saving investment were abandoned.

Could the energy crises of the 1970s recur? Low oil prices and abundant supplies during the 1990s encouraged complacency, but prices rose again in 2000–2001. Again, this was no global shortage of oil, but reflective of the OPEC cartel's increasing power, based on controlling a large share of global production.

As we look ahead to the longer term, we must consider the changing picture of both energy supply and demand. On the supply side, fossil fuel energy reserves have global limits, as well as much more stringent regional limits. On the demand side, global energy demand is steadily increasing. Although total demand in the currently developed economies is fairly stable, almost all developing economies show rapid rates of growth in energy demand. We can assess future economic and environmental implications of global energy use with a more specific look at current trends and future resource availability.

Energy Trends and Projections

Global energy use has grown rapidly (Figure 13-1). All fossil fuel use has expanded steadily, particularly oil consumption. Currently more than 80 percent of the world's energy comes from fossil fuel sources. If we consider commercial energy sources only, about 85 percent comes from fossil fuels.

Hydroelectric power and nuclear power are the major nonfossil fuel sources of industrial energy. Alternative sources such as wind, biomass, and solar power currently supply only a small fraction of total energy needs in industrialized countries (Figure 13-2). In many developing nations, biomass remains a significant portion of total energy supply, but in most of these countries commercial energy demand is swiftly increasing.

Crude oil is the largest single energy source, followed by coal and natural gas. Hydro and nuclear power contribute about 7 percent each, and biofuels (primarily in the developing world) about 13 percent. Energy uses are divided between transportation (24 percent), industry (38 percent), and residential and commercial (38 percent) as shown in Figure 13-2.

We can expect the continued steep upward slope of total world energy demand since 1950 to continue. World energy consumption in 2000 was close to double that of 1970, and World Bank projections show future world energy demand approaching another doubling by about 2030, with almost all the increase in presently developing

---

[7]Organization of Petroleum Exporting Countries.

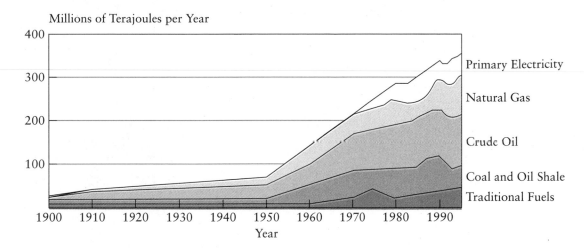

FIGURE 13-1 *World Energy Consumption*
Source: Meadows, 1992; U.S. Department of Energy, 1999, 2000.

nations. This would still leave per capita consumption in presently developing nations at less than one-third of what presently developed nations consume (Figure 13-3).

How will we meet this massive increase in world energy demand? Standard projections see fossil fuels mostly supplying the increase. "High-growth" energy use projections for 2050 by the World Energy Council and the International Institute for Applied Systems Analysis show huge increases in fossil fuel use, as well as in nuclear power (Figure 13-4a).

This is technically possible based on available fossil fuel reserves. The World Resources Institute has estimated that in 1990 about 40 years' proved reserves of oil remained, 50 years' supply of natural gas, and more than 200 years of coal reserves.[8] But is this energy future either economically feasible or environmentally desirable? An alternative projection, relying on conservation and greater use of renewable sources, shows little or no increase in fossil fuel use by 2050 (Figure 13-4b). A central issue is the future of world oil production, since oil is now the predominant fossil fuel.

Patterns of Energy Use

According to a theory advanced by petroleum geologist M. King Hubbert in 1956, the typical pattern of energy resource use over time resembles a bell curve. In the early period of resource exploitation, prices fall, discovery and production expand, and consumption grows exponentially. Eventually limited supplies and rising resource recovery costs force a turnaround, and consumption starts to fall.

---

[8]World Resources Institute, 1994, p. 169.

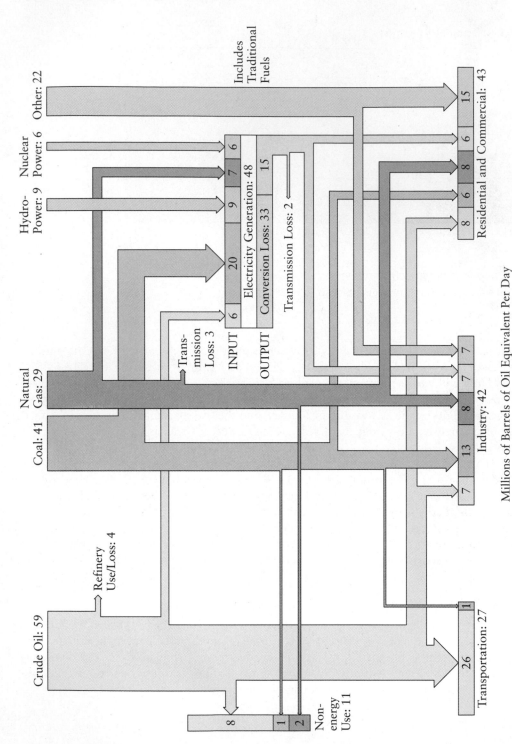

FIGURE 13-2 *World Energy Flows*

Source: Davis, 1990. Based on illustration by Slim Films. Reprinted by permission of Slim Films. (Since 1990, the share of coal in world energy supply has declined, and those of natural gas, hydro, and nuclear have increased. For current figures see http://www.eia.gov/.)

(a) Total Consumption

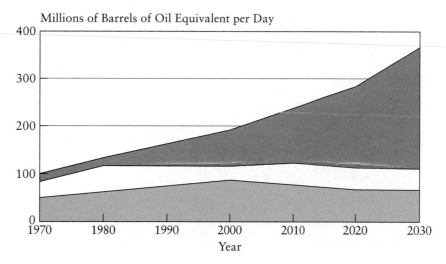

(b) Per Capita Consumption

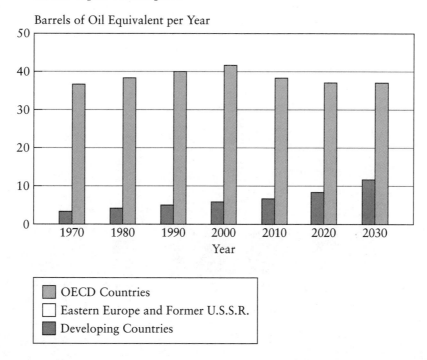

FIGURE 13-3 *Past and Projected Energy Consumption, 1970–2030*

Source: Adapted from *World Development Report 1992* by World Bank, copyright 1992 by the International Bank for Reconstruction and Development/The World Bank. Used by permission of Oxford University Press, Inc.

(a) World Total Primary Energy Consumption — High Growth; Ample Oil and Gas

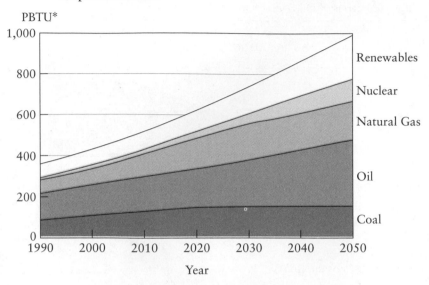

(b) World Total Primary Energy Consumption — Ecologically Driven; New Renewables with Nuclear Phaseout

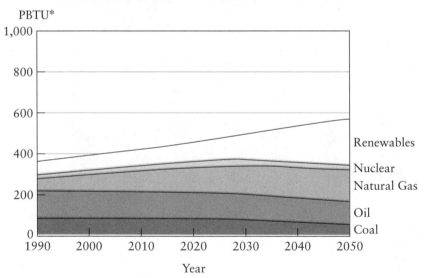

*PBTU = Quadrillion British Thermal Units

FIGURE 13-4 *Projections of World Energy Use to 2050 by Fuel Source*

Source: International Institute for Applied Systems (IIASA) and the World Energy Council (WEC), 1998.

As Figure 13-5 shows, the **Hubbert curve** projection has worked out well for U.S. oil production. Oil output in the continental United States peaked by 1980, and has been declining since then. If U.S. oil production continues to follow the Hubbert model, reserves will be essentially exhausted by 2040. Much the same pattern applies to natural gas production.

The picture for world oil production is a little different. Through about 1980, world oil production followed the steadily increasing pattern that represents the up-slope of a Hubbert curve (Figure 13-6). After the sharp oil price increases of the 1970s, global production and consumption of oil leveled off for about 20 years. According to the original Hubbert curve pattern, world oil production would have peaked about 2000, but this prolonged slowdown in consumption has extended the projected lifetime of world oil reserves.

World coal reserves are plentiful, and at present consumption rates would last for at least 200 years. Supply constraints are thus not an issue for coal use. Far more important are the environmental implications of expanded coal use. Coal mining, especially strip-mining, often generates significant environmental damage, and coal-burning is a major contributor both to regional acid rain and smog problems and to global carbon dioxide accumulation.

The Future of World Oil Production

Because oil currently supplies nearly 40 percent of global commercial energy needs (see Figure 13-2), oil supply and demand represent a crucial element of the future energy picture. Recent analyses indicate a renewed concern with future oil limits. The In-

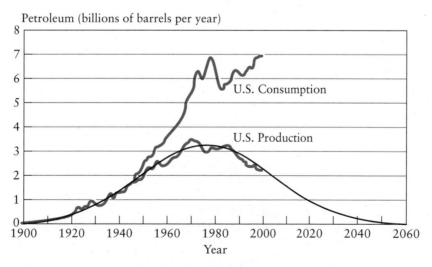

FIGURE 13-5 *The Hubbert Curve and Actual U.S. Oil Production*
Source: Gever, 1991; U.S. Department of Energy, 2000.

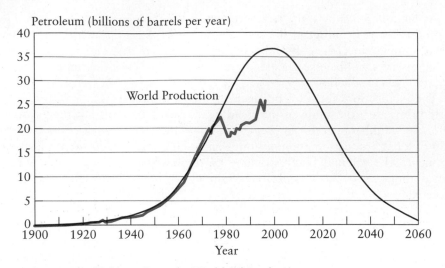

FIGURE 13-6 *Hubbert Curve for World Oil Production*
Sources: Gever, 1991; U.S. Department of Energy.

ternational Energy Agency projects a resumption of the Hubbert curve pattern of rising oil demand.[9] If such demand increases occur, the production curve peak, at which supply constraints start to choke off consumption, will occur within the next few decades. James MacKenzie uses a range of figures for **estimated ultimately recoverable supplies (EUR)** of oil to project peaking sometime between 2007 and 2020 (Figure 13-7).

Petroleum geologists Colin Campbell and Jean Laherrère argue that, unlike the 1970s energy crisis,

> The next oil crunch will not be so temporary. Our analysis of the discovery and production of oil fields around the world suggests that within the next decade, the supply of conventional oil will be unable to keep up with the demand.
>
> This conclusion contradicts the picture one gets from industry reports, which boasted of 1,020 billion barrels of oil (Gbo) in "proved" reserves at the start of 1998. Dividing that figure by the current production rate of about 23.6 Gbo a year might suggest that crude oil could remain plentiful and cheap for 43 more years—probably longer, because official charts show reserves growing.[10]

According to Campbell and Laherrère, optimistic official estimates suffer from three major errors. One is accepting inflated estimates of "proved" reserves provided by governments of former Soviet countries and others who may have political reasons to exaggerate their holdings. A second error is ignoring probable growth in demand. The third is omitting the well-established economic principle of **diminishing returns,**

---

[9]International Energy Agency, 2000.

[10]Campbell and Laherrère, 1998.

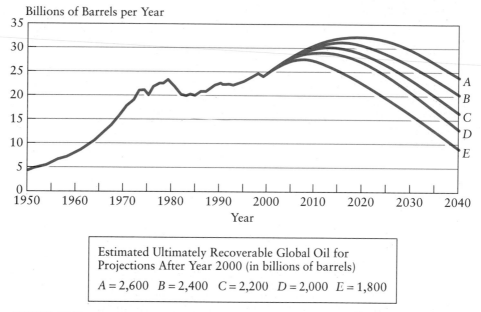

FIGURE 13-7 *Actual and Projected World Oil Production, 1950–2040*

Source: Adapted from MacKenzie, *Oil as a Finite Resource: When Is Global Production Likely to Peak?*, Washington, D.C.: World Resources Institute, 1996. Reprinted by permission of World Resources Institute.

which tells us that as oil fields are exploited, the per-unit costs of obtaining the remaining oil will rise. Campbell and Laherrère update Hubbert's analysis to project a peak in world oil production by 2010.

What would a peak in conventional oil production in the not-too-distant future imply? As we know from Chapter 12, an environment of rising prices would accompany this change in supply/demand balance. This in turn would encourage substitution of other fuels for oil.

A rise in use of natural gas would be likely (natural gas can be liquefied for use as a transport fuel in addition to its use in domestic heating and industrial power generation). The expected lifetime of natural gas reserves, however, is not much longer than that of oil reserves. It would also be possible to obtain oil from tar sands and oil shale deposits, although recovery from these sources, like coal strip-mining, has potentially high environmental costs.

A further issue with future oil production concerns the regional distribution rather than the total quantity of reserves. Oil reserves are disproportionately concentrated in the Middle East, and natural gas reserves are predominantly located in the Middle East and former Soviet countries. This gives rise to both economic and security concerns for countries lacking oil supplies or for countries like the United States with declining oil production and increasing import dependence (as shown by the gap between U.S. consumption and production in Figure 13-5).

As production in oil fields outside the Middle East starts to decline, the concentration of a larger proportion of the remaining oil production in a limited number of countries increases the likelihood of a successful cartel. This suggests that an economic infrastructure that relies heavily on oil could be vulnerable:

> . . . The growing dependence on imported oil in general and Persian Gulf oil in particular has several potentially serious implications for the nation's economic and national security. First, the United States is expected to be importing nearly 60 percent of its oil by [2006], with roughly a third of that oil coming from the Persian Gulf. Our trade deficit in oil is expected to double, to $100 billion a year, by that time—a large and continual drag on our economic health. To the extent that the Gulf's recapture of the dominant share of the global oil market will make price increases more likely, the U.S. economy is at risk.[11]

The Economics of Alternative Energy Futures

Two factors could dramatically alter the projections discussed above. On the demand side, significant energy conservation and increased end-use efficiency could considerably lower projections of demand growth. On the supply side, the renewable resources that currently provide only a small proportion of the world's energy needs (Figure 13-2) could become much more significant. However, these changes would require a combination of market price signals and government energy policies promoting energy efficiency and renewables.

Technologies for highly efficient energy use could achieve dramatic reductions in energy consumption with little or no effect on living standards. In most developed nations, energy use per dollar of GDP has declined steadily with technological progress and a shift to a more service-based economy. Developing nations have the opportunity to take advantage of existing technologies for more efficient and less environmentally damaging energy systems. Energy demand will certainly grow in the developing world, but this does not necessarily mean reliance on inefficient or highly polluting sources.[12]

Simply by using the most efficient known technologies, energy use in developed nations could be cut by up to 50 percent with no loss in living standard.[13] If this were to occur, global energy demand would be almost flat through 2020. The percentage of global energy use attributable to (presently) developed nations would decline from 70 to 35 percent, while (presently) developing nations could increase energy use from 30 to 65 percent of the global total. This would provide for the inevitable growth in population and allow a modest rise in per capita energy consumption (and a much bigger rise in living standards) among presently developing nations.

This scenario has many obvious advantages from an environmental point of view. All forms of pollution associated with energy use would drop, including atmospheric

---

[11]Romm and Curtis, 1996.

[12]See Reddy and Goldemberg, 1990.

[13]Intergovernmental Panel on Climate Change, 1996.

Windmills in San Gorgonio Pass, Palm Springs, California. California's energy policies encourage development of renewable energy sources.

carbon dioxide accumulation. Countries with limited domestic energy sources would benefit from greater self-sufficiency and less import dependence. And lifetimes of limited oil and other fossil fuels reserves would be extended significantly.

The Central Role of Energy Prices

Given these advantages, what stands in the way of a high-energy-efficiency future? The central economic issue is low current prices for energy. Even though increasing energy efficiency by a factor of 2 or more may be technically feasible, it is not necessarily economically profitable. This may seem strange, but recall our earlier distinction between economic and thermodynamic efficiency. So long as energy prices remain low, energy-intensive methods may remain the optimal economic strategy.

Significant costs accompany developing and installing energy efficient technologies. Why should a business firm bother to take on these costs if their current energy bills are already low? Why should a homeowner or car driver worry much about furnace and appliance efficiency or gas mileage if oil and gas cost only a dollar a gallon or so? We choose to spend our time, effort, and money in areas that bring us the greatest return. If energy costs are low, other areas of our lives and businesses are more likely to receive attention, and attract economic investment.

Energy pricing is equally central to developing nonfossil fuel energy sources. Costs of solar and renewable energy sources have declined rapidly since 1980 (Figure 13-8). Some alternative power sources, such as wind and biomass energy, have

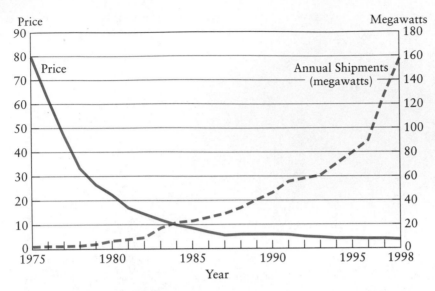

FIGURE 13-8 *World Photovoltaic Shipments and Prices 1975–1998*
Source: Worldwatch Institute Database, 1999.

reached the margin of competitiveness in the mass market, but in only a few instances have they crossed that margin into large-scale commercial feasibility. Solar power is competitive for hot water heating, but not yet for power supply. In addition to price, other institutional issues have been important in preventing alternative energy sources from gaining a significant market share.

The extensive infrastructure investment in fossil fuels—existing power stations, machinery, and transportation systems—creates considerable momentum for continued fossil fuel use. In addition, extensive direct and indirect government subsidies support fossil fuel industries. Worldwide, many governments artificially lower energy prices in order to promote industrial growth. Also, in many cases centralized power authorities are heavily committed to investment in standard coal or oil powered plants, and state regulatory policy makes it difficult for competitors to enter the market.

From an economic point of view, subsidizing fossil fuels is bad policy. As we saw in Chapter 3, the economic case for a subsidy must rest on external benefits associated with product use. But fossil fuels provide few external benefits and incur many external costs.

Low fossil fuel prices can properly be viewed as a **market failure,** omitting the external costs of health and environmental damages as well as military expenditures associated with maintaining access to oil. A rationale exists for internalizing user costs imposed by exhausting prime fossil fuel deposits, and for carbon taxes to reflect the long-term external costs of atmospheric carbon dioxide accumulation. Internalizing all these costs would shift the competitive balance between fossil fuels and renewables strongly in favor of renewables.

Policies for Future Energy Development

What kinds of government policies are most important to energy development? The answers differ somewhat for industrialized and developing nations. Industrialized nations already have an extensive energy infrastructure and strong momentum for continued fossil fuel use. Major infrastructure investments often have lifetimes of 50 years or more.

Large coal- or oil-fired power plants, electric grids reaching even remote areas, extensive highway systems, as well as cities designed for road traffic and energy-inefficient buildings dependent on fossil-fueled heating systems—all these encourage the continued use of presently cheap fossil fuels. Nonetheless, significant opportunities exist for modified or new infrastructure oriented towards conservation and alternative energy.

Historically, electric power generation has been treated as a regulated monopoly. This often leads to a perverse system of incentives whereby utilities are rewarded (with rate increases) for adding central power-station generating capacity and at the same time discouraged from conservation or efficiency initiatives that would lower power use. The barriers to entry in this system also make it difficult for more efficient producers and small-scale power generators to enter the market.

Regulators could create a rate structure that rewards utilities for conservation and requires them to purchase power from small producers. Recent emphasis, however, has been on **deregulation** of electric power.

Proponents of deregulation cite several favorable environmental effects. Market competition forces large, centralized power stations that use coal, oil, or nuclear fuel to compete with smaller power producers. Market incentives also favor the installation of highly efficient natural gas turbine **cogeneration** technology.

Gas turbine plants have significantly higher conversion efficiencies than conventional coal- or oil-fired plants—that is, they convert a higher proportion of the chemical energy of natural gas into electricity. Cogeneration means that the heat produced in the process is captured and used, rather than released as waste heat. Thus these plants combine thermodynamic and economic efficiency. Nitrogen oxide emissions drop by 90 percent, and carbon dioxide by 60 percent. Under deregulation, these new highly efficient plants will tend to replace older, less-efficient plants.

The outlook for renewable energy under deregulation is less clear. As Figure 13-8 shows, prices for solar and renewable sources have fallen toward the margin of competitiveness, but in most cases have not crossed this margin. To gain a significant market share, these sources need an extra boost in the form of subsidies, tax rebates, or content standards. U.S. deregulation laws have mainly been introduced at the state level, and they vary in structure, but many include some provisions to encourage use of renewables.

On the demand side, there is a possible conflict between deregulation and conservation. One goal of deregulation is to provide lower prices to consumers; but lower prices encourage higher usage and more energy-intensive technology. In some cases energy suppliers may offer customers a "package" of power supply and energy-saving

13-1   Nuclear Power: Coming or Going?

In the 1950s nuclear power was promoted as a safe, clean, and cheap source of energy. Proponents of nuclear power stated that it would be "too cheap to meter," and predicted that nuclear power would provide about one-quarter of the world's commercial energy and most of the world's electricity by 2000 (Miller, 1998).

Currently, nuclear power provides only about 7 percent of the world's energy and 17 percent of the world's electricity. Most forecasts predict a decline in nuclear energy production in the coming decades. No new nuclear power plants have been ordered in the United States since 1978. Among developed countries, only Japan, Korea, and possibly Finland are currently planning new nuclear plants.

Despite this projected decline, some have proposed a renewed expansion of nuclear power. Surprisingly, one of the touted benefits of nuclear power is environmental. Unlike fossil fuels, generating electricity using nuclear power does not emit carbon dioxide, the primary greenhouse gas. Is nuclear power an industry headed for extinction or is it entering a renaissance?

Accidents such as those at Three Mile Island and Chernobyl created significant public concern over the safety of nuclear power. These concerns remain—the results of a May 2001 Gallup survey indicate that 46 percent of Americans feel nuclear power is too dangerous even if it would solve the country's energy problems. Recent nuclear technologies such as pebble-bed reactors and passive safety features reduce the chance of a major nuclear accident, but the problem of storage of long-lived nuclear wastes is still unsolved.

The main weakness of nuclear power is economic. Existing nuclear power plants have lower operating costs than coal or natural gas plants, and new nuclear technologies promise even lower production costs. However, building new nuclear power plants requires considerable capital costs. Recent analysis by the International Energy Agency (IEA, 2001) estimates the capital costs of a modern nuclear power plant at $2,000 per kw, compared to $1,200 per kw for coal and $500 per kw for a combined-cycle gas plant. The IEA notes that "high capital cost is the single most important economic factor weakening the prospects for new nuclear power plants."

Nuclear power has benefitted from substantial government subsidies. Between 1974 and 1998, the U.S. government spent over $40 billion (in 1999 dollars) for research and development of nuclear technology. Another important subsidy is provided by the Price-Anderson Act, which limits the liability of nuclear power operators in the event of an accident. About half of all government-financed energy research and development in developed countries is currently directed towards nuclear power.

(continued on following page)

Electricity markets worldwide are in the process of deregulation. Subject to market forces and declining subsidies, nuclear power's revival may never materialize. The IEA states that "nuclear power must increasingly face the future on its economic merits and drawbacks as judged by electricity markets." New nuclear power plants may simply be too expensive to compete in the market.

SOURCES

International Energy Agency. IEA, 2001. Nuclear Power in OECD Countries.
Miller, G. Tyler, Jr. *Living in the Environment,* 10th edition. Belmont, Calif.: Wadsworth Publishing Company, 1998.
The Economist. "Special Report, Nuclear Power: A Renaissance That May Not Come." May 19, 2001, pp. 24–26.

technology. For instance, a supplier could offer a long-term contract including installation of efficient lighting and heating systems as well as power supply. The consumer's net cost would be less than the energy costs of a less-efficient system. However, such comprehensive power-and-conservation service may or may not thrive in a deregulated marketplace. So long as competition focuses primarily on lowering the price of delivered energy, incentives to conserve will be weak.

Other important policies that will affect the course of energy development include the following:

- *Subsidy shifts*—removing direct and hidden subsidies for fossil fuels and providing subsidies or tax incentives for alternative energy development. Such a shift is economically justifiable based on the external costs of fossil fuels and the relative environmental and security benefits of renewables. Temporary subsidies may help new technologies achieve sufficient market share and **economies of scale** to become commercially viable. Many renewable technologies can achieve significant cost reductions with increases in production volume. In the United States, California's energy policy has given renewables sufficient initial support to make them a significant part of that state's energy mix and to lower overall costs closer to commercially competitive levels.
- *Infrastructure investment.* Transportation—primarily automobile transport—has long been a major government spending area. Improving public transit and urban design to allow light rail and bicycle transportation, as well as "clean" fleets of buses running on alternative fuels, can contribute to significant reductions in energy use and pollution in this sector. High-speed inter-city rail can be nearly as fast as air transport, and is much more energy-efficient.

- **Research and development (R&D)**, including government sponsored research and tax policies that encourage corporate R&D in energy efficiency and renewables. Cutting-edge technologies that have high efficiencies and low to zero pollution, such as fuel cells, wind turbines, and photovoltaics, have begun to penetrate commercial markets, despite a relatively slim share of government R&D support, which has concentrated on fossil fuels and nuclear technology.
- **Efficiency standards.** High implicit consumer discount rates (Box 13-2) often mean that buildings, appliances, and vehicles remain energy inefficient even when efficient technologies are available and economical. Mandatory regulations such as building codes and fuel efficiency standards can help correct this market failure. Industries have historically resisted imposition of such regulations—for example, the automobile industry has always fought fuel efficiency standards. A compromise approach is mandatory **efficiency labeling,** common for appliances such as dishwashers and refrigerators. This provides better information to consumers—however, so long as energy prices remain low it may be ineffective in promoting a shift to use of higher-efficiency products.

Energy Policy Options for Developing Nations

The policies outlined above have particular importance for developing nations because of their rapidly expanding energy sectors. Developing nations are still creating energy infrastructure and have the opportunity to choose a different energy path from that of industrialized nations. As cities grow, for example, they can favor designs and plans for public transit and bicycle use over automobile-dependent transport systems.

Many developing nations are particularly well situated to take advantage of solar energy potential, both because of abundant sunshine and because the solar installation can substitute for the expansion of the electric grid to remote areas. Solar electric systems may be economically advantageous for villages not currently connected to a national grid. When the avoided costs of extending the grid are taken into account, solar systems are cost-effective.

Policies that are especially relevant to the energy sectors of developing nations:

- Eliminate widespread energy subsidies that primarily benefit fossil fuels development. These subsidies have been justified as a way of promoting industrialization, but waste scarce government funds and increase import dependence for nonoil-producing countries.
- Eliminate tariff systems that raise the cost of efficient equipment and technologies; facilitate technology transfer and developing technical expertise in energy efficiency and renewable technologies.
- Institute regulatory reform to break up powerful electricity generating boards whose policies strongly favor construction of centralized coal- and oil-fired or nuclear facilities.[14]

---

[14]Policies summarized from Kats, "Achieving Sustainability in Energy Use in Developing Countries." Chapter 9 in *Making Development Sustainable*, edited by Holmberg, 1992.

13-2	**Implicit Discount Rates and Energy Efficiency**

A major problem in increasing appliance energy efficiency arises from *high implicit discount rates*. Suppose that a consumer can purchase a standard refrigerator for $400 or an energy-efficient model for $600. The energy efficient model will save the consumer $10 per month in energy costs. From an economic point of view, we can say that the return on the extra $200 invested in the efficient model is $15 × 12 = $180/year or 60 percent.

Anyone who was offered a stock market investment that would bring a guaranteed 60 percent annual return would consider this a tremendous opportunity. But the refrigerator buyer will likely turn down the chance to make this fantastic return because she or he will place more weight on the immediate decision to spend $400 versus $600, and therefore choose the cheaper model. We could say that the consumer is implicitly using a discount rate of greater than 60 percent to make this judgment—a consumer behavior that is difficult to justify economically, yet it is very common.

In the long term, **solar hydrogen** systems might allow tropical countries in effect to export sunlight. Hydrogen can be produced with photovoltaic or wind power by water electrolysis. It can be used in fuel cells to generate power without the pollutants and carbon dioxide associated with fossil fuel use.[15]

Rather than becoming dependent on imported fossil fuels, countries with abundant sunlight could both supply their own energy needs and become net exporters. Technically feasible, this nonpolluting energy system would require a shift in the relative costs of fossil and renewable energy to become commercially viable.

The vast projected growth in energy demand in developing nations increases the need for a transition to renewable energy sources in the twenty-first century. Current government policies as well as temporary abundance and low oil and coal prices, however, keep us on a fossil fuel-dependent path.

Local and regional pollution from fossil fuel use, along with security considerations, may impel countries toward stronger policies promoting alternative paths. A decisive issue may well be global climate change implications of continued and expanded fossil fuel use. We address this topic, the subject of extensive research efforts and much controversy, in Chapter 18.

SUMMARY

Energy is an input fundamental to economic systems. Current economic activity depends overwhelmingly on nonrenewable fossil fuels including oil, coal,

---

[15]See Dunn, 2001, for an extensive discussion of hydrogen energy systems.

and natural gas. Renewable sources such as hydroelectric, wind, and solar power currently provide less than 10 percent of the energy supply in industrialized economies.

The laws of thermodynamics provide a basis for understanding the special role of energy. Energy can be used to expand the production of other nonrenewable resources, or to recycle them, but energy itself cannot be recycled. High-quality energy sources are essential to economic growth. Efficient energy use is desirable, but cheap energy often encourages thermodynamically inefficient uses.

World energy demand has expanded rapidly and is projected to double by 2030. Oil supplies are sufficient for several decades, but production could peak within a decade or two. World oil reserves are disproportionately located in the Middle East, and growing demand for limited supplies may strengthen producer cartels. Coal, which is more abundant, is often associated with significant environmental damage.

Alternative energy sources could grow in importance in the future. Prices for alternative sources such as wind and solar power have declined. Increased efficiency and energy conservation have great potential, but existing infrastructure and government subsidies continue to favor fossil fuel use. Policies that could promote a shift to alternative sources include eliminating fossil fuel subsidies, promoting research and development, and imposing efficiency standards.

Developing nations can reduce fossil fuel dependence by using renewable sources, acquiring energy-efficient capital, and promoting localized rather than centralized electric generating systems. Ultimately, a shift to a solar-based economy could benefit developing nations in tropical and subtropical areas, which could take advantage of their abundant sunshine to develop self-sufficient energy systems, and perhaps to export hydrogen fuel produced by solar energy.

KEY TERMS AND CONCEPTS

biomass
capital stock
cartel
cogeneration
deregulation
diminishing returns
economic efficiency
economic supply
economies of scale
efficiency labeling
efficiency standards
energy infrastructure
entropy
estimated ultimately recoverable
   (EUR) supplies

flow
Hubbert curve
hydropower
market failure
physical supply
research and development (R&D)
solar energy
solar flux
solar hydrogen
stock
thermodynamic efficiency
throughput

DISCUSSION QUESTIONS

1. Given that energy production represents only about 5 percent of economic output, why should we place any special importance on this sector? Is there any significant difference between an economic system that relies on nonrenewable energy supplies and one that uses primarily renewable sources? Should governments implement policy decisions about energy use, or should market allocation and pricing alone determine energy use patterns?

2. Discuss the concept of entropy as it relates to energy use. What do the thermodynamic laws imply for economic analysis of energy supplies, consumption, and environmental impact? How does this relate to the rapid expansion of energy use in the twentieth century and to projections for further expansion in the future?

3. In the 1970s, energy shortages had significant worldwide economic impact. Was this a one-time phenomenon or could it recur? Did it relate primarily to demand-side or supply-side factors? How have demand and supply for energy changed since the 1970s, and how have these changes affected energy prices and consumption patterns? Are further significant changes likely?

4. Many people argue that a transition to renewable energy sources would be good policy from both economic and environmental points of view. Yet such a transition has not occurred and does not seem imminent. Do you think a shift away from fossil fuel dependence would be beneficial? What economic factors and policy decisions are likely to significantly affect whether and how rapidly such a shift occurs?

REFERENCES

Campbell, Colin, and Jean Laherrère. "The End of Cheap Oil." *Scientific American,* March 1998.

Cleveland, Cutler. "Natural Resource Scarcity and Economic Growth Revisited: Economic and Biophysical Perspectives." Chapter 19 in *Ecological Economics,* edited by Robert Costanza. New York: Columbia University Press, 1991.

Daly, Herman E. *Steady-State Economics,* 2nd ed. Washington, D.C.: Island Press, 1991.

Davis, Ged. "Energy for Planet Earth." *Scientific American,* September 1990.

Dunn, Seth. *Hydrogen Futures: Toward a Sustainable Energy System.* Worldwatch Paper No. 157. Washington, D.C.: Worldwatch Institute, 2001.

Georgescu-Roegen, Nicholas. *The Entropy Law and the Economic Process.* Cambridge, Mass.: Harvard University Press, 1971.

Intergovernmental Panel on Climate Change (IPCC). *Climate Change 1995, Volume 3: Economic and Social Dimensions of Climate Change.* New York: Cambridge University Press, 1996.

International Energy Agency. *World Energy Outlook 2000.* Available at http://www.iea.org.

International Institute for Applied Systems (IIASA) and the World Energy Council (WEC). *Global Energy Perspectives.* Laxenburg, Austria, 1998. Available at http://www.worldenergy.org.

Kats, Gregory. "Achieving Sustainability in Energy Use in Developing Countries," Chapter 9 in *Making Development Sustainable,* edited by Johan Holmberg. Washington, D.C.: Island Press, 1992.

Krishnan, Rajaram, Jonathan M. Harris, and Neva Goodwin, eds. *A Survey of Ecological Economics.* Washington, D.C.: Island Press, 1995.

MacKenzie, James J. *Oil as a Finite Resource: When Is Global Production Likely to Peak?* Washington, D.C.: World Resources Institute, 1996.

Meadows, Donnella H., Dennis L. Meadows, and Jørgen Panders. *Beyond the Limits.* Post Mills, Vt.: Chelsea Green Publishing, 1992.

Reddy, Amulya, and José Goldemberg. "Energy for the Developing World." *Scientific American,* September 1990.

Romm, Joseph, and Charles Curtis. "Mideast Oil Forever?" *Atlantic Monthly,* April 1996.

U.S. Department of Energy, Energy Information Administration. *International Energy Annual.* Washington, D.C.: U.S. Government, 1999.

U.S. Department of Energy, Energy Information Administration. *Annual Energy Review.* Washington, D.C.: U.S. Government, 2000.

World Bank. *World Development Report 1992,* Chapter 6: "Energy and Industry." New York: Oxford University Press, 1992.

World Resources Institute. *World Resources 1994–95.* New York: Oxford University Press, 1994.

Worldwatch Institute Database Disk. Washington, D.C.: Worldwatch Institute, 1999.

WEB SITES

1. http://www.eia.doe.gov/ Web site for the Energy Information Administration, a division of U.S. Department of Energy. Provides a wealth of information about energy demand, supply, trends, and prices.
2. http://www.cnie.org/NLE/CRSreports/Energy/ Access to energy reports and issue briefs published by the Congressional Research Service.
3. http://www.nrel.gov/ The web site for the National Renewable Energy Laboratory in Colorado. NRE conducts research on renewable energy technologies including solar, wind, biomass, and fuel cell energy.
4. http://www.rmi.org/ Home page for the Rocky Mountain Institute, a nonprofit organization that "fosters the efficient and restorative use of resources to create a more secure, prosperous, and life-sustaining world." RMI's main focus has been promoting increased energy efficiency in industry and households.
5. http://www.eren.doe.gov/ Web site for the Energy Efficiency and Renewable Energy Network within the U.S. Department of Energy. The site includes a large amount of information of energy efficiency and renewable energy sources as well as links to thousands of other sites.

CHAPTER FOCUS QUESTIONS

- What ecological and economic principles govern fisheries?
- Why are so many of the world's fisheries suffering from overexploitation?
- What policies can be effective in conserving and rebuilding fisheries?

CHAPTER **14**

Renewable Resource Use: Fisheries

Principles of Renewable Resource Management

The expansion of human economic activity, as we noted in Chapter 2, has had major impact on the planet's renewable natural resources. In the early twenty-first century most of the world's major fisheries are depleted or in decline, tropical forest area continues to shrink at about 30 million acres per year, and groundwater withdrawals continue to deplete aquifers in all major water-scarce regions of the globe.[1] Clearly, management of renewable resources remains a major continuing issue. What economic and ecological principles underlie sustainable—or unsustainable—management of renewable resources?

We can view resources simply as inputs into the economic production process, or, in a broader view, analyze **renewable resources,** in terms of their own internal logic of equilibrium and regeneration. In some resource management approaches, these two perspectives are compatible, but in others they clash. For example, should the governing principle in managing natural systems be ecological diversity or maximum yield?

---

[1]World Resources Institute, 2000; UNEP, 1999.

277

The problem of integrating economic and ecological goals is essential to the management of natural resource systems.

In Chapter 1, we identified the relationships between the human economy and natural systems in terms of **source function** and **sink function**. The source function is the provision of materials for human use, and the sink function is the absorption of waste products from human activity. We have already considered aspects of these functions in dealing with agriculture, nonrenewable resources and atmospheric carbon absorption. **Sustainable management** of renewable resources involves maintaining the resource's source and sink functions in such a way that its quality and availability remain stable over time. Although this certainly seems like a desirable goal, some forms of management tend to encourage unsustainable use.

We have already seen an example of how managing a fishery as an **open-access resource** can lead to overfishing and depletion of stocks (Chapter 5). However, management by a private owner or by a government authority can also lead to unsustainable practices. The reason lies in the difference between economic principles and ecological principles.

Economic principles of resource management include profit maximization, efficient production, and efficient intertemporal resource allocation. We saw in Chapters 4 and 5 how these principles apply in general to resource use. When we examine fisheries, forests, and water systems in more detail we see that these economic principles are sometimes, but not always, consistent with sustainable management.

The ecological principles underlying renewable resource systems are a little more difficult to express in simple terms. One basic rule derived from ecological principles is that of **maximum sustainable yield** (*MSY*)—no more of the resource should be harvested or withdrawn annually than can be regenerated or replenished by the natural processes of resource cycling and the capture of solar energy. Maximum sustainable yield, as we have already seen in Chapter 5, can be included in an economic analysis and may be consistent with economic goals under some circumstances.

But we must also consider that most natural systems are characterized by **ecological complexity.** Fisheries typically include many species of fish as well as other forms of animal and vegetable marine life. Natural forests usually have a variety of tree species, provide habitat for many animal species, as well as symbiotic or parasitic insects, fungi, and microbial life. Water systems generally include different kinds of aquatic habitat, some of which, like wetlands, play a crucial role in balancing the water cycle and maintaining water quality.

Human management of natural ecosystems must of necessity be a compromise between economic and ecological goals. In almost every case, human use of natural ecosystems will alter their state to some degree. Even so, we can usually manage ecosystems without destroying their **resilience**—defined as the capacity to recover from adverse impacts—or exceeding their maximum sustainable yield. To do so, however, requires a degree of restraint that may or may not be consistent with economic principles of profit maximization and economic institutions of resource ownership. In this chapter and Chapter 15 we will investigate this tension between economic and ecological principles as it applies to the management of fisheries, forests, and water systems.

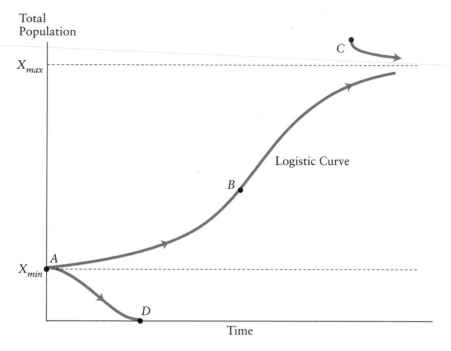

FIGURE 14-1 *Species Population Growth over Time*

Ecological and Economic Analyses of Fisheries

In our initial analysis of fisheries in Chapter 5, we viewed the fishery as a productive system whose output—fish—was an economic good. But fisheries are fundamentally biological systems, so a more complete view should start with a biological analysis and examine its economic implications.

The field of **population biology** identifies a general theory of population change for an organism, such as a species of fish, in the natural environment. Figure 14-1 shows a basic pattern of population change over time characteristic of many species in a natural state. This graph shows two paths for population change over time. Above a minimum critical population necessary for survival (X_{min}), population will grow from point A to a natural equilibrium, in balance with food supply, following a **logistic curve** of growth over time.

With a small population and abundant food supply, the population initially grows at a steady rate, in a near-exponential pattern. Limits on food supply and living space slow the rate of population growth. Beyond point B, known as an **inflection point,**[2]

---

[2]At an inflection point, the curvature of the line changes from positive (upward) to negative (downward). In the terminology of calculus, the second derivative goes from positive to negative, and is equal to zero at the inflection point.

annual growth declines and population eventually approaches an upper limit X_{max}. Should the population ever exceed this limit, for example reaching point C due to a temporary increase in available food, it will rapidly decline from point C back to X_{max} once normal food supply conditions return.

If the population falls below the critical X_{min} level, it will decline to extinction (point D). This can happen if disease, predation, or excessive harvesting by humans reduces the population to an unsustainably low level. The passenger pigeon in North America provides a classic case in which excessive harvesting led to extinction of a wild species. At one time, abundant food supply in the forests of North America made the passenger pigeon perhaps the most numerous species on the continent. Unrestrained hunting reduced it to a few scattered remnants, which died out by the late nineteenth century.

In general, species populations in a natural state are determined by the environment's **carrying capacity**—the supply of food and other life support naturally available. Human exploitation of renewable resources must be consistent with this carrying capacity to avoid ecological disruption and possible population collapse.

The population growth pattern shown in Figure 14-1 can be viewed in a different graphical format by relating the stock (population size) to its growth per year (Figure 14-2). Stock size now appears on the horizontal axis and annual growth on the vertical axis. The arrows indicate the direction of population change. When growth rates

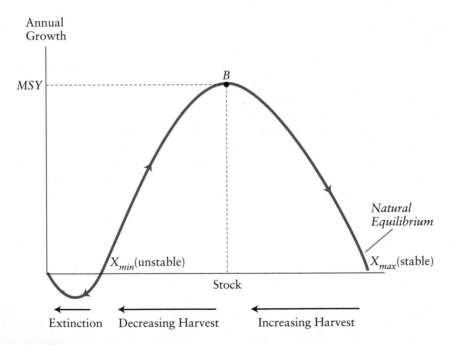

FIGURE 14-2 *Species Population and Annual Growth*

are positive (above X_{min}) the population is expanding toward X_{max}, while below X_{min} it is declining toward zero.

We can now see that X_{min} is an **unstable equilibrium.** At this population, a slight increase will set the species on the road to recovery; a slight decrease will head it to extinction. Many endangered species are in this position. For example, barely enough North American whooping cranes survive to maintain a nesting population, and scientists hope to nudge the number upward to recovery. But a single major incidence of natural disaster or disease could eliminate the species.

By contrast, X_{max} is a **stable equilibrium.** In a natural state, the population will tend to this equilibrium. A smaller population will grow, while a larger population will shrink. Thus while some oscillation might occur around the equilibrium, the population will not tend to explode or to crash.[3]

In this form, the population growth graph clearly shows the maximum sustainable yield (*MSY*) at the top of the curve. The potential sustainable harvest of fish equals the total annual growth. If this amount is taken for human use, the population will remain constant. It will therefore be possible to exploit the fish stock at any population level between X_{max} and X_{min}, with the maximum possible harvest at point B.

Deriving an Economic Analysis from Biological Principles

Note that so far we have followed a strictly biological analysis, without considering economic implications. But we have derived a graph close to the economic graph of **total product** used for the fishery in Chapter 5. If we view Figure 14-2 from right to left, starting at the natural population equilibrium X_{max}, we can see how the economic graph of total product is derived.

Suppose Figure 14-2 describes a fish population in its natural state—say, the codfish population off New England when the first European colonists arrived.[4] As fishing effort increases, the stock will decline. However, this leads to a *higher* annual increment of fish. This is because a somewhat smaller stock of fish, with an unchanged food supply, can reproduce more rapidly. This pattern continues until point B, the maximum sustainable yield or *MSY*.

If fishing continues beyond *MSY*, however, the pattern changes. Both the fish stock and the annual increment decline. Larger harvests progressively reduce both stock and yield until eventually the fish population may face danger of extinction as X_{min} is approached.

The economic view of this biologically derived pattern is shown in Figures 14-3 and 14-4. Figure 14-3 relates fishing effort (measured in number of boat-days) to total returns. The total product, measured in tons of fish, can be converted to money terms by multiplying by the price of fish.[5] The resulting total revenue (*TR*) curve has the

---

[3]For an advanced treatment of fisheries dynamics, see Clark, 1990.

[4]The levels of fishing engaged in by Native American tribes before European colonization would have had little impact on the natural equilibrium.

[5]For this example, we assume a stable market price for fish.

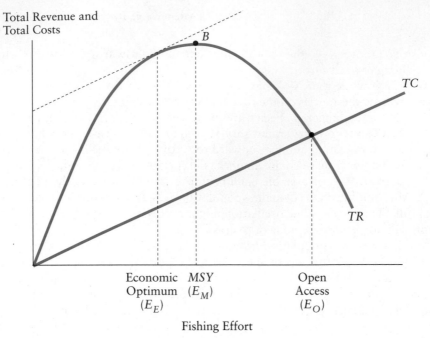

Total Revenue and
Total Costs

B

TC

TR

Economic   *MSY*
Optimum (E_M)
(E_E)

Open
Access
(E_O)

Fishing Effort

FIGURE 14-3 *Total Revenues and Costs in the Fishery*

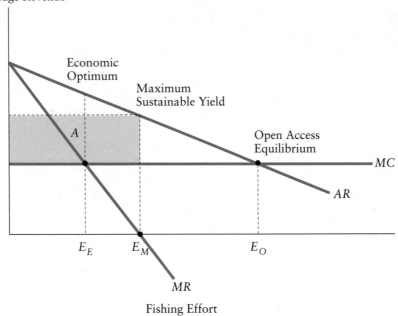

Marginal Costs,
Marginal Revenue, and
Average Revenue

Economic
Optimum

Maximum
Sustainable Yield

A

Open Access
Equilibrium

MC

AR

E_E E_M E_O

MR

Fishing Effort

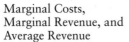

A: Rent or Net Social Benefit

FIGURE 14-4 *Marginal Revenues and Costs in the Fishery*

same general shape as the yield curve in Figure 14-2, and in fact corresponds closely to that curve. Increased fishing effort moves right to left in Figure 14-2, but left to right in Figure 14-3. We measure the horizontal axes on the two graphs in different units, because one measures fish population and the other fishing effort, but in general as fishing effort increases fish population decreases.

Fishing, of course, also involves costs. The total cost (TC) curve shown in Figure 14-3 is linear, implying a constant cost per unit of fishing effort. Other patterns for total cost curves are possible, but in general total costs will increase as fishing effort increases. The combination of costs and revenues shown here allows us to identify two possible equilibrium positions:

1. the **economic optimum, E_E,** where the slopes of the total revenue and total cost curves are equal, or Marginal Revenue = Marginal Cost;
2. the **open-access equilibrium, E_O,** where $TR = TC$, or Average Revenue = Marginal Cost.

These equilibria can be more easily identified using the marginal and average cost and revenue curves shown in Figure 14-4. The maximum sustainable yield appears on the economic graphs as E_M, where TR is maximized and $MR = 0$.

The open access equilibrium E_O, as discussed in Chapter 5, occurs only when average revenue equals marginal cost, which means that profits throughout the fishing industry have fallen to zero. So long as the industry is profitable, new entrants will continue to increase the pressure on the fish population, driving total revenues down until $TR = TC$. This position is both economically and ecologically undesirable, but is the likely outcome unless policies to limit entry are in place.

From the economist's point of view, open-access equilibrium leads to **rent dissipation**—the loss of much of the potential social benefit from the fishery. A single owner of the fishery could capture the potential rent by limiting operations to E_M. This potential rent is the shaded area A in Figure 14-4. The difference between average revenue and marginal cost shows the rent per unit of effort, and area A shows the total rent. With open access, this economic benefit is lost.

Note the relationship of the economic optimum (E_E), maximum sustainable yield (E_M), and open-access equilibrium (E_O) in Figure 14-4. The economic optimum lies to the left of maximum sustainable yield, and the open-access equilibrium lies to the right. As we saw in Chapter 5, the economic optimum might be achieved through use of a **license fee** or **quota system**.

In cases where the fishery is localized, such as on a small lake, the economic optimum could be achieved through **private ownership**. A profit-seeking owner, or group of owners acting together, would have an incentive to limit fishing effort to E_E. This would maximize profits, and would also have the effect of avoiding overexploitation of the fishery.

Referring back to the biological graph (Figure 14-2), we see that the economic optimum will lie to the right of *MSY* (point *B*), in a sustainable range. Although total fish stocks will drop as a result of the fishing effort, a high annual growth rate will allow the system to maintain resilience, or bounce-back capacity. The open-access equilibrium, in contrast, lies to the left of *MSY*.

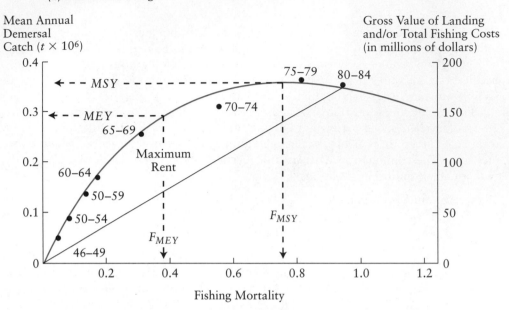

(a) Demersal Fishing

Mean Annual
Demersal
Catch ($t \times 10^6$)

Gross Value of Landing
and/or Total Fishing Costs
(in millions of dollars)

Fishing Mortality

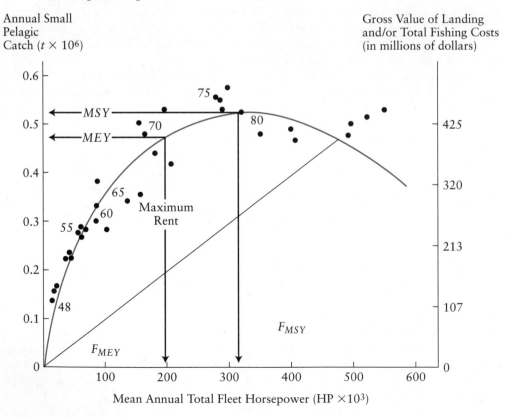

(b) Pelagic Fishing

Annual Small
Pelagic
Catch ($t \times 10^6$)

Gross Value of Landing
and/or Total Fishing Costs
(in millions of dollars)

Mean Annual Total Fleet Horsepower (HP $\times 10^3$)

FIGURE 14-5 *Open Access in Philippine Fisheries*
Source: Adapted from "The Overfishing of Marine Resources: Socioeconomic Background in Southeast Asia," by Pauly, D., and Thia-Eng, C., in *Ambio*, Vol. 17, no. 3, p. 203. Reprinted by permission of *Ambio*.

As we move further to the left of *MSY*, both harvest and annual growth decline, and eventually the fish stock may be in danger of extinction. As fish harvests decline, fish prices are likely to rise, increasing the marginal and average revenue curves in Figure 14-4, thus pushing the open-access equilibrium further to the right and hastening the spiral toward collapse of the fishery.

Unfortunately, the open-access equilibrium is common in fisheries throughout the world. Figure 14-5 shows data from Philippine fisheries, in which open-access has led to effort levels exceeding first the maximum economic yield *MEY* (corresponding to E_M in the above analysis), then the maximum sustainable yield *MSY*. It is interesting to note how this actual historical data corresponds closely to our theoretical patterns for the economics of a fishery. We can clearly see how, by the 1980s, fishing had exceeded the maximum sustainable yield and catches of both demersal (sea-bottom) and pelagic (ocean) fisheries had begun to decline.

The Economics of Fisheries in Practice

Fishing in open seas is a typical illustration of a situation where the **tragedy of the commons,** as discussed in Chapter 5, is likely to occur. Individual fishers tend to have little incentive to practice conservation, for they know that if they do not catch the available fish, someone else probably will. Without limits in place, fishers try to catch as many fish as they possibly can. Technological improvements that make it easier to find and catch fish only make matters worse.

Many traditional societies have evolved rules limiting the seasons or days when particular seafood species could be harvested (for example, prohibiting fishing at spawning season), or the amount to be taken. In recent years these rules have in many cases been swept aside, in part due to population pressures. Other reasons why the balance might break down include **institutional failure,** such as when an outside interest acquires the power to override the community's traditional patterns of property rights.[6]

In industrial societies, **overfishing** rapidly affects whole fisheries. Management institutions often are overwhelmed by rising demands. Today the problem is global in scope:

> In 1871, the U.S. government created its first federal conservation agency, the Commission of Fish and Fisheries, in response to the decline of fisheries off the coast of New England and in inland lakes. Fishery declines were nothing new even in 1871—in the mid-1800s drastic declines of whales had captured people's attention.

---

[6]See Schlager and Ostrom, 1993; McGinnis and Ostrom, 1996.

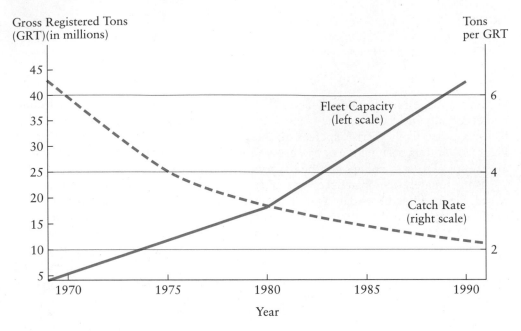

FIGURE 14-6 *Global Fleet Capacity and Catch Rate, 1970–90*

Source: Adapted from Anne Platt McGinn, *Rocking the Boat: Conserving Fisheries and Protecting Jobs.* Worldwatch Paper no. 142. Washington, D.C.: Worldwatch Institute, 1998. Reprinted by permission of Worldwatch Institute, http://www.worldwatch.org.

[Today] as a result of excessive exploitation and other abuses, most of the highly prized marine fisheries around the world are on the verge of collapse. The warning signs are clear: 11 of the world's 15 most important fishing areas and 60 percent of major fish species are in decline, according to the U.N. Food and Agriculture Organization (FAO).[7]

The scale of fishing operations has increased dramatically with the introduction of modern vessels such as commercial trawlers. Between 1970 and 1990, global fleet capacity more than quadrupled, whereas the average catch per boat (catch rate) dropped by a factor of three (see Figure 14-6).

Clearly, an open-access situation is economically irrational. It also poses further ecological problems because modern fishing methods often cause a high death rate among nontarget species. One fourth of all catches are discarded, because they are either undersized or nonmarketable. This wasted portion of the global harvest is called **bycatch.** "Global bycatch was estimated at more than 28 million tons in 1994 . . . bycatch is associated with industrialized fishers who use indiscriminate gear to catch as much as they can, but generally keep only the fish they are legally permitted to catch or those that make money."[8]

---

[7]McGinn, 1998, p. 11. See also McGoodwin, 1990; Fairlie, 1995.

[8]McGinn, 1998.

TABLE 14-1 *Declining Major Fisheries in the World*

Ocean Area	Estimated Annual Potential (million tons)	Year Potential Reached	Decline from Peak Yield
East Central Atlantic	4	1984	−22%
Northwest Atlantic	4	1971	−38%
Southeast Atlantic	3	1978	−53%
West Central Atlantic	2	1987	−28%
East Central Pacific	3	1988	−13%
Northeast Pacific	4	1990	−12%
Southwest Pacific	1	1991	−13%
Antarctic	0.2	1980	unavailable
World	82	1999	unavailable

Sources: FAO, 1997; McGinn, 1999.

Although identifying the maximum sustainable yield for a fishery can help maintain an individual species, the issues of ecological sustainability are more complex. Depleting one species may lead to an irreversible change in ocean ecology as other species fill the ecological niche formerly occupied by the harvested species.[9] For example, dogfish and skates have replaced overfished cod and haddock in major areas of the North Atlantic fishery, and are now themselves threatened with overfishing. Fishing techniques such as trawling, in which nets are dragged along the bottom of the ocean, are highly destructive to all kinds of benthic (bottom-dwelling) life. In large areas of the Atlantic, formerly productive ocean floor ecological communities have been severely damaged by repeated trawling.

While some fisheries remain in a healthy state, and others have recovered after fishing limitations have been imposed, many major ocean fisheries appear to have been exploited beyond the point of maximum sustainable yield (Table 14-1). The issue of open-access and proper fishery management is thus both a national and a global problem. Existing institutions for fishery management are often not sufficient to control the economic pressures leading to depletion of ocean resources.[10]

Policies for Sustainable Fisheries Management

From an economic point of view, the reason for **market failure** in open-access fisheries is that important productive resources—lakes and oceans—are treated as free resources, and are therefore overused. A simple solution is to place a price on the resource.

---

[9]See Hagler, 1995; Ogden, 2001.
[10]See Hanna, 1999.

Certainly no private owner of a small lake, for example, would allow unlimited numbers of people to fish for free, depleting the stock of fish until the resource was worthless. The owner would charge a fee to fish, yielding income for the owner (part of which might go to restocking the lake) and limiting the number of people who would fish. Although the owner's motivation would be to collect **economic rent**,[11] the people fishing would also benefit—despite having to pay a fee—because they would have access to continued good fishing instead of suffering depletion of the fish stock.

An ocean fishery does not allow the private ownership solution. The oceans have been called a common heritage resource—they belong to everyone and no one. But under the 1982 **Law of the Sea,** agreed to under United Nations auspices, nations can claim territorial rights to many important offshore fisheries. They can then limit access to these fisheries by requiring a fishing license within their Exclusive Economic Zones (EEZs), which extend 200 miles from their coastlines.

Fishing licenses can be sold for a set fee, or a limited number can be sold at auction. In effect, this establishes a price for access to the resource. Notice that we can also view this as *internalizing a negative externality*. Each fisher now must pay a price for the external costs imposed on one fishery by adding one extra boat. The economic signal such a price sends will result in fewer people entering the fishery.

This approach, however, will not necessarily solve the problem of overinvestment. A boat owner who buys a license will have added incentive to obtain the maximum catch by investing in new equipment such as sonar devices to track fish, bigger nets, and more powerful engines to travel further. He or she will be more likely to spend as much time as possible at sea, to earn the maximum return on the investment in the license and equipment. If all fishers do this, the depletion problem may remain serious. Governments can respond by imposing quotas on total catch, but area-wide quotas are often difficult to enforce and meet fierce resistance from fishers.[12]

One possible policy response that combines regulation with the use of market mechanisms is a system of **individual transferable quotas (ITQs).** Like transferable emissions permits, ITQs impose a maximum limit on the quantity of fish that can be taken. Anyone purchasing such a permit can catch and sell a certain number of fish—or can sell the permit and fishing rights to someone else. Assuming the quota limits can be enforced, the total catch from the fishery will not exceed a certain predetermined level.

To determine the maximum sustainable yield level, policymakers must consult marine biologists, who can estimate the sustainable level of fish population. Once ecological sustainability has been assured, the permit market will promote **economic efficiency.** Those who can fish most effectively will be able to outbid others to acquire the ITQs. Although ITQ systems have been successful in certain areas, they have also led to complaints that they promote concentration in the fishing industry and squeeze out small fishers.[13]

---

[11]Economic rent is the return that flows to the owner of a scarce resource.

[12]See Townsend, 1990, for a survey of the effects of entry restrictions in fisheries.

[13]See Duncan, 1995; Arnason, 1993; Young, 1999.

A more difficult problem concerns species that are highly migratory. Tuna and swordfish, for example, continually travel between national fishing areas and the open ocean. Even with good policies for resource management in national waters, these species can be harvested as an open-access global resource, which almost inevitably leads to stock declines. Only an international agreement can solve an issue concerning global commons.

In 1995, the first such agreement was signed: the Convention on Highly Migratory and Straddling Stocks. This convention embodies a principle of ecological economics introduced in Chapter 6: the **precautionary principle.** This principle suggests that, rather than waiting until depletion is obvious, fishery access should be controlled before problems appear, with measures to limit the total catch rate, establish data collection and reporting systems, and minimize bycatch through the use of more selective gear.[14]

Demand-Side Issues: Changing Consumption Patterns

People in developed countries currently consume 40 percent of the global fish catch; the other 60 percent is consumed in the developing world, where fish is an important protein source.[15] Increasing population and income in developing countries will likely produce steady growth in global demand for fish and fish products, but supply expansion, at least from wild fisheries, may be close to its limits.

After increasing rapidly between 1950 and 1990, the world fish catch now appears to have leveled off, and per capita catch has increased little over the past 30 years (Figure 14-7). Most ocean and inland fisheries are at or near their capacity limits, with many already in decline (see Table 14-1). Atlantic fisheries have been especially pressured as many fishing nations compete for access, and fishery management within the 200-mile EEZs has been inadequate.[16]

About one-third of world fish production—30 million tons—goes to nonfood uses such as fishmeal and oils.[17] Alternative use of soymeal and other sources of protein in animal and fish feed would relieve pressure on fisheries, and potentially make more fish available for direct human consumption. This would depend, of course, on increased output of land-grown protein products such as soybeans, which as we saw in Chapter 11 may pose other environmental issues.

Changes in human consumption patterns are also important. Public education campaigns that identify fish and seafood produced with environmentally damaging techniques may lead consumers to avoid these species. For example, a boycott of swordfish aimed at stopping the decline of this species has gained the support of numerous restaurant chefs and consumers.

Ecolabeling, which identifies products produced in a sustainable manner, has the potential to encourage sustainable fishing techniques. Products of certifiably sustainable

---

[14]McGinn, 1998.

[15]Ibid.

[16]See Harris, 1998.

[17]McGinn, 1998.

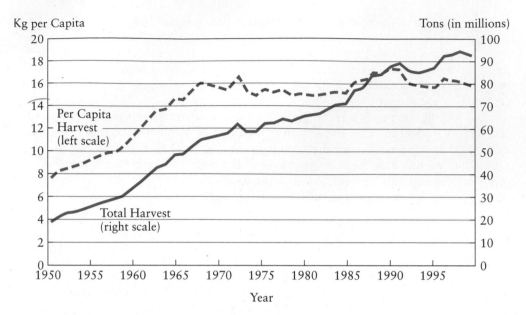

FIGURE 14-7 *World Fish Catch, Total and Per Capita*
Source: Worldwatch Institute, Worldwatch Database Disk, 1999.

fishing practices can often command a slightly higher market price. By accepting this price premium, consumers implicitly agree to pay for something more than the fish they eat. They pay a little extra for the health of the ocean ecosystem and the hope of a supply of fish to feed people in the future as well as in the present. These consumer choices give the fishing industry a financial incentive to use sustainable methods.

In economic terminology, we can say that consumers are *internalizing the positive externalities* associated with sustainable fishing techniques through their willingness to buy ecolabeled products. Governments or well-respected private agencies can oversee **certification** of sustainable fish products. A prominent example is "dolphin-safe" ecolabeling, which has been instrumental in reducing the numbers of dolphin killed as bycatch during tuna fishing.

Another area where governments policies can assist in internalizing positive externalities is the provision of **subsidies**—for example, to assist in developing or acquiring equipment designed especially to release bycatch, or to avoid major disturbances of the seabed. This may moderate political opposition from fishing communities to government intervention aimed at eliminating destructive fishing practices.

Aquaculture: New Solutions, New Problems

The most rapidly growing area of fish production is **aquaculture**—fish farming, often in large offshore pens. Aquaculture is largely responsible for recent increases in world fish production (see Figure 14-8). However, from an environmental point of view aquaculture may pose as many questions as it solves.

A salmon farm in Washington. While aquaculture offers significant potential for expanding fish supplies, it can also lead to ecological damage and degradation of wild stocks through interbreeding with escaped fish or the spread of disease.

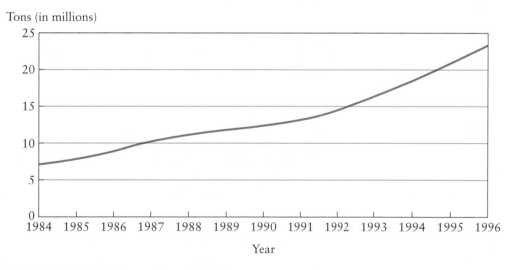

FIGURE 14-8 *World Aquaculture Production*
Source: Worldwatch Institute, Worldwatch Database Disk, 1999.

14.1 Scientists Criticize Salmon Aquaculture

Despite their image as potential saviors of the world's beleaguered fisheries, some of the most successful forms of fish farming may do more harm than good by depleting marine resources and polluting the water, according to a paper in the journal *Science.*

Researchers from Stanford University and the Environmental Defense Fund argue that salmon and shrimp aquaculture are especially damaging to the environment because the animals are carnivorous, consuming smaller fish that could have been eaten by humans or other marine life.

The world's salmon farmers fed their fish 1.8 million tons of wild fish to harvest just 644,000 tons of salmon. At the same time, water pollution from shrimp and salmon farms has grown. Salmon farms in Norway alone discharge nutrients in their feces equivalent to a city of at least 1.7 million people.

Shrimp farming, which has grown 700 percent since the 1980s, also leaves a trail of ecologically crippled ponds in China, Thailand, and Indonesia where low-income people formerly harvested shellfish.

"Rapid growth in shrimp and salmon farming has clearly caused environmental degradation, while contributing little to world food security" the paper concludes.

SOURCE

"Fish Farming Pollutes, Harms Marine Life," by Scott Allen. *Boston Globe*, October 30, 1998, p. A13. Copyright ©1998 by Globe Newspaper Co. (MA). Reproduced with permission of the Globe Newspaper Co. (MA) in the format textbook via Copyright Clearance Center.

While traditional aquaculture systems often raised several species of fish in ecologically healthy combination with crops and animals, modern systems rely on **monoculture** of economically profitable species such as salmon and shrimp. Such systems have significant negative externalities. Excess food and fish wastes contaminate the aquatic environment, and captive fish can spread disease to wild stocks or, if they escape, degrade the wild gene pool. Shrimp farms, which often replace mangrove forests, are especially ecologically destructive:

In the short term, intensive shrimp farming is highly profitable: in a year, an individual shrimp farmer can make up to $10,000 per hectare for intensive production rates of 4 to 5 tons per hectare. This compares to the roughly $1,000 per hectare that a species such as milkfish or carp generates. But these economic returns do not account for ecological—and economic—losses such as habitat degradation. By converting diverse ecosystems to simple ones, fish farmers and the public lose a host of ecological goods such as fish, shellfish, timber, charcoal, and other products. They also lose services that coastal ecosystems provide, such as filtering and purifying water, cycling nutrients, removing contaminants and buffering the land from coastal storms and severe weather. A study of the Matang mangrove in Malaysia revealed that its value for coastal protection alone exceeded the value of farmed shrimp by 170 percent.[18]

On a modest local scale, inland aquaculture can be environmentally beneficial, encouraging multiple use of water systems for crops such as rice as well as fish ponds. Asia has a long tradition of ecologically sound aquaculture, and Africa and other developing areas show considerable potential for its further development.[19] Whether ocean aquaculture can be practiced on a large scale without irreversible damage to ecosystems remains to be seen.

Given the rapid growth in aquaculture, regulatory policy should encourage less-resource-intensive forms of production. Reviving and encouraging traditional pond systems, which integrate well with local environments and available resources, would help minimize aquaculture's impact on the environment.

Aquaculture will undoubtedly be a component of a strategy for sustainable fisheries management, but it cannot compensate for the damage done by unrestricted access to wild fisheries. A comprehensive approach including supply management, demand modification, and sustainable forms of aquaculture will be required to meet the needs of a still-growing world population.

SUMMARY

A renewable natural resource system such as a fishery involves both economic and ecological principles. In a natural state, fish populations reach an equilibrium level based on the carrying capacity of the environment. Human exploitation of the resource can be sustainable provided it is consistent with this natural carrying capacity.

Economic analysis of the fishery suggests that economically efficient resource use should be compatible with ecological sustainability. However, open-access conditions in many fisheries create a strong tendency toward overexploitation.

On a global scale, fishing fleet capacity has exceeded maximum sustainable yield, leading to declining catch rates in most ocean fisheries. The total world fish catch increased steadily from 1950 to 1990, but has leveled off since then. Per capita catch rates have not increased over the past 30 years. Destructive fishing techniques have damaged marine habitat and altered ocean ecology, diminishing productivity.

Policies for maintaining sustainable yield and rebuilding depleted fisheries can involve a combination of regulation and market mechanisms. International conventions have set guidelines for territorial rights and management practices. Nations can require fishing licenses or impose quotas to limit access to the fishery. Area-wide quotas can be difficult to enforce, but systems of individual transferable quotas have been successfully implemented.

[18]McGinn 1998, pp. 48–49.

[19]See Brummett and Williams, 2000.

Fish is an important protein source, especially in the developing world, where demand can be expected to grow as population and income rise. More efficient consumption patterns and increased aquaculture will be important as wild fish catches reach or exceed sustainable limits.

Consumption patterns can be modified to promote more sustainable fisheries management through consumer awareness and certification or ecolabeling programs. Aquaculture has great potential, but can also involve significant environmental costs. Small-scale and traditional inland aquacultural systems often tend to be more environmentally beneficial than large-scale commercial operations.

KEY TERMS AND CONCEPTS

aquaculture
bycatch
carrying capacity
certification
ecolabeling
ecological complexity
economic efficiency
economic optimum
economic rent
individual transferable
   quotas (ITQs)
inflection point
institutional failure
Law of the Sea
license fee
logistic curve
market failure
maximum sustainable yield
   (*MSY*)

monoculture
open-access equilibrium
open-access resource
overfishing
population biology
precautionary principle
private ownership
quota system
renewable resources
rent dissipation
resilience
sink function
source function
stable equilibrium
subsidies
sustainable management
total product
tragedy of the commons
unstable equilibrium

DISCUSSION QUESTIONS

1. What is the basic reason for fishery depletion? What factors have made this problem especially severe in the modern period? Relate this issue to the difference between economic and ecological analyses of a fishery.

2. Discuss the advantages and disadvantages of the following policies for fisheries management: private ownership, government regulation through licensing, the use of individual transferable quotas (ITQs). In what circumstances might each one be appropriate?

3. Explain the interrelationship between the following concepts as they relate to fisheries: economic rent, maximum sustainable yield (MSY), economic efficiency, ecological sustainability. How should these concepts help guide fisheries management policies?

PROBLEMS

1. Suppose that a fishery is characterized by the following relationship between total fish stock and annual growth:

STOCK (thousand tons biomass)	10	20	30	40	50	60	70	80	90	100	120
GROWTH (tons)	0	800	1600	2400	2800	3000	2800	2200	1200	0	−1200

Construct a graph showing the relationship between stock and growth, and another graph showing the growth *rate* at each stock level (for example, at stock = 60,000 tons, yield = 3000 tons, growth rate = 5%). What stock level corresponds to the maximum growth rate? What stock level gives the maximum sustainable yield? What will be the stable and unstable equilibrium stock levels for this fish population in a natural state?

2. Now assume that we can translate this population/yield relationship into an economic relationship between fishing boats operating and total product:

BOATS	0	100	200	300	400	500	600	700	800	900
TOTAL PRODUCT (tons)	0	1200	2200	2800	3000	2800	2400	1600	800	0

Fish prices average $1000/ton, and the cost to operate a fishing boat for a year is $4,000.

Construct a graph showing total revenues and total costs in the fishery as a function of the number of boats operating. Now derive graphs showing marginal and average revenue and marginal cost. Use your graphs to analyze equilibrium in the fishery under the following conditions:

(a) A natural state with no fishing industry
(b) A fishing industry obtaining the maximum sustainable yield from the fishery
(c) A fishing industry operating under an efficient management plan, with economically optimal returns
(d) A fishing industry characterized by open access

What does this economic analysis suggest concerning government policy on fisheries management? Should such policies be based on the concept of maximum sustainable yield? Are other significant considerations not reflected in this analysis?

REFERENCES

Arnason, R. "The Icelandic Individual Transferable Quota System: A Descriptive Account." *Marine Resource Economics* 8 (1993): 201–218.

Brummett, Randall E., and Meryl J. Williams. "The Evolution of Aquaculture in African Rural and Economic Development." *Ecological Economics* 33 (May 2000): 193–203.

Clark, Colin. *The Optimal Management of Renewable Resources.* 2nd ed. New York: Wiley, 1990.

Duncan, Leith. "Closed Competition: Fish Quotas in New Zealand." *The Ecologist* 25 (March/April, May/June 1995): 97–104.

Fairlie, Simon, Mike Hagler, and Brian O'Riordan. "The Politics of Overfishing." *The Ecologist* 25 (March/April, May/June 1995): 46–73.

Food and Agriculture Organization of the United Nations (FAO). *The State of World Fisheries and Agriculture, 1996.* FAO: Rome, 1997.

Hagler, Mike. "Deforestation of the Deep: Fishing and the State of the Oceans." *The Ecologist* 25 (March/April, May/June 1995): 74–79.

Hanna, Susan S. "Strengthening Governance of Ocean Fishery Resources." *Ecological Economics* 31 (November 1999): 275–286.

Harris, Michael. *Lament for an Ocean: The Collapse of the Atlantic Cod Fishery.* Toronto, Ontario: M&S Publishing, 1998.

McGinn, Anne Platt. *Rocking the Boat: Conserving Fisheries and Protecting Jobs.* Worldwatch Paper No. 142. Washington, D.C.: Worldwatch Institute, 1998.

McGinn, Anne Platt. *Safeguarding the Health of Oceans.* Worldwatch Paper No. 145. Washington, D.C.: Worldwatch Institute, 1999.

McGinnis, Michael, and Elinor Ostrom. "Design Principles for Local and Global Commons." In *The International Political Economy and International Institutions,* Vol. 2. Edited by Oran P. Young. Cheltenham, England: Edward Elgar, 1996.

McGoodwin, James R. *Crisis in the World's Fisheries: People, Problems, and Politics.* California: Stanford University Press, 1990.

Ogden, John C. "Maintaining Diversity in the Oceans." *Environment* 43 (April 2001): 28–37.

Schlager, Edella, and Elinor Ostrom. "Property Rights and Coastal Fisheries: An Empirical Analysis." In *The Political Economy of Customs and Culture: Informal Solutions to the Commons Problem.* Edited by Terry L. Anderson and Randy T. Simmons. Lanham, Md.: Rowman and Littlefield, 1993.

Townsend, Ralph E. "Entry Restrictions in the Fishery: A Survey of the Evidence." *Land Economics* 66 (1990): 361–378.

United Nations Environmental Programme. *Global Environmental Outlook 2000.* London, England: Earthscan Publications, 1999.

United Nations Food and Agriculture Organization (FAO). *Review of the State of World Fishery Resources: Marine Fisheries.* Rome, Italy: FAO, 1997.

World Resources Institute, United Nations Development Programme, United Nations Environment Programme, and the World Bank. *World Resources 2000-2001: People and Ecosystems.* Washington, D.C.: World Resources Institute, 2000.

Young, Michael D. "The Design of Fishing Rights Systems: The New South Wales Experience." *Ecological Economics* 31 (November 1999): 305–316.

WEB SITES

1. http://www.nmfs.noaa.gov/ Web site for the National Marine Fisheries Service, a division of the National Oceanic and Atmospheric Administration that provides information on marine harvest, prices, and ecosystem health in the United States. The NMFS is also responsible for the management of endangered marine species.
2. http://osu.orst.edu/Dept/IIFET/ Home page for the International Institute of Fisheries Economics and Trade, an organization of researchers devoted to an exchange of information on issues of fishery economics and management.
3. http://fisheries.fws.gov/ Web site of the U.S. Fish and Wildlife Service devoted to freshwater fisheries and habitat conservation. Includes links to information on the relationship between environmental quality and fishery health.

Ecosystem Management: Forest and Water Systems

The Economics of Forest Management

Forests, like fisheries, are primarily biological systems. When we exploit them for human use, both ecological and economic analyses can help us understand principles of effective management. Just as with fisheries, natural growth rate is fundamental in forest ecology and provides a link between ecological and economic analyses. An important factor in forest management policy is the cumulative nature of forest growth: biomass accumulated years, decades, or even centuries ago will still remain available for use if left undisturbed. Thus choices about time of harvesting are important in forest management.

If we measure the volume of standing timber in a forest over time, we obtain a **logistic curve** similar to that for the growth of a fishery (Figure 15-1). However, the logic of harvesting is somewhat different. From an economic point of view, we can see a standing forest as an asset, or **stock,** that can also yield a **flow** of **use value** to humans. If a forest is privately owned, the owner will balance the asset value against the stream of income available from use. A simplified example will demonstrate the economic principle involved.

Consider a forest with 100,000 tons of standing timber, and a growth rate of 5,000 tons additional biomass per year. At a price of $100 per ton, the value of the forest if it is **clear-cut** (logged all at one time) is $10 million. A policy of sustainable

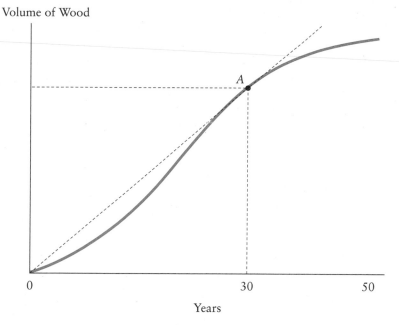

FIGURE 15-1 *Forest Growth over Time*

management, in which the annual harvest is no more than the annual growth, would yield $500,000 per year.

Which is economically preferable? It depends on the **discount rate.** At 4 percent, the present value (*PV*) of the sustainable yield alternative is

$$PV = \$500,000/.04 = \$12.5 \text{ million.}$$

At 6 percent it is

$$PV = \$500,000/.06 = \$8.33 \text{ million.}$$

Comparing these figures with the $10 million present value of an immediate clearcut, we find that at the lower discount rate, sustainable management is economically preferable, but at the higher rate the owner will do better with a clear-cut.

From the owner's point of view, the clear-cut revenue of $10 million can be invested at 6 percent to give $600,000 per year, a more lucrative option than the $500,000 from sustainable management. Thus a financial variable, the commercial rate of interest, will dominate private forest management policy. Forests with a growth rate below the going rate of interest are destined to be harvested as fast as possible. U.S. corporate forest management frequently applies this logic, especially when forest owners have high-interest debt to pay off.

This simple example fails to consider forest replanting and regrowth. We can apply a more sophisticated version to determine economically optimum harvesting periods (years from planting to cutting in plantation forestry).

Consider a forest's biological growth pattern. Figure 15-1 shows that a young forest grows more rapidly than a mature forest. The **mean annual increment (MAI)**, or average growth rate, is obtained by dividing the total **biomass**, or weight of timber, by the age of the forest. Graphically, the MAI at any point on the growth curve is shown by a straight line from the origin to that point. The maximum MAI occurs where a line from the origin is exactly tangent to the curve (point *A* in Figure 15-1).

One possible rule for harvesting would be to cut at a period that maximized the MAI (30 years in Figure 15-1). This would result in the highest total volume of timber and highest average annual revenues over time, assuming a constant price for timber.

To find an economic optimum, however, we must consider two other factors. One is the cost of harvesting—the labor, machinery, and energy required to cut the timber and transport it to market. The other important factor, as our earlier example showed, is the discount rate. Both revenues and costs must be discounted to calculate the present value of various harvesting policies.

The economic optimum can be determined by comparing total revenue to total cost for different possible harvesting periods (Figure 15-2),[1] then discounting this figure to obtain the present value of expected future profits (Figure 15-3). Total revenue minus total cost indicates the profit from harvesting at some future point. Profits expected at a future time must be discounted to calculate their present value. The point at which the discounted value of (*TR–TC*) is maximized gives the **optimum rotation period** for harvesting, from the point of view of economic profitability.[2]

At higher discount rates, the present value of expected future income shrinks. Thus the higher the discount rate, the shorter will be the optimum harvesting period. Figure 15-3 shows discounted *TR–TC* curves for two different discount rates. At the higher rate, the *TR–TC* curve is lower, and its maximum occurs at an earlier year. As discount rates rise, the optimum rotation period shortens, as indicated by the arrow.

This principle helps to explain why plantation forestry is generally based on fast-growing softwood trees. Slower-growing hardwoods or mixed forest might be profitable over the long term, but at a commercial rate of discount the present value of slower-growing trees will be too low to be attractive to timber companies. The determination of commercial interest rates depends on financial factors unrelated to ecological systems—but interest rates can have significant impact on ecosystem management.

This economic logic also helps explain pressure on old-growth forests. Standing forests that may have taken hundreds of years to grow represent an economic asset that can be harvested for immediate profit. Replantings tend to be in faster-growing species. Although replanting an entire forest with a single fast-growing species represents a significant ecological loss, commercially speaking it may be the most profitable option.

---

[1]Total cost includes the fixed cost of planting, then rises in proportion to the quantity of wood harvested.

[2]For a more detailed treatment of the economics of timber harvesting and optimal rotation periods, see Hartwick and Olewiler, 1998, Chapter 10.

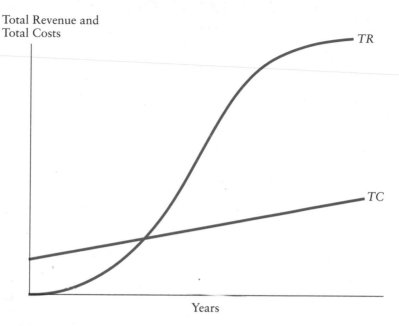

FIGURE 15-2 *Timber Revenues and Costs over Time*

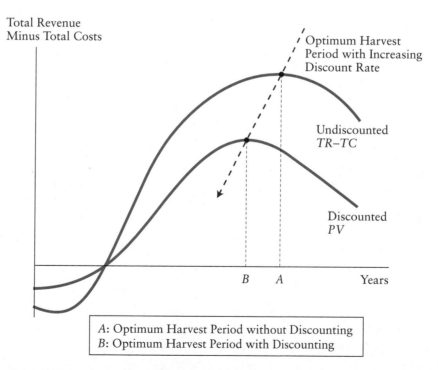

FIGURE 15-3 *Optimum Harvest Period with Discounting*

The principles of commercial forest management can often conflict with ecological goals. Although it may be possible to internalize some of the social costs and benefits related to forest management, for vast areas of privately owned or open-access forest, market profitability is the only management principle. This has led to serious problems of forest and biodiversity loss throughout the world.

Forest Loss and Biodiversity

Human activity has reduced forest area in some cases, increased it in others, as well as changed forest biodiversity. Worldwide, about two-thirds of tropical deforestation results from slash-and-burn agricultural techniques rather than directly from timbering. However, opening up forest areas with logging roads often allows access and encourages destructive agricultural techniques. In Asia and parts of Latin America, logging is directly responsible for half or more of the forest area lost.[3]

As human populations have increased, a typical pattern has been to cut down natural forests and replace them with planted forests. This gives rise to a U-shaped curve showing the change in total forested area as population densities increase (Figure 15-4). Most tropical areas of the world remain on the downward-sloping portion of this curve, suffering net forest loss. Many temperate zones have a stable or increasing forest area, having eliminated much of their natural forest and replaced it with planted forest.[4]

Losses of tropical forest have been severe over the past several decades. Estimates of forest loss range from 50,000 km^3 to 170,000 km^3 per year. From 1980 to 1995, Africa and Latin America lost about 10 percent of their forests, while Asia and Oceania lost more than 6 percent.[5]

Even in areas where forest area is stable or increasing, the threat to biodiversity from economic uses of forests may still be great. Cultivated forests tend to be **monocultures**—huge stands planted with a single species selected for maximum economic return. Such artificial forests displace natural forests, which provide habitat for many more species. Over a long period of time it is possible to regenerate diverse forests, but economic incentives to manage forests for diversity are often lacking.

The maximum sustainable yield principle may not be enough to achieve ecosystem sustainability. Forest managers can maintain sustainable yield merely by replanting all logged areas with a single species of fast-growing tree. This offers sustainable flows of timber and income for the forest owner but destroys the original complexity of the forest ecosystem to the detriment of many animals and plants that thrive in a multispecies forest.

---

[3]United Nations Environmental Programme (UNEP) 1999, p. 38.

[4]Myers, 1996, surveys the state of world forests.

[5]World Resources Institute 2000, pp. 90–91.

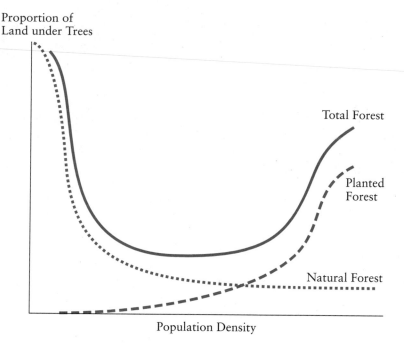

FIGURE 15-4 *Deforestation and Tree Cover*

Ecologist C. S. Holling has identified the principle of **resilience** as central to ecosystem sustainability.[6] Resilience is a "bounce-back" capacity—the ability of an ecosystem to recover from disruption (for example, a forest fire or pest infestation). In general, complex ecosystems display more resilience than simple systems. If a plantation forest contains only one species of tree, an attack by a single pest may destroy the entire forest. A forest with many species is much more likely to withstand pest attacks. The proportion of species within the forest may change, but its ecological integrity and health will survive.

Species extinction has accelerated in the past decades, and loss of **biodiversity** is likely to be one of the most critical environmental problems of the coming century (see Box 15-1).[7] Biological diversity can be viewed economically as a significant positive externality associated with preservation of existing forests and ecosystems—or as a negative externality associated with their loss. These externalities are not reflected in

---

[6]See Holling, 1986; Common and Perrings, 1995.

[7]See Wilson, 1988 and 1992; Ehrlich and Daily, 1993.

15-1   Loss of Biodiversity

Why does biodiversity matter? Loss of a single species of beetle may never be noticed, and seems to have no economic impact. But any species may have vital pharmaceutical or medical value, and cumulatively the existence of many species promotes crucial ecosystem resilience. In 1990, a compound derived from twigs and leaves from a tree in the Malaysian rainforest was found to stop the

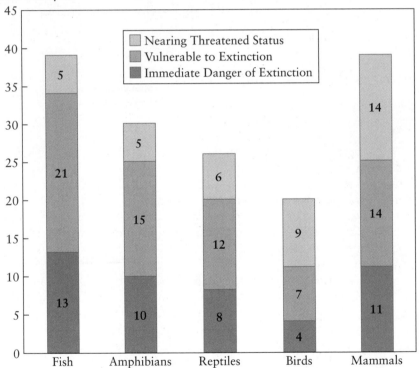

FIGURE 15-5 *Threatened and Endangered Species*
Source: World Conservation Union, *IUCN Red List of Threatened Animals*, 1996. Adapted from Tuxill, 1998.

(continued on following page)

spread of one of the two strains of HIV that causes AIDS. But when researchers re-turned for more samples, they found that the stand of trees had been felled, and no other trees in the vicinity yielded the crucial ingredient.[1] Our knowledge of the world's biodiversity, and of scale of biodiversity losses, is very limited.

> Perhaps the biggest unknown in the debate over mass extinctions is how many species exist. Scientists know that the 1.4 million named species represent a small portion of existing wildlife, though estimates of the total vary from 10 million to 100 million. Because species density is highest in tropical forests, every large swath that falls or burns is likely to contain beetles, plants, fungi, in-sects or animals that could vanish before ever coming to human notice.[2]

An extensive review of worldwide animal species conservation by the Interna-tional Union for the Conservation of Nature (IUCN) led to the publication of the *1996 Red List* of threatened and endangered species. This study concluded that about 10 percent of birds and 25 percent of mammals face threat of extinction. While the survey covers only a fifth of reptile species, an eighth of amphibians, and a tenth of fish, 20 percent of reptiles and amphibians and more than 33 percent of fishes were considered threatened.[3]

---

[1]Scott Allen, "Loss of a tree means loss of an HIV blocker," *Boston Globe*, November 10, 1992.
[2]*New York Times*, June 2, 1998, E7.
[3]Tuxill, 1998.

---

the commercial exploitation of forests for timber. We must account for them, however, in any policy for sustainable forest management.

Economic and Demographic Pressures on Forests

Economic forces that promote forest destruction include a steadily increasing global market for wood products, leading to declining forest area or conversion to ecologi-cally less-desirable plantation forestry. Rising demand alone, however, does not fully explain forest destruction. Overexploitation is often the result of **institutional failure.** Many governments either allow open access to forests, or encourage **under-pricing** of forest resources by selling logging rights well below their market value.[8]

In some cases, local communities have traditionally managed forests in a sustain-able manner—until they lose control over the resource to governments and logging companies. Governments often grant logging concessions and sometimes monopolies

---

[8]See Panayotou, 1993, Chapter 3, for a discussion of policy failures in forest management.

"Much forest exploitation and conversion is encouraged and subsidized by governments. In both developed and developing countries, these policies result in forests being sold at prices far below what the timber alone is worth. In Belize, a Malaysian logging firm paid about $1 a hectare for timber rights. Indonesia's give-away timber concessions cost the government $2.5 billion in lost revenues in 1990 alone. In the United States, timber sales from national forests lost over $1 billion from 1992 to 1994. . . . Subsidies for below-cost logging, processing, roads, and infrastructure are so large that governments are essentially paying private interests to take the timber and convert the land to other uses.

"Globalization and the lowering of barriers to international trade and investment allow corporations to roam the world seeking more profitable forest opportunities. Legal international trade in forest products has almost tripled since 1970. Meanwhile, illegal and unrecorded trade has likely expanded far faster, encouraged by lax enforcement of domestic forest laws and gaps in international ones. The Brazilian government, for example, estimates that 80 percent of the timber harvest in the Amazon violates the law.

"As some Asian nations have depleted their forest resources, they have turned elsewhere to satisfy their domestic consumption needs and the demands of their forest industries. Companies that have grown wealthy from domestic timber exploitation are using their capital to expand elsewhere. . . . One Malaysian company controls 60–85 percent of the logging concessions in Papua, New Guinea. In 1996, the area of Amazon forest under concession to Asian timber companies quadrupled to more than 12 million hectares.

"Few forest communities have been successful in gaining recognition for their customary rights. Their right of occupancy has been banned in some cases, and disregarded in others. . . . In Brazil and Venezuela, hard-won indigenous reserves have been invaded by miners, loggers, and settlers. In Indonesia, the government created a real-life **tragedy of the commons** when it declared in 1967 that it had sole jurisdiction over the nation's forests. Customary rights to common areas, which had evolved as a complex and sustainable management system over many generations, were not legally recognized. The government . . . was unable to police the nation's vast forests, and the communities who are in the forest no longer had the power to stop exploitation by outsiders. One analysis concluded that "the traditional rights of millions of people have been handed over to a relatively small number of commercial firms and state enterprises."

SOURCE

Adapted from Janet N. Abramovitz, *Taking a Stand: Cultivating a New Relationship with the World's Forests,* Worldwatch Paper no. 149, ©1998. Reprinted with permission of Worldwatch Institute. www.worldwatch.org.

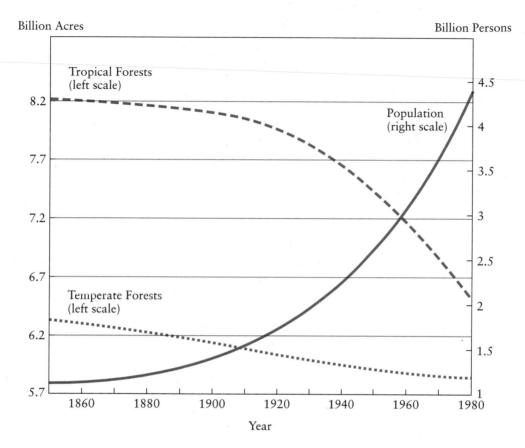

FIGURE 15-6 *Deforestation and Population Growth*
Sources: World Resources Institute, 1987, p. 272; United Nations, 2001.

to timber companies. They have also encouraged large agricultural firms to encroach on the forest for extensive cattle ranching, as in Brazil and Central America, or for cash-crop cultivation of coffee, tobacco, and other export crops, as in Indonesia, other Asian countries, and Latin America.

Demographic pressure also contributes to forest loss. Governments have encouraged settlements in formerly undisturbed forest areas as a means of accomodating population growth. These new settlers often lack knowledge of forest management, and their practices of exploitation and agricultural encroachment may have deep and lasting ecological impact.[9] Although poor policies are usually more to blame for forest loss than simple population pressure (Box 15-2), rising global population has been accompanied by a general trend of decline in forested area over a long period (Figure 15-6).

―――――
[9]See Abramovitz, 1998, for many specific examples of destructive government forest policies.

Policies for Sustainable Forest Management

Both economic and ecological theory can offer guidance in devising better approaches to forest management. Better policy approaches can be implemented both on the supply side, by promoting sustainable forestry, and on the demand side, by changing consumption patterns, reducing wastes and expanding recycling.

Supply Side: Property Rights and Pricing Policies

A major issue in forest management throughout the developing world is the need for secure **property rights.** Individuals and communities whose land tenure is insecure, including many migrants, have little incentive to conserve forests. Economic necessity forces them to exploit the forest for maximum short-term gain and then move on. If granted secure tenure, they will have an interest in a continuing flow of income from the forest, including forest products other than timber, such as fruits, latex (from rubber-tapping), or shade-grown coffee.[10]

Stable communities also have incentives to maintain forests in order to enjoy their accompanying positive externalities. A village or community situated in the mountains, for example, may undertake a program of reforestation both to sustain the supply of wood and also because trees retain soils on the slopes, preventing erosion. Forested ecosystems also help to provide a stable supply of fresh water and prevent flooding.

Some positive externalities associated with forest maintenance or reforestation are global in nature. Forests remove and store atmospheric carbon, reducing the concentration of carbon dioxide in the atmosphere and lowering the risks of global climate change. This may bring no immediate benefit to the local community, but future global climate change agreements may well provide compensation to nations that preserve or expand their forest cover.[11] In the future, a country might be able to earn income from its forests by keeping them in place rather than by cutting them down for timber export. The carbon storage function of tropical forests has been estimated at $3.7 trillion, assuming a carbon storage value of $20 per ton.[12]

Another critical issue is **full pricing** of forest concessions. Government policies of low-cost sales of timber constitute **subsidies** to major logging corporations, as well as an inducement to corrupt practices such as payoffs to government officials for valuable concessions. The many negative externalities of overexploiting forests make this

---

[10]Shade-grown coffee leaves forest trees standing, with coffee bushes beneath, whereas sun-grown coffee requires complete removal of forest cover.

[11]Under the Kyoto Protocol, negotiated in December 1997, nations committed to reducing their greenhouse gas emissions must include in their calculations the changes to their carbon stock resulting from "afforestation, deforestation, and reforestation." See discussion in Chapter 18.

[12]See Myers, 1996.

is a particularly inappropriate use of a subsidy, which should be used only where clear positive externalities exist.[13]

Economic theory supports secure property rights and full pricing of resources. The ecological perspective adds another important dimension to forest management issues: Forests must be recognized as complex ecosystems to be managed as such, both to preserve healthy ecosystems and to supply of a wide array of goods and services for current and future generations. These ecological goals often differ from the priorities of private landowners, who seek to manage the forest for profitability, often selecting fast-growing species and cutting timber on a short cycle rather the longer, natural cycle that allows a mature forest to develop.

Government policy can encourage sound forest management by such measures as tax breaks for sustainable forestry or limitations on clear-cutting. From an economic-theory perspective, the positive externalities associated with good forest management justify such policies. Programs have also begun for **certification** of sustainably produced wood so that consumers and public agencies can encourage sound practices by their purchasing choices. Experience shows that many consumers are willing to pay a premium above market price for sustainably produced wood.

In cases where complex and old-growth forest ecosystems can only be effectively protected through preservation as parkland, government or private conservation agencies can acquire them as **public goods.** In many developing nations buffer zones around parkland allow local communities to pursue sustainable exploitation of forest products. This can overcome local hostility to parks on the part of villagers who resent the loss of access to forest resources.

Often a key factor is the availability of credit on reasonable terms to villagers who invest in replanting and **agroforestry** (mixing tree crops with food crops). As we have seen, a high interest rate encourages a short planning horizon, and low-cost credit can encourage profitable investment in long-term resource conservation.

Demand Side: Changing Consumption Patterns

As we have noted, overall demand for wood products has risen steadily. The increase in paper demand has been especially rapid (Figure 15-7). Like other forms of consumption, paper consumption is unequally distributed: U.S. paper use is 341 kilograms per person per year, while in Germany per capita consumption is 200 kilograms, in Brazil 35 kilograms, and in India only 4 kilograms.

> If everyone in the world consumed as much as the average American, the world would be using nearly seven times as much paper. And by 2050 it would be 11 times as much. If, on the other hand, paper use stabilized at today's global average—50 kilograms a year per person—paper consumption in 2050 could be held to 1.7 times today's level.[14]

---

[13]See Panayotou, 1998, pp. 78–79, on policies for fully pricing forest concessions.

[14]Abramovitz, 1998.

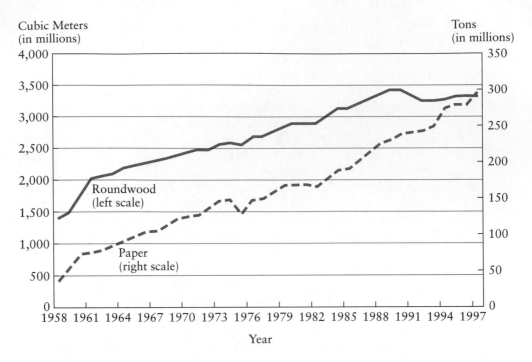

FIGURE 15-7 *Global Demand for Wood and Paper Products*
Source: Worldwatch Institute database, 1999.

Expanded recycling of paper and other wood products has significant potential to reduce pressure on forests. Worldwide, 43 percent of wastepaper is now recycled. Developing countries such as India typically recover and reuse many paper products and often import and recycle scrap paper from industrialized nations.

Low prices for paper and other wood products serve both as an incentive for greater consumption and a disincentive to expanded recycling. In some cases, direct and indirect subsidies for forest exploitation encourage use of virgin rather than recycled paper. Internalizing environmental externalities into prices would encourage greater efficiency at all stages of the production cycle. Properly pricing wood products would increase prices for nonrecycled paper and all one-time-use wood products relative to recycled-materials prices, thereby encouraging a higher recycling rate.[15]

[15]Data on paper consumption and recycling from Abramovitz, 1998; Abramovitz and Mattoon, 1999. For more on paper recycling, see Chapter 17.

15-3   Forest Carbon Storage Valuation in Zimbabwe

One of the many benefits of forests is that trees and other plants store carbon dioxide in their tissue, called carbon sequestration. Net increases in plant biomass generally increase carbon storage, essentially removing CO_2 from the earth's atmosphere. As discussed in Chapter 18, CO_2 is an important greenhouse gas that influences the global climate. Thus, efforts to increase forest cover or prevent forest loss provide a positive externality by tempering climate change.

One of the reasons for overexploitation of forests is that positive externality values are not reflected in market transactions. Estimates of these values can be used to support efforts to preserve forests. A 2000 article in the journal *Ecological Economics* (Kundhlande et al., 2000) provides estimates of the carbon sequestration benefits for the savanna region of Zimbabwe.

The authors use a value of $25 per ton for the benefits of carbon sequestration. Future benefits are discounted at a rate of 5% annually. The present value of carbon sequestration is estimated to be around $300 per hectare. This value is significant, but less than the potential agricultural value of land, which is around $600 per hectare. Thus, based on carbon storage benefits alone, policies to prevent the conversion of forests to agricultural land are not economically justified. In combination with other forest values, however, carbon storage values might alter the economic logic of forest conversion.

Forests also provide other values including watershed protection, wildlife habitat, recreational values, and marketable products. A complete accounting of forest benefits may indicate that forest preservation is justified but, as we saw in Chapter 6, obtaining valid estimates of all values may be difficult. Forest policies based solely on market behavior "fail to fully account for the numerous functions and values that are not captured through market transactions. Forest use decisions that ignore those benefits that are not normally exchanged in markets introduce distortions in resource allocation, often with detrimental environmental consequences."

SOURCE

Kundhlande, G., W. L. Adamowicz, and I. Mapaure. "Valuing Ecological Services in a Savanna Ecosystem: A Case Study from Zimbabwe," *Ecological Economics* 33 (2000): 401–412.

Water: Depletion and Renewal

Water, because it can be reused indefinitely if not severely polluted, can be characterized as a renewable resource. But stocks of water such as underground aquifers are also depletable resources. Some aquifers have such long replenishment times as to be essentially nonrenewable on a human time-scale.[16] Thus analysis of water systems combines elements of renewable- and nonrenewable-resource theory. Water also has a unique and essential ecological function.

Many of the principles of renewable resource management apply to water systems, but water availability is subject to absolute limits. Although water is reusable, the amount available in a given region is limited to the total **freshwater runoff,** of which only about a third is **stable supply.**

> Each year, evaporation fueled by the sun's energy lifts 500,000 cubic kilometers of moisture into the atmosphere each year—86 percent from the oceans and 14 percent from the land. An equal amount falls back to earth as rain, sleet, or snow, but it is distributed in different proportions: whereas the continents lose about 70,000 cubic kilometers through evaporation, they gain 110,000 through precipitation. As a result, roughly 40,000 cubic kilometers are transferred from the sea to the land each year. . . . Two-thirds runs off in floods, leaving about 14,000 cubic kilometers as a relatively stable source of supply.[17]

This stable supply is about 7,000 cubic meters per person, but it is unevenly distributed. Some areas are **water-abundant,** and others are **water-scarce.** Hydrologists[18] have established that, considering the water needs of modern societies, a threshold of 2,000 cubic meters per person per year represents the level above which a population can be sustained comfortably by the water available. Between 1,000 and 2,000 cubic meters per person, the situation is "water-stressed," below 1,000, "water-scarce," where "lack of water becomes a severe constraint on food production, economic development and protection of natural systems."[19]

Table 15-1 lists countries already experiencing water stress or scarcity. Considering that the developing countries on this list will continue to experience rapid population growth over the next half-century (with some projected to double in population) the water problem is likely to worsen in the coming decades.[20]

---

[16]Aquifers under the Sahara, for example, are thousands of years old and are sometimes referred to as "fossil water."

[17]Postel, 1992, p. 27.

[18]Hydrology is the scientific study of water's distribution and movement on the earth's surface, underground, and in the atmosphere.

[19]Postel, 1992, p. 29. See also Falkenmark and Widstrand, 1992.

[20]For an extensive recent analysis of the world's water resources, see Gleick, 2000.

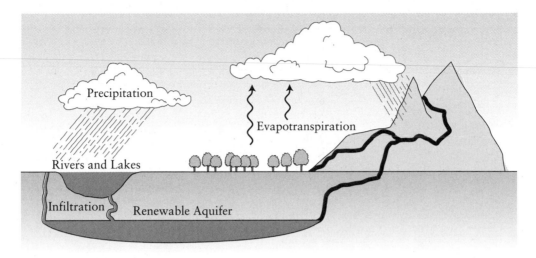

FIGURE 15-8 *The Water Cycle*

Increasing Supply: Aquifers and Dams

The two sides to the water-population equation are supply and demand. We can respond to scarcity by either increasing supply or decreasing demand. Past water management policies generally oriented toward increasing supply; systematic conservation policies have only recently begun to attract attention.

Many countries and regions that face water scarcity problems rely on water from underground aquifers. Aquifers are replenished or **recharged** by rainfall, but in most cases use rates greatly exceed recharge rates. Countries such as Saudi Arabia and Libya are relying on "fossil" groundwater from ancient aquifers in desert areas that have practically no recharge and are likely to be exhausted in the next 40 to 60 years.

Almost all major water-scarce areas of the world suffer from **groundwater overdraft**—withdrawal of water exceeding aquifer recharge capacity, resulting in declining water tables. In the Western United States, the Ogallala aquifer is severely depleted, and irrigated area has started to shrink. Similar problems affect aquifers in North China, India, Pakistan, Mexico, and many other countries.

Another way of increasing water supply is damming surface flows. Dams can capture floodwater that would otherwise be unavailable for human use, as well as providing hydroelectric power. Worldwide, 40,000 large dams and about 800,000 small

TABLE 15-1 Water-Scarce and Water-Stressed Countries

	Water-scarce countries (renewable water supply per capita <1,000 cubic meters)		Water-stressed countries (renewable water supply per capita < 2,000 cubic meters)	
Sub-Saharan Africa	Eritrea	789	Benin	1751
	Kenya	696	Botswana	1870
	Mauritania	163	Burkina Faso	1535
	Niger	346	Ethiopia	1771
	Rwanda	965	Ghana	1607
	Somalia	563	Malawi	1690
			Nigeria	1815
			South Africa	1011
			Sudan	1227
			Zimbabwe	1182
Middle East & North Africa	Algeria	460	Iran	1755
	Egypt	43*	Iraq	1615
	Israel	289	Morocco	1071
	Jordan	114		
	Libya	100		
	Saudi Arabia	119		
	Syria	456		
	Tunisia	371		
Europe	Belgium	822	Germany	1165
	Hungary	604	Poland	1278
	Netherlands	635	Ukraine	1029
			U.K.	1219
Asia	Singapore	172	Azerbaijan	1069
	Turkmenistan	232	India	1896
	Uzbekistan	704	Korea	1434
			Pakistan	1678

*Not including Nile River flows originating in other countries. Including Nile flows = 896 m³ per cap.
Source: World Resources Institute, 1998.

An irrigation and drainage system in Saudi Arabia. Agriculture in water-scarce countries is heavily dependent on irrigation.

dams are now in operation.[21] More dams are being built, but the best sites are already in use. Existing dams often suffer problems of siltation, and new large dam proposals have been criticized for the environmental and social damage resulting from the flooding of large areas.[22]

Given the vast amounts of seawater on the planet, **desalination** has appeal as a potential source of virtually unlimited supply. Here, however, cost is a significant barrier. Desalination is expensive: one to two dollars per cubic meter, four to eight times average urban water costs and ten to twenty times the current cost of water for agricultural use. Although desalination is an important source of supply in some arid regions, it is likely to provide only a small proportion of global freshwater supply.[23]

---

[21]Postel, 1999, p. 81..

[22]See World Commission on Dams, 2000.

[23]Postel, 1992, pp. 45–46; Gleick, 2000, Chapter 5.

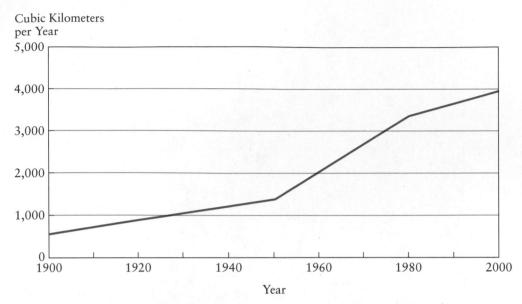

Cubic Kilometers
per Year

FIGURE 15-9 *Global Water Demand*
Source: Adapted from Postel, 1992, based on I. A. Shiklomanov, "Global Water Resources," *Nature and Resources,* vol. 26, no. 3, 1990. 2000 projections are as adjusted by Shiklomanov in 1998, cited in Gleick, 2000, pp. 50–53.

Demand: Always More Water?

The three major sectors of water use are agricultural, industrial, and domestic use. Agriculture is by far the biggest consumer of water, accounting for two-thirds of freshwater demand worldwide. Although 83 percent of the world's cropland is rain-fed, the 17 percent that requires irrigation produces more than 40 percent of the world's food supply.[24] Arid and semi-arid countries, most of which are in the developing world, rely heavily on irrigation for food production.

Irrigation is thus a cornerstone of global food security. However, current irrigation demands are pressing against or exceeding water supply limits in many areas, and the rate of expansion of irrigated land—a key factor in agricultural output growth—has slowed significantly.

Industrial demand has also grown rapidly in the developing world. Many industries in the early phases of economic development are water-intensive. Urbanization and improvement of standards of living have promoted increased domestic water demand. Between 1900 and 1995, freshwater consumption rose sixfold, more than double the rate of population growth (see Figure 15-9).[25] In future, the combined growth of urban, industrial, and agricultural demand will clearly increase water demand significantly, especially in the developing world.

---

[24]Postel, 1999, p. 42.

[25]UNEP, 1999, p. 4.

Policies for Sustainable Water Management

We can alter the current trend of ever-increasing water demand through policies to increase water use efficiency. Whereas traditional irrigation by flooding or channeling water by gravity is inefficient (60 percent of the water is lost by evaporation or infiltration), new techniques of **microirrigation** by drip systems allow an efficiency of 95 percent.[26]

Recycling and reuse of wastewater can reduce water demand in many industries. Leak detection and repair, as well as efficient appliances, can help improve urban and domestic water efficiency.

The most important way to induce more efficient water use is through appropriate water pricing. Prices should serve as indicators of economic scarcity, reflecting physical limits and environmental externalities. For various social and political reasons however, governments have maintained low water prices, particularly for agricultural supply.

Governments often build, maintain, and operate irrigation systems with public funds and then charge prices well below actual cost. These policies of subsidizing water have created an artificial climate of water abundance—even in arid areas like the western part of the United States—that has favored wasteful and inefficient water use. Setting prices closer to the real cost of supplying water would encourage farmers to shift to more efficient methods of irrigation, as well as giving city dwellers and manufacturers an incentive to conserve, recycle, and reuse their supplies.

Figure 15-10 shows how pricing policies affect water supply and demand. The figure shows total water demand (D) together with the marginal cost of supplying water (MC). In addition, the full marginal social cost (MSC) is shown, taking into account such factors as damage to ecosystems or depletion of aquifers. It is reasonable to assume that these costs increase with larger water withdrawals.

Setting a water price (P) below true marginal cost leads to excessive demand of Q_D. This can create problems. Because quantity demanded exceeds quantity supplied, some form of government allocation or rationing will be required. But the government will also feel pressure to subsidize the supply of water. In this example, an increase in supply to Q_S—meeting part, but not all, of the excess demand—would require a government subsidy equal to area C. Significant external or user costs may also be associated with excessive water consumption, shown by area B.

Full marginal-cost pricing would lead to an equilibrium at the lower supply level of Q_E, with a price of P_E. If we include full social costs, the price would be P^*, with quantity consumed of Q^*. This would be the best solution, leading to a net social benefit equal to area A, and avoiding the external costs B and subsidy payment C. This pricing policy would promote economic efficiency as well as internalization of environmental costs. Political pressures for a lower water price, however, are likely to make this full-pricing policy difficult to implement.[27]

Government policy can also promote the development of water markets. Establishing clear rules regarding water rights will facilitate a water trading system through

[26]Postel, 1992, p. 104.

[27]Panayotou, 1998, pp. 165–168, provides examples of the role of pricing in water resource management.

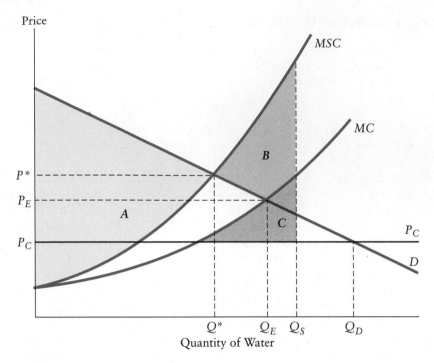

FIGURE 15-10 *Effects of Subsidized Water Pricing*

which a market price for water can be established. This can promote both conservation and further development of water resources. Possible drawbacks to such a system include encouraging excessive withdrawals from rivers and groundwater, and placing insufficient value on in-stream uses of water, including recreational and ecological functions. In addition, water rights systems raise significant issues of equity, because more affluent users can bid water away from lower-income farmers or domestic consumers.

Conclusion: Reconciling Economic and Ecological Principles

A general conclusion from the basic economic theory of renewable resource management is that *economically* efficient use of natural resources, although generally more sustainable than open-access exploitation, is not necessarily sustainable from an *ecological* perspective. An important goal of natural resource management, therefore, must be to reconcile the differing principles of economics and ecology.

As we have noted, ecological sustainability has dimensions not reflected in the economic analyses of resource use. Whereas economic sustainability is concerned primarily with sustaining a flow of income over time, ecological sustainability depends

15-4   Water Scarcity, Pollution , and Politics in Mexico

In Mexico, a growing population struggles to cope with problems of scarce and polluted water supplies. About 15 million Mexicans, or 16 percent of the population, do not have access to drinking water services. In rural areas of Mexico only 52 percent of the people have access to drinking water services.

While local water shortages do exist in some arid regions of Mexico, the more prominent problems concern water quality and politics. Nearly every river and stream in Mexico is polluted and 73 percent of the nation's water supply, including both surface and ground water, is contaminated. The health costs of drinking water contamination in Mexico have been estimated at $3.6 billion annually. While Mexico needs to build more water treatment plants, it does not even have the money to maintain existing plants. None of the 13 treatment plants in Chiapas State are operating because of a lack of money to perform necessary repairs.

The aquifer that supplies Mexico City is nearly depleted, and water is pumped nearly a mile uphill, from as much as 125 miles away. Enough water leaks annually from cracks in supply pipes to provide for the water needs of Los Angeles. Groundwater pumping in Mexico City is lowering its underground aquifer by as much as 11 feet per year, causing streets and buildings to bend and sink.

Water is a powerful political issue in Mexico. Allocation of water has been based on political alliances, and water supply can be cut off to punish political opponents. The 2000 presidential election of Vincente Fox, ending over 70 years of rule by the Institutional Revolutionary Party (PRI), was partly a result of his promise to increase water supplies. One possibility for funding improvements in drinking water supplies is to reduce implicit and explicit government subsidies—water subsidies comprise over 1 percent of the federal budget. Large mining, ranching, and farming businesses, who consume at least 70 percent of the nation's water, currently obtain water for free; a proposed law would start charging these companies for water.

A solution to Mexico's water problems will require institutional and market reforms. For many years in Mexico, water, like power, has flowed towards the wealthy. Proposed reform include increased private sector involvement in providing water. A movement is also underway to decentralize water management and increase public participation in decisions regarding water issues.

SOURCES

Hazin, Lilian Saade. "Toward More Efficient Urban Water Management in Mexico" (2001). Available at http://www.iwrn.net/mexsaade.htm.
Weiner, Tim. "Mexico Grows Parched, with Pollution and Politics," *New York Times,* April 14, 2001.

on resilience—the "bounce-back" capacity of ecosystems affected by economic exploitation or by natural phenomena such as disease or weather extremes. Resilience depends on **ecological complexity,** an essential element of sustainable natural systems. Economic harvesting with maximum profit in mind often destroys complexity.

A key determinant of natural resource management is technology. We saw in Chapter 14 that as fishing technologies become more "productive" in an economic sense, fisheries are more likely to be overexploited. Technological progress accelerates economic growth, but relatively slow-growing natural resource systems come under greater pressure from the demands of economic "efficiency."

Similarly, old-growth forests are doomed to clear-cutting in a forestry regime that places a premium on rapid growth and shorter harvesting periods, and that can bring to bear powerful equipment for timber removal. Total forested area may not decline, but natural forest will be replaced with fast-growing plantation monocultures. In rapidly growing developing economies, many natural resource systems, traditionally harvested in a relatively sustainable manner, come under much heavier pressure as a market logic prevails and modern technology penetrates remote areas.

On the other hand, technologies such as paper recycling and efficient irrigation have great potential for conservation of scarce resources. Given the proper incentives, ecologically friendly technology can promote less wasteful resource use, recycling, and more efficient consumption.

A related issue is **social sustainability.** Indigenous communities dependent on forest products are threatened by more intensive, "modernized" methods of forest exploitation. Local fishing communities have often been devastated by economically more productive trawlers that push fish stocks to collapse. Social sustainability and resource sustainability are mutually dependent.

Policies for natural resource management must also consider continuing growth in overall demand. We have seen how growing demand has increased the impact of market failures in fisheries, forests, and water systems. Although policies aimed at increasing economic efficiency can improve resource management at the *micro*economic level, they can also increase overall stress on natural systems at the *macro*economic level. More efficient resource use requires less resource input per unit of consumption, but may also encourage expanded consumption by lowering prices.

An **ecosystems management** model stressing the ecological integrity of fisheries, forests, and water systems may provide more appropriate policy guidance. In such a model, economic efficiency principles can be extremely important, as reflected in the need for secure land tenure institutions, suitable price incentives, and credit extension to rural communities. But the principles of economic efficiency alone can also conflict with long-term natural resource sustainability. Effective natural resource systems management must therefore consider both economic and ecological principles.

SUMMARY

Forest management policies can be derived from the ecological principles of forest growth. Forest growth patterns imply an optimum rotation period for commercial timber. However, this commercial optimum neglects other ecological functions of forests.

Deforestation and conversion of natural forest to plantation cause significant biodiversity loss. Values associated with biodiversity represent significant externalities rarely reflected in market prices.

Growing demand for wood and wood products increases pressure on forests. Open access to many forests creates incentives for short-term exploitation without investment in replanting or sustainable forestry. In addition, many governments subsidize excessive forest clearance by making public lands available to timber companies at low prices.

Policies that encourage secure tenure and support for small-scale forestry enterprises and agroforestry can create incentives to maintain environmentally stable forests. In addition to timber, forests can provide income from other products such as fruit and latex. Certification programs for sustainably produced forest products can benefit from some consumers' willingness to pay a premium for certified wood. Public good and carbon storage functions also represent positive economic values of standing forest.

Like forests, water systems are under pressure from steadily growing agricultural, industrial, and urban demand. Many countries experience permanent water stress, defined as less than 2,000 cubic meters per capita available supply. Shortages will become more serious as population grows.

Increasing supply by pumping from aquifers has led to groundwater overdraft in major water-scarce areas throughout the world. Construction of dams also increases available supply, but most major dam sites are already being exploited, and new dam construction often involves major environmental and social costs.

Proper water pricing can promote conservation and encourage technologies for efficient water use. Government policies, however, often subsidize water, thereby encouraging over-use. A better approach for both forests and water systems is ecosystems management, aimed at balancing economic and ecological functions.

KEY TERMS AND CONCEPTS

agroforestry	microirrigation
asset	monoculture
biodiversity	optimum rotation period
biomass	property rights
certification	public goods
clear-cut	recharge of aquifers
desalination	resilience
discount rate	social sustainability
ecological complexity	stable water supply
ecosystems management	stock
flow	subsidies
freshwater runoff	tragedy of the commons
full pricing	under-pricing
groundwater overdraft	use value

institutional failure
logistic curve
mean annual increment (MAI)

water-abundant and
   water-scarce areas
water cycle

DISCUSSION QUESTIONS

1. Unlike ocean fisheries, forests can be privately owned, and in fact many millions of acres of forests are owned and managed by private corporations. In economic theory, private ownership should create incentives for efficient management. To what extent is this true of privately owned forests? Is efficient management also beneficial to the environment?

2. How can the timber values of forests be balanced with their value in supporting biodiversity? What changes in property regimes and forest management policies could help achieve the dual goals of economic profitability and environmental preservation?

3. In what ways do economic and ecological analyses of water systems resemble those of forests and fisheries? How do they differ? Which water management problems can be addressed through market mechanisms, and which require some form of government or social management?

PROBLEMS

1. XYZ Forest Products owns a 2,000-acre tract of forest land. 1,000 acres are currently planted in hardwood trees (oak, beech, etc.) and 1,000 in softwoods (pine). An acre of either kind of forest contains a biomass (standing timber) of 200 tons/acre. Hardwoods, however, grow more slowly: an acre of hardwoods will add 10 tons/acre/year of new growth, whereas an acre of softwoods will add 20 tons/acre/year. The current age of the hardwoods is 40 years, and of the softwoods 20 years; both are currently at their maximum levels of mean annual increment.

   The going prices are $500 per ton for hardwood and $300 per ton for softwood. These prices are expected to remain stable for the indefinite future (in real terms). Two management practices are possible: clear-cutting or sustainable timbering, in which the amount of biomass removed annually just equals annual growth. Costs of clear-cutting are $40 per ton (for either kind of tree), and costs of sustainable timbering are $70 per ton.

   Analyze the profit-maximizing forest management policy XYZ corporation will pursue if

   (a) Real interest rates are 3 percent per annum;
   (b) Real interest rates are 5 percent per annum.

2. Now assume that XYZ is taken over by the Gargantua conglomerate, which has $100 million in debt at an 8 percent real interest rate. Analyze their probable forest management practice.

      Comment on the role of the interest rate here and suggest a government policy on forest management. What other considerations not apparent in the data given here would affect policy formulation? What would you recommend if the forest were publicly rather than privately owned? How might your recommendations differ for forest management in developed versus developing nations?

REFERENCES

Abramovitz, Janet N. *Taking a Stand: Cultivating a New Relationship with the World's Forests*. Worldwatch Paper No. 140. Washington, D.C.: Worldwatch Institute, 1998.

Abramovitz, Janet N., and Ashley T. Mattoon. *Paper Cuts: Recovering the Paper Landscape*. Worldwatch Paper No. 149. Washington, D.C.: Worldwatch Institute, 1999.

Common, Mick, and Charles Perrings. "Towards an Ecological Economics of Sustainability," *Ecological Economics* 6 (July 1992): 7–34.

Ehrlich, Paul R., and Gretchen C. Daily. "Population Extinction and Saving Biodiversity," *Ambio* 22 (May 1993): 64–68. Summarized in *A Survey of Sustainable Development*, edited by Harris et al., 176–178. Washington, D.C.: Island Press, 2000.

Falkenmark, Malin, and Carl Widstrand. *Population and Water Resources: A Delicate Balance*. Washington, D.C.: Population Reference Bureau, 1992.

Gleick, Peter H. *The World's Water 2000–2001: The Biennial Report on Freshwater Resources*. Washington, D.C.: Island Press, 2000.

Hartwick, John M., and Nancy D. Olewiler. *The Economics of Natural Resource Use*, 2nd ed. New York: Addison Wesley, 1998.

Holling, C. S. "The Resilience of Terrestrial Ecosystems: Local Surprise and Global Change." In *Sustainable Development of the Biosphere*, edited by W. C. Clark and R. E. Munn. Cambridge, England: Cambridge University Press, 1986.

Myers, Norman. "The World's Forests: Problems and Potentials." *Environmental Conservation* 23 no. 2 (1996): 156–168. Summarized in *A Survey of Sustainable Development*, edited by Harris et al., 183–188. Washington, D.C.: Island Press, 2000.

Panayotou, Theodore. *Green Markets: The Economics of Sustainable Development*. San Francisco: Institute for Contemporary Studies Press, 1993.

Panayotou, Theodore. *Instruments of Change: Motivating and Financing Sustainable Development*. London: Earthscan Publications, 1998.

Postel, Sandra. *Last Oasis: Facing Water Scarcity*. Worldwatch Environmental Alert Series, edited by Linda Starke. New York: Norton, 1992.

Postel, Sandra. *Pillar of Sand: Can the Irrigation Miracle Last?* New York: Norton, 1999.

Tuxill, John. *Losing Strands in the Web of Life: Vertebrate Declines and the Conservation of Biological Diversity*. Worldwatch Paper No. 141. Washington, D.C.: Worldwatch Institute, 1998.

United Nations Economic and Social Council. *World Population Prospects: The 1998 Revision*. United Nations, 1998.

Wilson, E. O., ed. *Biodiversity*. Washington, D.C.: National Academy Press, 1988.

Wilson, E. O. *The Diversity of Life*. New York: Norton, 1992.

World Commission on Dams. *Dams and Development: A New Framework for Decision-Making*. London: Earthscan Publications, 2000. Also at www.dams.org.

World Resources Institute and The International Institute for Environment and Development, *World Resources 1987*. New York: Basic Books, 1987.

World Resources Institute, United Nations Development Programme, United Nations Environment Programme, and the World Bank. *World Resources 1998–99: A Guide to the Global Environment*. Washington, D.C.: World Resources Institute, 1998.

World Resources Institute, United Nations Development Programme, United Nations Environment Programme, and the World Bank. *World Resources 2000–2001: A Guide to the Global Environment*. Washington, D.C.: World Resources Institute, 2000.

United Nations Department of Economic and Social Affairs, Population Division. *World Population Prospects: The 2000 Revision*. United Nations, 2001.

United Nations Environmental Programme. *Global Environmental Outlook 2000*. London: Earthscan Publications, 1999.

WEB SITES

1. **http://www.fs.fed.us/sustained/siteindex.html** The U.S. Forest Service's web site, with links to information on sustainable forest management.
2. **http://www.fscoax.org/** Home page for the Forest Stewardship Council, a leader in the development of an international forest products labeling plan that certifies products grown in a sustainable manner.
3. **http://www.ran.org/info_center/index.html** Links to information about rainforests from the Rainforest Action Network, an environmental group that campaigns to protect rainforests around the world.
4. **http://www.wri.org/water/** The World Resources Institute's web site about freshwater issues. The site includes discussion papers on freshwater issues as well as extensive data.

Pollution: Impacts and Policy Responses

CHAPTER FOCUS QUESTIONS

■ What policies are best for controlling pollution?
■ How can we balance the cost and benefits of pollution regulation?
■ Should industries be allowed to purchase permits to pollute?
■ How can we deal with long-lived and cumulative pollutants?

CHAPTER

16

Pollution: Analysis and Policy

The Economics of Pollution Control

One of the services provided by natural systems is a **sink function**—the capacity to absorb wastes and pollution. Although essential to human life and economic systems, this function has often been abused by excessive pollution. This raises two questions for environmental policy. First, how much pollution is acceptable—given that any society must emit some waste products? Second, how can we best control or reduce pollution to this acceptable level?

How Much Pollution Is Too Much?

If we take an economic approach to answering this question, we need to compare marginal costs and benefits associated with a pollution-generating activity. We saw in Chapter 3 that this leads to the concept of an **optimal pollution level**—the amount of pollution that exactly balances marginal social benefits and marginal social costs. Another way of looking at this is to consider the marginal cost of pollution control versus the marginal cost of pollution damage (Figure 16-1). In this approach, pollution reduction is worthwhile so long as control costs are less than the benefits gained in terms of reduced damage.

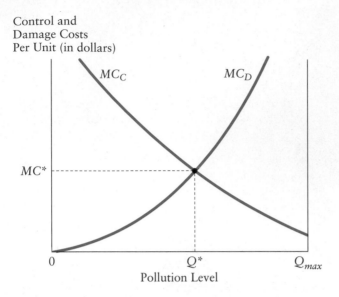

FIGURE 16-1 *Marginal Costs of Pollution Damage and Control*

Picking a Pollution Control Policy

In Chapter 3 we discussed **pollution taxes** or charges levied per unit emitted. Other options include regulation, in which the government sets specific limits on emissions, or **transferable pollution permits,** which allow firms to emit only the level of pollution for which they have permits. Transferability implies that firms can buy and sell these permits, with low-emitting firms able to sell extra permits, and high-emitting firms able to purchase additional permits.

In this chapter, we will approach the questions of the level and method of pollution control primarily in terms of economic analysis. At the same time, we will bear in mind the limitations of a purely economic perspective. In dealing with the impacts of pollution, we may not be able to measure all relevant costs and benefits in economic terms. This is especially true when multiple pollutants affect the environment, when cumulative ecosystem damage and degradation is at issue, or when subtle effects of persistent pollutants are poorly understood.

In such cases, economic analysis may not capture the full scope of ecosystem effects. Economic analysis, however, is essential to understand how pollution control policies affect firms and individuals, and the role that economic incentives play in altering behavior with regard to the production and consumption of pollution-generating products.

Marginal Costs and Benefits of Pollution Control

Let us look first at the question of pollution levels. Figure 16-1 shows a general analysis applicable to many pollution control issues. The horizontal axis shows the quantity of pollution emitted in a particular industry, with pollution levels increasing from left to right. The maximum level, Q_{max}, shows the expected amount of pollution with no pollution control. As pollution control policies are implemented, the amount of pollution will drop below Q_{max}, moving from right to left on the horizontal axis.

MC_D, the marginal cost of damage, shows the marginal costs associated with pollution emissions. These tend to rise in a nonlinear, upward-curving pattern, indicating that incremental emissions are proportionately more damaging once the environment is already polluted. This is consistent with both common sense and scientific evidence—a small amount of automobile exhaust on a clear day may be a mere annoyance, but the same amount added to a smog-choked intersection at rush-hour could trigger significant breathing and health problems.

MC_C, the marginal cost of control, rises as pollution levels fall (moving from right to left on the graph). This also makes sense in terms of practical experience. It is generally easier to clean up the first few units of pollution than to reduce pollution to low levels. As we approach zero emissions the control costs are likely to soar, and for many pollutants a zero level would require shutting down production entirely.

Economic theory indicates that the optimum level of control is Q^*—where the marginal damage cost exactly equals the marginal control cost (MC^*). At Q^*, the cost of cleaning up one more unit of pollution is greater than the benefit it brings in reduced damages. On the other hand, cleaning up one less unit will increase damages by more than it reduces control costs. Therefore Q^* is the most efficient level of cleanup. This balancing of marginal control cost with marginal damage cost is known as the **equimarginal principle.**[1]

It is easy enough to find Q^* on our graph, but how can we identify it in real life? This is not so easy, because we are unlikely to know the shape and location of the MC curves with any precision. As we saw in Chapter 6, valuation of environmental damages is an imprecise science and involves many judgment calls. Control costs may be easier to estimate based on industry experience, but these too are often uncertain.

Industries often estimate control costs at higher levels than actually occur when control policies go into effect. For example, the automobile industry has often argued that controlling tailpipe emissions would boost vehicle costs by a large margin. In practice, the implementation of significantly tighter vehicle emission standards has had little impact on costs.

Similarly, the electric power industry predicted high costs for sulfur oxide (SO_X) reduction, but the real costs (as shown by the price of SO_X emissions permits, discussed below) were considerably lower. On the other hand, control costs can run much higher than estimated, as has often proved the case for cleaning up toxic waste facilities.

Despite these uncertainties, the equimarginal principle is central to the economic analysis of pollution control policies. Even if we cannot define the precise goal, we

---

[1]The equimarginal principle can also apply to marginal control costs for different firms, as we will see in our discussion of pollution control policies. Tietenberg (2000) distinguishes between the "first equimarginal principle" of equating marginal costs and benefits and the "second equimarginal principle" of equalizing marginal costs. See Tietenberg, 2000, Chapters 2 and 3.

know that it will be better to use efficient policies—those that give the greatest result for the lowest cost—rather than inefficient policies that bring relatively higher costs and reduced benefits. Economic analysis can help us formulate efficient policies and analyze the advantages and disadvantages of different approaches. In the following sections, we will consider some of the possible options for pollution control from this point of view.

Pollution Control Policies: Standards, Taxes, Permits

One option for pollution control is direct regulation of pollution-creating activities. Government departments such as the U.S. Environmental Protection Agency can set **emissions standards** for particular industries or products, subject to legislative guidelines. Many people experience such standards at an annual automobile inspection. Cars must meet certain standards for tailpipe emissions; a car that fails must correct the problem before receiving an inspection sticker.

What are the advantages and disadvantages of standards from the economic perspective? The clear advantage is that standards can specify a definite result. This is particularly important in the case of substances that pose a clear hazard to public health. By imposing a uniform rule on all producers, we can be sure that no factory or product will produce hazardous levels of pollutants.

Systems that require all economic actors to meet the same standard, however, may have the problem of inflexibility.[2] Fixed standards work well when pollution-generating activities are similar. For example, different models of automobiles are sufficiently alike to impose the same emissions rules on all.[3] But consider an industry with many plants of different sizes and ages. Will it make sense to have the same rule for every plant? A particular standard might be too difficult for the older plants to meet, forcing owners to shut them down. On the other hand, the same standard might be too lax for more modern plants, allowing them to emit pollution that could have been eliminated at low cost.

In the case of an industry with many different plants, a **market-based pollution control** system may make sense. One such system is a tax, or per unit charge, for emissions. As we saw in Chapter 3, a pollution tax reflects the principle of **internalizing externalities.** If producers must bear the costs associated with pollution by paying a per unit charge, they will find it in their interests to reduce pollution so long as the marginal control costs are less than the tax.

---

[2]Some economists refer to government-set standards as **command-and-control** systems, comparing them unfavorably to market-based mechanisms. We avoid this terminology here, because it conveys unnecessary bias. "Command and control" summons up images of failed communist economic systems. Rather, we will seek to evaluate different policies on their merits, without preconceptions as to which is better. Goodstein (1999, Chapter 12) shares this reservation about the use of the term.

[3]A problem has arisen, though, with sport utility vehicles, which are defined as light trucks and thus avoid strict emissions control standards. For this reason, the Environmental Protection Agency has moved to tighten standards for SUVs.

Once again, Q_{max} is the level of pollution emitted with no controls. If, as shown in Figure 16-2, a uniform charge or pollution tax equal to T_1 is imposed, pollution will fall to Q_1. Producers will find it preferable to reduce pollution to this level, at a total cost of E (the area under the marginal control cost curve between Q_1 and Q_{max}), rather than paying a fee equal to $E + F$ on these units. They will also have to pay a total charge equal to $B + D$ on the quantity Q_1 of pollution they continue to emit. Thus their total cost arising from pollution control plus charges will be $B + D + E$. This is less than $B + D + E + F$, which they would have to pay if they undertook no pollution reduction.

If the per-unit charge is set higher, at T_2, producers will reduce pollution to Q_2. This will involve control costs of $C + D + E$, and pollution charges of $A + B$. The extra units of pollution reduction involve higher marginal costs, but so long as these costs are less than T_2 producers will find it worthwhile to undertake the extra expense and thus avoid paying the fee on the units of pollution between Q_1 and Q_2.

Which of these pollution tax levels is correct? To find out, we must measure the real costs of pollution damage. Notice that the marginal cost of damage curve shown in Figure 16-1 has been omitted in Figure 16-2. This is consistent with real-life policy-making, in which we rarely have a precise measure of damages in economic terms. This raises the possibility that the pollution charge will be set too high, or too low.

Notice, however, that for any given tax level producers' response will be **economically efficient**. In the case where different producers have different control costs, they can decide independently as to which level of pollution control makes sense for them. Those who have high control costs will reduce less, but pay a higher total charge for

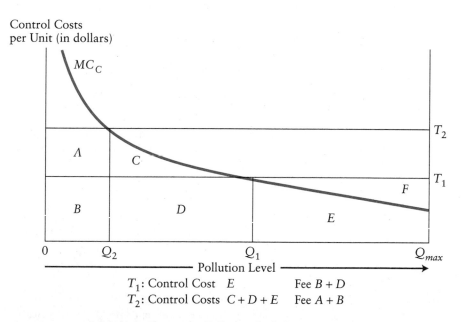

T_1: Control Cost E Fee $B + D$
T_2: Control Costs $C + D + E$ Fee $A + B$

FIGURE 16-2 *A Per-Unit Charge for Pollution Emissions*

pollution emitted. Those who can cut pollution at low cost will reduce more, thereby reducing the charges they must pay.

This cost-minimizing logic ensures that cleanup expenses are directed to wherever they can achieve the most. Here we have a different application of the equimarginal principle—marginal control costs are being equalized among all producers.[4] If the tax level reflects the true damage costs, it will also be true that marginal control costs for all producers are equal to marginal benefits from damage reduction.

Transferable Pollution Permits

Economic efficiency in pollution control is clearly an advantage. One disadvantage of pollution charges, however, is that it is generally impossible to predict the total amount of pollution reduction a given charge will produce. It depends on the shape of the MC_C curve shown in Figure 16-2, which as we have noted is usually not known to policymakers.

Suppose that the policy goal is a more precise and definite reduction in pollution levels within a region. For example, in 1990 the U.S. Environmental Protection Agency set a goal of 50 percent reduction in sulfur and nitrogen oxide (SO_X and NO_X) emissions that cause acid rain. What is the best way to achieve such a specific target, while also achieving economic efficiency?

One approach, used in the U.S. Clean Air Act Amendments of 1990, is to set up a system of transferable pollution permits. The total number of permits issued equals the desired target level of pollution. These permits can then be allocated to existing firms or sold at auction. Once allocated, they are fully transferable, or tradable, among firms or other interested parties. Firms can choose for themselves whether to reduce pollution or to purchase permits for the pollution they emit—but the total volume of pollution emitted by all firms cannot exceed a maximum amount set by the total number of permits.[5]

Within this system, however, private groups interested in reducing pollution can purchase permits and permanently retire them, thus reducing total emissions below the original target level. The permits also may be issued for a specific time period, after which fewer permits will be issued, resulting in lower overall pollution levels. Figure 16-3 illustrates a simplified version of a transferable permit system.

In this simplified example we assume only two firms, each emitting 50 units of pollution. The policy goal is a total reduction of 40 units of pollution. The sum of reductions by the two firms must therefore equal 40. However, the marginal control costs for the two firms differ. Figure 16-3 shows the different ways in which a total reduction of 40 units can be distributed between the two firms.

The marginal cost of control (MC_C) curves for the two firms are plotted in different directions on the same axis, with pollution reduction by Firm 1 going from left to

---

[4]Tietenberg, 2000, refers to this as the "second equimarginal principle."

[5]For an in-depth account of the background and implementation of the 1990 Clean Air Act Amendments, see Goodstein, 1999, Chapters 12 and 15.

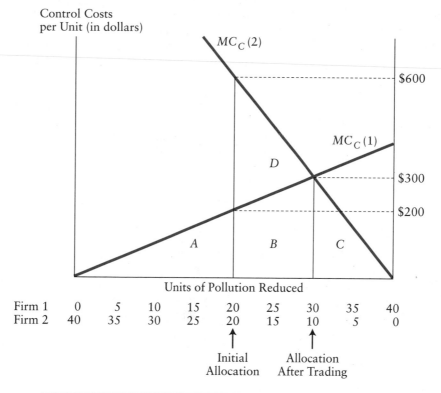

FIGURE 16-3 *A Transferable Pollution Permit System*

right, and for Firm 2 from right to left. This is merely a graphical trick to make it easy to identify the point at which the equimarginal principle is satisfied (that is, the point at which the marginal control costs for the two firms are equal).

The two firms together are emitting 100 units of pollution. To achieve the 40-unit reduction goal, a total of 60 permits must be issued. Suppose that the initial allocation of permits is 30 to each firm. If permits cannot be traded, each firm must cut back its emission from 50 to 30—a net reduction of 20. This is shown in the middle of the graph. At this point, the marginal control cost is $200 for Firm 1 and $600 for Firm 2. This is the same result that would occur if a uniform regulation limited each firm to a maximum of 30 emissions units.

This result achieves the policy goal in terms of emissions reductions, but it is economically inefficient. Each firm's total control cost can be seen on the graph as the area under the MC_C curve.[6] Firm 1's total cost for pollution control is area A (= $2,000), and the total cost for Firm 2 is areas $B + C + D$ (= $6,000). The combined cost to achieve 40 units of pollution reduction is $A + B + C + D$ (= $8,000). However, the firms can improve their own positions, and overall economic efficiency, by trading permits.

It will be advantageous for Firm 1, which has lower control costs, to reduce pollution by 10 additional units (for a total of 30 reduced), thus using only 10 permits and selling the extra 10 permits to Firm 2. Firm 2 will find it worthwhile to purchase 10 permits, allowing it to reduce pollution by only 10 units. The equilibrium price for the permits will be $300, which represents the value of marginal control costs for both firms at the point where Firm 1 is reducing by 30 units and Firm 2 by 10 units.

At this new equilibrium, total control cost for Firm 1 is areas $A + B$ (= $4,500), and total cost for Firm 2 is area C (= $1,500). The combined cost is $6,000. The same pollution reduction goal has been achieved at a lower cost. Area D (= $3,000) represents the net savings from this more efficient solution. Figure 16-3 shows the costs with and without trading. Notice that trading reduces the total costs for each firm, as well as the combined costs.

In a sense, a transferable permit system combines the advantages of direct regulation and an emissions charge system. It allows policymakers to set a definite limit on total pollution levels, while using the market process to seek an efficient method of achieving the goal. It is economically advantageous for the firms involved, as our example shows, allowing a given amount of pollution reduction for the minimum economic cost. In addition, other interested parties can strengthen pollution control by purchasing and retiring permits, and pollution controls can be tightened over time by reducing the overall number of permits issued.

The trading equilibrium shown in Figure 16-3 is consistent with the equimarginal principle, because at the trading equilibrium the marginal control costs for all firms

[6]In mathematical terms, total cost $= TC = \int_0^q MC\, dq$ where q is units of pollution reduced.

are equal. (Our example used only two firms for simplicity, but the principle can easily apply to an industry with many firms.) This uniform marginal control cost will also be the equilibrium price of a pollution permit. Firms will benefit by purchasing permits whenever the permit price is below marginal control costs or selling permits whenever the permit price exceeds these costs.

It does not necessarily follow, however, that a transferable permit system is always the ideal pollution control policy. Transferable permits have been used successfully for sulfur dioxide reduction under the Clean Air Act Amendments of 1990, and have been widely discussed as a tool for reduction of global carbon dioxide emissions (more on this in Chapter 18). But numerous factors must be considered in deciding whether pollution taxes, permits, or direct regulation are the best policy tools for a particular goal. In the next section, we review some of these issues and look at some examples of pollution control in practice.

Pollution Control Policies in Practice

One major factor in formulating effective pollution control policies is the nature of the pollution involved. Are its effects primarily **local, regional,** or **global?** Do the effects increase linearly with the amount of pollutant, or are there **nonlinear or threshold effects?** (See Figure 16-4.)

Consider, for example, a heavy metal pollutant such as lead. If a productive facility is emitting lead as a pollutant, this poses a grave health threat to those living in the vicinity of the plant. A small amount of lead in the blood can lead to serious neurological and mental damage, especially in children. We can say that the threshold for acceptable levels of lead in the environment is low, and above this threshold damage can be severe (Figure 16-4b).

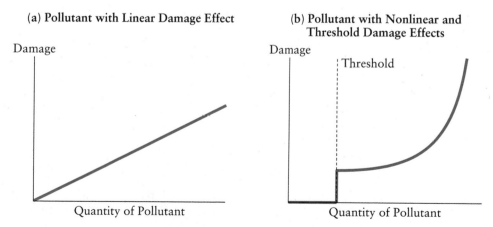

(a) Pollutant with Linear Damage Effect

(b) Pollutant with Nonlinear and Threshold Damage Effects

FIGURE 16-4 *Linear and Nonlinear Pollution Damage Effects*

Environmental activists rally for tighter emissions controls at power plants in Massachusetts. Six older plants are responsible for 90 percent of the state's power plant pollution. In 2001 Massachusetts imposed tougher regulations which will require cuts of as much as 75 percent in nitrous oxide and sulfur dioxide pollutants.

Another important factor in this case is the distribution of the pollutant's impact. The worst effects are likely to be local—although lead pollution can spread throughout the environment, the highest concentrations are likely to be near to the producing plant.[7]

Market mechanisms such as pollution taxes or permits are generally ineffective in preventing damage from lead pollution. Under a permit system a high-polluting but profitable plant could simply purchase permits and continue polluting, with serious consequences for local residents. Similarly, the managers of such a plant might choose to pay a pollution tax rather than cut back emissions. These market-based systems might achieve regional or national control of overall lead emissions, but they would fail to protect local residents. In a case like this, regulations must specify strong emis-

---

[7] In the case of leaded gasoline, the pollution is spread widely through automobile exhaust, and in this case lead becomes a regional pollutant.

sions standards for every plant in order to protect the public. For leaded gasoline or lead paint, complete prohibition is the only effective policy.

Market-based policies work better in the case of **uniformly mixed pollutants.** Sulfur oxides (SO_X) are an example. These gases, which contribute to acid rain, are emitted by many productive facilities, especially coal- and oil-fired power plants. They travel on the wind over wide areas, creating regional pollution. In devising policies to limit these regional damages, it makes little difference which sources reduce pollution output, provided that the desired reduction targets are met. This is therefore a good case for the application of a tax or permit scheme.

As we have noted, the Clean Air Act Amendments of 1990 utilized transferable permits with successful results. Considerable overall reduction in SO_X emissions has been achieved, and the price of an emissions permit has fallen as emissions reduction technology has improved (see Box 16-1).[8]

Policy issues become more complex regarding **nonuniformly mixed pollutants.** Consider the case of water pollution in a large river that runs past many urban, industrial, and agricultural areas. The river will carry different types of pollution from many different sources. Some of these are likely to be **point-source pollution** emitters, like waste pipes from factories or sewage treatment plants. A large portion may also be **nonpoint source pollution.** This could include agricultural fertilizer and pesticide runoff, as well as runoff of oil, salt, and other pollutants from roads and urban areas.

In this case the important factor may be the **ambient pollution level** in the river, meaning the concentration of pollutants per cubic meter of water. Some acceptable threshold level may exist for ambient pollution (as shown in Figure 16-4b). If pollution exceeds this level, regulations for point source pollution reduction must be calculated based on the contribution of particular sources to the ambient level. This may vary depending on the location and nature of the source. Because of the difficulty in devising a pollution charge or tradable permit system in this case, point source water pollution control has generally depended on specific regulations for different kinds of emitters, including sewage facilities and industrial plants.

Nonpoint source pollution has proved more difficult to control. The widespread origins of this kind of pollution require **watershed management,** which involves modified industrial and agricultural practices as well as protection of land surrounding public water supplies. Watershed management can involve various policy instruments, including market-based instruments such as taxes on fertilizer and pesticides, or subsidies for erosion control or pollution-reduction technology. In addition, zoning regulations to prevent the location of new polluting facilities and federal or state purchase of conservation land are likely to be important elements of a watershed management policy.[9]

---

[8]Sanchez, 1998, discusses how the Clean Air Act Amendments promoted technological progress in emissions reduction; Joskow et al., 1998, and Stavins, 1998, examine the operation of the market for emissions rights. Burtraw, 1997, finds that Clean Air Act Amendments benefits considerably outweigh costs, and Jorgenson and Wilcoxen, 1998, evaluate the act's overall economic impact.

[9]For an extensive analysis of nonpoint source pollution, see Rigano, 1994; and Miltz et al., 1998.

16-1   Sulfur Dioxide Emissions Trading

The 1990 Clean Air Act Amendments created a national program to allow trading and banking of sulfur dioxide (SO_2) emissions. Electricity firms that emit SO_2 may trade permits, or allowances, to other firms. Unused allowances may be "banked" for use in future years. By reducing the total number of allowances allocated, national SO_2 emissions can be gradually reduced.

Economic theory suggests that a system of transferable pollution permits can produce the same level of pollution reduction as a universal standard but at lower cost. Dallas Burtraw, an economist with Resources for the Future, notes that the "SO_2 allowance market presents the first real test of economists' advice and therefore merits careful evaluation" (Burtraw, 2000, p. 2). After more than 10 years of practice, has the SO_2 trading system produced significant cost savings?

To evaluate the policy, the effects of emissions trading must be isolated from other factors. Declining prices for low-sulfur coal in the 1990s and technological advances would have reduced the costs of lowering emissions even without a trading system. Further complicating the analysis, Burtraw notes that the trading scheme is responsible for spurring innovation in pollution reduction technologies and organizational behavior. Separating the savings induced by the emissions trading program from other factors is difficult.

Using statistical techniques, a group of researchers estimated the annual cost savings directly associated with trading as $250 billion, in 1995 dollars, for the period 1995–2000 (Carlson, 2000). The cost savings increase to $784 billion annually after 2000 as all electricity plants are covered by the program (from 1995–2000 only the dirtiest plants were covered). The number of trades in the first few years of the program was lower than expected because of price uncertainty, regulatory factors, state mandates of coal use, and other factors (U.S. GAO, 1994). Cost savings could be increased as policies are changed to encourage more trading.

Overall, the SO_2 trading plan has been effective in reducing national emissions. Actual SO_2 emissions are about 35% below the allowable cap (U.S. GAO, 1997) but banked allowances could be utilized in the future to increase emissions. Although the cost savings are not as large as originally expected, they "are substantial and contribute to the tremendous success of the program" (Burtraw, 2000, 24).

Lessons learned from the SO_2 trading policy can be applied to other environmental issues, particularly CO_2 trading to reduce global warming. Agreements for other pollutants should reduce "administrative complexities," "set more objectively based reduction goals, and encourage a more rapid phase-in of the reduction process" (Ackerman and Moomaw, 1997, p. 66).

(continued on following page)

SOURCES

Ackerman, Frank, and William Moomaw. "SO$_2$ Emissions Trading: Does it Work?",
   Electricity Journal, vol. 10 (1997): 61–66.
Burtraw, Dallas. "Innovation Under the Tradable Sulfur Dioxide Emission Permits Pro-
   gram in the U.S. Electricity Sector," Resources for the Future Discussion Paper
   00–38, 2000.
Carlson, Curtis, Dallas Burtraw, Maureen Cropper, and Karen L. Palmer. "Sulfur Dioxide
   Control by Electric Utilities: What Are the Gains from Trade?", *Journal of Political
   Economy,* vol. 108 (2000): 1292–1326.
U.S. General Accounting Office. Overview and Issures on Emissions Allowance Trading
   Programs, GAO/T-RCED-97-183, 1997.
U.S. General Accounting Office. Allowance Trading Offers an Opportunity to Reduce
   Emissions at Less Cost, GAO/RGED-95-30, 1994.

Policy Choice: Pollution Taxes Versus Tradable Permits

Clearly, market-based policies can play a significant role in pollution control. Both pollution taxes and tradable permits can promote efficiency, although as we have seen they are not always the most appropriate policies.[10] When market-based policies are indicated, a further question arises: which market-based policy is best? Also, if we choose taxes, at what level should they be set? And if we choose permits, how many should be issued and to whom?

The choice of taxes versus permits relates closely to the shapes of the marginal cost of control and marginal cost of damage curves shown in Figure 16-1. In analyzing the way in which these policies work, we focused on issues related to the marginal cost of control curve. But in the choice of policies, we must also consider the marginal cost of damage and the interrelationships between the two curves. A couple of examples will show why this is important.

Suppose that for a particular pollutant the marginal costs of damage are steep, or inelastic: that is to say, they rise quickly as the level of pollution increases. On the other hand, the per unit costs of control for this pollutant tend to be fairly stable, with marginal cost rising only slowly as pollution reduction increases. This is shown in Figure 16-5.

In this case, a pollution tax is risky, because a small error in setting the tax level can lead to a large increase in pollution damage. In Figure 16-5, the appropriate tax level to balance marginal damage and control costs would be T_0, with resulting pollution level Q_0. But setting the tax slightly lower, at T_1, would cause firms to cut back on

---

[10]An overview of the applicability of market-based environmental policies is provided by Stavins and Whitehead, 1997. The analysis presented in this section is based on Weitzman, 1974.

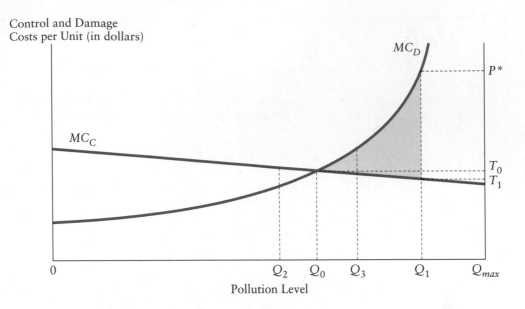

FIGURE 16-5 *Pollution Control with Steep Marginal Damage Costs*

pollution control to Q_1, with marginal damage costs rising to P^*. The large shaded triangle shows the net social loss from this extra pollution damage.

This pattern of damage costs might be associated with a pollutant such as methyl mercury, which can cause serious nerve damage above a very low tolerance threshold. In this case, a quantity-based control system would be a much more effective policy. Transferable permits or direct regulation could limit emissions to Q_0. A small error in either direction in setting the quantity control level (Q_2 or Q_3) would cause a much smaller net social loss (the small triangular areas between the marginal cost and damage curves from Q_0 to Q_2 or from Q_0 to Q_3).

A contrasting case occurs when the marginal cost of damage curve is relatively flat, but the marginal cost of control curve is steep, as shown in Figure 16-6. Here, control costs rise rapidly above a certain level, while damage costs are fairly stable.

In this case quantity controls pose the more serious risk of error. The ideal quantity control would be at Q_0, but an excessively strict control at Q_1 would cause a rapid rise in marginal control costs, to P^*, with net social loss shown by the large shaded triangle. On the other hand, a tax policy could deviate from the appropriate level of T_0 without having much negative effect either in excessive cost or excessive damage. The impact of a tax policy with a tax level set too high (T_1) or too low (T_2) causes only a small deviation from the Q_0 control level, with net social losses equal to the small triangles between MC_C and MC_D between Q_0 and Q_2 or Q_0 and Q_5.

Industry spokespersons often argue that excessively rigid government regulations force high control costs for limited benefits. As we have seen, these arguments sometimes amount to crying wolf. Where industrywide control costs may genuinely be high, however, a tax or pollution charge will allow firms to make their own decisions

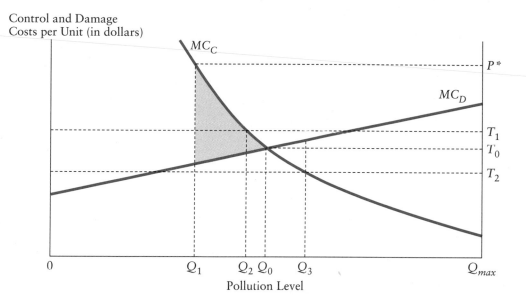

Control and Damage
Costs per Unit (in dollars)

FIGURE 16-6 *Pollution Control with Steep Marginal Control Costs*

about pollution control. They will not be forced to undertake exorbitant expenditures, but at the same time the tax will require them to account for the internalized social costs of pollution. For example, a tax on fertilizer or pesticides could encourage farmers to seek more environmentally friendly production techniques while allowing the use of chemical inputs where cost-effective.

Structuring Pollution Control Policies

A further issue in the use of market-based pollution control concerns how we allocate permits in a tradable permit system. One approach is to issue permits to existing firms requiring new firms entering the industry to purchase permits on the open market. This obviously favors existing firms, who receive something of value (the permits) at no charge. However, it may be the most politically acceptable policy, because it will minimize industry opposition.

An alternative approach is a permit auction, in which permits are sold to the highest bidder. This has the advantage of bringing in government revenues that could be used to lower taxes elsewhere in the economy (we will discuss this possibility in greater detail in Chapters 17 and 18). Tradable permits sold at auction are economically similar to pollution taxes; the market-determined permit price is equivalent in effect to a per-unit pollution charge.

A related issue is **grandfathering** of existing plants. This refers to a system in which strict pollution control regulations are applied to new plants, but existing plants are allowed to comply with less-demanding standards (or no standards at all).

This is intended to avoid excessively high marginal control costs, but is clearly biased toward existing plants, and is open to abuse (see Box 16-2).

The Impact of Technological Change

Finally, when considering the effectiveness of different policies we should evaluate their relationship to technological progress in pollution control. The marginal control cost curves we have used in our analysis are not fixed over time. With technological progress, control costs can be reduced. This raises two issues. First, how will changing control costs affect the policies we have discussed? Second, what incentives do these policies create for the development of improved pollution control technologies?

Figure 16-7 shows how the level of pollution control will vary with different policies and technological change. Suppose we start with a cleanup level of Q_0 units, achieved either by a pollution charge equal to T_0 or a permit allocation with a market-determined permit price of P_0. Then technological progress lowers control costs to MC_C^*. How will firms react?

16-2   Grandfathering and Air Pollution Control

The Clean Air Act of 1970 "grandfathered" coal-fired power plants built before 1970, exempting them from the law's pollution standards in the expectation that they would eventually be closed. But as of 2000, many of these plants were still in business, producing far more pollution than more modern plants.

The act also specified that when older plants were modernized to make appreciably more energy, they had to comply with the same emission standards as new plants. The State of New York and the federal Environmental Protection Agency sued more than 100 plants, claiming that they had made major modifications without installing required pollution controls.

The first results of these suits came when the Virginia Electric Power Company agreed to spend $1.2 billion to cut harmful pollutants from eight coal-burning plants, and the Tampa Electric Company pledged to spend $1 billion to switch a plant from coal to cleaner natural gas.

Federal and state regulators thus acted to close the loophole created by the "grandfathering" language of the 1970 act. The results of these suits may eventually lead to significant clean-up at many more plants across the country.

SOURCE

"Power Plants to Cut Emissions Faulted in Northeast Smog," *New York Times,* November 16, 2000; editorial, November 20, 2000.

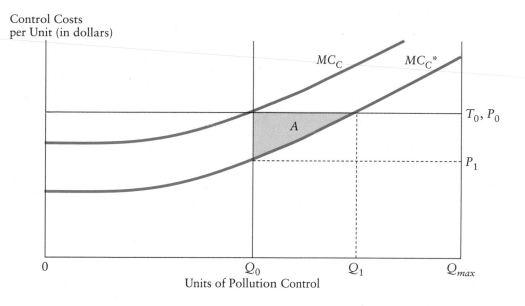

FIGURE 16-7 *The Impact of Technological Change*

In the pollution tax case, firms will have an incentive to increase pollution control to Q_1. By doing so they save area A (the difference between the new control costs and the pollution taxes they were formerly paying on units Q_0 to Q_1). With permits, however, the result will be different. Given the lower control costs, the permit price will fall to P_1. (Recall from Figure 16-3 that the equilibrium permit price is equal to marginal control costs.) The total units of pollution reduced will remain the same—equal to the total number of permits issued.

In fact, the permit system may have a seemingly perverse effect. If control costs fall drastically for some firms (those using newer technology), the permit price will fall, allowing plants with older technology to purchase more permits and actually increase emissions. This surprising effect of better pollution control technology leading to *more* pollution by some firms could, however, be avoided by reducing the total number of permits issued.

Following the same logic, we can conclude that pollution taxes provide a better incentive for the development of improved technology. With a fixed pollution charge, any firm can save money by installing improved control technology. With permits, some firms can "free-ride" on the technological progress of others, while actually increasing their emissions. For this reason, the authorities responsible for a permit scheme must be alert to changes in technology, tightening the allocation of permits over time to provide an incentive for the development of better pollution-control methods.

Cumulative and Global Pollutants

Pollution problems are often long-lived. Organochloride pesticides such as DDT, polychlorinated biphenyls (PCBs), and chlorofluorocarbons (CFCs) remain in the environment for many decades. As emissions of such **cumulative pollutants** continue, their total accumulations in land, air, water, and living things steadily increase.

The kinds of analyses that we have discussed regarding marginal costs of pollution damage are appropriate for **flow pollutants**—those that have a short-term impact and then dissipate or are absorbed harmlessly into the environment. For cumulative or **stock pollutants,** however, we need a different kind of analysis and different control policies.

The issues of cumulative pollution are especially important for **global pollutants.** Carbon, methane, and chlorofluorocarbons emitted into the atmosphere last for decades and have worldwide effects. Pollutants such as DDT and other persistent pesticides also spread worldwide and are found in high concentrations in the bodies of people and animals in the Arctic, where these substances have never been used.

Polychlorinated biphenyls (PCBs) formerly used as insulators in electrical systems have caused severe river pollution that remains a major problem decades after their use was banned. Methyl mercury absorbed by fish in rivers and oceans can prevail for many years, becoming more concentrated as it moves up the food chain. As the importance of such issues increases, we must consider appropriate responses. Often these may be quite different from the policies used to respond to shorter-term air and water pollution.

Let us consider the case of ozone-depleting substances (ODS), which include chlorofluorocarbons (CFCs) as well as other chemicals such as the pesticide methyl bromide. The damaging effects of CFCs were first identified in the 1970s, but many years passed before the scale of the problem was sufficiently well understood to motivate significant action on a global scale. These gases, used for cooling equipment such as automobile air conditioners as well as in other industrial applications, eventually migrate to the upper levels of the atmosphere, where they attack the earth's protective ozone layer.

As the ozone layer thins, damaging solar radiation penetrates, causing problems such as increased incidence of skin cancer as well as complex ecological damage. Complete destruction of the ozone layer would end most life on earth, as few organisms could withstand the intense radiation that would result. Thus the problem is extremely grave, and alarm has increased as holes in the ozone layer have widened over the polar regions (Box 16-3).

To analyze the issue of ozone depletion, we must consider both emissions and accumulation of CFCs. Figure 16-8 shows the relationship between the two in simplified form. Unlike our previous graphs, this one includes time, shown on the horizontal axis. The graph shows an emission pattern over three time periods of 20 years each. In the first period, emissions increase steadily. In the second, a freeze is imposed on emissions levels, with no further increase permitted—but emissions continue at the level

16-3	**Has Ozone Depletion Peaked?**

In October 2000, NASA data showed that the ozone hole over Antarctica had reached a size of nearly 11 million square miles, an area more than three times the size of the United States. This was the largest measurement ever reported. Record-low temperatures in the stratosphere are believed to have promoted the expansion of the ozone hole during the Southern Hemisphere's spring season.

For two days, a small part of the hole extended north from Antarctica to Punta Arenas, a southern Chile city of about 120,000 people, exposing residents to very high levels of ultraviolet (UV) radiation. This was the first time the ozone hole had extended over a major population center. Too much UV radiation can cause skin cancer and destroy tiny plants at the beginning of the food chain.

Somewhat better news was reported in October 2001. The hole did not grow any larger, and may have peaked in 2000. "This is consistent with human-produced chlorine compounds that destroy ozone reaching their peak concentrations in the atmosphere, leveling off, and beginning a very slow decline," according to NASA scientist Samuel Oltmans. However, recovery of the ozone layer to levels observed before 1980 is expected to take at least 50 years.

SOURCES

Lilley, Ray. Associated Press, "Ozone Hole Opens over Chile City," *Boston Globe,* October 6, 2000.

Schmid, Randolph. "New Data Show Ozone Hole Is No Longer Getting Worse," *Boston Globe,* October 17, 2001.

they had already reached. In the third period, emissions drop steadily to an eventual zero level.[11]

Note the relationship between emissions and accumulations.[12] As emissions rise at a steady rate, shown by the straight line in the first part of the upper graph, accumulations rise at an exponentially increasing rate. Accumulations continue to rise steadily

---

[11]This is rather over-optimistic for CFCs and other ozone-depleters. Loopholes in international agreements, as well as illegal production and trade, have made the goal of zero emissions an elusive one.

[12]In mathematical terms, this relationship can be expressed as $A = \int_0^t e\, dt$, meaning that accumulation can be measured as the integral of emissions over time.

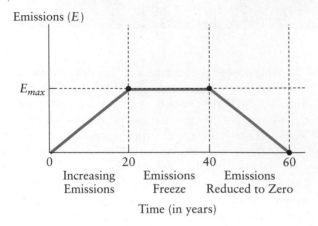

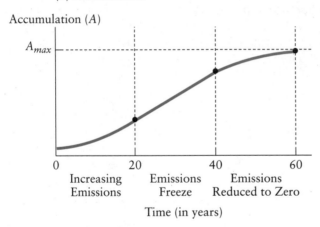

FIGURE 16-8 *Emissions and Accumulation of a Stock Pollutant*

even when a freeze is imposed on emissions during the second period. Only when emissions are cut to zero in the third period does the rate of increase in accumulations start to slow, finally reaching a maximum accumulation that occurs 40 years after the maximum emission level was reached.

This simplified diagram conveys the essence of the problem. Since damages are related to accumulations, not emissions, environmental impact becomes steadily more severe, continuing for many years after control measures are taken. Dealing with cumulative pollutants requires urgent action and stringent policy measures. Even with such measures irreversible damage may occur. The environmental accumulations on our graph will take many decades after year 60 before they decline to a safe level.

The extreme urgency of the ozone depletion problem prompted an international agreement known as the Montreal Protocol, reached in 1987, to phase out the use of ozone-depleting substances. Subsequent amendments to the protocol strengthened and accelerated its implementation. Despite this unprecedented and generally effective international agreement, serious problems with loopholes have allowed continued production by some developing nations, and illegal trade in CFCs and other ozone de-pleters has been difficult to control. While emissions have declined as a result of the protocol, accumulations have continued to rise.[13]

The history of the ozone depletion problem shows the difficulty of responding adequately to cumulative pollutants. This is especially true when impacts are global, because effective action requires agreement among many governments. Unfortunately, ozone depletion is by no means the only problem with cumulative and global implications. Global climate change, as we will see in Chapter 18, shows a similar pattern of steadily accumulating **greenhouse gases** that cause atmospheric warming. Many industrial chemicals also are long-lived and persistent in the environment, making it impossible to limit policy analysis to short-term marginal damage effects.

The kinds of analysis and policy we have reviewed in this chapter have limited value in dealing with cumulative pollution problems. Market-based systems such as tradable permits have been used for transitional periods; for example, during the U.S. phase out of CFCs. A tradable permit system has been proposed for carbon emissions related to global warming. An effective response to the long-lived environmental impact of many human industrial and agricultural activities, however, requires fundamental changes in industrial systems.

In Chapters 17 and 18 we view pollution problems in a broader perspective. Chapter 17 deals with **industrial ecology**, which aims at an overall reduction of human environmental impact, and Chapter 18 focuses in greater depth on the problem of **global climate change** resulting from emissions of carbon dioxide and other gases.

SUMMARY

The principle of economic efficiency in environmental policy implies a balance between the marginal costs and benefits of pollution control. This has implications both for the level of control and the policies used to achieve it. Although the principle of balancing marginal costs and benefits is simple in theory, its application to real-world issues is often complex and involves judgment about both goals and policies.

---

[13]For an overview of the implementation of the Montreal Protocol, see Brack, 1996; Benedick, 1998; and LePrestre et al., 1998.

One possible market-based policy is a per-unit tax on pollution emissions. The tax level should reflect the damage caused by the pollution. A pollution tax allows individual firms to decide how much pollution reduction to undertake. Least-cost pollution control options will be selected first. However, choosing the tax level requires an accurate estimate of damage costs, which may be difficult to reduce to monetary terms.

Transferable pollution permits, another market-based policy, allow setting a target for total pollution reduction. The permit price is then set through the market mechanism, as firms trade permits amongst themselves. This, in theory, combines the advantages of a definite amount of pollution reduction with an economically efficient process. However, it is only suitable for specific pollution control efforts under particular conditions.

Market-based policies often fail to control pollutants that exhibit nonlinear and threshold damage effects, as well as pollutants with local rather than regional impact. Specific emissions standards may be needed for these pollutants, especially those that produce potentially severe health or ecological damage. For nonuniformly mixed water pollutants, ambient pollution level rather than emission levels must be the focus of policy. This may require different kinds of policies for different emitters.

Important considerations in the choice of pollution policy include the patterns of costs and damages as well as options for improved pollution-control technology. Policies should be selected with a view to minimizing unnecessary costs or damages, and promoting technological progress in pollution control.

An especially difficult problem arises in the case of long-lived, cumulative pollutants such as DDT, PCBs, and ozone-depleting substances. In these cases, controlling emissions levels is insufficient, and it will often be necessary to reduce emissions to zero to avoid unacceptable levels of damage.

KEY TERMS AND CONCEPTS

ambient pollution level
command-and-control policies
cumulative pollutant
economic efficiency
emissions standards
equimarginal principle
flow pollutant
global climate change
global pollutant
grandfathering
greenhouse gases
industrial ecology
internalizing externalities

local and regional pollutants
market-based pollution control
nonlinear or threshold effects
nonpoint source pollution
nonuniformly mixed pollutants
optimal pollution level
point source pollution
pollution tax
sink function
stock pollutant
transferable pollution permits
uniformly mixed pollutants
watershed management

DISCUSSION QUESTIONS

1. How practical is the idea of an optimum pollution control level? How is it possible to establish such a level in practice? Can this be done solely based on economic analysis, or must we take into account other factors?

2. Suppose that your state has a problem with pollution in rivers and lakes, from both residential and industrial sources. You are asked to advise on appropriate pollution control policies. Which kinds of policies would be appropriate? How would you decide whether to recommend standards, pollution taxes, or permits, or some other policy? What factors (for example, different kinds of pollution) would go into your decision?

3. Why is an emissions freeze not an adequate policy response to a cumulative pollutant such as chlorofluorocarbons (CFCs)? What kinds of policies are more appropriate, and why are these policies often especially difficult to implement?

PROBLEM

Two power plants are currently emitting 80 units of pollution each (for a total of 160 units). Control costs for Plant 1 are given by $MC_c(1)=2Q$ and for Plant 2 by $MC_c(2)=3Q$, where Q represents the number of units of pollution reduction. Analyze the effects of the following policies in terms of control costs for each firm, total control costs, government revenues, and total pollution reduction:

(a) A regulation requiring each plant to reduce its pollution by 50 units.
(b) A pollution tax of $120 per unit of pollution emitted.
(c) A transferable permit system in which 60 pollution permits are issued, 30 to each plant (Use a diagram similar to Figure 16-3, showing 100 units of pollution reduction).

REFERENCES

Benedick, Richard Elliott. *Ozone Diplomacy; New Directions in Safeguarding the Planet.* Cambridge, Mass.: Harvard University Press, 1998.

Brack, Duncan. *International Trade and the Montreal Protocol.* Royal Institute of International Affairs, Energy and Environment Programme. London: Earthscan Publications, 1996.

Burtraw, Dallas, et al. "Costs and Benefits of Reducing Air Pollutants Related to Acid Rain." *Contemporary Economic Policy* 16 (October 1998): 379–400.

Goodstein, Eban. *Economics and the Environment,* 2nd ed. New York: Wiley, 1999.

Jorgenson, Dale W., and Peter J. Wilcoxen. "The Economic Impact of the Clean Air Act Amendments of 1990." In *Energy, the Environment, and Economic Growth,* edited by Dale Jorgenson. Cambridge, Mass., and London: MIT Press, 1998.

Joskow, Paul L., Richard Schmalensee, and Elizabeth M. Bailey. "The Market for Sulfur Dioxide Emissions." *American Economic Review* 88 (September 1998): 669–685.

LePrestre, Phillipe G., et al. *Protecting the Ozone Layer: Lessons, Models, and Prospects*. Boston: Kluwer, 1998.

Miltz, D. et al. "Standards versus Prices Revisited: The Case of Agricultural NonPoint Source Pollution." *Journal of Agricultural Economics* 39 (September 1998): 360–368.

Rigano, James P. "The Regulation of Non-Point Source Pollution." In *The Environment: Global Problems, Local Solutions,* edited by James E. Hickey and Linda A. Longmire. Westport, Conn., and London: Greenwood Press, 1994.

Sanchez, Carol M. "The Impact of Environmental Regulations on the Adoption of Innovation: How Electric Utilities Responded to the Clean Air Act Amendments of 1990." In *Research in Corporate Social Performance and Policy,* vol. 15, edited by James E. Post. Stamford, Conn., and London: JAI Press, 1998.

Stavins, Robert. "What Can We Learn from the Grand Policy Experiment? Lessons from SO$_2$ Allowance Trading." *Journal of Economic Perspectives* 12 (Summer 1998): 69–88.

Stavins, Robert, and Bradley Whitehead. "Market Based Environmental Policies." In *Thinking Ecologically: The Next Generation of Environmental Policy,* edited by Marian R. Chertow and Daniel C. Esty. New Haven, Conn.: Yale University Press, 1997.

Tietenberg, Tom. *Environmental and Natural Resource Economics*, 5th ed. New York: Addison-Wesley, 2000.

Weitzman, Martin. "Prices versus Quantities." *Review of Economic Studies* 41 no. 4 (October 1974): 477–491.

WEB SITES

1. http://www.epa.gov/airmarkets/ The EPA's web site for acid rain regulation. Includes extensive information about the SO$_2$ emissions trading program.
2. http://www.etei.org/ Home page for the Emissions Trading Education Initiative, a project of the Environmental Defense Fund and the Emissions Marketing Association. The site includes some case studies as well as extensive links and a bibliography.
3. http://www.epa.gov/ozone/ The EPA's web site about the ozone layer and ozone depletion. The site includes scientific information on ozone depletion, information about the Montreal Protocol and CFC substitutes, and a glossary of terms.
4. http://www.rff.org/environment/air.htm Links to many research and discussion papers, published by Resources for the Future, dealing with the benefits of pollution reduction and different approaches for regulating pollution.

- Can the principle of recycling apply to the entire industrial system?
- Can modern agriculture become compatible with ecological systems?
- Can growing world demands for materials be met without disrupting the global environment?

CHAPTER

17

Industrial Ecology

Economic and Ecological Views of Production

We started this book with the observation that economic systems inevitably use resources and produce wastes. In Chapters 4, 5, and 12–15 we discussed the economics of resources, and in Chapters 3 and 16 we looked at methods of internalizing environmental costs and controlling pollution. Although the standard environmental economics approach is to examine these issues separately, they are clearly connected.

In this chapter we survey the flows of resources and wastes through the economic system—what we call **throughput**—and develop a new perspective on policies to improve resource management and reduce wastes and pollution.

Robert and Leslie Ayres, in an exposition of the basic principles of **industrial ecology,** summarize the relationship between resource use and waste generation as follows:

> As a point of departure, we note that every substance extracted from the earth's crust, or harvested from a forest, a fishery, or from agriculture, is a potential waste. Not only is it a potential waste, it soon becomes an actual waste in almost all cases, with a delay of a few weeks to a few years at most. The only exceptions worth mentioning are long-lived construction materials.

In other words, materials consumed by the industrial economic system do not physically disappear. They are merely transformed to less useful forms. . . . It follows from this simple relationship between inputs and outputs—a consequence of the law of conservation of mass—that economic growth tends to be accompanied by equivalent growth in waste generation and pollution.[1]

The economic view of production is as a process of transforming raw materials into finished products. This "straight-line" process—from raw materials to final product—must necessarily create the unwanted by-products of pollution and wastes. In addition, once products wear out, they too become wastes.

For many years, economic theory generally paid little attention to what happens to these wastes. Environmental and resource economics may be seen as an effort to respond to the "loose ends" of the production process—the inputs of resources and outputs of wastes. More generally, we can think of the entire economic process as being embedded within a broader set of ecosystem processes, as we indicated with the expanded circular flow diagram on page 8 in Chapter 1.

Natural systems, in contrast to economic systems, typically follow a cyclical pattern, with wastes being recycled and reused. Healthy natural systems show no buildup of pollution and wastes. Inorganic elements such as water and nitrogen cycle through the system. Dead and decayed organic materials form the basis of fertile soils from which new vegetable life can grow, in turn supporting new animal life. Rather than creating a problem requiring solution or disposal, wastes become inputs at a new stage in the cycle.

Can this principle apply to the economic system? Many resource inputs are **nonrenewable,** but opportunities often exist for resource **recycling.** As we saw in Chapter 12, recycling promotes resource conservation—fewer new resources are needed—and it also reduces the volume of wastes generated by the industrial system. Taking a broader view, we can think of the entire economic production process as a circular flow in which wastes (except for waste energy) can potentially become the raw materials for future production.

Making Wastes into Inputs

Figure 17-1 illustrates the economic view of the industrial process. Industrial ecology applies ecosystem principles of recycling to the industrial realm, replacing the straightline process with a circular pattern, as shown in Figure 17-2. "In industrial ecology, economic systems are viewed not in isolation from their surrounding systems, but in concert with them . . . it is the study of all interactions between industrial systems and the environment."[2]

Think of individual industries as composed of an interlocking pattern of different materials cycles. Figure 17-3 shows a more complete view of a typical industrial cycle,

---

[1]Ayres and Ayres, 1996, p. 1.
[2]Graedel, 1996, p. 23.

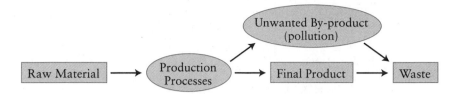

FIGURE 17-1 *"Straight-Line" Pattern of Traditional Industrial Processes*

taking into account the various stages in the processes of production and consumption. The complexity of real-life industrial processes offers many potential **feedback loops** within the total process: opportunities to reuse waste materials from production or consumption as inputs at an earlier stage in the process.

A specific example gives some insight into the policy challenges associated with creating a system of industrial ecology. Producing plastic beverage bottles (Box 17-1) offers various opportunities for recycling materials either into new bottles or into other products. Whether or not consumers and producers will take advantage of such opportunities depends on if they find it profitable to do so. Important economic issues include incentives for recycling—such as bottle deposit/return systems—and the institutions that support recycling, such as curbside collection of used bottles and other recyclables.

Closing the Loops: The Potential of Industrial Ecology

Current economic systems have developed primarily based on incentives associated with the "straight-line" production pattern shown in Figure 17-1. Reorienting the economic system toward more environmentally benign industrial ecology goals requires major **technological innovation** aimed at

- Minimizing the output of unwanted by-products such as pollution and CO_2 emissions.

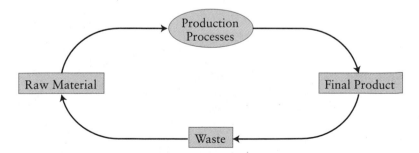

FIGURE 17-2 *Cyclic Production Processes of Industrial Ecology*

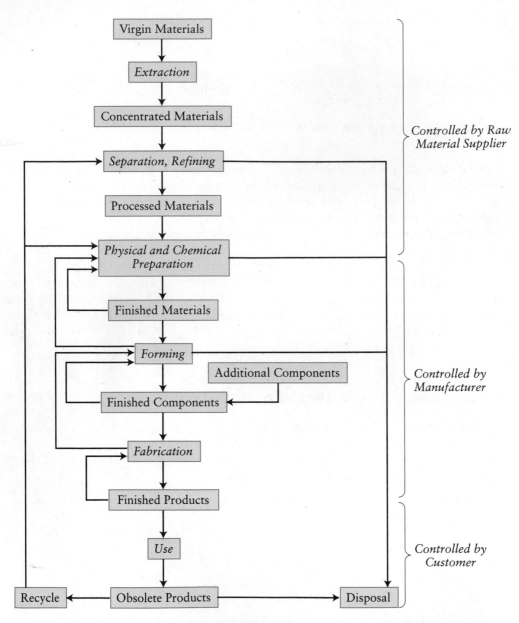

FIGURE 17-3 *The Total Industrial Ecology Cycle*

Source: Adapted from R. Socolow et al., eds. *Industrial Ecology and Global Change.* Cambridge: CUP, 1994. Reprinted with the permission of Cambridge University Press.

| **17-1** | **Beverage Bottle Recycling** |

The basic ingredient in widely used plastic beverage bottles is polyethylene teraphthalate (PET). Used PET is easily recyclable into fibers for carpets or insulation for sleeping bags, pillows, and ski jackets. With chemical treatment, it can make polyurethane foam insulation or polyester resin bathtubs, and can also be re-polymerized for new bottles and other PET products.

The U.S. PET bottle recycling rate is about 40 percent. About 35 percent of all synthetic carpeting sold in the United States contains material from used soft-drink bottles. With improved economic incentives, plastics recycling shows significant further expansion possibilities.

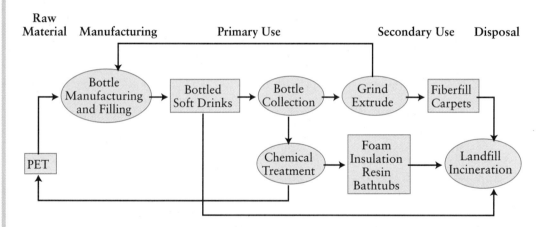

FIGURE 17-4 *Beverage Bottle Industrial Life Cycle*

Source: From R. Socolow et al., eds. *Industrial Ecology and Global Change.* Cambridge University Press, 1994, p. 344. Reprinted with the permission of Cambridge University Press. Frosch and Gallopoulos, 1992.

- Recycling the wastes from industrial processes and worn-out goods into raw materials for further production.

Robert and Leslie Ayres identify four major strategies for increasing the ecological efficiency of resource use and reducing wastes and pollution:

- **Dematerialization:** achieving the same economic goal using less material by increasing materials use efficiency.
- **Materials substitution:** replacing a scarce, hazardous, or high-polluting material with a more environmentally benign substitute.

- Repair, reuse, **remanufacturing,** and recycling: variations on the feedback loops shown in Figure 17-3. (*Remanufacturing* refers to the installation of new parts in used appliances and machines to extend their useful life.)
- **Waste mining:** retrieving usable materials from urban, industrial, or agricultural waste streams.[3]

Each of these strategies implies specific economic incentives and institutions. *Dematerialization* has occurred in many industries simply as a consequence of increased efficiency. Aluminum beverage cans, for example, contain 30 percent less metal than they did in the 1970s, and aluminum cans themselves replaced cans made of much heavier metal used in earlier decades. Achieving the same function (delivering the beverage to the consumer) using less material benefits the supplier, as well as the environment, cutting resource use and reducing the waste stream even if cans are not recycled.

Market incentives have led to *materials substitution*. Many uses of copper, for example, have been replaced by plastics, optical fibers, and lighter metals such as aluminum. Government regulation has contributed to the partial replacement of metal-based pigments in paint with organic pigments, reducing the dangers of lead paint poisoning and the amounts of lead and other heavy metals in the waste stream.[4]

Some market-driven substitutions, however, may be worse for the environment. For example, organo-chloride compounds such as poly-vinyl chloride (PVC), associated with environmental hazards and health risks, have expanded in use due to their relatively low cost in many industrial and commercial products.

An extensive review of the evidence on dematerialization and materials substitution concludes that, while considerable evidence indicates that many economic production processes have grown "lighter," using less material per unit of output, this does not necessarily result in less overall environmental impact. Trends of declining input use per dollar of GDP must be balanced against increasing overall demand as GDP grows. To separate, or "decouple," GDP growth from materials inputs would require that output can grow while input use remains constant. However, " . . . there is no compelling macroeconomic evidence that the U.S. economy is "decoupled" from material inputs; and we know even less about the net environmental effects of many changes in materials use."[5]

Although *recycling* has shown some increase in recent years, economic incentives to recycle materials vary considerably. Recycling some materials, such as aluminum, is profitable because of considerable savings in energy use and other costs as compared to the use of virgin materials. As we noted in Chapter 12, a significant portion of other metal production also uses scrap or recycled inputs.

Materials such as paper and plastics can be recycled effectively, but the profitability of recycling these materials varies. Thus successful paper and plastic recycling programs often depend on some degree of government support. *Repair and remanufac-*

---

[3]Ayres and Ayres, 1996, p. 13–14.

[4]Ayres and Ayres, 1996, p. 12.

[5]Cleveland and Ruth, 1999, p. 45.

turing tend to be labor-intensive. Countries with relatively high labor costs often forgo these activities in favor of replacement with new products.

Waste mining is "the recovery of low-value byproducts and wastes for use as industrial raw materials . . . such sources are often somewhat more difficult, or more costly to exploit than natural sources"[6] For this reason, effective waste mining requires government policy either to internalize the costs of generating wastes or to encourage their reuse. Both *technological innovation* and *institutional support* (such as curbside recycling programs or government purchase of recycled materials) are important in developing a thriving market for recyclables.[7]

The development of "green technologies" to reduce materials use and waste generation can be encouraged by economic incentives. Examples include **green taxes** (Pigovian taxes on negative externalities) and **green subsidies** (subsidies for environmentally friendly technologies that provide positive externalities), as well as **transferable permit** systems. Table 17-1 gives some examples of environmentally oriented economic policies in practice.

Making Agriculture Compatible with Natural Ecosystems

The connection between agricultural production and ecological systems is obvious; yet modernized agriculture borrows many of its operating principles from industry. Economic and ecological values may conflict in the drive to maximize agricultural output.

Modern production techniques generally focus on increasing agricultural yields per acre cultivated through the use of inputs such as chemical fertilizers, pesticides, and intensive irrigation (Figure 17-5). However, as we saw in Chapter 11, this type of agriculture can damage the environment. Chemical inputs can pollute groundwater and rivers, and pesticides can kill beneficial species and disturb the food chain of the surrounding ecosystems. Excessive irrigation can deplete water supplies and contribute to erosion, soil degradation, and groundwater pollution.

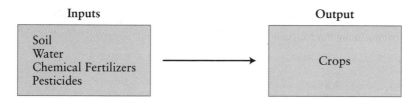

FIGURE 17-5 *The Economic "Straight-Line" View of Agricultural Production*

---

[6]Ayres and Ayres, 1996, p. 15.

[7]See Ackerman, 1996.

TABLE 17-1 Selected "Green" Tax and Permit Systems

Environmental Problem	Policy	Country, Year	Description
Excessive water demand	Tradable water rights	Chile, 1981	Existing users grandfathered. Rights to new suppliers auctioned. Total water use capped.
Solid waste	Toxic waste charge	Germany, 1991	Toxic waste production fell more than 15 percent in three years
	Solid waste charge	Denmark, 1986	Recycling rate for demolition waste, increased from 12 to 82 percent over 6–8 years.
Water pollution	Fees to cover waste-water treatment costs	Netherlands, 1970	Main factor behind 86–97 percent drop in industrial heavy metals discharges and substantial drops in organic emissions
	Fertilizer sales taxes	Sweden, 1982 and 1984	One charge, 1982–92, funded agricultural subsidies; the other pays for education programs on fertilizer use reduction. Use of nitrogen dropped 25 percent; potassium, 60 percent; phosphorus 64 percent.
Acid rain	Nitrogen oxide charge on electricity producers	Sweden, 1992	Refunded as electricity production subsidy. Contributed to 35 percent emissions reduction in two years.
SO_2 air pollution	Sulfur permit system	U.S., 1995	Nearly all permits allocated free to past emitters. Forcing total emissions to about half the 1980 level by 2000; cost of compliance far lower than predicted.
Ozone depletion	Ozone-depleting substance tax	U.S., 1990	Smoothing and enforcing phase-outs.
	Chlorofluoro-carbon permit system	Singapore, 1989	Half of permits auctioned, half allocated to past producers and importers. Smoothing and enforcing phase-out.
Global climate change	Carbon dioxide tax	Norway, 1991	Emissions appear 3–4 percent lower than they would have been without the tax.

(continued on following page)

TABLE 17-1 *(Continued)*

Environmental Problem	Policy	Country, Year	Description
Uncontrolled development	Tradable development rights	U.S., New Jersey pinelands, 1982	Land use plan sets density limits on development in forested, agricultural, and designated growth zones. In growth zones, developers may build beyond density limits if they buy credits from landowners agreeing to develop less than they could. Owners of 5,870 hectares in more protected areas have sold off development rights.
General	Linking investment tax credits to environmental and employment records	U.S., Louisiana, 1991	Tax credits reduced up to 50 percent for firms that pollute most and employ least. 12 firms agreed to cut toxic emissions enough to lower the state's total by 8.2 percent. Repealed after one year.

Source: Roodman, 1997.

An ecological view of agricultural production sees crop output as one part of a diverse **agroecological system,** including water, carbon, nitrogen and other nutrient cycles (Figure 17-6). To maintain the long-term sustainability of this system, cultivation practices must minimize chemical inputs and rely more on **organic techniques,** which return nutrients to the soil, control pests by natural methods, and are not harmful to other species. Agriculture of this type may not offer such high single-crop yields in the short term, but will allow farmers to raise a variety of crops and animals without damaging ecosystems or polluting water supplies.

Just as with industrial systems, economic incentives are key in developing more ecologically balanced agricultural production. Subsidies for fertilizer, pesticides, and water encourage the "straight-line" approach of high input use accompanied by problems such as chemical runoff and water overdraft. Removing such subsidies encourages more efficient use of inputs and recycling of natural organic nutrients.

Subsidy removal, however, can cause hardship for farmers who depend on purchased inputs. For this reason, other policies such as provision of information on organic techniques, agricultural credit for soil conservation and small-scale irrigation development, and transportation and marketing assistance must accompany the removal of subsidies, particularly in developing countries where many farmers are poor and have limited access to credit and markets.

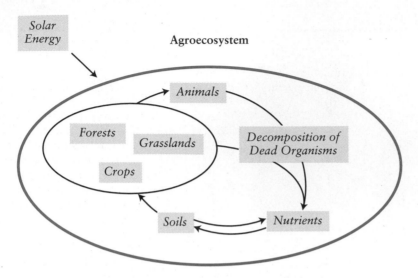

FIGURE 17-6 *The Ecological View of Agroecological Cycles*

Many traditional agricultural systems operated in greater harmony with natural cycles, using a diverse pattern of multiple crops and animal husbandry (Box 17-2). The challenge today is to preserve or regain the ecological benefits of such systems while also achieving the high yields essential to providing an adequate diet to still-growing populations.

Industrial Ecology on a Global Scale

Efforts to improve materials use efficiency take place against a backdrop of steadily increasing material consumption. Figure 17-8 shows the steady growth of world materials production over a 30-year period. "In 1995, nearly 10 billion tons of industrial and construction minerals, metals, wood products, and synthetic materials were extracted or produced globally. This is more than double the level of 1963. This 10 billion tons does not include hidden flows of material—the billions of tons that never entered the economy but were left at mine sites or smelters. Factoring in these flows would at least double and possibly triple the global total materials load."[8]

As shown in Table 17-2, per capita material consumption rates differ widely between developed and developing countries. Each U.S. citizen consumes about 10 tons of materials per year (not including mining wastes), about six times the world average.

[8]Gardner and Sampat, 1998, p. 14.

Thus if everyone in the world consumed at U.S. levels, materials consumption would hypothetically increase sixfold. Material flows at this level would be impossible to sustain, but even short of this seemingly impossible level, population and GDP growth will certainly lead to significantly greater demands in the coming decades.

It is therefore important to examine the potential impact of vastly increased materials flows on planetary ecosystems. This is a broader issue than the question of nonrenewable resource supplies that we examined in Chapter 12. Even if supplies of most resources are adequate, the mining, fabrication, use, and disposal of materials has environmental impacts at each stage of the cycle.

On a planetary scale, evidence is mounting that materials consumption by humans is causing significant disruptions in the **global materials cycles** that support life on earth:

> In the grand cycles, atoms of carbon, nitrogen, sulfur, and phosphorous cycle back and forth from living plants and animals to the soil, atmosphere and oceans. The winds and water currents of earth move these atoms global distances. . . . All four grand cycles are now strongly influenced by human activity. . . .
>
> The carbon cycle has been perturbed by fossil fuel use, deforestation, and changes in agriculture and animal husbandry. . . . The nitrogen cycle has been perturbed especially by worldwide fertilizer use, which has grown rapidly and steadily for more than 40 years. Secondary impacts on the nitrogen cycle have resulted from high-temperature combustion and from [other] agricultural practices.[9]

The sulfur and phosphorous cycles are also strongly affected by industrial emission of sulfur compounds and by mining of phosphate rock for fertilizer. Nitrogen and phosphorous cycles provide plant nutrients that are beneficial to agriculture but are also capable of creating ecological havoc by promoting excessive growth of algae and other opportunistic species that choke out other plant and animal life. Sulfur compounds cause acid rain and other damaging effects on ecosystems, and also affect weather patterns. In Chapter 18 we will examine some of the effects of the disruption of the global carbon cycle on climate and ecosystems.

Clearly, the projected continuing rise in world materials consumption will pose even greater problems of ecosystem disruption on regional and global scales. The most likely strategies for counteracting this trend include increased efficiency and recycling to reduce human global impact. The record to date, however, is not encouraging. Significant improvements in efficiency and reduction in the **intensity of materials use (IU)**, defined as the quantity of material used per unit of economic output,[10] have tended to be offset by economic growth and additional materials-related environmental impact (see Table 17-3).

---

[9]Socolow et al., 1994, p. 117. See Ayres et al., 1994, on carbon and nitrogen cycles.
[10]Cleveland and Ruth, 1999.

17-2 Integrated Farming Systems in Asia

Integrated Farming Systems (IFS) involving aquaculture have been used in Asia for many centuries. The IFS uses "natural processes involving natural organisms

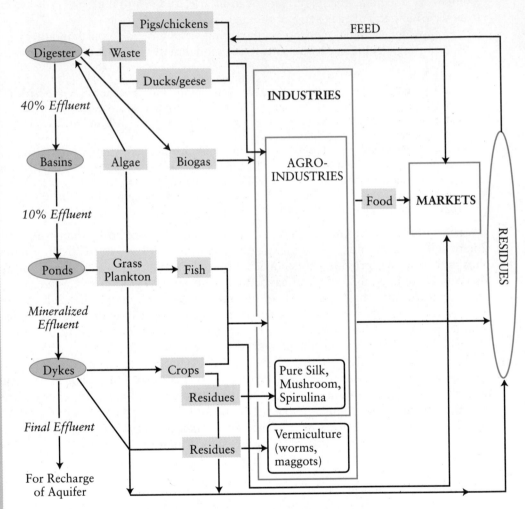

FIGURE 17-7 *Feedback Loops in an Integrated Farming System*

Source: Adapted from George L. Chan, "Aquaculture, Ecological Engineering: Lessons from China." *Ambio,* November 1993, p. 492. Reprinted by permission of *Ambio.*

(continued on following page)

under the most favorable conditions for optimum yields. The main objective is to enhance nutrient cycling and energy flow in ecosystems in order to obtain maximum benefits in food and fiber and to recycle residues completely and economically." The system "combines livestock, aquaculture, agriculture, and agroindustry on every farm, and reinforces the microbial or biochemical process as input for subsequent ones."[1]

"For food, the fish rely largely on the nutrient-rich residues and wastes from pigs or other animals, food preparation, or algae. In exchange, water in the fishpond provides backup irrigation for farm crops during the dry season. Plants grown in the fishponds provide additional food for the fish and can also be harvested to feed pigs or other animals. Several times a year, the renewable rich bottom soil is scooped out of the fishponds and applied to nearby fields, thus rounding out the on-farm organic loop."[2]

[1]McGinn, 1998.
[2]Chan, 1993.

Fish farms and rice paddies along the border of Shenzhen and Hong Kong. Recycling of nutrients and wastes can maintain ecological balance in agricultural systems producing multiple outputs.

Billions of Tons

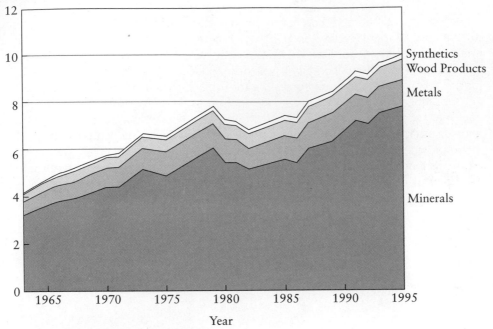

FIGURE 17-8 *World Materials Production, 1963–1995*

Source: Adapted from Gardner and Sampat, *Mind Over Matter: Recasting the Role of Materials in Our Lives.*
Worldwatch Paper no. 144. Washington, D.C.: Worldwatch Institute, 1998. Reprinted by permission of Worldwatch Institute, http://www.worldwatch.org.

Measuring the Impacts of Global Growth

In Chapter 10 we introduced the $I = PAT$ equation that links environmental impact,
population, affluence, and technology. The global industrial ecology challenge can be
viewed in terms of this equation as follows:

change in P = increase in population (at least 30 percent growth predicted 2000–
2025)

change in A = economic growth (2.5 percent per capita per year would give 85 percent growth by 2025)

total change in $(P \times A) = (1.3)(1.85) =$ a factor of 2.40 over 2000 levels by 2025.

The technology factor T is defined as the environmental impact per unit of output. If the technology factor—closely related to the intensity of materials use (material
use per unit of economic output or IU)—remained unchanged, by 2025 environmental impact would be multiplied by a factor of 2.4 over 2000 levels.

In order to hold environmental impact unchanged, IU would have to be reduced
by about 60 percent. In other words, if total output is 2.4 times as great in 2025, but
the impact per unit of output is 0.4 of the current level, the net impact would be

TABLE 17-2A World and U.S. Materials Use: Growth in World Materials Production, 1960–1995

Material	Production in 1995 (million tons)	Per Capita Production (tons per capita)	Increase over Early 1960's (factor of change)
Minerals	7,641	1.34	2.5-fold
Metals	1,196	0.20	2.1-fold
Wood Products	724	0.12	2.3-fold
Synthetics	252	0.04	5.6-fold
All Materials	9,813	1.72	2.4-fold

TABLE 17-2B World and U.S. Materials Use: Growth in U.S. Materials Consumption, 1900–1995

Material	Consumption in 1995 (million tons)	Per Capita Consumption (tons per capita)	Increase over 1900 (factor of change)
Minerals	2,410	9.16	29-fold
Metals	132	0.50	3-fold
Wood Products	170	0.64	14-fold
Synthetics	131	0.49	82-fold
All Materials	2,843	10.81	18-fold

Source: Adapted from Gardner and Sampat, *Mind Over Matter: Recasting the Role of Materials in Our Lives.* Worldwatch Paper no. 144. Washington, D.C.: Worldwatch Institute, 1998, p. 16. Reprinted by permission of Worldwatch Institute. www.worldwatch.org. Per capita production figures based on population estimates from Population Reference Bureau, 1995.

(0.4)(2.4), which approximately equals 1, indicating no change in net impact. To reduce the environmental impacts of economic activity below today's level, the reduction in *IU* would have to be even greater.

How likely is it that this kind of gain will occur? A study of industrial economies shows that energy intensity (energy use per dollar of GDP) has declined steadily since 1970 (see Figure 17-9). In almost all cases, this has been offset by GDP growth, so that net energy use has increased. But countries can take widely divergent energy paths, some with much less impact on the global carbon cycle than others.[11] With deliberate policy effort, much greater reductions in energy and materials intensity could be achieved.

A Worldwatch Institute report identifies strategies for promoting recycling and increased efficiency.[12] These include integrating recycling into all industrial stages, as

[11]Moomaw and Tullis, 1994.

[12]Gardner and Sampat, 1998.

TABLE 17-3 Gains in Materials Efficiency and Offsetting Factors

Product	Efficiency Gains	Offsetting Factors
Plastics in Cars	Use of plastics in U.S. cars increased by 26 percent between 1980 and 1994, replacing steel in many uses and reducing car weight by 6 percent.	Cars contain 25 chemically incompatible plastics that, unlike steel, cannot be easily recycled. Thus most plastic in cars winds up in landfills.
Bottles and Cans	Aluminum cans weigh 30 percent less today than they did 20 years ago.	Cans replaced an environmentally superior product—refillable bottles.
Lead Batteries	A typical automobile battery used 30 pounds of lead in 1974, but only 20 pounds in 1994, with improved performance.	U.S. domestic battery shipments increased by 76 percent in the same period, more than offsetting the efficiency gains.
Radial Tires	Radial tires are 25 percent lighter and last twice as long as bias-ply tires.	Radials are more difficult to retread. Sales of passenger car retreads fell by 52 percent in the United States between 1977 and 1997.
Mobile Phones	Weight of mobile phones dropped tenfold between 1991 and 1996.	Subscribers to cellular telephone service jumped more than eightfold in the same period, nearly offsetting the gains from lightweighting.

Source: Adapted from Gardner and Sampat, *Mind Over Matter: Recasting the Role of Materials in Our Lives.* Worldwatch Paper no. 144. Washington, D.C.: Worldwatch Institute, 1998, p. 29. Reprinted by permission of Worldwatch Institute. www.worldwatch.org.

the industrial ecology paradigm implies. In addition, redefining "output" in terms of services rather than goods could make firms seek to lower, rather than increase, physical product sales.

For example, if utilities oriented toward delivering heating, cooling, and light rather than gas or electricity, they could specialize in retrofitting homes and businesses for high efficiency, thereby profiting by selling *less* of their physical output. Substitution of new materials and nonfossil fuel energy sources in production and goods could considerably reduce environmental impacts. To be truly effective, these changes on the production side would need to be complemented by a new consumer ethic of **sufficiency**—a goal of having enough to support a comfortable life, but no more—rather than ever-growing consumption. (We will discuss this important issue of restraint in consumption in Chapter 20.)

Policies to Promote Industrial Ecology

In Chapters 12 and 16 we discussed many microeconomic policies aimed at conserving resources, internalizing the full costs of resource extraction, and reducing pollution. All of these policies are relevant to promoting industrial ecology. We cannot, however, respond on the necessary scale to global issues surrounding expansion of materials use and waste generation without macroeconomic policies as well.

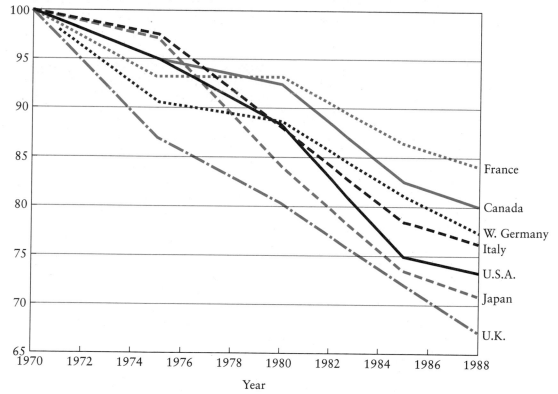

Energy Use per Dollar
GNP: Index 1970

Year

FIGURE 17-9 *Declining Energy Intensity in Industrial Economies*
Source: OECD, 1991. From Turner, R. Kerry, David Pearce, and Ian Bateman, *Environmental Economics: An Elementary Introduction,* p. 45, ©1993. Reprinted by permission of The Johns Hopkins University Press.

Industrial ecology advocates have called for nothing less than a reorientation of the structure and goals of the entire economic system. This would require a combination of microeconomic and macroeconomic policies including the following:

- Systematic "green" tax reform to shift the tax burden from income and capital to resource consumption and waste emissions.
- Global and national limits on carbon emissions, possibly implemented through a system of tradable permits (more on this in Chapter 18).
- Local and regional planning processes to restructure industrial and transportation systems for maximum recycling and minimum energy use and waste generation (see Box 17-3 on the Kalundborg industrial ecosystem).
- Promotion of **environmental design**—engineering products for environmental compatibility, recyclability, and minimal toxicity. Incentives for environmental

17-3   The Kalundborg Industrial Ecosystem

Creating a system of industrial ecology requires coordination among many different firms as well as government policy support. An outstanding example of such **industrial symbiosis** is the town of Kalundborg, Denmark, as described by John Ehrenfeld and Nicolas Gertler in the *Journal of Industrial Ecology.*

Eleven physical linkages comprise much of the tangible aspect of industrial symbiosis in Kalundborg. The town's four main industries—Asnaes Power Station, a 1,500-megawatt coal-fired power plant; a large oil refinery operated by Statoil; Novo Nordisk, a manufacturer of pharmaceuticals and enzymes; and Gyproc, a plasterboard manufacturer—and several users within the municipality trade and make use of waste streams and energy resources, and turn by-products into raw materials.

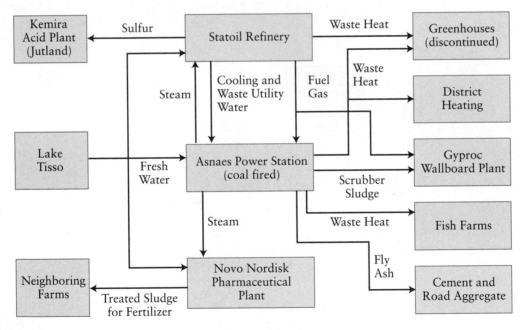

FIGURE 17-10 *Industrial Linkages at Kalundborg*

Source: From John Ehrenfeld and Nicholas Gertler, "Industrial Ecology in Practice: The Evolution of Interdependence at Kalundborg," *Journal of Industrial Ecology*, 1:1 (Winter 1997), pp. 67–79. ©1997 by Yale University and the Massachusetts Institute of Technology. Reprinted by permission.

(continued on following page)

Firms outside the area also participate as recipients of by-product-to-raw material exchanges. The symbioses evolved gradually and without a grand design over the past 25 years, as the firms sought to make economic use of their by-products and to minimize the costs of compliance with new, ever-stricter environmental regulations.

Figure 17-10 shows the system of interactive flows between industries in Kalundborg. A study of the Kalundborg system concludes that the development of these interactions required simultaneous positive economic and environmental incentives among firms, sometimes called "green twinning." These conditions will not generally occur without conscious public policy:

> Broad public policy initiatives can nudge the process along by creating the overall conditions that promote the emergence of positive factors in individual cases over time, but may falter where the promoters of an eco-industrial park are attempting to create all the linkages up front. An integrated and continuous planning process that explicitly seeks to identify opportunities and barriers to symbiotic development should increase the likelihood of attracting firms willing to make the necessary arrangements. Such a middle-ground approach between pure laissez-faire and heavy-handed policy intervention would seem to offer the best chance of success to institutional developers.

SOURCE

From John Ehrenfeld and Nicholas Gertler, "Industrial Ecology in Practice: The Evolution of Interdependence at Kalundborg," *Journal of Industrial Ecology,* 1:1 (Winter 1997), pp. 67–79. ©1997 by Yale University and the Massachusetts Institute of Technology. Reprinted by permission.

design can include **certification** of "green" products by government or independent agencies.

- Research and development of new technologies such as **solar hydrogen** and **fuel cells**[13] that capture and use solar energy to replace fossil fuels.
- Macroeconomic policies aimed at stability, sufficiency, and equity rather than continual economic growth.

Clearly, this vision is far from current reality. Present pollution control policies primarily respond to specific problems, but not the "macro" problems of economic growth and ecosystem disruption. However, industrial ecology theorists argue that we are not far from important **technological thresholds** that could introduce radically different—and much less environmentally damaging—industrial, agricultural, and energy systems.[14]

---

[13]Solar hydrogen systems use solar energy to split water into hydrogen and oxygen. The hydrogen and oxygen are then recombined in a fuel cell to provide energy with only water vapor emissions. Fuel cells can also use fossil fuels such as methane, but without the pollution resulting from burning fuels.

[14]See Ayres and Ayres, 1998, pp. 304–306.

The **Industrial Revolution** of the nineteenth century fundamentally altered both production systems and perceptions of economic goals. It may well be that in the twenty-first century the survival of planetary ecosystems will depend on a similar revolution in thought and practice, replacing standard industrial production and modernized agriculture with ecologically oriented systems. If so, we are only in the beginning stages of this transformation. Most of our policies and practices remain more suited to the earlier industrial era in which ecosystem impact were formed only a minor consideration.

In the next chapter, we will examine one of the most prominent issues related to industrial impacts on global ecological cycles—greenhouse gas emissions and global climate change.

SUMMARY

Industrial ecology adopts an overview of the entire process of resource use and waste generation in all sectors of the economy. Rather than viewing this as a series of "straight-line" processes from raw materials to final products and wastes, industrial ecology applies the cyclical logic of natural ecosystems. In a fully cyclical process, almost all wastes are recycled to become inputs to new processes.

Natural systems are based on complete cycles, with no buildup of pollution or wastes. Industrial systems may be designed to follow a similar cyclical pattern, by maximizing opportunities to recycle wastes at every point in the industrial production and consumption process.

Strategies for making the economic process more compatible with natural systems include increasing material use efficiency, finding substitutes for high-polluting or hazardous materials, reuse and recycling, and retrieving materials from urban, industrial, and agricultural waste streams. These strategies may be promoted through market processes, government policies, or economic incentives such as "green" taxes or subsidies.

Modern agriculture shares the "straight-line" focus on increased output that characterizes industrial systems. This has led to patterns of high input use and serious resource and environmental impact. A more environmentally benign agricultural system could be based on low-input techniques that conserve and recycle nutrients and water. Many traditional agricultural systems follow this approach, and traditional agriculture principles can combine with modern technological innovations to promote sustainable agroecological systems.

On a global scale, the effects of improved efficiency of materials use are outweighed by increased demand resulting from population and economic growth. Considerable further growth will occur throughout the developing world in coming decades, increasing pressures on resources and the environment. Human intervention significantly affects major planetary cycles including carbon, nitrogen, sulfur, and phosphorous.

Offsetting growth in population and per capita consumption will require dramatic reductions in intensity of materials use and environmental impact. Technological possibilities exist for achieving this goal, but local, regional, national, and global policy initiatives are needed to promote technologies that can make industry compatible with planetary ecosystems.

KEY TERMS AND CONCEPTS

agroecological systems
certification
dematerialization
environmental design
feedback loops
fuel cells
global materials cycles
green subsidies
green taxes
industrial ecology
Industrial Revolution
industrial symbiosis
intensity of materials use (IU)

materials substitution
nonrenewable resources
organic techniques
recycling
remanufacturing
solar hydrogen
sufficiency
technological innovation
technological thresholds
throughput
transferable (pollution) permits
waste mining

DISCUSSION QUESTIONS

1. What opportunities can you think of for developing industrial ecology in particular industries or regions? What kinds of economic incentives and government policies would be most effective in promoting ecosystem-friendly economic production?

2. What is the consumer's role in industrial ecology? In standard economic theory, consumers maximize their utility by consuming goods and services. How must this perspective be modified in an economic system oriented towards industrial ecology?

3. What are some barriers to developing agroecosystems that use organic techniques? Note that the organic food industry, once a small "niche" market, has expanded to become a multibillion-dollar industry. Yet "industrialized agriculture" still produces most of our food with high synthetic chemical input. What economic factors will determine the future course of agricultural production?

REFERENCES

Ackerman, Frank. *Why Do We Recycle? Markets, Values, and Public Policy.* Washington, D.C.: Island Press, 1996.

Ayres, Robert U., and Leslie W. Ayres. *Industrial Ecology: Towards Closing the Materials Cycle.* Cheltenham, England: Elgar, 1996.

Ayres, Robert U., William H. Schlesinger, and Robert H. Socolow. "Human Impacts on the Carbon and Nitrogen Cycles," Chapter 9 in Socolow, ed., 1994.

Chan, George L. "Aquaculture, Ecological Engineering: Lessons from China." *Ambio*, November 1993.

Cleveland, Cutler, and Matthias Ruth. "Indicators of Dematerialization and the Materials Intensity of Use." *Journal of Industrial Ecology* 2, no. 3 (1999): 15–50.

Ehrenfeld, John, and Nicholas Gertler. "Industrial Ecology in Practice: The Evolution of Interdependence at Kalundborg." *Journal of Industrial Ecology* 1, no. 1 (1997): 67–79.

France, Wayne, and Valerie Thomas. "Industrial Ecology in the Manufacturing of Consumer Products." Chapter 25 in Socolow et al., eds., 1994.

Frosch, R. A., and N. E. Gallopoulos. "Towards an Industrial Ecology." In *The Treatment and Handling of Wastes*, edited by A. D. Bradshaw et al. London: Chapman and Hall for the Royal Society, 1992.

Gardner, Gary. "Preserving Agricultural Resources." In *State of the World 1996*, edited by Brown et al. Washington, D.C.: Worldwatch Institute, 1996.

Gardner, Gary, and Payal Sampat. *Mind Over Matter: Recasting the Role of Materials in Our Lives*. Worldwatch Paper 144. Washington, D.C.: Worldwatch Institute, 1998.

Graedel, Thomas. "Industrial Ecology: Definition and Implementation." Chapter 3 in Socolow et al., 1994.

McGinn, Anne Platt. *Rocking the Boat: Conserving Fisheries and Protecting Jobs*. Worldwatch Paper no. 142. Washington, D.C.: Worldwatch Institute, 1998.

Moomaw, William, and Mark Tullis. "Charting Development Paths: A Multicountry Comparison of Carbon Dioxide Emissions." Chapter 10 in Socolow et al., 1994.

Organization for Economic Cooperation and Development (OECD). *Environmental Indicators: A Preliminary Set*. Paris, France: OECD, 1991.

Roodman, David M. *Getting the Signals Right: Tax Reform to Protect the Environment and the Economy*. Worldwatch Paper No. 134, May 1997.

Socolow, R., C. Andrews, F. Berkhout, and V. Thomas, eds. *Industrial Ecology and Global Change*. Cambridge, England: Cambridge University Press, 1994.

Turner, R. Kerry, David Pearce, and Ian Bateman. *Environmental Economics*. Baltimore: Johns Hopkins University Press, 1993.

World Population Data Sheet 1995. Washington, D.C.: Population Reference Bureau, 1995.

WEB SITES

1. **http://mitpress.mit.edu/catalog/item.default.asp?ttype=4&tid=32** Home page for the *Journal of Industrial Ecology*, a journal "designed to foster both understanding and practice in the emerging field of industrial ecology." The site includes abstracts and some sample articles.

2. **http://www.epa.gov/opptintr/dfe/** The EPA's web site for the Design for the Environment Program, an initiative that "helps businesses incorporate environmental considerations into the design and redesign of products, processes, and technical and management systems." The site includes descriptions of many successful applications of industrial ecology.

3. **http://www.worldbank.org/research/greening/cover.htm** An online version of "Greening Industry," a World Bank report on ways to resolve apparent conflicts between economic development and environmental quality in developing countries.

CHAPTER FOCUS QUESTIONS

■ How serious a problem is global warming/
global climate change?
■ Can economic theory help evaluate the impact of climate change?
■ What policies most effectively address climate change?

CHAPTER **18**

Global Climate Change

Causes and Consequences of Climate Change

Concern has grown in recent years over the issue of global climate change.[1] In terms of economic analysis, **greenhouse gas** emissions, which cause planetary warming, represent both **environmental externalities** and overuse of a **common property resource.**

The atmosphere is a **global commons** into which individuals and firms can release pollution in the shape of gases and particulates. Global pollution creates a "public bad" affecting everyone—a negative externality with wide impact. Many countries have environmental protection laws to limit release of **local and regional pollutants.** In economic terminology, such laws to some degree **internalize externalities** associated with local and regional pollutants.

Few controls exist for carbon dioxide (CO_2), the major greenhouse gas, which has no short-term damaging effects at ground level. Atmospheric accumulations of carbon dioxide and other greenhouse gases, however, will have significant effects on world weather, although there is uncertainty about the probable scale and timing of these effects (see Box 18-1).

If indeed the effects of climate change are likely to be severe, it is in everyone's interest to lower emissions for the common good. But where no agreement or rules on

---

[1]The problem, frequently called **global warming**, is more accurately referred to as **global climate change.** A basic warming effect will produce complex effects on climate patterns—with warming in some areas, cooling in others, and increased climatic variability.

The sun's rays travel through a greenhouse's glass to warm the air inside, but the glass acts as a barrier to the escape of heat. Thus plants that require warm weather can be grown in cold climates. The global greenhouse effect, in which the earth's atmosphere acts like the glass in a greenhouse, was first described by French scientist Jean Baptiste Fourier in 1824.

Clouds, water vapor, and the natural greenhouse gases carbon dioxide (CO_2), methane, nitrous oxide, and ozone allow inbound solar radiation to pass through, but serve as a barrier to outgoing infrared heat. This creates the natural **greenhouse effect** that makes the planet suitable for life. Without it, the average surface temperature on the planet would average about -18 degrees Celsius (0 degrees Fahrenheit), instead of approximately 15 degrees Celsius (60 degrees Fahrenheit).

"The possibility of an *enhanced* or *manmade* greenhouse effect was introduced by the Swedish scientist Svante Arrhenius in 1896. Arrhenius hypothesized that the increased coal burning, which had paralleled the process of industrialization, would lead to an increased concentration of carbon dioxide in the atmosphere and warm the earth."[1] Since Arrhenius's time, greenhouse gas emissions have grown dramatically. Carbon dioxide concentrations in the atmosphere have increased by 25 percent over preindustrial levels. In addition to increased burning of fossil fuels such as coal, oil and natural gas, manmade chemical substances such as chlorofluorocarbons (CFCs) as well as methane and nitrous oxide emissions from agriculture and industry contribute to the greenhouse effect.

In 1988, the United Nations Environment Programme and the World Meteorological Organization together established the Intergovernmental Panel on Climate Change (IPCC) to provide an authoritative international statement of scientific opinion on climate change. With respect to human-caused greenhouse effect, the IPCC concluded that "there has been a real, but irregular, increase of global surface temperature since the late nineteenth century" amounting to 0.5 degrees Celsius on average.

Current emissions trends will lead to a doubling of greenhouse gas concentration over preindustrial levels by about 2050. Using general circulation models—large mathematical models of the atmosphere—scientists can simulate the effect of increased greenhouse gas concentrations. The IPCC projects a global average temperature increase of 1 to 6 degrees Celsius, or 2 to 10 degrees Fahrenheit, which would have significant impact on climate throughout the world.

SOURCES

Cline, 1992; Fankhauser, 1995; IPCC, 1996, 2001.

---

[1]Fankhauser, 1995.

emissions exist, no individual firm, city, or nation will choose to bear the economic brunt of being first to reduce its emissions. In this situation, only a strong international agreement binding nations to act for the common good can prevent serious environmental consequences.

Because CO_2 and other greenhouse gases continuously accumulate in the atmosphere, stabilizing or "freezing" emissions will not solve the problem. This is a case of a **stock pollutant**: only major reductions in emissions levels will prevent ever-increasing atmospheric accumulations. Development of national and international policies to combat global climate change is a huge challenge, involving many scientific, economic, and social issues. In this chapter we will address these issues of analysis and policy, using some techniques and concepts developed in earlier chapters.

Trends and Projections for Temperature Change

Despite two global conferences dealing with the issue—the 1992 United Nations Conference on Environment and Development (UNCED) at Rio de Janeiro and a 1997 meeting in Kyoto, Japan—as well as follow-up negotiating sessions, progress on combating global climate change has been slow. Global greenhouse gas emissions continue to rise (see Figure 18-1).

Increasing accumulations of greenhouse gases have caused the earth's surface temperature to rise perceptibly. Although some warming may be a natural trend, the In-

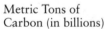

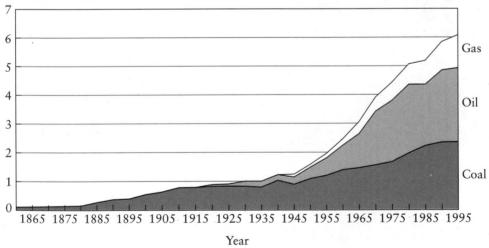

FIGURE 18-1 *Carbon Emissions Due to Fossil Fuel Consumption, 1860–1995*
Source: Adapted from Manne and Richels, *Buying Greenhouse Insurance: The Economic Costs of CO_2 Emission Limits.* Cambridge, MA: MIT Press, 1994. Updated with data only from Carbon Dioxide Information Analysis Center (CDIAC), http://cdiac.esd.ornl.gov/. Courtesy of CDIAC.

Temperature Variation (in °C)

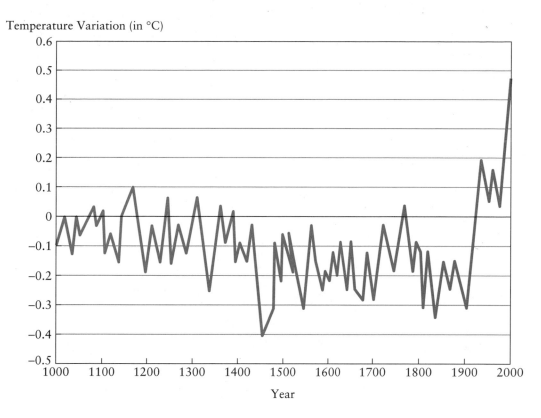

FIGURE 18-2 *Temperature Trend, Northern Hemisphere 1000–2000*

Source: Adapted from *The Economist,* November 18–24, 2000; data from the Carbon Dioxide Information Analysis Center (CDIAC), http://cdiac.esd.ornl.gov/.

tergovernmental Panel on Climate Change (IPCC) has determined that human-caused impact on the atmosphere has "contributed substantially to the observed warming over the last 50 years."[2] Temperatures have now reached levels unprecedented in the past thousand years (see Figure 18-2).

The IPCC scientists project that continued greenhouse gas emissions will further increase average temperatures between 1 and 6 degrees Celsius (about 2 to 10 degrees Fahrenheit) over the next century (Figure 18-3). This steady rise in earth's average temperature will have many significant effects on climate. For example, one effect of climate change is likely to be a rise in sea level as polar ice caps and

---

[2] "A Shift in Stance on Global Warming Theory: International Panel Highlights Role of Humans in Climate Change." *New York Times,* October 26, 2000. See also Trenberth, 2001.

Temperature (in °C)

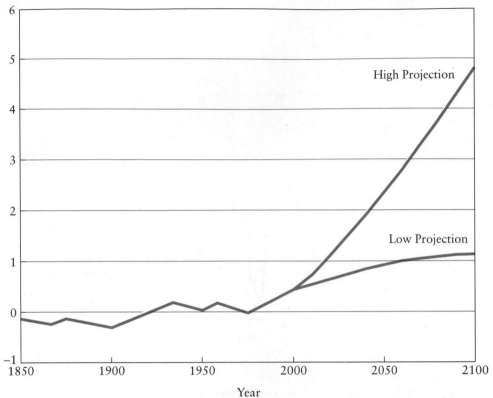

FIGURE 18-3 *Global Temperature Trends Projected to 2100*
Source: IPCC, 1996. IPCC, 2001, projects a slightly higher range of temperature increase, from 2.4°C to 5.8°C by 2100.

glaciers melt. This will have serious effects on islands and low-lying coastal areas (see Box 18-2).

The onset of climate change poses a choice between **preventive strategies and adaptive strategies.** Consider, for example, the damage caused by rising sea levels. The only way to stop this would be to prevent the climate change itself. It might be possible to adapt to changed conditions by building dikes and sea walls to hold back the higher waters. Those who live close to the sea—including whole island nations that could lose most of their territory to sea-level rise—are unlikely to endorse this mitigation strategy. But a successful prevention strategy would require convincing most of the world's countries to participate. Is it in their interest to do so? To answer this question, we must find a way to evaluate the effects of climate change.

18-2   Pacific Islands Disappear as Oceans Rise

Two islands in the Pacific Ocean nation of Kiribati—Tebua Tarawa and Abanuea—have disappeared as a result of rising sea level. Others, both in Kiribati and in the neighboring island nation of Tuvalu, are nearly gone. So far the seas have completely engulfed only uninhabited, relatively small islands, but the crisis is growing all along the shores of the world's atolls.

Populated islands are already suffering. The main islands of Kiribati, Tuvalu, and the Marshall Islands (also in the Pacific) have suffered severe floods as high tides demolish sea walls, bridges and roads, and swamp homes and plantations. Almost the entire coastline of the 29 Marshall Islands atolls is eroding. World War II graves on its main Majuro atoll are washing away, roads and subsoils have been swept into the sea, and the airport has flooded several times despite the supposed protection of a high sea wall.

The people of Tuvalu are finding it difficult to grow their crops because the rising seas are poisoning the soil with salt. In both Kiribati and the Marshall Islands families are desperately trying to keep the waves at bay by dumping trucks, cars and other old machinery in the sea and surrounding them with rocks.

The story is much the same far away in the Maldives. The Indian Ocean is sweeping away the beaches of one-third of its 200 inhabited islands. "Sea-level rise is not a fashionable scientific hypothesis," says President Gayoom. "It is a fact."

The seas are rising partly because global warming is melting glaciers and nibbling away at the polar ice caps, but mainly because the oceans expand as their water warms. Scientists' best estimate is that these processes will raise sea levels by about 1.5 feet over the next century, quite enough to destroy several island nations.

The higher the seas rise, the more often storms will sweep the waves across the narrow atolls and carry away the land—and storms are expected to increase as the world warms up. Many islands will become uninhabitable long before they physically disappear, as sea contaminates the underground freshwater supplies on which they depend.

SOURCE

Adapted from Geoffrey Lean, "They're Going Under; Two Islands Have Disappeared Beneath the Pacific Ocean—Sunk by Global Warming." *The Independent* (June 13, 1999): 15. Extracted from an article by Geoffrey Lean first published in *The Independent on* Sunday 13 June 1999. Reprinted by permission.

Economic Analysis of Climate Change

Scientists have modeled the results of a projected doubling of accumulated carbon dioxide in the earth's atmosphere. Some predicted effects are

- Land area loss, including beaches and wetlands, to sea-level rise
- Loss of species and forest area
- Disruption of water supplies to cities and agriculture
- Increased air conditioning costs
- Health damage and deaths from heat waves and spread of tropical diseases
- Loss of agricultural output due to drought

Some beneficial outcomes might include

- Increased agricultural production in cold climates
- Lower heating costs

In addition, some other less-predictable but possibly more damaging effects include

- Disruption of weather patterns, with increased frequency of hurricanes and other extreme weather events
- Sudden major climate changes, such as a shift in the Atlantic Gulf Stream, that could leave Europe's climate similar to Alaska's.
- Positive **feedback effects**,[3] such as increased carbon dioxide release from warming arctic tundra, which would speed up global warming.

How can we evaluate such possible impacts? In attempting to respond to this question, economists have employed **cost-benefit analysis,** which we introduced in Chapter 6. Others have criticized this approach as an attempt to put a monetary valuation on issues with social, political, and ecological implications that go far beyond dollar value. We will examine economists' efforts to place the issue in a cost-benefit context, then return to the debate over whether this effort is appropriate and what policies should be implemented.

We can evaluate policy responses to climate change by first considering a **business as usual** scenario in which no action is taken to limit greenhouse gas emissions. According to World Bank projections, global energy use will have nearly doubled by about 2030, with the greatest growth coming from developing nations.[4] Figure 18-4 illustrates the resulting dramatic increase in carbon emissions.

Today, the developed nations are responsible for most carbon emissions, but the largest projected increase in emissions will be in the currently developing nations. By 2020, developing nations will at least equal developed nations in emissions. But note that even with this large increase, per capita emissions levels will remain much lower in developing nations (Figure 18-5). With expected population and economic growth,

---

[3]A feedback effect occurs when an original change in a system causes further changes that either reinforce the original change (positive feedback) or counteract it (negative feedback).

[4]World Bank, 1992.

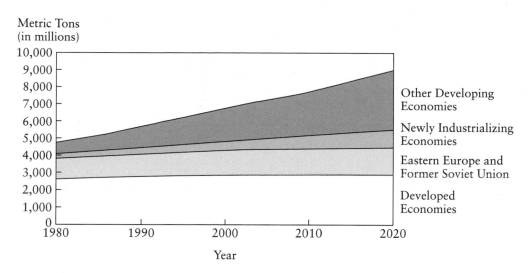

FIGURE 18-4 *Projected Carbon Emissions Through 2020, Business as Usual Scenario*
Source: Adapted from Duchin and Lange, 1994.

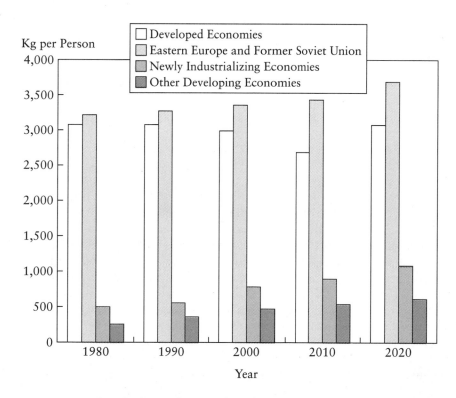

FIGURE 18-5 *Per Capita Emissions of Carbon by Region, Business as Usual Scenario*
Source: Adapted from Duchin and Lange, 1994.

emissions increases in the developing world are unavoidable. Thus global emissions reductions will require significant policy action by developed nations, as well as eventual limits on developing-nation emissions.

Cost-Benefit Studies of Global Climate Change

In performing a cost-benefit analysis, we must weigh the consequences of allowing this uncontrolled emissions scenario to proceed versus the costs of policy action to prevent it. We can do this by estimating the damages from uncontrolled global climate change. Strong policy action to prevent climate change will bring benefits equal to the value of these damages.[5] Then we must compare these to benefits to the costs of taking action. Various economic studies have attempted to estimate these benefits and costs. Table 18-1 shows the results of one such study for the U.S. economy.

The study is based on an estimated doubling of CO_2 over preindustrial levels. When the monetized costs are added up, the total annual U.S. damages are an estimated $60 billion (1990 dollars). This is about 1 percent of U.S. GNP. Although different economic studies come up with different estimates, most of them are in the range of 1 to 2 percent GNP. Cost estimates for larger temperature change over the longer term rise to about 5 percent of GNP (Table 18-1, column 2).

Note, however, the Xs, Ys, and Δs in the totals—unknown quantities that cannot easily be measured. The value of species loss, for example, is difficult to estimate in dollar terms: the estimates used here show a cost of at least $4 billion in the short term and $16 billion in the long term, with an additional unknown cost denoted as Δ.

Other monetized estimates could also be challenged on the grounds that they fail to capture the full value of potential losses. For example, oceanfront land is more than just real estate. Beaches and coastal wetlands have great social, cultural, and ecological value. Their market value fails to reflect the full scope of damage society will suffer if they are lost.

In addition, these estimates omit the possibility of the much more catastrophic consequences that *could* result if weather disruption is much worse than anticipated. A single hurricane, for example, can cause more than $10 billion in damage, in addition to loss of life. For example, in November 1998, a severe hurricane caused massive devastation and the loss of more than 7,000 lives in Central America. If climate changes cause severe hurricanes to become much more frequent, the estimate here of less than $1 billion in annual losses could be much too low. Another "X" value—human life losses from disease—could be very large if warmer weather conditions allow tropical diseases to significantly extend their range.

Clearly, these damage estimates are imprecise and open to many criticisms, but suppose we decide to accept them—at least as a rough estimate. We must then weigh the estimated benefits of policies to prevent climate change against the costs of such

---

[5]These benefits of preventing damage can also be referred to as **avoided costs.**

TABLE 18-1 Estimates of Annual Damages to the U.S. Economy from Global Climate Change (Billions 1990 $)

	$2 \times CO_2$ (+2.5°C)	Long-term warming (+10°C)
Agriculture	17.5	95.0
Forest loss	3.3	7.0
Species loss	$4.0 + \Delta$	$16.0 + \Delta'$
Sea-level rise		35.0
Building dikes, levees	1.2	
Wetlands loss	4.1	
Drylands loss	1.7	
Electricity requirements	11.2	64.1
Nonelectric heating	−1.3	−4.0
Human amenity	Xa	Ya
Human life	5.8	33.0
Human morbidity	Xm	Ym
Migration	0.5	2.8
Hurricanes	0.8	6.4
Construction	$+/- Xc$	$+/- Yc$
Leisure activities	1.7	4.0
Water supply	7.0	56.0
Urban infrastructure	0.1	0.6
Air pollution		
Tropospheric ozone	3.5	19.8
Other	Xo	Yo
Total	$61.1 + Xa + Xm + Xo + \Delta' +/- Xc$	$335.7 + Ya + Ym + Yo + \Delta +/- Yc$

Source: Adapted from William R. Cline, *The Economics of Global Warming*, Washington, D.C.: Institute for International Economics, 1992. Reprinted by permission of Institute for International Economics.

policies. To estimate these costs, economists use models that show how inputs such as labor, capital, and resources produce economic output.

To lower carbon emissions, we must cut back the use of fossil fuels, substituting other energy sources that may be more expensive. Some economic models predict that this substitution would reduce GNP growth. One major study showed GNP losses ranging from 1 to 3 percent of GNP for most countries, with higher potential long-term losses for coal-dependent developing nations such as China.[6]

If both costs and benefits of an aggressive carbon abatement policy fall in the range of 1 to 3 percent of GNP, how can we decide what to do? Much depends on our

---

[6]Manne and Richels, 1992.

A family walks through the destruction left by Hurricane Mitch in Honduras in 1998. More severe hurricanes are a possible result of global climate change.

evaluation of future costs and benefits. The costs of taking action must be borne today or in the near future. The benefits of taking action (the avoided costs of damages) are further in the future. Our task, then, is to decide today how to balance these future costs and benefits.

As we saw in Chapter 9, economists evaluate future costs and benefits by the use of a **discount rate.** The problems and implicit value judgments associated with discounting add to the uncertainties that we have already noted in valuing costs and benefits. This suggests that we should consider some alternative approaches—including techniques that incorporate ecological as well as economic costs and benefits.

Analyzing Long-Term Environmental Effects

Two major economic studies dealing with cost/benefit analysis of climate change have come to significantly different conclusions about policy. According to a study by William Nordhaus,[7] the **economic optimum** would be a small reduction in greenhouse

---

[7]Nordhaus, 1993. An updated report on modeling the economic effects of climate change is presented in Nordhaus and Boyer, 2000.

gas emissions below the business-as-usual emissions growth shown in Figure 18-4. This would require few changes in the carbon-based energy path typical of current economic development.

In contrast, a study by William Cline recommends "a worldwide program of aggressive action to limit global warming" that includes cutting carbon emissions well below present levels and freezing them there with no future increase.[8] This would involve major changes in current patterns of energy use. What explains the dramatic difference between these two cost/benefit analyses?

The two studies used similar methods to assess benefits and costs. The main differences were that the Cline study considered long-term effects and used a low discount rate (1.5 percent) to balance present and future costs. Thus even though costs of aggressive action appeared higher than benefits for several decades, the high potential long-term damages sway the balance in favor of aggressive action today.

As we saw in Chapter 6, the present value (PV) of a long-term stream of benefits or costs depends on the discount rate. A high discount rate will lead to a low present valuation for benefits that are mainly in the longer-term, and a high present valuation for short-term costs. On the other hand, a low discount rate will lead to a higher present valuation for long-term benefits. The estimated net present value of an aggressive abatement policy will thus be much higher if we choose a low discount rate.

While both the Cline and Nordhaus studies used standard economic methodology, Cline's approach gives greater weight to long-term ecological effects. These effects are significant both for their monetary and nonmonetary effects. In the long term, damage done to the environment by global climate change will have significant negative effects on the economy, too. Thus these long-term effects have a high monetary value, as shown in Figure 18-6. But a standard discount rate of 5 to 10 percent reduces the present value of significant future damages to relative insignificance.

An ecologically oriented economist would argue that the fundamental issue is the stability of the physical and ecological systems that serve as a planetary climate-control mechanism. This means that **climate stabilization** should be the goal, rather than economic optimization of costs and benefits. Stabilizing greenhouse gas emissions is insufficient; at the current rate of emissions carbon dioxide and other greenhouse gases will continue to accumulate in the atmosphere. Stabilizing the accumulations of greenhouse gases will require a significant cut below present emission levels.

Any measure taken to prevent global climate change will have economic effects on GDP, consumption, and employment, which explains the reluctance of governments to take drastic measures to reduce CO_2 emissions. But these effects may not necessarily be negative.

A comprehensive review of economic models of climate change policy shows that the economic outcomes predicted for carbon reduction policies depend heavily on the

----

[8]Cline, 1992.

Percent of GDP

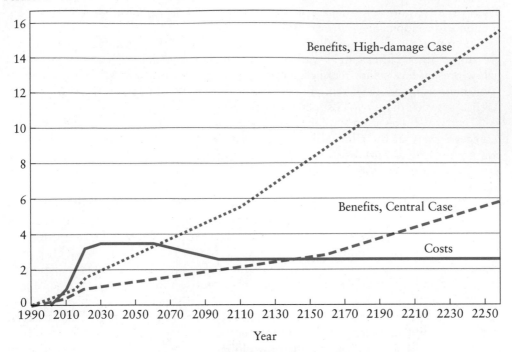

FIGURE 18-6 *Long-Term Costs and Benefits of Abating Global Climate Change*
Source: Adapted from William R. Cline, *The Economics of Global Warming,* Washington, D.C.: Institute for International Economics, 1992. Reprinted by permission of Institute for International Economics.

modeling assumptions used.[9] The predicted effects of stabilizing emissions at 1990 levels range from a 2 percent decrease to a 2 percent *increase* in GDP. The outcomes depend on a range of assumptions including:

- The efficiency or inefficiency of economic responses to energy price signals.
- The availability of noncarbon "backstop" energy technologies.
- Whether or not nations can trade least-cost options for carbon reduction.
- Whether or not revenues from taxes on carbon-based fuels are used to lower other taxes.
- Whether or not **external benefits** of carbon reduction, including reduction in ground-level air pollution, are taken into account.

Thus emissions reduction policies could range from a minimalist approach of slightly reducing emissions growth to a dramatic CO_2 emissions reduction of 40 or 50

---

[9]Repetto and Austin, WRI, 1997.

percent. Most economists who have analyzed the problem agree that action is necessary (see Box 18-3), but there is a wide range of opinion on how drastic this action
should be and how soon it should occur. The world's nations have acknowledged the
problem and are negotiating over plans to achieve emissions reductions. The scope of
the reductions now being discussed, however, falls well short of that necessary for climate stabilization.

Whatever the outcome of these negotiations, any serious effort to reduce carbon
emissions will require the kinds of economic policies to deal with negative externalities that we discussed in Chapter 3. We will now turn to an analysis of some possible
policies.

18-3   Economists' Statement on Climate Change

I. The review conducted by a distinguished international panel of scientists
under the auspices of the Intergovernmental Panel on Climate Change has
determined that "the balance of evidence suggests a discernible human influence on global climate." As economists, we believe that global climate
change carries with it significant environmental, economic, social, and
geopolitical risks, and that preventive steps are justified.

II. Economic studies have found that there are many potential policies to reduce greenhouse-gas emissions for which the total benefits outweigh the
total costs. For the United States in particular, sound economic analysis
shows that there are policy options that would slow climate change without harming American living standards, and these measures may in fact
improve U.S. productivity in the longer run.

III. The most efficient approach to slowing climate change is through market-
based policies. In order for the world to achieve its climatic objectives at
minimum cost, a cooperative approach among nations is required—such
as an international emissions trading agreement. The United States and
other nations can most efficiently implement their climate policies through
market mechanisms, such as carbon taxes or the auction of emissions permits. The revenues generated from such policies can effectively be used to
reduce the deficit or to lower existing taxes.

Note: The above statement has been endorsed by more than 2,500 economists, including eight
Nobel Laureates.

SOURCE

From Redefining Progress, Oakland, California, http://www.RedefiningProgress.org.

Policy Responses to Climate Change

Two types of measures can be used to address climate change: preventive measures tend to lower or mitigate the greenhouse effect, and adaptive measures deal with the consequences of the greenhouse effect and try to minimize their impact.

Preventive measures include the following:

- Reducing emissions of greenhouse gases, either by reducing the level of emissions-related economic activities or by shifting to more energy-efficient technologies that allow the same level of economic activity at a lower level of CO_2 emissions.
- Enhancing greenhouse gas sinks.[10] Forests recycle CO_2 into oxygen; preserving forested areas and expanding reforestation have a significant effect on net CO_2 emissions.

Adaptive measures include the following:

- Construction of dikes and seawalls to protect against rising sea levels and extreme weather events such as floods and hurricanes.
- Shifting cultivation patterns in agriculture to adapt to changed weather conditions in different areas.

An economic approach suggests that we should apply cost-effectiveness analysis in considering such policies. This differs from cost-benefit analysis in having a more modest goal: rather than attempting to decide whether or not a policy should be implemented, cost-effectiveness analysis asks what is the most efficient way to reach a policy goal.

In general, economists favor approaches that work through market mechanisms to achieve their goals. Market-oriented approaches are considered cost-effective—rather than attempting to control market actors directly, they shift incentives so that individuals and firms will change their behavior to take account of external costs and benefits. We have already mentioned the examples of **pollution taxes** and **transferable, or tradable, permits.** Both of these are potentially useful tools for greenhouse gas reduction. Other relevant economic policies include measures to create incentives for the adoption of **renewable energy sources** and **energy-efficient technology.**

Policy Tools: Carbon Taxes

The release of greenhouse gases in the atmosphere is a clear example of a negative externality that imposes significant costs on a global scale. In the language of economic theory, the market for carbon-based fuels such as coal, oil, and natural gas takes into account only private costs and benefits, which leads to a market equilibrium that fails to correspond to the **social optimum.**

---

[10]Carbon sinks are areas where excess carbon may be stored. Natural sinks include the oceans and forests. Human intervention can either reduce or expand these sinks through forest management and agricultural practices.

As we have seen, a standard remedy for internalizing external costs is a per-unit tax on the pollutant. For carbon dioxide emissions, this would be a **carbon tax,** levied exclusively on carbon-based fossil fuels. Such a tax will raise the price of carbon-based energy sources, and so give consumers incentive to conserve energy and to shift demand to alternative sources (Figure 18-7). Demand may also shift from carbon-based fuels with a higher proportion of carbon, such as coal, to those with relatively lower carbon content, such as natural gas.

Carbon taxes would appear to consumers as energy price increases. But since taxes would be levied on primary energy, which represents only one part of the cost of delivered energy (such as gasoline or electricity) and more important, since one fuel can in many cases be substituted for another, overall price increases may not be jolting. Consumers can respond to new prices by reducing energy use and buying fewer carbon-intensive products (those that require great amounts of carbon-based fuels to produce). In addition, some of these savings could be used to buy other less carbon-intensive goods and services.

Clearly, a carbon tax creates an incentive for producers and consumers to avoid paying the tax by reducing their use of carbon-intensive fuels. Contrary to other taxed items

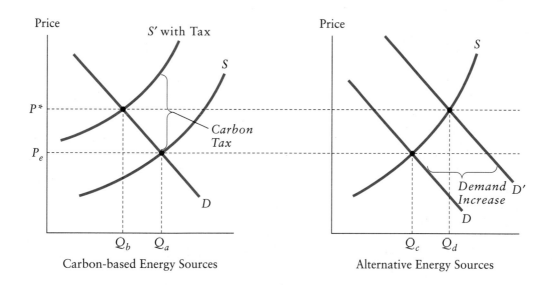

P_e = Equilibrium price of energy without carbon tax
P^* = Equilibrium price of energy with carbon tax
Q_a = Quantity of carbon-based fuels used without carbon tax
Q_b = Quantity of carbon-based fuels used with carbon tax
Q_c = Quantity of alternative energy used without carbon tax
Q_d = Quantity of alternative energy used with carbon tax

FIGURE 18-7 *The Economic Effects of a Carbon Tax*

TABLE 18-2 Alternative Taxes on Fossil Fuels

	Coal	Oil	Natural Gas
Unit of measure	ton	barrel	ccf (hundred cubic feet)
Tons of carbon per unit of fuel	.605	.130	.016
Average mine-mouth or wellhead price, 1989	$23.02	$17.70	$1.78
Carbon tax:			
Absolute tax:	$/ton	$/barrel	$/ccf
$10/ton of carbon	$6.34	$1.30	$0.16
$100/ton of carbon	$63.4	$13.00	$1.60
Tax as percent of price:			
$10/ton of carbon	26 percent	8 percent	9 percent
$100/ton of carbon	260 percent	80 percent	90 percent

Adapted from Poterba, 1993.

and activities, this avoidance has social benefits—reduced energy use and reduced CO_2 emissions. Thus, declining tax revenues over time indicate policy success—just the opposite of what happens when tax policy seeks to maintain steady or increasing revenues.[11]

Consider Table 18-2, which shows the impact different levels of carbon tax will have on prices of coal, oil, and gas. A $10 per ton carbon tax, for example, raises the price of a barrel of oil by $1.30, which is about 3 cents a gallon. Will this affect people's driving or home heating habits much? Probably not—we would not expect a high **elasticity of demand** for gasoline or heating oil, since these commonalities are viewed as necessities.

Figure 18-8 shows a cross-country relationship between gasoline prices and per capita use. Notice that the pattern of this relationship resembles a demand curve: higher prices are associated with lower consumption, lower prices with higher consumption. The relationship shown here, however, is not the same as a demand curve; because we are looking at data from different countries, the assumption of "other things equal," needed to construct a demand curve, doesn't hold.

People in the United States, for example, may drive more partly because travel distances (especially in the western states) are greater than in many European countries. But Figure 18-8 does indicate a clear price/consumption relationship. The data shown here suggest that it would take a fairly big price hike—in the range of $0.50–$1.00 per gallon or more—to affect fuel use substantially.

A much larger tax would be needed to promote a major shift away from fossil fuels. According to most studies, stabilizing global CO_2 emissions would require a carbon tax of at least $200 per ton.[12] This would more than double the price of oil and quadruple

[11]From Robert Dower and Mary Zimmerman, *The Right Climate For Carbon Taxes.* World Resources Institute, 1992. Reprinted by permission of World Resources Institute, Washington, D.C.

[12]Manne and Richels, 1992; Nordhaus and Boyer, 2000.

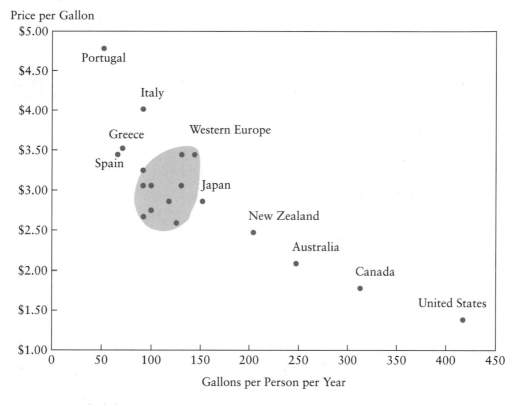

Price per Gallon

Note: Shaded area represents European price/consumption range.

FIGURE 18-8 *Gasoline Price Versus Use in Industrial Countries, 1994*
Source: Adapted from Roodman, 1997.

the price of coal, which would certainly affect consumption patterns. In addition, the long-term elasticity of demand would be significantly greater, as higher prices for carbon-based fuels promoted development of alternative technologies.

But would such a tax ever be politically feasible? Especially in the United States, high taxes on gasoline and other fuels would face much opposition, especially if people saw it as infringing on their freedom to drive. Note that in Figure 18-8 the United States has by far by the lowest price and the highest fuel consumption per person.

But let's note two things about the proposal for substantial carbon taxes:

First, **revenue recycling** could redirect the revenue from such taxes to lower other taxes. Much political opposition to high energy taxes comes from the perception that they would be an *extra* tax—on top of the income, property, and social security taxes that people already pay. If a carbon tax was matched, for example, with a substantial cut in income and social security taxes, it might be more politically acceptable.

The idea of increasing taxes on economic "bads" such as pollution and reducing taxes on things we want to encourage, such as labor and capital investment, is fully consistent with principles of economic efficiency.[13] Rather than a net tax increase, this would be a **revenue-neutral tax shift**—the total amount of taxes paid to the government is unchanged.

Second, if such a tax shift did take place, individuals or businesses whose operations were more energy-efficient would actually save money. The higher cost of energy would also create a powerful incentive for energy-saving technological innovation. Economic adaptation would be easier if the higher carbon taxes (and lower income and capital taxes) were phased in over time.

Policy Tools: Tradable Permits

As we have seen, one alternative to a pollution tax is a system of tradable pollution permits. In the international negotiations over greenhouse gas reduction, the United States has advocated implementation of a tradable permit system for carbon emissions. Such a system would work as follows:

- Each nation would be allocated a certain permissible level of carbon emissions. The total number of carbon permits issued would be equal to the desired goal. For example, if global carbon emissions are 6 billion tons and the goal is to reduce this by 1 billion, permits for 5 billion tons of emissions would be issued.
- Permit allocation would meet agreed-on targets for national or regional reductions. For example, under the 1997 Kyoto agreement, the United States agreed to set a goal of cutting its greenhouse emissions 7 percent below 1990 levels by 2008–2012. Japan agreed to a 6 percent cut, and Europe to an 8 percent cut.
- Nations could trade permits among themselves. For example, if the United States failed to meet its target, but Europe exceeded its target, the United States could purchase permits from Europe.
- The permits might also be tradable among firms, with countries setting targets for major industrial sectors, and allocating permits accordingly. Firms could then trade among themselves, or internationally.
- Nations and firms could also receive credit for reductions that they help to finance in other countries. For example, U.S. firms could earn credit for installing efficient electric generating equipment in China, replacing highly polluting coal plants.

From an economic point of view, a tradable permit system would encourage implementing least-cost carbon reduction options. Depending on permit allocations, it might also mean that developing nations could transform permits into a new export commodity by choosing a noncarbon path for their energy development. They could then sell permits to industrialized nations that had not met their reduction requirements.

The stumbling block to an international tradable permit system is obtaining agreement on the target levels. Developing nations have resisted *any* limitations on their emissions—which are currently much lower per capita than those of industrialized nations—until the

---

[13]To encourage higher investment, carbon tax revenues could be used to lower capital gains or corporate taxes.

developed nations show significant progress in reducing theirs. But some developed nations, such as the United States and Australia, are reluctant to implement any reduction policy until developing nations have signed on to some commitments (see Box 18-4).

The Economics of Tradable Carbon Permits

To demonstrate the economic impact of a tradable carbon permit system, we can use the analytical concept of **marginal net benefit** introduced in Chapter 4. Figure 18-10a shows the marginal net benefit of carbon emissions to producers and consumers.[14] The emissions level Q_E will result with no emissions limits—this is the market equilibrium, where consumers and producers maximize total net benefits, without taking into account environmental externalities.

Under a permit system, Q^* represents the total number of permits issued. The equilibrium permit price will then be P^*, reflecting the marginal net benefit of carbon emissions at Q^*. Emitters who gain benefits greater than P^* from their emissions will want to purchase permits, while those whose emissions benefits are less than P^* will do better to reduce emissions and sell any excess permits.

Figure 18-10b shows three possible carbon reduction strategies. Replacement of plants using existing carbon-emitting technologies is possible, but will tend to have high marginal costs. Reducing emissions through greater energy efficiency has lower marginal costs, as does carbon storage through forest area expansion. The permit price P^* will govern the relative levels of implementation of each of these strategies.

Nations and corporations subject to the trading scheme can decide for themselves how much of each control strategy to implement and will naturally favor the least-cost methods. This will probably involve a combination of approaches. If, for example, one nation undertakes extensive reforestation, they are likely to have excess permits, which they can sell to a nation with few low-cost reduction options. The net effect will be the worldwide implementation of the least-cost reduction techniques.

This system combines the advantages of economic efficiency with a guaranteed result—reduction to overall emissions level Q^*. The problem, of course, is to achieve agreement on the initial allocation of permits. Measurement problems may also arise, as well as issues such as whether to count only commercial carbon emissions or to include emissions changes resulting from forest and land use patterns.

Policy Tools: Subsidies, Standards, R&D, and Technology Transfer

Although political problems may prevent the adoption of sweeping carbon taxes or transferable permit systems, other policy measures have potential to lower carbon emissions. These include

---

[14]As we saw in Chapter 4, the marginal net benefit curve is derived from the demand and supply curve (in this case for carbon-based fuels), showing the marginal benefits of the product minus the marginal costs of supply.

18-4   The Kyoto Process

The December 1997 Kyoto Conference, held under the auspices of the United Nations, produced an agreement on greenhouse gas reduction called the Kyoto Protocol. Unlike the entirely voluntary Framework Convention on Climate Change (FCCC), agreed to at the Rio Conference on Environment and Development in 1992, the Kyoto Protocol is intended to be binding on its signatory nations. Industrialized countries accepted goals for emissions reduction over a 15-year period. Developing countries would not accept specific emissions limits, arguing that developed nations must first live up to their responsibility to cut their much greater per capita emissions.

Under the Kyoto Protocol, the **Clean Development Mechanism** allows cooperative projects, such as construction of highly efficient power plants in developing countries, through which an industrialized country can receive emissions reduction credit for aid given to a developing country. Another cooperative or **joint implementation** mechanism is sink enhancement, where common efforts between industrialized countries and developing countries promote forest conservation and reforestation.

These mechanisms do not add up to a global tradable permit system. Limited trading may be possible between nations that have agreed to specific emissions limits. For a global emission trading system to work, all nations must agree to emissions caps, which would require breaking the deadlock between developed and developing nations.

In meetings at The Hague in November 2000, climate change negotiations between the United States and the European Union broke down over two contentious points: whether to give countries credit for **carbon sinks** such as forests, and the limits to be placed on the so-called flexibility mechanisms.

U.S. emissions have increased by 12 percent since 1990, and are projected to increase further by 2010. (See Figure 18-9.) Drastic policy changes would be needed for the United States to meet its original Kyoto obligation of a 7 percent cut below 1990 levels by 2010.

In the negotiations at The Hague, the United States took the position that all of the carbon held in its existing forest and farmland should be counted towards its commitment. This would allow domestic industry to continue to emit at nearly the same levels seen today, and it represents nearly half of the original United States commitment (Figure 18-9). A compromise proposal agreed to by Britain would allow counting a portion of forested area. This plan was also rejected by the EU as a whole.

Disagreement also arose over how countries will meet their obligations after counting the appropriate sinks. The three principal "flexibility mechanisms" are: emissions trading, joint implementation, and the clean development mechanism.

(continued on following page)

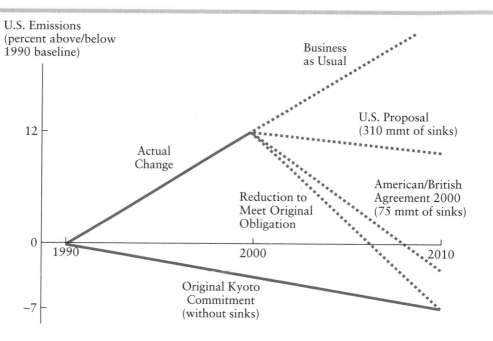

FIGURE 18-9 *United States Greenhouse Gas Emissions, 1990–2010*

Source: Percentage growth and proposed emissions cuts cited in "American Demands Something for Nothing, But the World Needs an End to its Hot Air," *The Independent* (London), November 27, 2000.

All of these would allow an industrial nation to finance emission reductions in other countries and apply them to its own Kyoto commitment.

The European Union sought to limit the amount of any country's commitment that can be satisfied through "flexibility," while the United States wanted no limits. This has important implications for actual domestic emission reductions. If unlimited flexibility is allowed, all required reductions could theoretically occur without any change in domestic emissions. According to the United States negotiators, increased flexibility would help achieve the ultimate goal of reducing global greenhouse gas emissions. But European nations argued that unlimited flexibility would allow the United States to avoid taking any serious measures to reduce its own carbon emissions.

In 2001, the Bush administration rejected the Kyoto agreement, arguing that negotiations had failed, and a new approach was necessary. They sought to emphasize voluntary rather than mandatory carbon limits. This dealt a serious blow to efforts to control global greenhouse gas emissions. Some observers argued, however, that the Kyoto process had already failed, and that a fresh start was needed in any case. As the 2008–2012 target dates grow closer, it seems clear that the original Kyoto targets will remain unmet, but it is unclear what will replace them.

(a) Determination of Carbon Permit Price

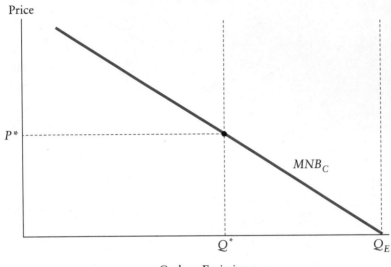

MNB$_C$ = Marginal net benefits of carbon emissions

Q$_E$ = Quality of carbon emissions without permit system

Q* = Quantity of carbon permits issued

P* = Equilibrium price of carbon permit

FIGURE 18-10A *Least-Cost Carbon Reduction with Tradable Permits—*
Determination of Carbon Permit Price

- *Shifting **subsidies** from carbon-based to noncarbon-based fuels.* As noted in Chapter 13, many countries currently provide direct or indirect subsidies to fossil fuels. Eliminating these subsidies would alter the competitive balance in favor of alternative fuel sources. If these subsidy expenditures were redirected to renewable sources, especially in the form of tax rebates for investment, it could promote a boom in investment in solar, photovoltaics, fuel cells, biomass and wind power—all technologies currently at the margin of competitiveness in various areas.
- The use of ***efficiency standards*** *to require utilities and major manufacturers to increase efficiency and renewable content in power sources.* A normal coal-fired generating plant achieves about 35 percent efficiency, and a high-efficiency gas-fired cogeneration facility achieves from 75 percent to 90 percent

(b) Carbon Reduction with a Permit System

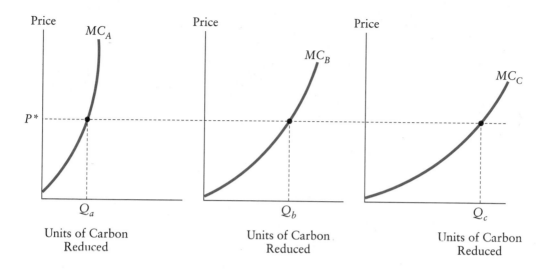

MC_A = Marginal costs of carbon reduction by plant replacement
MC_B = Marginal costs of carbon reduction by increased energy efficiency
MC_C = Marginal costs of carbon reduction by forest area expansion
P^* = Equilibrium price of carbon permit
Q_a = Units of carbon reduced by plant replacement
Q_b = Units of carbon reduced by increased energy efficiency
Q_c = Units of carbon reduced by forest area expansion

FIGURE 18-10B *Carbon Reduction with a Permit System*

efficiency. Current automobile fuel-efficiency standards do not exceed 27.5 miles per gallon, but efficiencies of up to 50 miles per gallon or more can be achieved with proven technology. Tightening standards over time for plants, buildings, vehicles, and appliances would hasten the turnover of existing, energy-inefficient capital stock.

- *Research and development (R&D) expenditures directed toward the commercialization of alternative technologies.* Both government R&D programs and favorable tax treatment of corporate R&D for alternative energy can speed commercialization. The existence of a noncarbon "backstop" technology significantly reduces the economic cost of measures such as carbon taxes, and if the backstop became fully competitive with fossil fuels carbon taxes would be unnecessary.

- **Technology transfer** to developing nations. As we have seen, the bulk of projected growth in carbon emissions will come in the developing world. Many energy development projects are now funded by agencies such as the World Bank and regional development banks. To the extent that these funds can be directed toward noncarbon energy systems, supplemented by other funds dedicated specifically to alternative energy development, it will be economically feasible for developing nations to turn away from fossil-fuel intensive paths, achieving significant local environmental benefits at the same time.

The future course of energy and global climate change policy will undoubtedly respond to further scientific evidence regarding atmospheric carbon dioxide accumulation. Political barriers that prevent significant policy action may eventually diminish. Some combination of the policies discussed in this chapter will certainly be centrally relevant to energy policies for the next half-century and beyond.

SUMMARY

Climate change, arising from the greenhouse effect of heat-trapping gases, is a global problem. All nations are involved in both its causes and consequences. Current developed nations are the largest greenhouse gas emitters, but emissions by developing nations will grow considerably in coming decades.

The most recent scientific evidence indicates that effects during the twenty-first century may range from a global temperature increase of 1 degree Celsius (2 degrees Fahrenheit) to as much as 6 degrees Celsius (10 degrees Fahrenheit). In addition to simply warming the planet, other predicted effects include disruption of weather patterns and possible sudden major climate shifts.

An analysis of costs and benefits can serve as an economic analysis of climate change. The benefits in this case are the damages potentially averted through action to prevent climate change; the costs are the economic costs of shifting away from fossil fuel dependence, as well as other economic implications of greenhouse gas reduction.

Cost-benefit studies have estimated both costs and benefits in the range of several percent of GDP. However, relative evaluation of costs and benefits depends heavily on the discount rate selected. Because damages tend to worsen with time, the use of a high discount rate leads to a lower evaluation of the benefits of avoiding climate change. In addition, some effects such as species loss and effects on life and health are difficult to measure in monetary terms. Also, depending on the assumptions used in economic models, the impact of policies to avoid climate change on GDP could range from a 2 percent decrease to a 2 percent increase in GDP.

Policies to respond to global climate change could be preventive or adaptive. One widely discussed policy is a carbon tax, which would fall most heavily on fuels causing the highest carbon emissions. Revenues from such a tax could be recycled to lower taxes elsewhere in the economy. Another policy option is tradable carbon emissions permits, which could be bought and sold by firms or nations, depending on their level of carbon emissions. Both these policies have the advantage of economic efficiency, but it has been difficult to obtain the political support necessary to implement them. Other possible policy measures include shifting subsidies away from fossil fuels, strengthening energy efficiency standards, and increasing research and development of alternative energy technologies.

The international negotiation process on climate change has led to some pledges for emissions reduction, but progress has stalled due to disagreements on the assignment of responsibility for cuts. The original targets for greenhouse gas reduction will probably go unmet, and new approaches are needed to devise a global response to the problem.

KEY TERMS AND CONCEPTS

avoided costs
business as usual
carbon sinks
carbon tax
Clean Development Mechanism
climate stabilization
common property resource
cost-benefit analysis
cost-effectiveness analysis
discount rate
economic optimum
efficiency standards
elasticity of demand
energy-efficient technology
environmental externalities
externalities/external costs and benefits
feedback effect
global climate change
global commons

global warming
greenhouse effect
greenhouse gases
internalizing externalities
joint implementation
local and regional pollutants
marginal net benefit
pollution taxes
preventive and adaptive strategies
renewable energy sources
research and development (R&D)
revenue recycling
revenue-neutral tax shift
social optimum
stock pollutant
subsidies
technology transfer
transferable (tradable) pollution permits

DISCUSSION QUESTIONS

1. Do you consider cost-benefit analysis a useful means of addressing the problem of climate change? How can we adequately value the melting of arctic ice caps, inundation of island nations, and similar climactic impacts? What is the appropriate role of economic analysis in dealing with questions that affect global ecosystems and future generations?

2. Which policies might most effectively address climate change? How can we decide which combination of policies to use? What kinds of policies would economists especially recommend? What are the main barriers to effective policy implementation?

3. The process for formulating and implementing international agreements on climate change policy has been plagued with disagreements and deadlocks. What are the main difficulties in agreeing on specific policy actions? From an economic point of view, what kinds of incentives might induce nations to enter and carry out agreements? What kinds of "win-win" policies might overcome negotiating barriers?

PROBLEMS

1. Suppose that the terms of an international agreement require reduction of U.S. CO_2 emissions by 200 million tons and those of Brazil by 50 million tons. These are the emissions reduction policy options for each country:

Policy Options	Total Emissions Reduction (million tons carbon)	Cost ($ billion)
United States:		
A: Efficient machinery	60	12
B: Reforestation	40	20
C: Replace coal fueled power plants	120	30
Brazil:		
A: Efficient machinery	50	20
B: Protection of Amazon forest	30	3
C: Replace coal-fueled power plants	40	8

a. What policies appear most efficient for helping the United States and Brazil meet their targets? What will be the cost to each nation if they must operate independently?

b. Suppose a market of transferable permits allows the United States and Brazil to trade permits to emit CO_2. Who has an interest in buying permits? Who has an interest in selling permits? What agreement can they reach to meet the overall emissions reduction target of 250 million tons at the least cost? Can you estimate a range for the permit price to emit one ton of carbon? (Hint: calculate the average cost per unit for each reduction policy.)

2. Suppose that the annual consumption of an average American household is 2,000 gallons of oil in heating and transportation and 2,000 ccf (hundred cubic feet) of gas in cooking. Use the figures in Table 18-2 on the effects of a carbon tax to calculate how much an average American household would pay per year with an added tax of $10 per ton of carbon. (One barrel of oil contains 42 gallons.)

Figuring about 100 million such households in the United States, what revenue would such a tax generate for the U.S. Treasury? What national revenue would a tax of $100 per ton of carbon generate? (Consider the issue of possible changes in consumption.) How might the government use such revenues? What impact might this tax have on the average family?

REFERENCES

Cline, William R. *The Economics of Global Warming*. Washington, D.C.: Institute for International Economics, 1992.

Dower, Roger C., and Zimmerman, Mary. *The Right Climate for Carbon Taxes, Creating Economic Incentives to Protect the Atmosphere*. Washington, D.C.: World Resources Institute, 1992.

Duchin, Faye, and Glenn-Marie Lange. *The Future of the Environment, Ecological Economics and Technological Change*. Oxford, England: Oxford University Press, 1994.

Fankhauser, Samuel. *Valuing Climate Change: The Economics of the Greenhouse*. London: Earthscan Publications, 1995.

Intergovernmental Panel on Climate Change (IPCC). *Climate Change 1995, Volume 1: The Science of Climate Change*. Cambridge, England: Cambridge University Press, 1996.

Intergovernmental Panel on Climate Change (IPCC). *Climate Change 2001, Volume 1: The Scientific Basis*. Cambridge, England: Cambridge University Press, 2001.

Manne, Alan S., and Richard G. Richels. *Buying Greenhouse Insurance: The Economic Costs of CO_2 Emissions Limits*. Cambridge, Mass.: MIT Press, 1992.

Nordhaus, William D. "Reflections on the Economics of Climate Change." *Journal of Economic Perspectives* 7 (Fall 1993): 11–25.

Nordhaus, William D., and Joseph Boyer. *Warming the World: Economic Models of Global Warming*. Cambridge, Mass.: MIT Press, 2000.

Poterba, James. "Global Warming Policy: A Public Finance Perspective," *Journal of Economic Perspectives* 7 (Fall 1993): 47–63.

Repetto, Robert, and Duncan Austin. *The Costs of Climate Protection: A Guide for the Perplexed*. Washington, D.C.: World Resources Institute, 1997.

Roodman, David M. *Getting the Signals Right: Tax Reform to Protect the Environment and the Economy*. Worldwatch Paper 134. Washington, D.C.: Worldwatch Institute, 1997.

Trenberth, Kevin E. "Stronger Evidence of Human Influence on Climate: The 2001 IPCC Assessment," *Environment* 43 (May 2001): 8–19.

World Bank. *World Development Report 1992: Development and the Environment*. Washington, D.C.: World Bank, 1992.

WEB SITES

1. **http://www.epa.gov/globalwarming/** The global warming web site of the U.S. Environmental Protection Agency. The site provides links to information on the causes, impact, and trends related to global climate change.

2. **http://www.ipcc.ch/** The web site for the Intergovernmental Panel on Climate Change, a United Nations–sponsored agency "to assess the scientific, technical, and socioeconomic information relevant for the understanding of the risk of human-induced climate change." Their web site includes assessment reports detailing the relationships between human actions and global climate change.

3. **http://www.wri.org/climate/** World Resource Institute's web site on climate and atmosphere. The site includes several articles and case studies, including research on Clean Development Mechanisms.

4. **http://www.unfccc.de/** Home page for the United Nations Framework Convention on Climate Change. The site provides data on the climate change issue and information about the ongoing process of negotiating international agreements related to climate change.

5. **http://www.weathervane.rff.org/** A web site sponsored by Resources for the Future devoted to climate change issues. The site includes several research papers on the trading of greenhouse gas emissions permits.

Environment, Trade, and Development

CHAPTER FOCUS QUESTIONS

- What effects does expanded trade have on the environment?
- Should regional and global trade agreements include environmental protection?
- What policies can promote sustainable trade?

World Trade and the Environment

Environmental Impact of Trade

World trade expansion has raised the issue of the relationship between trade and the environment. Is trade good or bad for the environment? The answer is not obvious. The production of goods for import and export, like other production, often has environmental effects. Will these effects increase or decrease with expanded trade? How will they affect the exporting nation, the importing nation, or the world as a whole? Who is responsible for responding to environmental problems associated with trade? Questions such as these have received increasing attention in recent years.

International attention first focused on these issues in 1991, when the Mexican government challenged a U.S. law banning tuna imports from Mexico. The U.S. Marine Mammal Protection Act prohibited tuna-fishing methods that killed large numbers of dolphins, and banned tuna imports from countries that used such fishing methods. The Mexican government argued that this U.S. law violated the rules of the **General Agreement on Tariffs and Trade (GATT)**.

According to the free-trade principles that provided the basis for GATT and for its successor, the **World Trade Organization (WTO)**, countries cannot restrict imports except in limited cases such as protecting the health and safety of their own citizens. A GATT dispute panel ruled that the United States could not use domestic legislation to protect dolphins outside its own territorial limits.

Although Mexico did not press for enforcement of this decision, the tuna/dolphin case opened a major controversy over issues of trade and environment. In a similar case in 1999, the World Trade Organization ruled that the United States could not prohibit shrimp imports from countries using fishing methods that killed endangered sea turtles.

The implications of this and the earlier tuna/dolphin decision could affect many other international environmental issues, including forest protection, ozone depletion, hazardous wastes, and global climate change. All these issues relate to international trade. If individual countries cannot use trade measures to protect the global environment, how will it be possible to devise effective policies to respond to these issues?

To address these questions, we need to reexamine the theory and practice of international trade. Most economists believe that expanded trade is generally beneficial, promoting increased efficiency and greater wealth among trading nations. But what if expanded trade causes environmental damage?

At the national level, the standard economic policy response to environmental impact is to implement policies that internalize externalities, as discussed in earlier chapters. At the international level, however, the picture is more confused. The burden of environmental externalities associated with trade may be borne by importers, exporters, or by others not directly involved in producing or consuming traded goods. The authority to formulate and enforce environmental policies usually exists only at the national level. This can create significant problems when environmental impacts are transnational, because most international trade agreements make no provision for environmental protection.

Comparative Advantage and Environmental Externalities

We can use economic theory to analyze some of the gains and losses associated with environmental effects of trade. The theory of **comparative advantage** tells us that both trading partners gain from trade by specializing in goods they can produce most efficiently. This basic theory does not consider **environmental externalities** associated with the production or consumption of goods. Consider Figure 19-1, which uses automobiles as an example of an imported good's welfare effects.

The supply curve S takes into account private costs, whereas S' shows social costs including both private costs and externalities. P^* is the domestic price in the absence of trade, whereas P_w is the world price, which will also be the domestic price under free trade conditions.[1] Q^* is the quantity produced domestically with no trade; Q_1 is

---

[1]This example shows trade in a relatively small country whose demand has no affect on world price—hence world price is shown as constant.

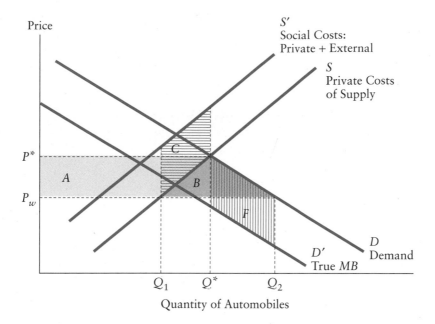

FIGURE 19-1 *Gains and Losses from Importing Automobiles*

the quantity produced domestically with free trade; and $(Q_2 - Q_1)$ is the quantity imported, for a total domestic consumption of Q_2.

How does trade affect domestic economic welfare? Domestic producers of automobiles lose area A because they now sell fewer cars at a lower price. Domestic consumers gain areas $A + B$ because they can now buy more cars at the same lower price. The net gain from trade is therefore $(A + B) - A = B$.

But this leaves out any environmental externalities associated with trade. If the automobile production causes environmental damage, by lowering production the country gains area C in reduced environmental costs—costs shifted to countries producing cars for export. On the other hand, if automobile consumption and use causes environmental damage and lowers the true marginal benefits from consumption to D', trade increases the negative externalities associated with consumption by area F.

This has important implications for trade theory. In the basic trade case without externalities, we can unambiguously claim overall **gains from trade.** Even though one group (automobile producers) loses, consumers' gains outweigh these losses. Once we introduce externalities, however, we can no longer be so sure that there are net gains from trade. It depends on the nature and size of the environmental damages C and F. Policy actions by the importing and exporting countries could internalize these external costs, but unless we know such policies will be implemented, we cannot be sure of a net gain from trade.

Environmental Effects of Expanding Resource Exports

Environmental effects must also figure in the analysis of how trade affects an exporting country. In Figure 19-2 we use timber exports as our example. In the ordinary analysis of trade without externalities, production of timber increases from Q^* to Q_2, while domestic consumption decreases to Q_1, leaving $(Q_2 - Q_1)$ for export. Timber producers gain areas $A' + B'$ because with trade they can produce and sell more timber at the higher world price P_w. Domestic timber consumers lose A', being able to afford less timber at the higher price. The net gain to the country is B'.

The external costs associated with additional timber production—which could include land and watershed degradation as well as user costs, option values, and ecological costs—are shown by the area of C'. We cannot tell for sure how B' and C' compare in size. Thus we cannot unambiguously claim net benefits from trade to this exporting country. In more commonsense terms, it is not clear that the economic benefits of increased exports outweigh the environmental damage associated with expanded logging.

Our examples, of course, represent a simple model of trade, but the conclusion that environmental costs may seriously affect net gains from trade is far-reaching. In the real world, hundreds of countries trade trillions of dollars' worth of products. Where significant environmental externalities occur, trade will reallocate these externalities among countries.

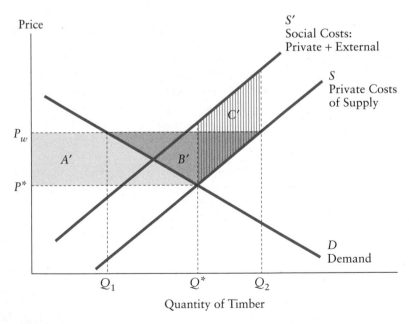

FIGURE 19-2 *Gains and Losses from Exporting Timber*

It may be possible to **export pollution** by importing goods whose production creates heavy environmental impact. In addition, expanded trade tends to increase the scale of production for the individual countries and world as a whole, meaning that the total volume of pollution and environmental damage is likely to increase. Trade also necessarily involves energy use for transportation, with resulting air pollution and other environmental consequences. Indirect environmental effects of trade might also occur, for example when larger-scale export agriculture displaces peasant farmers onto marginal lands such as hillsides and forest margins, leading to deforestation and soil erosion. Specific kinds of trade, such as trade in toxic wastes or endangered species, can have obvious negative environmental impact.

Trade may also have environmentally beneficial effects. Freer trade may help spread environmentally friendly technology, and the tendency of trade to promote more efficient production may reduce materials and energy use per unit of output. In addition, trading nations may come under pressure to improve environmental standards when product quality or transboundary impacts are at issue.[2] How can we balance the economic gains from trade against the reality that trade shifts environmental impact, sometimes increasing and sometimes decreasing total external costs?

Trade and Environment: Policy and Practice

Many developing countries grow agricultural crops for domestic sale as well as for export. With increased trade—often a major feature of "structural adjustment" policies required by international agencies such as the International Monetary Fund and the World Bank—the area devoted to export crops increases. What are the environmental effects of shifting to export crops? In some cases they can be significant, and harmful. A study of Mali, for example, finds that development of cotton as a cash export crop "has substantially increased the cultivated area and markedly reduced the fallow period . . . the profitability of cotton led farmers to increase greatly the area cultivated, extending onto marginal land. . . . Almost no fallowing is practiced in the region. The environmental effects are evident in land degradation and soil erosion owing to overcultivation, insufficient fallow, and the use of marginal land against a backdrop of increasing aridity."[3]

On the other hand, export crops may sometimes be more environmentally friendly than the domestic crops they replace. In Latin America and Africa, tree crops such as coffee and cocoa can help to prevent erosion, and in Kenya horticulture (growing flowers for the European market) provides a high-value export with little negative environmental effect. In the Kenyan case, the flowers are flown to Europe by jet, so transportation energy use could raise an environmental issue—but the energy consumed in jet fuel is less than the energy needed to grow similar flowers in heated greenhouses in Europe.

---

[2]Examples could include pesticide residues in food or water pollution.

[3]Reed, ed., 1996, pp. 86 and 96.

Much depends not on trade alone, but on domestic political conditions. **Dualistic land ownership,** with large landowners wielding considerable political power and small farmers being displaced by export-oriented agriculture, can be doubly damaging to the environment. In Central America, for example, improved transportation and trade infrastructure led to "a technical shift to higher-profit, input-dependent farming. Maize and beans gave way to cotton, tomatoes, strawberries, and bananas. The value of farmland naturally increased, which benefited privileged land-owning elites but led many poor farmers to be promptly evicted. These farmers had no choice but to move on to drier lands, forests, hillsides, or lands with shallow and less fertile soils." At the same time the affluent farmers "use their influence to demand environmentally damaging input subsidies, which in turn lead them to overmechanize, overirrigate, and overspray."[4]

Health and safety issues arising in trade are not always easily resolved at either the domestic or international levels. Domestic regulations that prohibit the sale of, for example, a toxic pesticide, do not apply internationally. "Goods that are restricted in domestic markets, on the grounds that they present a danger to human, animal or plant life or health, or to the environment, may often be legally exported. This may cause a problem for the importing country, where information is lacking on whether and why the product is banned: exporters may make false declarations, customs authorities (particularly in developing countries) may lack adequate product testing facilities."[5]

According to **GATT Article XX,** countries may restrict trade in order to "conserve exhaustible natural resources" or to protect "human, animal or plant life or health." However, interpretation of this special exception to free trade rules has led to fiercely contested disputes among countries.

For example, European nations have refused to allow imports of U.S. beef produced with hormone supplements. The United States has argued that since there is no proven harm to human health this is an illegal barrier to trade. The Europeans, however, cite the **precautionary principle:** because their consumers are concerned about the possible effects of hormones, shouldn't they have the prerogative to decide what they will allow for domestic consumption?

Product and Process Issues

A similar issue has arisen over the use of genetically engineered crops. Although the United States allows unlabeled genetically engineered foods, these are widely opposed in Europe. Should European countries be able to ban the import of genetically engineered foods? The issue has enormous implications both for agribusinesses that see great profit potential in genetic engineering and for many consumers who strongly oppose it.

---

[4]Paarlberg, 2000, p. 177.

[5]Brack, 1998, p. 7.

The issue is further complicated because much of the opposition to genetic engineering is based not on possible human health effects (which, if proved, would be a valid reason for trade restrictions under Article XX), but on the likely environmental repercussions of genetically engineered crops. Pollen from such crops can easily spread into the environment, disrupting fragile ecosystems and possibly creating "superweeds" resistant to herbicides. But under GATT and WTO rules, the production *process* is not an acceptable cause for trade restrictions. Only if the *product* itself is harmful can a country impose controls.

For example, if pesticide residues at dangerous levels are detected on fruit or vegetables, import of those products can be banned. But if pesticide overuse is causing environmental damage in the producing areas, the importing nation has no right to act. Similarly, if unrestricted logging is destroying rainforests, countries may not impose a ban on the import of unsustainably produced timber.

This **process and production methods (PPM) rule** removes an important potential weapon for international environmental protection. If a nation fails to act to protect its own environment, other countries have no trade leverage to promote better environmental practices. Only if a specific **multilateral environmental agreement (MEA)** such as the Convention on International Trade in Endangered Species (CITES) is in place are import restrictions permissible.

This principle was at issue in the tuna/dolphin and shrimp/turtle decisions, in which trade authorities ruled that nations had no jurisdiction over extraterritorial environmental issues. But such issues are more and more common in an increasingly globalized world. Simply waiting for the producing country to "clean up its act" is likely to be insufficient.

Trade can affect domestic as well as international policy, weakening the autonomy of nations to define their own environmental and social policies. Concerns have arisen of a **"race to the bottom,"** in which nations reduce environmental and social standards in order to gain competitive advantage.

> Producers located in member states enforcing strict process standards will suffer a competitive disadvantage compared with producers located in member states enforcing less strict standards. All things being equal, this may result in increased sales, market share, and profitability for those producers located in low-standard member states. . . . [F]aced with the prospect of their industries suffering a competitive disadvantage when compared with companies located in low-standard jurisdictions, member states may choose not to elevate environmental standards or may even relax current standards.[6]

The North American Free Trade Agreement (NAFTA) has produced cases in which corporations have challenged environmental regulations as barriers to trade.[7] The Canadian asbestos industry sought to remove U.S. restrictions on the sale of

---

[6]Brack, 1998, p. 113.

[7]The parties to the NAFTA are the United States, Canada, and Mexico. Discussions are underway to create a Free Trade Area of the Americas (FTAA), which would extend NAFTA-like trade rules to all of North and South America.

cancer-causing asbestos products, and the U.S. pesticide industry challenged strong Canadian pesticide regulations. In one case, the Ethyl Corporation (based in the United States) successfully overturned a Canadian ban on importation and sale of the gasoline additive MDMA, a chemical suspected to cause nerve damage. Canada was required not only to eliminate the ban, but also to pay $10 million to compensate Ethyl Corp. for legal costs and lost sales.

Trade expansion may also have direct or indirect beneficial effects on the environment. According to comparative advantage theory, trade causes countries to become more efficient in their use of resources, thereby conserving resources and avoiding waste. Trade liberalization also removes distortionary subsidies and pricing policies, improving the efficiency of resource allocation. For example, widespread subsidies on chemical fertilizers and pesticides promote environmentally harmful farming methods—but trade agreements often prohibit such subsidies to domestic producers. Eliminating these subsidies would promote both economic efficiency and environmental sustainability.

Trade may also encourage the spread of environmentally friendly technology. In energy production, for example, many developing and formerly communist nations depend heavily on old, inefficient, high-polluting power plants. Trade can facilitate the replacement of these plants with modern, highly efficient facilities or (as in India) encourage a growing wind-power sector. Multinational companies, sometimes seen as offenders in the exploitation of developing country resources, can also introduce efficient technologies into industrial sectors. Multinationals may respond to domestic political pressures to develop cleaner industrial processes and then disseminate those processes throughout their worldwide operations.

> Foreign investment affects the environment in many ways. In resource-based industries, especially oil extraction and mineral mining, it can lead to significant local environmental degradation as demonstrated in, for example, Nigeria, Indonesia, and Papua New Guinea. Foreign investment in the manufacturing sector, on the other hand, can lead to the employment of later vintage and possibly less resource- and pollution-intensive technology.[8]

Globalization of trade can also create "boomerang" effects through the transboundary exchange of externalities. For example, pesticides banned in the United States are often exported to developing countries. Poor laborers who apply pesticides without safety precautions suffer harmful effects, as do adults and children who drink water from streams polluted by runoff. In addition, harmful effects return to the United States through trade in fruits containing residues of dangerous chemicals.

Trade Agreements and the Environment

A variety of institutional and policy approaches have been suggested to balance the goals of trade benefits and environmental protection, some similar to the standard free-trade model, and some significantly different. Let's examine some of them.

---

[8]Neumayer, 2001, p. x.

Indonesian environmental activists protest air pollution levels in Jakarta, calling for use of unleaded fuels. Signs on the masks say "no lead." Many cities in developing nations have very high levels of air pollution.

The World Trade Organization Approach

This approach retains the overarching policy goal of free or "liberalized" trade, pursued for five decades through "rounds" of trade agreements under the General Agreement on Tariffs and Trade, which became the World Trade Organization in 1994. The GATT and WTO, whose membership now includes over 120 nations, have worked to lower tariffs and nontariff barriers to trade, as well as eliminate subsidies for export industries.

Although the WTO recognizes a special exception to trade rules under Article XX for resource conservation and environmental protection, its panel rulings have interpreted this narrowly. WTO authorities tend to be suspicious of "green protectionism"—the use of trade barriers to protect domestic industry from competition under the guise of environmental regulation. They are also unsympathetic to nations' efforts to affect environmental policy outside their borders through trade measures.

19-1 The Environmental Kuznets Curve Debate

Defenders of expanding global trade have often relied on the **Environmental Kuznets Curve (EKC)** principle, which asserts that environmental damage increases in the early stages of growth, but diminishes once nations reach higher levels of income (see Figure 19-3). According to this theory, after passing through a "dirty" stage of development, nations will put effort into "cleaning up" and may also shift to less-polluting production methods. More open trade will therefore accelerate the process of achieving both economic growth and a cleaner environment.

Do empirical data support the EKC principle? The picture is mixed. A study by Grossman and Krueger found it effective for a limited number of air and water pollutants.[1] Other important environmental pollutants such as nitrogen oxides, car-

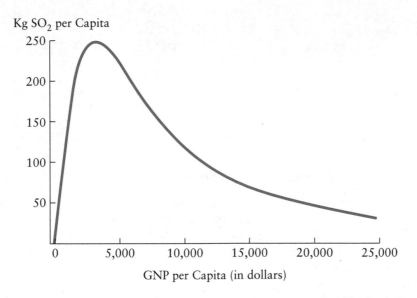

FIGURE 19-3 *Environmental Kuznets Curve for Sulfur Dioxide Emissions*
Source: Adapted from Panayotou, T., *Empirical Tests and Policy Analysis of Environmental Degradation at Different Levels of Development*, 1993. Reprinted by permission of the author.

---

[1]Grossman and Krueger, 1995. The pollutants they tested were sulfur dioxide, smoke, and particulate matter in air; oxygen loss, fecal contamination, and heavy metal contamination in water.

(continued on following page)

bon monoxide, carbon dioxide, methane, and tropospheric ozone, were not included, nor were municipal wastes or measures of ecosystem degradation such as species loss, soil degradation, or groundwater depletion.

According to a World Bank study, carbon dioxide emissions and municipal wastes continued to increase with economic growth. And even those pollutants that seem to conform to an EKC have high enough "turning points," ranging from $2,000 to $12,000 in income, to imply a considerable increase in pollution for most of the world's developing nations before any improvement would be noted.

According to one EKC study, the estimated global "turning point" for sulfur dioxide would not come until 2085, by which time global emissions would be 354 percent above 1986 levels. Suspended particulate matter would peak in 2089 at 421 percent higher emissions, and nitrogen oxides in 2079 with 226 percent higher emissions.[2] Another review of EKC studies suggested that ". . . using different indicators, more explanatory variables than income alone and the estimation of different models, the EKC results are not generally reproduced. This should be a warning to those who too superficially have concluded that economic growth is, by nature, a benefit for the environment and that economic growth can be prescribed as the remedy to environmental problems."[3]

Clearly, trade-led growth can have significant environmental impacts. Although economic growth may increase the capabilities of nations to promote environmental protection, avoiding unacceptable levels of environmental damage will require specific policies to reduce pollution.

---

[2]Selden and Song, 1994.

[3]Rothman and de Bruyn, 1998, p. 145. See also Stern, 1998.

From the WTO perspective, environmental policy responsibility should remain at the national level. As far as possible, decisions on international trade policy should not be complicated with environmental issues. This is consistent with an economic principle known as the **specificity rule:** policy solutions should directly target the source of the problem. Using trade measures to accomplish environmental policy goals is therefore a **second-best solution** likely to cause other, undesired effects such as economic losses from trade restriction.

This argument, placing the responsibility for environmental policies on national governments, has been criticized on several grounds. It fails to consider the competitive pressures that may encourage trading nations to reduce environmental protections, as well as the weak regulatory institutions in many developing countries. It is also inadequate for dealing with truly **transboundary** or **global pollution** problems.

The North American Free Trade Agreement (NAFTA) Approach

In 1993, the United States, Canada, and Mexico signed the NAFTA agreement, lowering trade barriers across the continent. During negotiations, environmental groups argued strongly that freer trade could lead to negative environmental consequences, pointing to the severe environmental problems already affecting the *maquiladoras*—tariff-free industrial zones along the Mexican border. As a result, a side agreement, the North American Agreement on Environmental Cooperation (NAAEC), set up the tripartite Commission for Environmental Cooperation (CEC), and another side agreement, the North American Agreement on Labor Cooperation (NAALC), dealt with labor issues.

This specific attention to social and environmental aspects of trade was remarkable and almost unprecedented in trade agreements. Although this unusual aspect of NAFTA persuaded some environmental groups in the United States to support the agreement, the CEC has few enforcement powers. It may respond to a country's failure to enforce existing environmental regulations, but its role is generally limited to producing a fact-finding report and recommendations to the government involved. In addition, promises of funding to clean up environmentally damaged areas along the Mexican/U.S. border have generally not been fulfilled, and border conditions have continued to deteriorate.[9]

The opening of agricultural sector trade under NAFTA has both social and environmental effects, as small corn farmers in Mexico are unable to compete with cheaper grain imported from the U.S. The migration of displaced farmers from rural to urban areas will intensify urban environmental pressures, as well as creating greater pressure for illegal migration across the U.S./Mexico border. In addition, the genetic diversity characteristic of small-scale farming may be threatened, which could result in the loss of a "living seed bank" of great importance to world agriculture.[10]

In the area of industrial pollution, NAFTA has had both positive and negative impacts. Mexican environmental enforcement has improved, but increased industrial concentrations have led to worsened local environmental quality in some areas. A recent review of NAFTA's environmental provisions concludes that they have "fallen well short of the aspirations of the environmental community" and "should be strengthened in the next phase of NAFTA."[11]

---

[9]Varady and Mack, 1996.

[10]See CEC, 1999, Issue Study 1: Maize in Mexico; and Nadal, 2000.

[11]Hufbauer et al., 2000, p. 62.

The European Union Approach

The European Union is unusual in being a free-trade area with its own legislative and administrative institutions. Unlike the North American CEC, the European Union has the power to make environmental regulations binding on its member countries. This is known as **harmonization of environmental standards.** Note, however, that this policy solution involves more than free trade; it entails the creation of a supranational authority with the power to set environmental standards.

Regional trade area policies also raise the issue of "harmonizing up" versus "harmonizing down." Some countries may be forced to tighten their environmental policies to meet EU standards, but others may find their environmental standards weakened. The EU overturned a law requiring returnable bottles in Denmark as a barrier to trade, and Norway chose not to join the EU in part out of fear that they would be compelled to modify strict domestic environmental regulations.

It is relatively rare for trade agreements to include the kind of enforceable supranational environmental regulations that exist in the European Union. Although the Standards Code adopted after the Uruguay Round GATT negotiations in 1992 calls for international harmonization of environmental standards, no basis exists for this process to be other than voluntary. Indeed, critics have argued that harmonization undertaken in the closed, business-dominated atmosphere of the WTO standards committees would in many cases be likely to harmonize standards down rather than up.

Multilateral Environmental Agreements (MEAs)

It has long been recognized that some environmental problems require international solutions. The first international treaty dealing with trade and the environment was the *Phylloxera* agreement of 1878, restricting trade in grapevines to prevent the spread of pests that damage vineyards. In 1906 an international convention was adopted banning the use of phosphorus in matches. Phosphorus was responsible for serious occupational disease among match workers, but it was the cheapest ingredient for matches. Only an international convention could prevent any exporting country from gaining competitive advantage by using phosphorus in match production.[12]

Since then, numerous international treaties have responded to specific environmental issues. These include conventions protecting fur seals, migratory birds, polar bears, whales, and endangered species. Transboundary and global environmental issues have been addressed in the Montreal Protocol on Substances that Deplete the Ozone Layer (1987), the Basel Convention on Hazardous Wastes (1989), the Antarctica Treaty (1991), and the Convention on Straddling and Highly Migratory Fish Stocks (1995). In 1997 the Kyoto Protocol on Climate Change established guidelines for reducing greenhouse gas emissions, including important trade-related measures.

---

[12]Charnovitz, 1996, pp. 176–177.

These international treaties have addressed the environmental consequences of production methods in ways that individual nations cannot. "The local imposition of PPM (Process and Production Measures) standards on domestic manufacturing industry is obviously a national prerogative, but it should not be used to restrict imported products, whatever the process used for their production. This kind of action would be in conflict with the GATT. If PPMs are included as appropriate measures within a Multilateral Environmental Agreement (MEA), however, this would be much more acceptable, as their imposition would be multilateral rather than unilateral."[13]

Serious questions remain, however, about the compatibility of MEAs with WTO rules. Which set of international agreements should take precedence in the case of a conflict? For example, the Kyoto Protocol encourages the subsidized transfer of energy-efficient technology to developing nations—but this provision could violate the WTO's prohibition of export subsidies. Whereas national laws such as the U.S. Marine Mammal Protection Act have been found incompatible with WTO rules, so far no major test case has addressed conflict between an MEA and a trade agreement.

Strategies for Sustainable Trade

The emerging twenty-first century global economy will be characterized both by resource and environmental limits and by a much more important role for the presently developing nations. Expanded global trade will bring benefits in terms of increased efficiency, technology transfer, and the import and export of sustainably produced products. But we must also evaluate the effects of trade in terms of social and ecological impacts.

A World Bank review of trade and environment issues finds that "many participants in the debate now agree that (a) more open trade improves growth and economic welfare, and (b) increased trade and growth without appropriate environmental policies in place may have unwanted effects on the environment."[14] This implies that future trade agreements must take environmental sustainability more explicitly into account. Introducing sustainability into trade policy will require institutional changes at global, regional, and local levels.

"Greening" Global Environmental Organizations

At the global level, advocates of institutional reform have proposed setting up a **World Environmental Organization (WEO)**[15] that would counterbalance the World Trade Organization much as national environmental protection agencies balance departments of finance and commerce. This would create a global environmental advocacy organization but might also lead to conflict and deadlock with other transnational institutions.

---

[13]Brack, 1998, p. 65.

[14]Fredriksson, 1999, p. 1.

[15]See Runge, 1994, Chapter 6; and Esty, 1994, Chapter 4.

Another approach would be to "green" existing institutions, broadening the environmental and social provisions of the GATT's Article XX and altering the missions of the World Bank and International Monetary Fund to emphasize sustainable trade development objectives (discussed further in Chapter 20).

The idea of a World Environmental Organization may seem visionary, but it has gained significant support. According to Sir Leon Brittan, vice president of the European Commission: "Setting environmental standards within a territory may be fine, but what about damage that spills over national borders? In a rapidly globalizing world, more and more of these problems cannot be effectively solved at the national or bilateral level, or even at the level of regional trading blocs like the European Union. Global problems require global solutions."[16]

A World Environmental Organization could serve as an umbrella for the implementation of existing multinational environmental agreements, as well as promoting further agreements consistent with global sustainable development strategies. **Global public goods** such as biodiversity, ozone layer protection, climate stabilization, and protection of oceans and water systems, would be the responsibility of the WEO.

A WEO could also play a role in negotiating trade agreements on agricultural subsidies, seeking to redirect farm subsidies to soil conservation and development of low-input agricultural techniques. As global CO_2 emissions continue to rise, energy sector trade may need to accommodate a carbon tax or tradable permit scheme, as discussed in Chapter 18. Global agreements on forest and biodiversity preservation are also likely to involve specific trade restrictions, tariff preferences, or labeling systems. In all these areas, a powerful advocate for environmental interests would have a major impact on the shaping of trade treaties and regulations.

Local, Regional, and Private Sector Policies

The trend toward globalization, which increasingly subjects communities to the logic of the global marketplace, may conflict with the goal of strengthening local and regional policies promoting sustainable development. Reserving powers of resource conservation and management to local and national institutions is important to sustainable resource management. Most environmental protection policies are implemented at the national level, and it is important to maintain national authority to enforce environmental standards.

In regional groupings such as NAFTA, that involve no supranational rule-making body, trade agreements could give special status to national policies aimed at sustainable agriculture and resource management. NAFTA rules currently give precedence to international environmental treaties (such as the Basel Convention on hazardous wastes, the Montreal Protocol on ozone depleting substances, and CITES on endangered species). This principle could be expanded to all national environmental protection policies, and effective sanctions for environmental violations could be established.

---

[16]Brack, 1998, pp. 19–20.

Regional trade and customs unions such as the European Union, with elected supranational policy-making bodies, can be responsible for environmental and social regulation to the extent that their legitimate democratic mandate allows. Transboundary issues are a logical area for supranational bodies to carry out environmental rule-making. Where they are empowered to intervene in national policy-making, the process can be oriented toward "harmonizing up" rather than "harmonizing down" environmental standards. This means that countries within a free-trade area must retain the power to impose higher social and environmental standards where they see fit.

The development of **certification** and labeling requirements for sustainably produced products can arise from public or private initiative. Germany's "green dot" system for recyclable and recycled goods is one example. Private, nongovernmental organizations have also set up certification systems for goods such as coffee and timber. To be effective in a globalized world, however, such certification systems must be international. This requires support both at the national level and from corporations and international agencies.

In conclusion, it is evident that there are many different approaches to reconciling the goals of trade and environment policy. In an article reviewing the debate on trade and environment, Daniel Esty concludes that ". . . there is no real choice about whether to address the trade and environment linkage; this linkage is a matter of fact . . . Environmental rules cannot be seen simply as pollution control or natural resource management standards; they also provide the ground rules for international commerce and serve as an essential bulwark against market failure in the international economic system. Building environmental sensitivity into the trade regime in a thoughtful and systematic fashion should therefore be of interest to the trade community as well as environmental advocates."[17] Achieving this goal will be a major challenge for trade negotiators at both regional and global levels for the foreseeable future.

SUMMARY

Trade expansion can often have environmental implications. Trade may increase environmental externalities at the national, regional, or global level. Although it is usually economically advantageous for countries to pursue their comparative advantage through trade, trade may have environmental repercussions such as increased pollution or natural resource degradation.

The environmental impacts of trade affect both importers and exporters. Agricultural cropping patterns altered by the introduction of export crops may involve environmental benefit or harm. Secondary effects of trade may arise from the disruption of existing communities, increased migration, and impact on marginal lands. Industrial pollution may increase, decrease, or shift in regional impact.

International trade agreements make some provisions for resource conservation and environmental protection, but these are usually limited exceptions to a general

[17]Esty, 2001, pp. 114 and 126–127. See also Harris, 2000.

principle of free trade. In the World Trade Organization, countries may consider the environmental impact of a product, but not of its production processes. This has led to numerous trade disputes over whether specific measures are justified on the grounds of protection of life and health, or are simply disguised protectionism.

Policy responses to trade and environment issues can occur at the national, regional, or global level. The European Union is an example of a free-trade area that includes institutions for transnational environmental standards enforcement. The North American Free Trade Agreement was accompanied by a side agreement setting up an environmental monitoring authority, the Commission for Environmental Cooperation, but this body has little enforcement power.

Multilateral environmental agreements (MEAs) address specific transboundary or global environmental issues. Conflicts between MEAs and World Trade Organization rules are possible, but have so far been avoided. Proposals have also been made for a World Environmental Organization to oversee global environmental policy and to advocate for environmental interests in the world trade system.

Where effective environmental protection policies are lacking at the regional or global level, national policies must address trade-related environmental issues. Certification and labeling requirements, instituted by governments or by private nongovernmental organizations, can help to promote consumer awareness and "greener" corporate practices in international trade.

KEY TERMS AND CONCEPTS

comparative advantage
certification
dualistic land ownership
environmental externalities
Environmental Kuznets Curve (EKC)
exporting pollution
gains from trade
GATT Article XX
General Agreement on Tariffs
    and Trade (GATT)
global pollution
global public goods

harmonization of environmental standards
multilateral environmental agreements
    (MEAs)
precautionary principle
process and production methods
    (PPM) rules
race to the bottom
second-best solution
specificity rule
transboundary pollution
World Environmental Organization (WEO)
World Trade Organization (WTO)

DISCUSSION QUESTIONS

1. What are the welfare implications of trade in toxic wastes? Should such trade be banned or can it serve a useful function? Who should regulate trade in toxic wastes, individual nations, local communities, or a global authority?

2. Can harmonizing environmental standards solve the problem of environmental externalities in trade? How would harmonization issues differ in NAFTA, the European Union, and the World Trade Organization? Would harmonization promote economic efficiency as well as environmental improvement, or might it lead to lower environmental standards?

3. What should be done if the provisions of a multilateral environmental agreement in conflict with the principles of the World Trade Organization? Which should take precedence, and who should have the authority to decide? Which economic, social, and ecological principles should influence such issues?

REFERENCES

Brack, Duncan, ed. *Trade and Environment: Conflict or Compatibility?* London: Royal Institute of International Affairs, 1998.

Commission for Environmental Cooperation (CEC). *Assessing Environmental Effects of the North American Free Trade Agreement: An Analytic Framework and Issue Studies.* Montréal, Québec, Canada: CEC, 1999.

Charnovitz, Steve. "Trade Measures and the Design of International Regimes." *Journal of Environment and Development 5*, no. 2 (1996): 168–169.

Esty, Daniel C. *Greening the GATT: Trade, Environment, and the Future.* Washington, D.C.: Institute for International Economics, 1994.

Esty, Daniel C. "Bridging the Trade-Environment Divide." *Journal of Economic Perspectives* 15, no. 3 (2001): 113–130

Fredriksson, Per G., ed. *Trade, Global Policy, and the Environment.* World Bank Discussion Paper No. 402. Washington, D.C.: The World Bank, 1999.

Grossman, Gene, and Alan Krueger. "Economic Growth and the Environment." *Quarterly Journal of Economics* 110, no. 2 (1995): 353–377.

Harris, Jonathan M. "Free Trade or Sustainable Trade? An Ecological Economics Perspective." Chapter 5 in *Rethinking Sustainability: Power, Knowledge, and Institutions,* edited by Jonathan Harris. Ann Arbor, Mich.: University of Michigan Press, 2000.

Hufbauer, Gary C., Daniel C. Esty, Diana Orejas, Luis Rubio, and Jeffrey J. Scott. *NAFTA and the Environment: Seven Years Later.* Policy Analyses in International Economics 61. Washington, D.C.: Institute for International Economics, 2000.

Nadal, Alejandro. *The Environmental and Social Impacts of Economic Liberalization on Corn Production in Mexico.* London, England: World Wildlife Fund and Oxfam UK, 2000.

Neumayer, Eric. *Greening Trade and Investment: Environmental Protection without Protectionism.* London, England: Earthscan Publications, 2001.

Paarlberg, Robert. "Political Power and Environmental Sustainability in Agriculture," Chapter 7 in Harris, ed., 2000.

Panayotou, Theodore. "Empirical Tests and Policy Analysis of Environmental Degradation at Different Levels of Development." Geneva, Switzerland: International Labour Office Working Paper WP238, 1993.

Reed, David, ed. *Structural Adjustment, the Environment, and Sustainable Development.* London: World Wide Fund for Nature, 1996.

Rothman, Dale, and Sander de Bruyn. "Probing into the Environmental Kuznets Curve Hypothesis" (Introduction to Special Issue on the Environmental Kuznets Curve), *Ecological Economics* 25, no. 2 (1998): 143–145.

Runge, C. Ford. *Freer Trade, Protected Environment: Balancing Trade Liberalization and Environmental Interests.* New York: Council on Foreign Relations Press, 1994.

Selden, Thomas M., and Daqing Song. "Environmental Quality and Development: Is There a Kuznets Curve for Air Pollution?" *Journal of Environmental Economics and Management* 27, no. 2 (1994): 147–162.

Stern, David I. "Progress on the Environmental Kuznets Curve." *Environment and Development Economics* 3 (1998): 173–196.

Varady, Robert, and Maura Mack. "Transboundary Water Resources and Public Health in the U.S./Mexico Border Region." *Journal of Environmental Health* 17, no. 4 (1996): 23–25.

WEB SITES

1. **http://www.wto.org/english/tratop_e/envir_e/envir_e.htm** The World Trade Organization's web site devoted to the relationship between international trade issues and environmental quality. The site includes links to many research reports and other information.
2. **http://www.oecd.org/ech/** The web site for the trade division of the Organisation for Economic Co-operation and Development. The site includes many publications on trade issues, including trade and the environment.
3. **www.cec.org/** Home page for the Commission for Environmental Cooperation, created under the North American Free Trade Agreement "to address regional environmental concerns, help prevent potential trade and environmental conflicts, and to promote the effective enforcement of environmental law." The site includes numerous publications on issues of trade and the environment.

CHAPTER

20

Institutions for Sustainable Development

The Economics of Sustainable Development

All nations seek economic development. Economic development policies, however, have taken little heed of the environment until relatively recently. Only within the past 40 years have currently developed nations recognized the need for specific policies to protect the environment. In many nations, the concept of environmental protection is even more recent.

The United States, for example, set up its Environmental Protection Agency in 1970. Prior to this, a conservation movement, active for nearly a century, had focused primarily on protection of public lands. The idea that the industrial system should be subject to some sort of environmental controls was not an integral part of economic development theory or practice for most of the twentieth century.

In the twenty-first century, it is clear that the issues of environment and development cannot be separated. This has given rise to the concept of **sustainable development**. In 1987, the World Commission on Environment and Development addressed the issue of conflicts between environment and development by proposing a definition:

> Sustainable development is development that meets the needs of the present without compromising the ability of future generations to meet their own needs.[1]

This view of development suggests that the standard perspective of equating economic development with economic growth may need to be altered. From an economic point of view, development improves the situation of future generations by increasing their **capital stock.** Having more capital enables a country to produce more goods and deliver a higher standard of living to its citizens. But if, in the process of producing this stock of manufactured capital, we degrade or destroy **natural capital,** we may actually leave future generations worse off. Indeed, we may leave ourselves worse off, because some environmental pollution damage may immediately affect our lives and health.

The implications of making development sustainable differ for developed and developing nations. Currently developed nations typically have large capital stocks and extensive infrastructure including power plants, highways, factories, extensive urban and suburban business and residential construction, dams, irrigation systems, and many other elements essential to modern economic production. This is both an advantage and a disadvantage in trying to achieve environmental sustainability.

On the one hand, greater economic capacity and advanced technology makes instituting environmental protection systems more possible and affordable. On the other, developed nations with large existing stocks of resource-using, waste- and pollution-generating capital and consumer demand for a continual flow of products may encounter **technological lock-in** such as a dependence on fossil fuels and the technologies associated with them. A lock-in may also be social—an example might be American reluctance to consider alternatives to automobile-based transport.

Developing nations have a different set of problems in achieving sustainability. Starting from much lower income levels, a major social and economic goal is increasing production. As we have seen, developing nations also tend to have considerable population growth momentum. The combination of increased population and economic growth creates strong pressure for rising resource use and increased generation of wastes and pollution.

At the same time, developing nations may have greater choice as to the development path they will pursue. They are not necessarily committed to following a resource-intensive, high waste-generating pattern of economic growth. As later participants in development, they may have access to improved technologies and avoid costly environmental errors made by the developed nations. They will also, however, find themselves competing with developed nations for limited resources and limited environmental absorption capacities for global pollutants such as CO_2 (see Box 20-1).

---

[1]World Commission on Environment and Development, 1987, p. 8.

20-1   China and the Future of the Global Environment

A major factor affecting the future of the global environment is China's ability to develop economically without causing serious and irreversible ecological damage. With a population of over 1.2 billion, China already uses about 11 percent of the world's commercial energy and is responsible for emitting about 14 percent of global CO_2 emissions. However, China is also experiencing rapid economic growth. Between 1988 and 1997 China's GDP grew at an average annual rate of 8.2 percent (WRI, 2001). For comparison, GDP in the United States grew at an annual average rate of 2.5 percent during the same period.

Significant further economic development appears likely for China. Consider that per capita motor vehicle ownership in China is only about 1/100 of the U.S. level. Per capita energy use and CO_2 emissions in China are much lower than the comparable values for Mexico and Thailand (see table). What will happen to the environment if China's growth continues?

Even with relatively low per capita impacts, the large total population in China (about 21 percent of global population) means that China already causes significant global environmental impacts. China is soon expected to pass the United States as the world's largest energy consumer and emitter of carbon dioxide. If China used the same amount of energy per capita as Americans do, global energy use would nearly double.

China, still a relatively poor country, resists suggestions by developed countries to limit economic development for the benefit of the global environment. As noted by Mark Hertsgaard (1999, p. 210), "China has little patience with Western finger-pointing on the climate-change issue, regarding it as a cynical means of constraining China's economic development." Currently, China appears willing to sacrifice environmental quality for economic growth.

Hope may lie in China's continued integration into the international community. Financial and technical assistance could provide China with the ability to develop efficient processes that reduce energy consumption by half (Hertsgaard, 1999). All nations have a stake in the issue because the negative environmental consequences of increased resource use and pollution by China will be global in scope. The credibility of Western nations in helping to find an environmentally friendly development path for China will depend on their willingness to take effective measures to reduce their own environmental impacts.

(continued on following page)

Environmental Data for Selected Countries

Country	2001 Population (millions)	Energy Consumption[1] Per Capita	Total[4]	CO_2 Emissions[2] Per Capita	Total[5]	Motor Vehicles[3] Per 1,000 People	Total[6]
Bangladesh	140	198	28	0.2	28	1	0.1
China	1,285	883	1,135	2.8	3,598	8	10.3
France	59	4,233	250	5.8	342	530	31.3
India	1,025	477	489	1.1	1,128	7	7.2
Japan	127	4,085	519	9.2	1,168	560	71.1
Mexico	100	1,501	150	3.9	390	144	14.4
Thailand	64	1,339	86	3.5	224	103	6.6
United States	286	7,947	2,273	20.0	5,720	767	219.4
WORLD	6,134	1,671	10,250	4.2	25,763	124	760.6

[1]Commercial energy consumption from all sources, measured in kilograms of oil equivalent, 1997 data

[2]Emissions from industrial processes, measured in metric tons, 1997 data

[3]Includes automobiles, buses, and freight vehicles, date of data varies

[4]Measured in billions of kilograms of oil equivalent

[5]Measured in millions of metric tons

[6]Measured in millions of vehicles

Source: United Nations, 2001.

SOURCES

Hertsgaard, Mark. "Our Real China Problem," in *Annual Editions, Environment 99/00,* edited by John L. Allen. Guilford, Conn.: Dushkin/McGraw-Hill, 1999.

United Nations, Population Division, Department of Economic and Social Affairs. *Population, Environment, and Development, 2001.* Wall chart available on the Internet at http://www.un.org/esa/population/unpop.htm.

World Resources Institute. *World Resources 2000–2001: People and Ecosystems: The Fraying Web of Life.* Washington, D.C.: World Resources Institute, 2001. Available on the Internet at http://www.wri.org/wr2000/index.html.

A critical issue is whether developed and developing nations can cooperate to promote environmentally sustainable development paths. As we saw in the Chapter 18 discussion of global climate, agreement can be difficult to reach. Developing nations argue that the richer countries should "clean up their act" first. Developed countries worry that the vast growth of production expected in the developing world will swallow up gains from efficiency and pollution control, unless developing nations modify their economic goals. This difference in perspectives need not lead to deadlock. Many possibilities exist for mutual progress toward environmental improvement—but the scale of the problems is daunting.

New Goals and New Production Methods

To bring the argument down to earth and develop a sense of what the principles summarized at the beginning of this section mean for development policies, we can examine some specific areas of economic activity. In each, sustainability implies a major shift from existing techniques and organization of production.

- **Agriculture.** Feeding an expanding population at higher per-capita levels of consumption will impose significant strain on global soil and water systems.[2] The response to this must be twofold. On the production side, current high-input techniques associated with soil degradation and water pollution and overdraft must give way to organic soil rebuilding, integrated pest management, and efficient irrigation. This in turn implies much greater reliance on local knowledge and participatory input into the development of farming systems.[3]

  On the consumption side, probable resource limitations on production will necessitate both population growth limits and greater food distribution equity and efficiency. As discussed in Chapter 10, effective policies can simultaneously promote social equity and moderate population growth, including women's education and health and family planning services. Distribution and dietary patterns will need to emphasize affordable basic foodstuffs and vegetable-based proteins and nutrients.

- **Energy.** Both supply limits and environmental impact, in particular the accumulation of greenhouse gases, will require a transition away from fossil fuels well before 2050. A restructured energy system would be significantly less centralized, adapted to local conditions and taking advantage of opportunities for wind, biomass, and off-grid solar power systems. This is unlikely to occur without a major mobilization of capital resources for development of **renewable energy sources** in countries now rapidly expanding their energy systems.

---

[2]Harris and Kennedy, 1999; Pinstrup-Andersen and Pandya-Lorch, 1998.
[3]Pretty and Chambers, 2000.

- **Industry.** As the scale of global industrial production grows well beyond current levels, which themselves represent a quadrupling over 1950 levels, the inadequacy of "end-of-pipe" pollution control will be increasingly apparent. As we saw in Chapter 17, the concept of **industrial ecology** implies the restructuring of whole industrial sectors based on a goal of reducing emissions and reusing materials at all stages of the production cycle. A broad cooperative effort between corporations and government is essential to achieve this goal.
- **Renewable resource systems.** As we have discussed, world fisheries, forests, and water systems are severely overstressed. With even greater demands on all systems expected in the twenty-first century, reform is needed at all levels of institutional management. Multilateral agreements and global funding must conserve transboundary resources; national resource management systems must shift from exploitative goals to conservation and sustainable harvesting; and local communities must participate fully in resource conservation (see Box 20-2).

Each of these areas poses social and institutional as well as economic challenges. Environmental sustainability is thus linked to **social sustainability.** Existing institutions of all kinds, including corporations, local and national governments, and transnational organizations, must adopt policies for sustainable development if the problems that motivated development of the concept are not to grow worse. Democratic governance, participation, and the satisfaction of basic needs are an essential part of a new approach to development.[4]

Reforming Global Institutions

Major global institutions such as the World Bank, the International Monetary Fund (IMF), and the World Trade Organization (WTO) have as their goal promoting economic development. Only relatively recently have environmental considerations acquired a prominent role in World Bank policy-making. As we saw in Chapter 19, environmental issues remain controversial at the WTO. The IMF does not include environmental factors in its mandate, but its monetary policies have significant implications both for the environment and for relations between developed and developing countries.

A major theme in both IMF and World Bank policy has been **structural adjustment.** This refers to a package of conditions linked to loans to developing countries, intended to promote market-oriented economic reform. Generally these conditions include fiscal and monetary measures aimed at balancing government budgets and restraining money supplies to avoid inflation. In addition, countries often must reduce barriers to trade, correct overvalued exchange rates, and privatize state-controlled enterprises.

---

[4] See Harris et al., 2000.

20-2   Community Resource Management in India

The role of local communities is often central in developing sustainable agriculture and forestry policies. A case in point is the Arabari experiment in India's West Bengal. This region was suffering rapid deforestation in the 1970s, leading to a government program to offer villagers alternatives to the illegal cutting of firewood. Local residents were offered employment opportunities planting trees and grass in deforested areas. Through a revenue-sharing arrangement with the Forest Department, the villagers received 25% of the income from sales of sustainably-produced trees. In return, they were given the responsibility of protecting the forest from illegal cutting.

After 15 years, degraded forest areas had been rehabilitated, and economic conditions for the villagers had improved significantly. The success of the initial experiment led to its expansion to over 700 villages. By 1989 Village Protection Committees were managing the restoration of more than 70,000 hectares of degraded lands in West Bengal.

In Haryana, India, a cooperative project between government agencies, nongovernmental organizations, and villagers led to the construction of a system of small dams for irrigation and erosion protection, and to the protection of local forests. Instead of cutting the forests for grazing lands, villagers were encouraged to grow fiber and fodder grasses as well as trees. This provided the basis for the success of small rope-making businesses and milk sales, as well as dramatically increased crop yields.

Similar successes with small-scale local farming and land management programs has been reported in Nepal, Indonesia, Kenya, Niger, and Sri Lanka, among other developing countries. Effective group management structure and cooperation among all parties is essential to the success of such programs.

SOURCES

Panayotou, Theodore. *Green Markets: The Economics of Sustainable Development.* San Francisco, Calif.: Institute for Contemporary Studies (ICS) Press, 1993.

Pretty, Jules N., and Robert Chambers. "Toward a Learning Paradigm: New Professionalism and Institutions for Agriculture," *Rethinking Sustainability: Power, Knowledge, and Institutions,* edited by Jonathan M. Harris. Ann Arbor, Mich.: University of Michigan Press, 2000.

Poffenberger, M. *Joint Management of Forest Lands: Experiences from South Asia.* New Delhi: The Ford Foundation, 1990.

A Nicaraguan worker picks cotton. Structural adjustment programs can have varied effects on agricultural production and the environment. Some export crops are less erosive, but increased pesticide use on crops such as cotton can be harmful to workers and ecosystems, and can pollute water supplies.

A study by the Worldwide Fund for Nature (WWF) reviewed the social and environmental impact of structural adjustment policies promoted by the IMF and World Bank.[5] The WWF researchers found that environmental effects were mixed, but negative effects seemed predominant in many cases. Environmentally positive results included the following:

- Shifting terms of trade to favor the agricultural sector provides farmers with more income to finance on-farm investment.
- Increased farm income reduces poverty-induced degradation of marginal lands.
- Reduced subsidies for agricultural inputs reduce fertilizer and pesticide overuse.
- Some export crops produce less erosion than the local crops they replace.
- Better macroeconomic management increases investment flows.
- Market-oriented microeconomic policies improve industrial efficiency.

---

[5]Reed, 1997.

On the other hand, negative environmental effects included the following:

- Small farmers displaced by imports or unable to take advantage of export opportunities increase rural-to-urban migration and pressures on marginal lands and forests.
- Rising prices for agricultural inputs promote unsustainable extension of agricultural production onto marginal lands.
- Faster growth in the mining and industrial sectors leads to increased environmental damage and larger waste flows.
- Extension of pasture for cattle production and beef export promotes faster deforestation.
- Imports of inefficient used vehicles greatly increase urban pollution.
- Government agricultural extension services, environmental protection expenditures, and social services all decline under conditions of budget stringency.
- Reduced educational and health spending leads to lower school attendance, increased disease, and weakened population and family planning policy implementation.

The study concludes that structural adjustment policies have led to increased consumption of renewable and nonrenewable resources, greater pressure on environmental **sink functions** of pollution absorption, a drawdown of natural capital, and a weakening of environmental institutional capacity. "The weakening of environmental institutions represents a major setback in moving countries towards sustainable development paths."[6]

The WWF study recommends integrating environmental issues into the planning of macroeconomic reforms. Specific proposals include

- Implementation of national environmental accounting systems.
- Reinvestment of incomes from nonrenewable resource extraction.
- Increased agricultural extension and credit policies.
- Stronger environmental regulation for emerging industries.
- Increased social services and health care spending, with a special focus on women's education and health care.
- Targeted small-scale lending policies (microlending) to encourage small local enterprises.
- Targeted food assistance and distributional equity policies.

This analysis suggests that economic reform and environmental goals are compatible, but only if policies are specifically designed for sustainable outcomes. Neglecting the environment leads to long-term problems that can undermine economic goals as well. Also, environmental and social issues are clearly linked. Deteriorating conditions for the poor are likely to accentuate environmental problems, which in turn worsen poverty. Thus development policy must include the dual goals of poverty reduction and environmental improvement.

---

[6]Reed, 1997, p. 351.

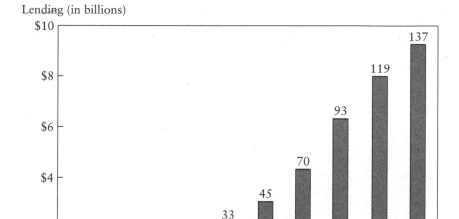

Note: Numbers on columns indicate active environmental lending projects.

FIGURE 20-1 *The Active World Bank Environmental Portfolio*

Source: Adapted from World Bank, *Monitoring Environmental Progress: A Report on Work in Progress.* Copyright ©1995 by World Bank. Reproduced by permission of World Bank in the format textbook via Copyright Clearance Center.

Promoting Environmentally Sustainable Development

In the 1980s and 1990s the World Bank was frequently a target of protest for funding environmentally destructive projects such as large dams and forest clearance. Partly as a result, the bank shifted its lending policies to give much greater prominence to the environment. Funding for environmentally oriented projects increased from less than $1 billion in 1988 to more than $15 billion in 2000 (Figure 20-1).[7]

These projects include both a "brown agenda" (pollution management) and a "green agenda" (natural resource conservation). They include projects on forest management, integrated pest management, watershed rehabilitation, energy efficiency and renewables, and water management and sewer systems. Some of these loans are coupled with grants from the Global Environmental Facility (GEF), jointly managed by the World Bank, the United Nations Environment Programme (UNEP), and the United Nations Development Programme (UNDP).

In addition, all World Bank projects are screened for potential environmental impact. "A growing number of sector projects include environmental components or

---

[7]World Bank, 1995 and 2000.

20-3   The Global Environmental Facility

The Global Environmental Facility (GEF), initiated in 1990, is jointly administered by the United Nations Environment Programme (UNEP), the United Nations Development Programme (UNDP) and the World Bank. In 1994 the GEF was restructured and expanded, with $2 billion in funding. Its mission is to support global environmental projects including biodiversity conservation, ocean ecosystem protection, and reduction of greenhouse gases and ozone-depleting substances.

Unlike the World Bank and the IMF, the GEF provides grants and concessional funds rather than loans. Often a GEF grant may be paired with a World Bank environmental loan to increase its impact at lower cost to the receiving nation.

The GEF operates on the economic rationale that the global community as a whole should bear the **incremental costs** of environmental protection beyond what developing nations are prepared to pay. For example, the installation of energy-efficient and renewable power systems has local benefits, but also contributes to the global effort to limit greenhouse gas emissions. It seems reasonable, therefore, that the recipient nation should pay some of the cost in the form of loan repayments, but wealthier nations should also underwrite part of the cost through GEF.

In practice, applying this incremental-cost concept has been tricky. Critics have argued that it is difficult to separate global and national benefits. Also, the pairing of regular World Bank grants with GEF loans may actually promote greater environmental damage in some cases. For example, in Ecuador, a logging company received $4 million in World Bank funds as well as a $2.5 million GEF grant. The company was required to set up a forest reserve, but also expanded logging on a much greater area. In Egypt, a $242 million World Bank loan to develop a coastal resort was paired with a $4.75 million GEF loan for conservation activity. In such cases, the GEF component may serve as a rationale for accelerated resource exploitation.

SOURCES

Barnes et al., 1995; World Bank, 1995 and 2000; Shiva, 2000.

incorporate environmental considerations into the project design."[8] Rural development projects increasingly emphasize land resource management, soil and water conservation, and training in sustainable farming techniques. Urban development projects include water and sanitation upgrading and solid waste management. Energy lending

---

[8]World Bank, 2000, p. 10.

includes promotion of energy efficiency and renewable energy sources, as well as development of cleaner fossil fuels such as natural gas.

Despite significant improvement in the environmental content of World Bank policies, critics still maintain that "the World Bank and the IMF pay insufficient heed to the profound effects of [their] policies on the ecological health and the social fabric of the recipient countries."[9] Because these institutions provide loans, not grants, the funds must eventually be repaid. To promote debt repayment, the lenders emphasize export promotion, but "the pressure to export can lead countries to liquidate natural assets such as forest and fisheries, thereby undermining longer-term economic prospects."[10] In addition, large bureaucratic institutions dealing in billions of dollars often are poorly prepared to connect to sustainable initiatives at the local level.

Local Development Projects

Some of the most encouraging stories of sustainable development projects are those funded by **nongovernmental organizations** (**NGOs**) and European governments. A review by Friends of the Earth and the National Wildlife Federation cites dozens of successful local development projects.[11] These include

- Organic farming cooperatives in the Philippines
- **Extractive reserves** in the Brazilian rainforest promoting multiple-product forest management and conservation
- Aquatic ecosystem management including rice and fish cultivation
- Sustainable forestry and rehabilitation of deforested lands in the Peruvian Amazon
- Forest conservation, rehabilitation, and biodiversity classification in Costa Rica
- Rural solar power installation in the Dominican Republic
- Soil restoration and conservation technologies in Honduras
- Oilseed production and processing in Tanzania and Zimbabwe
- Promoting bicycle transportation in Lima, Peru
- Family planning and health services in Colombia and Pakistan
- Women's cooperatives for farming, food processing, and light industry in Nigeria
- **Agroforestry** programs in Guatemala, Haiti, and Indonesia
- Recycled paper production in India

These examples of sustainable development in practice demonstrate that the goals of economic development, poverty reduction, and environmental improvement can be successfully combined. However, the principles embodied in these small-scale projects are rarely reflected in national and global economic priorities. This suggests the continuing need for a major reorientation of economic development policies.

---

[9]French, 2000, p. 196.

[10]Ibid.

[11]Barnes et al., 1995.

20-4   Sustainable Urban Management in Curitiba, Brazil

About half of the world's population currently lives in urban areas and urbanization rates are expected to increase in the future. Achieving environmental sustainability will require an integration of ecological principles into urban management. While most cities have grown without significant regard to environmental impacts, exceptions exist as role models for other communities.

The city of Curitiba, Brazil, has grown in population from 300,000 in 1950 to around 2 million today. Faced with this growth pressure, the city has demonstrated that urban environmental problems can be addressed with creativity, strong leadership, and public participation despite limited financial resources. Rather than relying on a single master plan, city officials have taken a flexible approach with constant input from local residents.

A key component of Curitiba's success is the attention given to transportation issues. Zoning laws foster high-density development along transportation corridors served by buses. The bus system transports over 1 million passengers per day. Gasoline use per capita and air pollution levels in Curitiba are among the lowest in Brazil.

The city has protected drainage areas to control flooding by converting these areas into public parks. Curitiba could not afford a large-scale recycling plant but public education programs have been successful in reducing wastes and increasing recycling rates. In areas where streets are too narrow for garbage trucks to enter, incentives for community garbage collection have been created by exchanging filled garbage bags for bus tokens, parcels of surplus food, and school notebooks. In another program, older public buses are converted to mobile schools and travel to low-income neighborhoods.

The example of Curitiba shows that progress towards environmental sustainability is possible even in an urban area with increasing population and high poverty rates. "The lesson to be learned from Curitiba is that creativity can substitute for financial resources. Any city, rich or poor, can draw on the skills of its residents to tackle urban environmental problems" (World Resources Institute, 1996).

SOURCE

World Resources Institute. *World Resources 1996–97: The Urban Environment.* New York: Oxford University Press, 1996.

Policies for Sustainable Development

The goals of sustainable development policies can be viewed in terms of **strong and weak sustainability.** In general, advocates of *strong sustainability* argue that natural systems should be maintained intact wherever possible. They identify **critical natural capital**—such as water supplies—as resources to preserve under all circumstances. In this view, for example, maintaining soil's natural fertility is essential—even if it is possible to compensate for degraded soils with extra fertilizer. Under the more moderate approach of *weak sustainability,* some degradation or loss of natural capital is acceptable if it is compensated for by accumulation of manufactured capital.

Either concept of sustainability—but especially the strong version—implies some limits to economic growth. Economic activity that relies heavily on natural resources, raw materials, and fossil fuels cannot grow indefinitely. Because the planetary ecosystem has certain limits, limits must also apply on a macroeconomic scale—the overall level of resource use and goods output. Herman Daly has argued for the long-term need to reach a plateau, a **steady state economy** in terms of the consumption of material and energy resources.[12]

This concept differs radically from the standard view of economic growth, in which GDP increases indefinitely on an **exponential growth** path—for example 4 percent GDP growth per year. In the limits-to-growth perspective, national and global economic systems must follow what is called a **logistic curve** pattern in which economic activity approaches some maximum, at least in terms of resource consumption (Figure 20-2).

This analysis necessarily implies some constraints on material consumption, but activities that involve no resource consumption or are environmentally neutral or environmentally friendly, could grow indefinitely. Such activities could include services, arts, communication, and education. Once basic needs are met and moderate levels of consumption achieved, the concept of sustainable development implies that economic development should be increasingly oriented toward these kinds of inherently "sustainable" activities.[13]

Currently much of development theory and policy promotes continuous economic growth. What kind of policies would promote sustainability? Are the goals of economic growth and sustainability compatible?

Some ecological economists view "sustainable growth" as a contradiction in terms. They point out that no system can grow without limit. However, some kinds of economic growth are certainly essential. The large number of people in the world who lack basic needs require more and better food, housing, and other goods.

In high-consumption societies, improved well-being might be achieved through expanded educational and cultural services that, as we have noted, have no negative environmental impact. But unregulated economic growth is unlikely to be either equitable

---

[12]See Daly, 1996.
[13]See Durning, 1992.

Resource-using
Economic Activities

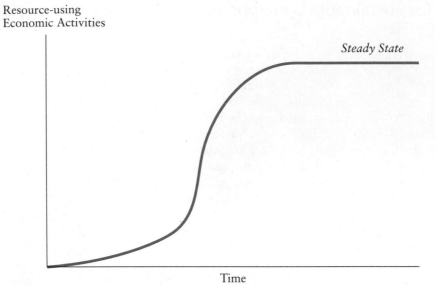

FIGURE 20-2 *Growth Reaching a Steady State*

or environmentally benign. We therefore need specific policies to promote sustainable development.

Specific Policy Proposals

Such policies might include approaches that we have already touched on in previous chapters:

- *Green taxes that would shift the tax burden away from income and capital taxation and onto fossil fuel use, resource extraction, and pollution generation.* This would discourage energy- and material-intensive economic activities while favoring the provision of services and labor-intensive activities.[14] A **revenue-neutral tax shift** could match every dollar collected in new energy and resource taxes with a dollar of income, payroll, corporate or capital gains tax reduction.[15]
- *Elimination of agricultural and energy subsidies that encourage overuse of energy, fertilizer, pesticides, and irrigation water.* This could be matched with pro-

[14]Labor-intensive production systems use large amounts of labor relative to other factors of production. Similarly, energy-intensive systems use large amounts of energy. For example, automobile transport is energy-intensive; bicycle transport is labor-intensive.

[15]See Hamond et al., 1997, summarized in Harris et al., 2001.

motion of sustainable agricultural systems including nutrient recycling, crop diversification, and natural pest controls, minimizing the use of artificial chemicals and fertilizer.

- *Greater **recycling** of materials and use of renewable energy.* The principles of industrial ecology suggest redesigning industrial systems to imitate the closed-cycle patterns of natural systems and reuse as many materials as possible with minimal waste output.

- *Efficient transportation systems that replace energy-intensive automotive transport with high-speed trains, public transit, increased bicycle use, and redesign of cities and suburbs to minimize transportation needs.* The use of highly fuel-efficient cars would be important in countries such as the United States with extensively developed automobile-centered systems. Some developing countries might avoid large-scale automobile dependence by relying instead on bicycles and efficient public transit.

- *Accelerated development of renewable energy systems such as solar, hydroelectric, wind, and geothermal power, as well as new technologies such as fuel cells and high-efficiency industrial systems.* As we saw in Chapter 13, redirection of current fossil fuel subsidies to create market incentives for alternative energy sources is essential to this process.

Analysis of development policy must take account of long-term sustainability. Policies oriented toward economic growth alone risk damage to the broader "circular flow" of the **biosphere,** unless they include consideration of environmental impact and sustainable scale. This adds a new dimension to the debate over development policy, a dimension that will be increasingly important for both developed and developing economies.

As world population continues to grow, and economic activity expands at an even faster rate, sustainability will become both more important and more difficult to achieve. This is the major challenge of the twenty-first century, and both economic and ecological understanding will be needed to formulate global, national, and local responses.

SUMMARY

Sustainable development has been defined as development that meets present needs without damaging the basis for meeting future needs. This implies increasing and improving manufactured capital without destroying natural capital. The needs of a growing population must be met without increasing resource demands and pollution generation beyond the supportive capacity of ecosystems.

For developed nations, this implies both moderation in consumption growth and adoption of more environmentally friendly technologies. Developing nations, for whom growth in consumption is essential, can avoid production methods that have high resource demands and environmental repercussions. Mutual cooperation between developed and developing nations toward these goals is essential but often difficult to achieve.

Major reforms must occur in agricultural, industrial, and energy systems, as well as in renewable resource management. Low-input and organic agriculture, energy-efficient and ecologically sound industrial development, as well as better fishery and forest management, are all important components of a balanced economic/environmental system. In addition, population stabilization is central to sustainability in all these areas.

An inherent tension exists between the ideas of sustainability and economic growth. Although the two are not necessarily incompatible, we cannot have unlimited economic growth with finite resources. Future economic growth must therefore turn more toward areas such as services, communication, arts, and education that contribute to human welfare but have relatively low resource requirements.

Major global finance institutions such as the World Bank have begun to recognize the necessity of specific policy initiatives to promote more sustainable development and reorient their development lending accordingly. However, resource-intensive and pollution-generating development strategies remain common. Small-scale projects financed privately or by individual countries have often been more successful in achieving the dual goals of poverty reduction and environmental conservation.

Sustainable development strategies attempt to balance the imperatives of economic growth with the limits of planetary resources and pollution absorption capacity. Modification of global goals of economic growth will be essential for sustainability in the twenty-first century.

KEY TERMS AND CONCEPTS

agroforestry	nongovernmental organizations (NGOs)
biosphere	recycling
capital stock	renewable energy sources
critical natural capital	revenue-neutral tax shift
exponential growth	sink functions
extractive reserves	social sustainability
green taxes	steady state economy
incremental costs	strong sustainability
industrial ecology	structural adjustment
logistic curve	sustainable development
macroeconomic scale	technological lock-in
natural capital	weak sustainability

DISCUSSION QUESTIONS

1. Comment on the original definition of sustainable development: "development which meets the needs of the present without compromising the ability of future generations to meet their own needs." Do you consider this definition useful or so

ambiguous or vague as to lack applicability? How might you make it more precise? What alternative definitions might you use?

2. How would you seek to balance the goals of economic growth and environmental sustainability? To what extent are these goals necessarily in conflict?

3. Which specific policies do you consider of greatest importance in promoting environmentally sustainable development? In which areas is the world making progress toward sustainability, and where are the most serious problems?

REFERENCES

Barnes, James N., Brent Blackwelder, Barbara J. Bramble, Ellen Grossman, and Walter V. Reid. *Bankrolling Successes: A Portfolio of Sustainable Development Projects.* Washington, D.C.: Friends of the Earth and the National Wildlife Federation, 1995.

Daly, Herman E. *Beyond Growth: The Economics of Sustainable Development.* Boston: Beacon Press, 1996.

Durning, Alan. *How Much Is Enough: The Consumer Society and the Future of the Earth.* Worldwatch Environmental Alert Series, edited by Linda Starke. New York: Norton, 1992.

French, Hilary. "Coping with Ecological Globalization." Chapter 10 in *State of the World 2000,* edited by Brown et al. New York: Norton, 2000.

Hamond, M. Jeff, Stephen J. DeCanio, Peggy Duxbury, Alan H. Sanstad, and Christopher H. Stinson. *Tax Waste, Not Work.* Washington, D.C.: Redefining Progress, 1997.

Harris, Jonathan M., and Scott Kennedy. "Carrying Capacity in Agriculture: Global and Regional Issues." *Ecological Economics* 29, no. 3 (1999): 443–461.

Harris, Jonathan M., Timothy A. Wise, Kevin P. Gallagher, and Neva R. Goodwin, eds. *A Survey of Sustainable Development: Social and Economic Dimensions.* Washington, D.C.: Island Press, 2001.

Pinstrup-Andersen, Per, and Rajul Pandya-Lorch. "Food Security and Sustainable Use of Natural Resources: A 2020 Vision." *Ecological Economics* 26, no. 1 (1998): 1–10.

Pretty, Jules, and Robert Chambers. "Towards a Learning Paradigm: New Professionalism and Institutions for Agriculture." In *Rethinking Sustainability: Power, Knowledge, and Institutions,* edited by Jonathan M. Harris. Ann Arbor, Mich.: University of Michigan Press, 2000.

Reed, David, ed. *Structural Adjustment, the Environment, and Sustainable Development.* London: Earthscan Publications, 1997.

Shiva, Vandana. "Conflicts of Global Ecology: Environmental Activism in a Period of Global Reach." Original publication in *Alternatives* 19 (1994): 195–207; summarized version in Harris et al., eds., *A Survey of Sustainable Development,* 2000.

United Nations Department for Economic and Social Information and Policy Analysis, Statistical Division. *Integrated Environmental and Economic Accounting.* New York: United Nations, 1993.

World Bank. *Monitoring Environmental Progress: A Report on Work in Progress.* Washington, D.C.: World Bank, 1995.

World Bank. *Environment Matters: Annual Review.* Washington, D.C.: World Bank, 2000.

World Commission on Environment and Development. *Our Common Future.* New York: Oxford University Press, 1987.

WEB SITES

1. **http://www.gefweb.org/** Home page for the Global Environmental Facility, a funding agency "established to forge international cooperation and finance actions to address four critical threats to the global environment: biodiversity loss, climate change, degradation of international waters, and ozone depletion." The site includes publications and a summary of projects that are funded by the GEF.
2. **http://www.panda.org/resources/programmes/mpo** Home page for the World Wildlife Fund's Macroeconomics for Sustainability Programme, designed to "analyze the impact of macroeconomic practices, and to promote alternative approaches that integrate environmental and social concerns into macroeconomic planning and application." The site includes publications and case studies.
3. **http://www.unep.org/Documents/Default.asp?DocumentID=52** The United Nation's web site for Agenda 21, a "roadmap" for sustainable development drafted during the 1992 Earth Conference in Rio de Janeiro. Agenda 21 "addresses the pressing problems of today and also aims at preparing the world for the challenges of the next century."

Glossary

absolutely diminishing returns an increase in one or more inputs results in a decrease in output. (5)

absorptive capacity of environment the ability of the environment to absorb and render harmless waste products. (2, 7)

adjusted net national product (NNP*)/net domestic product (NDP*) the value obtained by subtracting both humanmade and natural resource depreciation from gross national product or gross domestic product. (8)

agroecological systems systems of agricultural production in which crop output is integrated with a diverse ecological system. (17)

agroforestry growing both tree and food crops on the same piece of land. (11, 15, 20)

ambient pollution level the concentration of a pollutant measured in terms of pollutant quantity per volume of air, water, or soil. (16)

aquaculture raising fish for harvest in controlled conditions. (14)

asset(s) something with market value, including financial assets, physical assets, and natural assets. (1, 15)

average revenue total revenue divided by quantity sold. (5)

avoided cost(s) costs avoidable through environmental preservation or improvement. (6, 18)

backstop resource a resource that can substitute for a preferred resource but at a higher price. (12)

benefit/cost ratio the ratio of total benefits to total costs; a ratio greater than one indicates net benefits. (6)

bequest value value people place on the knowledge that a resource will be available for future generations. (6)

biodiversity the maintenance of many different interrelated species in an ecological community. (1, 11, 15)

biomass energy supply from wood, plant, and animal wastes. (2, 13, 15)

biophysical cycles the circular flow of organic and inorganic materials in ecosystems. (11)

biosphere all areas on earth that contain life forms, including air, soil, land, and water. (20)

business as usual a policy of maintaining the status quo; for example, estimates of greenhouse gas emissions levels if no policy measures counteract global climate change. (18)

bycatch fishery catch discarded because it is undersized or non-marketable. (14)

capital depreciation a deduction in national income accounting for the wearing-out of capital over time. (7)

capital shallowing a decrease in the availability of capital per worker leading to reduced productivity per worker. (10)

capital stock the existing quantity of capital in a given region, including manufactured, human, and natural capital. (2, 13, 20)

carbon sinks portions of the ecosystem with the ability to absorb certain quantities of carbon dioxide, such as forests and oceans. (18)

carbon tax a per-unit tax on goods and services based on the quantity of carbon dioxide emitted during the production or consumption process. (18)

carrying capacity the level of population and consumption sustainable by the available natural resource base. (1, 2, 10, 11, 14)

cartel a group of independent organizations working together to regulate production and prices; the OPEC cartel nations significantly influence oil production and price. (13)

certification the process of certifying products that meet certain standards, such as certifying produce grown using organic farming techniques. (14, 15, 17, 19)

choke price the minimum price of a good or service that would result in a zero quantity demanded. (12)

circular flow a diagram that indicates the ways resources, such as goods, money, wastes, and energy, move through an economy or ecosystem. (1)

Clean Development Mechanism a component of the Kyoto Protocol that allows industrial countries to receive credits for helping developing countries reduce their carbon emissions. (18)

clear-cut the process of harvesting all trees within a given area. (15)

climate stabilization the policy of reducing fossil fuel use to a level that would not increase the potential for global climate change. (18)

closed system a system that exchanges no energy or resources with another system; except for solar energy and waste heat, the global ecosystem is a closed system. (7)

Coase theorem the proposition that if property rights are well defined and there are no transactions costs, an efficient allocation of resources will result, even if externalities exist. (3)

cogeneration the process of using waste energy to produce heat from electricity generation. (12, 13)

command-and-control policies regulation policies that dictate standards or equipment, such as a policy that limits allowable automobile emissions or requires catalytic converters. (16)

common property resource(s) a resource not subject to private ownership and available to all, such as a public park or the oceans. (1, 5, 11, 18)

comparative advantage the theory that trade benefits both parties by allowing each to specialize in goods they can produce with relative efficiency. (19)

complementary goods goods that tend be used together, such as gasoline and automobiles. (3)

constant returns (to scale) a proportional increase (or decrease) in one or more inputs results in the same proportional increase (or decrease) in output. (5, 10)

consumer surplus the benefits consumers receive from a product in excess of the amount they pay for it. (3)

contingent valuation an economic technique that surveys people regarding their willingness to pay for a good or service such as preservation of hiking opportunities or air quality. (6)

cost-benefit analysis (CBA) a tool for policy analysis that attempts to monetize all the costs and benefits of a proposed action to determine the net benefit. (1, 6, 18)

cost-effectiveness analysis a policy tool that determines the least-cost approach for achieving a given goal. (6, 18)

critical natural capital elements of natural capital for which no good human-made substitutes exist, such as basic water supplies and breathable air. (8, 20)

crop rotation and fallowing an agricultural system involving growing different crops on the same piece of land at different times and regularly taking part of the land out of production. (11)

crop value index an index indicating the relative value of production of different crops on a given quantity of land. (11)

cross-boundary flows the transport of materials or information across a given physical boundary. (9)

cumulative pollutant(s)/pollution pollutants that do not significantly dissipate or degrade over time. (2, 8, 16)

defensive expenditures expenditures made to clean up pollution or repair or compensate for environmental damage. (8)

demand-side management an approach to energy management that stresses increasing energy efficiency and reducing energy consumption. (2)

dematerialization the process of achieving an economic goal through a decrease in the use of physical materials, such as making aluminum cans with less metal. (17)

demographic transition the tendency for first death rates and then birth rates to fall as a society develops economically; population growth rates first increase and eventually decrease. (10)

dependency ratios the ratio of the number of people in a society who depend on others for their livelihood divided by the number who do not depend on others. (10)

depletable resource a renewable resource that can be exploited and depleted, such as soil or clean air. (11)

deposit/return systems systems that encourage recycling by charging consumers a deposit when they purchase certain goods such as beverages in recyclable containers or batteries; the deposit is returned when the consumer returns the recyclable material to an appropriate location. (12)

deregulation the process of converting a market dominated by a regulated monopoly or oligopoly to a market with competition. (13)

desalination the removal of salt from ocean water to make it usable for irrigation, industrial, or municipal water supplies. (15)

diminishing returns a proportional increase (or decrease) in one or more inputs results in a smaller proportional increase (or decrease) in output. (5, 13)

direct use value the value one obtains by directly using a natural resource, such as visiting a national park. (6)

discount rate the annual rate at which future benefits or costs are discounted relative to current benefits or costs. (1, 4, 6, 11, 15, 18)

dualistic land ownership an ownership pattern, common in developing countries, where large landowners wield considerable power and small landowners tend to be displaced. (19)

dynamic equilibrium a market equilibrium that results when present and future costs and benefits are considered. (4)

ecolabeling a label on a good that provides information concerning the environmental impact of producing the good. (14)

ecological complexity the presence of many different living and nonliving elements in an ecosystem interacting in complex patterns; ecosystem complexity implies that human impact on ecosystems may be unpredictable. (7, 14, 15)

ecological cycles the flow of energy and natural resources through ecosystems. (1)

ecological economics an economic perspective that views the economic system as a subset of the broader ecosystem and subject to biophysical laws. (1)

ecological value the value of ecosystem resources and services not expressed in markets. (6, 8)

economic efficiency an allocation of resources that maximizes net social benefits; perfectly competitive markets in the absence of externalities are efficient. (3, 13, 14, 16)

economic optimum a result that maximizes an economic criterion, such as efficiency or profits. (5, 14, 18)

economic rent income that accrues to the owner of a scarce resource. (14)

economic reserves (economically recoverable reserves) the quantity of a resource identified as economically feasible to extract given current prices and technology. (12)

economic supply (of a resource) the amount of a resource that is available based on current prices and technology. (12, 13)

economic value/valuation the value of a good or service, expressed in monetary terms. (1, 6)

economies of scale expanded output increases returns per unit of input. (10, 13)

ecosystems management a system of resource management that stresses long-term ecosystem sustainability. (15)

effective demand the total demand for goods and services based on ability to pay; consumers must have sufficient income to translate needs into effective demand. (5)

efficiency labeling labels on goods that indicate energy efficiency, such as a label on a refrigerator indicating annual energy use. (13)

efficiency standards regulations that mandate efficiency criteria for goods, such as fuel economy standards for automobiles. (13, 18)

elasticity of demand the sensitivity of quantity demanded to prices; an elastic demand means that a proportional increase in price results in a larger proportional change in quantity demanded; an inelastic demand means that a proportional increase in price results in a smaller proportional change in quantity demanded. (18)

elasticity of supply the sensitivity of quantity supplied to prices; an elastic supply means that a proportional increase in price results in a larger proportional change in quantity supplied; an inelastic supply means that a proportional increase in price results in a smaller proportional change in quantity supplied. (11)

embodied energy the total energy required to produce a good or service, including both direct and indirect uses of energy. (9)

emissions standards regulations that set the maximum amount of pollutants that may be legally emitted by an industrial facility or product. (16)

empty-world and full-world economics the view that economic approaches to environmental issues should differ depending whether the scale of the economy relative to the ecosystem is small (an empty world) or large (a full world). (7)

end-of-year stocks the stock of natural resources, such as timber and oil, at the end of a year; used as a supplement to national income accounting. (8)

energy infrastructure a system that supports the use of a particular energy source, such as gas stations and roads that support gasoline-powered automobiles. (13)

energy supply augmentation an approach to energy management emphasizing increase in energy supplies, such as building more power plants or increasing oil drilling. (2)

energy-efficient technology a technology that minimizes the amount of energy used to perform a specific task, such as the use of compact fluorescent light bulbs to supply light. (18)

engineering cost method an approach to economic valuation that determines the monetary costs of duplicating or replacing environmental services. (6)

entropy   a measure of the unavailable energy in a system; according to the second law of thermodynamics entropy increases in all physical processes. (9, 13)

environmental design   the design of products or processes to limit environmental impact, such as manufacturing a product for eventual recycling or reducing materials requirements. (17)

environmental externalities   environmental impacts of an economic activity that are not reflected in the market costs or prices associated with the activity. (3, 18, 19)

Environmental Kuznets Curve (EKC)   the theory that a nation's environmental impact increases in the early stages of economic development but eventually decreases above a certain level of income. (19)

environmental macroeconomics   an analysis that places the human economic system in an ecological context to balance the scale of the economic system within ecological constraints. (1)

environmental microeconomics   the use of microeconomic techniques such as economic valuation, property rights rules, and discounting to determine an efficient allocation of natural resources and environmental services. (1)

environmental services   ecosystem services such as nutrient cycling, water purification, and soil stabilization; these services benefit humans and support economic production. (1, 8)

environmental sustainability   the continued existence of an ecosystem in a healthy state; ecosystems may change over time but do not significantly degrade. (2, 11)

environmental valuation   assigning monetary values to environmental goods and services using economic techniques. (3)

equimarginal principle   the concept that benefits are maximized when marginal benefits equal marginal costs, or when marginal costs of achieving a given goal by different methods are equalized. (16)

equity   fairness in the relative distribution of goods or services across a population; can be applied to income and environmental quality. (3)

estimated ultimately recoverable (EUR) supplies   an estimate of the total amount of a nonre-

newable resource that will ultimately be extracted. (13)

existence value   the value people place on the continued existence of a resource, such as the benefit one obtains from knowing an area of rainforest is preserved even though one will never visit it. (6)

expected value   an estimate of the value of an event or outcome whose likelihood is uncertain, calculated by mutiplying its probability by its cost or benefit. (6)

exponential growth   a value that increases by the same percentage in each time period, such as a population increasing by the same percentage every year. (10, 20)

exponential reserve index   an estimate of a resource lifetime based on existing economic reserves and a projected continuing percentage increase in resource use rates. (12)

exporting pollution   importing goods whose production involves environmental impact, thereby avoiding domestic impacts. (19)

external benefit(s)   a benefit, not necessarily monetary, not reflected in a market transaction. (1, 3, 18)

external cost(s)   a cost, not necessarily monetary, not reflected in a market transaction. (1, 3, 11, 18)

externalities   an effect of a market transaction on individuals or firms other than those involved in the transaction. (1, 11, 18)

extraction path   the extraction rate of a resource over time. (12)

extractive reserves   a forested area that is managed for sustainable harvests of non-timber products such as nuts, sap, and extracts. (20)

feedback loops/effects   the process of changes in a system leading to other changes that either counteract or reinforce the original change. (6, 17, 18)

fertility rate   the average number of live births per woman in a society. (10)

first law of thermodynamics   the physical law stating that matter and energy cannot be created or destroyed, only transformed. (9)

fixed factors   production factors whose quantity cannot be changed in the short run. (10)

flow   the quantity of a variable measured over a period of time, such as the flow of a river past a given point measured in cubic-feet per second. (13, 15)

flow pollutant   a pollutant that has a short-term impact and then dissipates or is absorbed harmlessly into the environment. (16)

free market environmentalism   the view that a more complete system of property rights and expanded use of market mechanisms is the best approach to solving issues of resource use and pollution control. (3)

free rider effect   the incentive for people to avoid paying for a resource when the benefits they obtain from the resource are unaffected by whether they pay; results in the undersupply of public goods. (3, 5)

freshwater runoff   the amount of freshwater that flows across a given area in a period of time, including water usable for human water supplies and flood waters. (15)

fuel cells   using a chemical reaction between a fuel and an oxidant to produce electricity directly. (17)

full pricing   the inclusion of both internal and external costs in the price of a product. (15)

gains from trade   the net social benefits that result from trade. (19)

GATT Article XX   the GATT provision stating that a country can restrict trade to conserve exhaustible natural resources or to protect human and animal life or health. (19)

General Agreement on Tariffs and Trade (GATT)   a multilateral trade agreement providing a framework for the gradual elimination of tariffs and other barriers to trade; the predecessor to the World Trade Organization. (19)

genuine saving (S*)   a measure that estimates the amount of national income being saved, taking into account natural-resource depletion, net foreign borrowing, and net additions to capital stock. (8)

global climate change   the changes in global climate, including temperature, precipitation, and storm frequency and intensity, that result with changes in greenhouse gas concentrations in the atmosphere. (2, 16, 18)

global commons   global common property resources such as the atmosphere and the oceans. (2, 5, 18)

global environmental problems   environmental problems with global impact, such as global climate change and species extinction. (1)

global materials cycles   the natural cycling of atoms of certain chemicals, such as nitrogen, carbon, and sulfur, between living beings, soil, air, and water. (17)

global pollution/pollutant(s)   pollutants that can have global impact such as carbon dioxide and chlorofluorocarbons (CFCs). (8, 16, 19)

global public goods   environmental goods or services that benefit all people, such as biodiversity and climate stabilization. (19)

global warming   the increase in average global temperature as a result of emissions from human activities. (18)

GNP growth rate   the annual change in GNP, expressed as a percentage. (2)

government procurement   programs that guarantee a certain government demand for a good or service. (12)

government regulation   direct government control through the use of a specific rule or standard, as applied for example to permissible pollution emission levels. (3)

grandfathering   a policy of exempting existing industrial facilities from complying with new environmental standards or regulations. (16)

green accounting   approaches to national income accounting that attempt to incorporate the depletion of natural capital and other environmental benefits and costs. (8)

green subsidies   subsidies on a good or service based on the reduction of environmental impact. (17, 20)

green taxes   taxes based on the environmental impact of a good or service. (17, 20)

greenhouse effect   the effect of certain gases in the earth's atmosphere trapping solar radiation, resulting in an increase in global temperatures and other climatic changes. (10, 18)

greenhouse gases   gases such as carbon dioxide and methane whose atmospheric concentrations influence global climate by trapping solar radiation. (16, 18)

gross annual population increase   the total numerical increase in population for a given region over one year. (10)

groundwater overdraft   the withdrawal of water from an underground aquifer at a rate greater than the recharge rate. (15)

harmonization of environmental standards   the equalization of environmental standards across countries, as in the European Union. (19)

hedonic pricing   the use of statistical analysis to explain a good's price or service as a function of several components, such as explaining the price of a home as a function of the number of rooms, the caliber of local schools, and the surrounding air quality. (6)

holdout effect   the ability of a single entity to hinder a multi-party agreement by making disproportionate demands. (3)

Hotelling's rule   a theory stating that in equilibrium the net price (price minus production costs) of a resource must rise at a rate equal to the rate of interest. (4, 12)

Hubbert curve   a bell-shaped curve showing the production rate of a nonrenewable energy resource over time. (13)

Human Development Index (HDI)   a national income accounting technique, developed by the United Nations Development Programme, that combines GDP with data on life expectancy, literacy, and school enrollment to obtain an HDI score. (8)

hydropower   the generation of electricity from the energy in flowing water. (13)

hypothetical and speculative resources   the quantity of a resource not identified with certainty but hypothesized to exist. (12)

identified reserves   the identified quantity of a resource; includes both economic and subeconomic reserves. (12)

incremental costs   costs of environmental protection in developing countries in excess of what the country is prepared to pay without foreign assistance. (20)

Index of Sustainable Economic Welfare (ISEW)   a national income accounting measure that subtracts defensive expenditures from output and accounts for natural resource depletion, pollution damages, income inequality, and nonmarketed services. (8)

indicated or inferred reserves   resources that have been identified but whose exact quantity is not known with certainty. (12)

indirect use values   ecosystem benefits not valued in markets, such as flood prevention and pollution absorption. (6)

individual demand schedule   the relationship between price and quantity demanded for a particular individual. (5)

individual transferable quotas (ITQs)   tradable rights to harvest a resource, such as a permit to harvest a particular quantity of fish. (14)

induced innovation   innovation in a particular industry resulting from changes in the relative prices of inputs. (11)

industrial ecology   the application of ecological principles to the management of industrial activity. (2, 9, 12, 16, 17, 20)

Industrial Revolution   the period during the late eighteenth and nineteenth centuries marking a significant increase in industrial output. (17)

industrial symbiosis   the process of linking industrial production such that the wastes from one industry become production inputs for other industries. (17)

inflection point   the point on a curve where the second derivative equals zero, indicating a change from positive to negative curvature or vice versa. (14)

information asymmetry   a situation where different agents in a market have different knowledge or access to information. (11)

information-intensive techniques   production techniques that require specialized knowledge; usually these techniques substitute knowledge for energy, produced capital, or material inputs, often reducing environmental impact. (11)

input-intensive agriculture   agricultural production that relies heavily on machinery, artificial fertilizers, pesticides, and irrigation. (2)

input-output analysis (static and dynamic)   a modeling approach that determines the physical or economic relationships between sectors of an economy; a static analysis does not account for changes in technology and capital stock, but a dynamic model does account for these changes. (9)

institutional failure   the failure of governments or other institutions to prevent resource overexploitation, or the use of policies that promote resource overexploitation and environmental damage. (14, 15)

integrated pest management   the use of methods such as natural predators, crop rotations, and pest removal to reduce pesticide application rates. (11)

intensification of production   increasing production rates with a limited supply of resources, such as increasing agricultural yield per acre. (2)

intensity of materials use (IU)   the quantity of physical materials used per unit of economic output. (17)

microirrigation irrigation systems that increase water use efficiency by applying water in small quantities close to the plants. (15)

micronutrients nutrients present in low concentrations in soil, required for plant growth or health. (11)

monoculture an agricultural system involving the growing of the same crop exclusively on a piece of land year after year. (11, 14, 15)

multilateral environmental agreements (MEAs) international treaties between nations on environmental issues, such as the Convention on International Trade in Endangered Species. (19)

multiple cropping an agricultural system involving growing more than one crop on a piece of land. (11)

natural capital the available endowment of land and resources including air, water, soil, forests, fisheries, minerals, and ecological life-support systems. (2, 7, 20)

natural capital depreciation a deduction in national accounting for loss of natural capital, such as a reduction in the supply of timber, wildlife habitat, or mineral resources. (7, 8)

natural capital sustainability conserving natural capital by limiting depletion rates and investing in resource renewal. (7)

neo-Malthusianism the modern version of T. R. Malthus's argument that human population growth can lead to catastrophic ecological consequences and an increase in the human death rate. (10)

net foreign borrowing (NFB) the amount borrowed by a country less the amount lent to other countries; gross investment is adjusted by NFB and depreciation to determine net domestic investment or savings. (8)

net investment the process of adding to productive capital over time, calculated by subtracting depreciation from gross, or total, investment. (7, 8)

net national product (NNP)/net domestic product (NDP) the value obtained by subtracting the depreciation of humanmade capital from gross national product or gross domestic product. (8)

net present value the present value of a stream of benefits minus the present value of a stream of costs. (6)

net price (of a resource) the price of a resource minus production costs. (4)

net primary product of photosynthesis (NPP) the biomass energy directly produced by photosynthesis. (7)

net receipts returns from the sale of a resource, equal to revenues minus production costs. (8)

net social benefit the social gain that results when total benefits exceed total costs, including external benefits and costs. (3, 5)

net social loss the social loss that results when total costs exceed total benefits, including external benefits and costs. (3)

nitrogen cycle the conversion of nitrogen into different forms in the ecosystem, including the fixation of nitrogen by symbiotic bacteria in certain plants such as legumes. (11)

nominal GNP gross national product measured using current dollars. (2)

nonexclusive good a good available to all users; one of the two characteristics of public goods. (5)

nongovernmental organizations (NGOs) privately-funded, and commonly nonprofit, organizations involved in research, lobbying, provision of services, or development projects. (20)

nonlinear or threshold effects effects such as the health damage from a pollutant that do not increase linearly with the quantity of the pollutant. (16)

nonmarket values the values people place on goods or services not traded in markets. (6)

nonpoint source pollution pollution difficult to identify as originating from a particular source, such as groundwater contamination from agricultural chemicals used over a wide area. (16)

nonrenewable resources resources available in fixed supply, such as metal ores and oil. (1, 2, 4, 12, 17)

nonrival good a good whose use by one person does not limit its use by others; one of the two characteristics of public goods. (5)

nonuniformly mixed pollutants pollutants that have different effects in different areas, depending on where they are emitted. (16)

nonuse values values people obtain without actually using a resource; nonuse values include existence and bequest values. (6)

nutrient recycling the ability of ecological systems to transform nutrients such as carbon,

intercropping an agricultural system involving growing more than one crop on a piece of land at the same time. (11)

intergenerational equity the distribution of resources, including humanmade and natural capital, across human generations. (6, 7)

internalizing externalities using approaches such as taxation to incorporate external costs and benefits into market decisions. (1, 3, 16, 18)

intertemporal resource allocation the way resource consumption is distributed over time. (1)

irreversibility environmental damage that cannot be reversed, such as the extinction of species. (6, 7)

joint implementation cooperative agreements between nations to reduce carbon emissions. (18)

labor-intensive techniques production techniques that rely heavily on labor input. (11)

law of diminishing returns the principle that a continual increase in production inputs will eventually yield decreasing marginal output. (10)

Law of the Sea a 1982 international treaty regulating marine fisheries. (14)

license fee the fee paid for access to a resource, such as a fishing license. (5, 14)

local and regional pollutants pollutants that cause damage only within the area where they are emitted. (16, 18)

logistic curve an S-shaped growth curve tending toward an upper limit. (14, 15, 20)

macroeconomic (system) scale the total scale of an economy; ecological economics suggests that the ecosystem imposes scale limits on the macroeconomy. (1, 2, 7, 20)

marginal benefit the benefit of producing or consuming one more unit of something. (3)

marginal cost the cost of producing or consuming one more unit of something. (3, 5)

marginal extraction cost the cost of extracting an additional unit of a nonrenewable resource. (12)

marginal net benefit the net benefit of the consumption or production of an additional unit of a resource; equal to marginal benefit minus marginal cost. (4, 18)

marginal physical product the additional tity of output produced by increasing an level by one unit. (11)

marginal revenue the additional revenue ob tained by selling one more unit of a good or service. (5)

marginal revenue product the additional revenue obtained by increasing input by one unit equal to marginal physical product multiplied by marginal revenue. (11)

market demand schedule the relationship between the price of a good or service and the quantity consumers are willing to purchase. (3, 5)

market equilibrium the interaction of supply and demand resulting in a price at which no excess demand or supply exists. (3)

market failure the failure of certain markets to provide a socially efficient allocation of resources. (10, 13, 14)

market supply schedule the relationship between the price of a good or service and the quantity producers are willing to produce. (3)

market-based pollution control the use of market incentives to control pollution levels, such as pollution taxes or tradable permits. (16)

materials substitution changing the materials used to produce a product, such as using plastic pipe instead of copper in plumbing systems. (17)

maximum net present value criterion a decision rule stating that policies should be designed to maximize net present values; the maximum net present values occurs when the marginal benefits of an action just equal the marginal costs. (6)

maximum sustainable yield (MSY) the maximum quantity of a natural resource that can be harvested annually without depleting the resource stock or population. (5, 14)

mean annual increment (MAI) the average growth rate of a forest; obtained by dividing the total weight of timber by the age of the forest. (15)

measured reserves identified resources whose quantity is known with certainty. (12)

methodological pluralism the view that a more comprehensive understanding of problems can be obtained by using a combination of perspectives rather than just one perspective. (9)

nitrogen, and phosphorus into different chemical forms. (11)

nutritional deficit failure to meet human demands for basic levels of nutrition. (11)

open system a system that exchanges energy or natural resources with another system; the economic system is considered an open system because it receives energy and natural resources from the ecosystem and deposits wastes into the ecosystem. (7)

open-access equilibrium the level of use of an open-access resource that results from a market with free entry; this use level may lead to resource depletion. (5, 14)

open-access resource(s) a resource that offers unrestricted access such as an ocean fishery or the atmosphere. (2, 5, 14)

opportunity cost of capital the rate of return available for alternative investment projects. (6)

optimal depletion rate the depletion rate for a natural resource that maximizes the resource's net present value. (4)

optimal pollution (level) the pollution level that maximizes net social benefits. (3, 16)

optimum rotation period the rotation period for a renewable resource that maximizes the financial gain from harvest; determined by maximizing the discounted difference between total revenues and total costs. (15)

option value the value people place on maintaining future resource use options. (6)

organic techniques agricultural production systems that maintain soil fertility using organic materials and use natural methods of pest control. (17)

overfishing a level of fishing effort that depletes fishery stock over time. (5, 14)

over-harvesting of renewable resources rates of harvest that decrease resource stock or population over time. (2)

pay-by-the-bag systems waste disposal systems in which customers pay a fee for each unit of waste discarded. (12)

per capita GNP growth rate the annual change in per capita GNP, expressed as a percentage. (2)

per capita output the total product of a society divided by population. (10)

physical accounting a supplement to national income accounting that estimates natural resource stock or services in physical, rather than economic, terms. (7)

physical supply (of a resource) available reserves measured in physical terms, without regard to the economic feasibility of recovery. (12)

Pigovian tax a per-unit tax set equal to the external damage caused by an activity, such as a tax per ton of pollution emitted equal to the external damage of a ton of pollution. (3)

point source pollution pollution emitted from an identifiable source such as a smokestack or waste pipe. (16)

polluter pays principle the view that those responsible for pollution should pay for associated external costs such as health costs and damage to wildlife habitats. (3)

pollution tax(es) a per-unit tax based on the level of pollution. (3, 16, 18)

population age profile estimated numbers of people classified by age groups in a given place and time. (10)

population biology the study of how a species population changes as a result of environmental conditions. (14)

population cohort the group of people born within a specific time period in a country. (10)

population growth rate the annual change in the population of a given area, expressed as a percentage of the total population. (2, 10)

population momentum the tendency for a population to continue to grow, even if the fertility rate falls to the replacement level, as long as a high proportion of the population is young. (2, 10)

positional analysis a policy analysis tool that combines economic valuation with considerations such as equity, individual rights, and social priorities; it does not aim to reduce all effects to monetary terms. (6)

positive net present value criterion a decision rule stating that projects should be undertaken if they provide positive discounted net benefits (present value of benefits minus present value of costs). (6)

precautionary principle the view that policies should account for uncertainty by taking steps to avoid outcomes that are damaging to health or the environment, especially when such outcomes are irreversible. (6, 7, 14, 19)

present value the current value of a stream of future costs and/or benefits, calculated through the use of a discount rate. (4, 6, 11)

preventive and adaptive strategies   the contrasting perspectives of trying to prevent environmental damage versus trying to adapt to damage once it occurs. (18)

price path   the price of a resource, typically a nonrenewable resource, over time. (12)

price taker   a seller in a competitive market who has no control over the product price. (12)

private choice   individual preferences usually expressed through market behavior. (3)

private optimum   the optimal allocation or production of a resource based on market behavior. (3)

private ownership   the provision of certain exclusive rights to a particular resource, such as the right of a landowner to restrict trespassing. (14)

process and production methods (PPM) rules   international trade rules stating that an importing country cannot use trade barriers or penalties against another country for failure to meet environmental or social standards related to the process of production. (19)

producer surplus   the net benefit accruing to producers of a good, measured by the difference between the price received and costs of production. (3)

production function method   an approach to economic valuation that determines the monetary costs of duplicating or replacing environmental services. (6)

productivity loss estimates   an estimate of the reduction in the productive capacity of renewable natural resources, such as soil; used to supplement national income accounting. (8)

property rights   the set of rights that belong to the resource owner, such as a landowner's right to prohibit trespassing. (1, 3, 15)

proxy variable   a variable used to represent a broader concept, such as the use of fertilizer application rates to represent the input-intensity of agricultural production. (11)

psychic benefit   a benefit derived without the actual use of a resource, such as the existence benefits of species preservation. (5)

public choice   social preferences for policies; these preferences may not be expressed in market behavior. (3)

public good(s)   goods available to all (nonexclusive), whose use by one person does not reduce their availability to others (nonrival). (1, 5, 15)

quota (system)   a system of limiting resource access through user limits on the permissible resource harvest. (5, 14)

race to the bottom   the tendency for nations to weaken national environmental standards to attract foreign businesses or to keep existing businesses from moving to other nations. (19)

real GNP   gross national product corrected for inflation using a price index. (2)

recharge of aquifers   the refilling of groundwater reservoirs through seepage of surface and subsurface water through the earth's strata. (15)

recycling   the process of using waste materials as inputs into a production process. (12, 17, 20)

remanufacturing   replacing only the worn parts of a discarded product while retaining structural components in order to make the product reusable. (17)

renewable energy sources   energy sources supplied on a continual basis such as wind, water, biomass, and direct solar energy. (2, 18, 20)

renewable resource(s)   resources supplied on a continuing basis by ecosystems; renewable resources such as forests and fisheries can be depleted through exploitation. (1, 2, 4, 11, 14)

rent dissipation   the loss of potential social and economic benefits in a market because of market failure. (14)

replacement cost   an approach to measuring environmental damages that estimates the costs necessary to restore or replace the resource, such as applying fertilizer to restore soil fertility. (8)

replacement fertility level   the fertility level that would result in a stable population. (10)

research and development (R&D)   efforts to increase technical knowledge for the production of new products or improvement of existing products. (13, 18)

reserve base index   an estimate of available resource reserves divided by the annual consumption rate; uses a broad estimate of available reserves. (12)

resilience   ecosystem capacity to recover from adverse impact. (14, 15)

resistant pest species   pest species that evolve resistance to pesticides, requiring either higher pesticide application rates or new pesticides to control the species. (11)

resource depletion   a decline in resource stocks through human exploitation. (1)

resource depletion tax   a tax imposed on the extraction or sale of a natural resource. (4)

resource lifetime   the number of years the economic reserves of a resource are projected to last under expected consumption rates. (12)

resource recovery   mining or extraction of resources for economic use. (2)

resource rents   income derived from ownership of a scarce resource. (12)

resource substitution   the use of one resource in a production process as a substitute for another resource, such as the use of aluminum instead of copper in electrical wiring. (12)

resource use profile   the consumption rates for a resource over time, typically applied to nonrenewable resources. (12)

revenue recycling   using revenues from tax increases on certain products or activities to reduce other taxes. (18)

revenue-neutral tax shift   policies designed to balance tax increases on certain products or activities with reductions in other taxes, such as a reduction in income taxes that offsets a carbon-based tax. (18, 20)

right to pollute   a system that gives an entity a right to emit a certain quantity of a pollutant, such as a tradable emissions permit. (3)

risk aversion   the tendency to prefer certainty instead of risky outcomes, particularly in cases where actions may cause significant negative consequences. (6)

safe minimum standard   the principle that environmental policies on issues involving uncertainty should be set to avoid possible catastrophic consequences. (6)

salinization and alkalinization of soils   the buildup of salt or alkali concentrations in soil with the effect of reducing soil productivity. (11)

satellite accounts   accounts that estimate the supply of natural capital in physical rather than monetary terms; used to supplement traditional national income accounting. (7, 8)

second law of thermodynamics   the physical law stating that all physical processes lead to a decrease in available energy, that is, an increase in entropy. (9)

second-best solution   a policy solution to a problem that fails to maximize potential net social benefits but may be appropriate if the optimal solution cannot be achieved. (19)

sensitivity analysis   an analytical tool that studies how the outputs of a model change as the assumptions of the model change. (6)

sink function   the environment's ability to absorb and render harmless the by-products of human activity. (1, 14, 16, 20)

social benefit   the market and nonmarket benefits associated with a good or service. (3, 5)

social cost   the market and nonmarket costs associated with a good or service. (3, 4)

social demand   the vertical addition of individual demand schedules to obtain total willingness to pay for a given level of a resource. (5)

social discount rate   a discount rate that reflects social rather than market valuation of future costs and benefits. (6)

social optimum   an allocation of resources that maximizes net social benefits (equal to social benefits minus social costs). (3, 18)

social rate of time preference (SRTP)   a discount rate that attempts to reflect the appropriate social valuation of the future; the SRTP tends to be less than market or individual discount rates. (6)

social sustainability   the maintenance of social structure and traditions, for example among indigenous peoples. (15, 20)

solar energy   the energy supplied continually by the sun, including direct solar energy as well as indirect forms such as wind energy and flowing water. (1, 2, 13)

solar flux   the continual flow of solar energy to the earth. (9, 10, 13)

solar hydrogen   a virtually emissions-free system of energy relying on solar energy to release hydrogen gas from water, burning hydrogen to obtain useful energy, and obtaining water as a by-product. (13, 17)

source function   the environment's ability to make services and raw materials available for human use. (1, 14)

specificity rule   the view that policy solutions should be targeted directly at the source of a problem. (19)

stable equilibrium   an equilibrium of, for example, a renewable resource stock level, to which the system will tend to return after short-term changes in conditions. (14)

stable water supply   the quantity of water available to a region for human use on a continual basis. (15)

static equilibrium   a market equilibrium that results when only present costs and benefits are considered. (4)

static reserve index   an index that divides the economic reserves of a resource by the current rate of use for the resource. (12)

steady state economy   an economy that maintains a constant level of natural capital by limiting the throughput of material and energy resources. (20)

stock   the quantity of a variable at a given point in time, such as the amount of timber in a forest at a given time. (13, 15)

stock pollutant   a pollutant that accumulates in the environment, such as carbon dioxide and chlorofluorocarbons (CFCs). (16, 18)

strategic bias   the tendency for people to state their preferences or values inaccurately in order to influence policy decisions. (6)

strong sustainability   the view that natural and humanmade capital are generally not substitutable and, therefore, natural capital levels should be maintained. (7, 8, 20)

structural adjustment   policies to promote market-oriented economic reform in developing countries by making loans conditional on reforms such as controlling inflation, reducing trade barriers, and privatization of businesses. (20)

subeconomic resources   a resource quantity that cannot be economically extracted at current prices and technology. (12)

subsidies   government assistance to an industry or economic activity; subsidies can be direct, through financial assistance, or indirect, through protective policies. (3, 14, 15, 18)

substitutability (of natural and manufactured capital)   the ability of humanmade capital to compensate for the depletion of some types of natural capital, such as the ability of fertilizer to compensate for the loss of soil fertility. (7, 8)

sufficiency   the goal of limiting consumption to an amount necessary to live a comfortable but not extravagant lifestyle. (17)

supply constraint   an upper limit on supply of, for example, a nonrenewable resource. (4)

sustainable agriculture   systems of agricultural production that do not deplete the productivity of the land or environmental quality, including such techniques as integrated pest management, organic techniques, and multiple cropping. (2, 11)

sustainable development   development that meets the needs of the present without compromising the ability of future generations to meet their own needs. (1, 2, 20)

sustainable (natural resource) management   management of natural resources such that natural capital remains constant over time, including maintenance of both stocks and flows. (2, 14)

sustainable yield   a yield or harvest level that can be maintained without diminishing the resource stock or population. (7)

system boundary   a boundary defining an area for study, such as a wetland or urban area; used in economic/ecological modeling. (9)

technological innovation   increases in knowledge used to develop new products or improve existing products. (2, 10, 17)

technological lock-in   the tendency of an industry to continue to use a given technology despite the availability of more efficient or cheaper technologies. (12, 20)

technological thresholds   important industrial, agricultural, and energy technological innovations that make possible new production methods and may dramatically reduce environmental impact. (17)

technology transfer   the process of sharing technological information or equipment, particularly among nations. (18)

theoretical paradigm   the basic conceptual approach used to study a particular issue. (2)

thermodynamic efficiency   minimizing the energy used to produce a given output or achieve a given task. (13)

third-party effects   effects of market transactions that affect people other than those involved in the transaction, such as industrial pollution that affects a local community. (1)

throughput   the total use of energy and materials as both inputs and outputs of a process. (1, 7, 12, 13, 17)

total cost of pollution   a monetary measure of pollution damage, including both financial and social costs. (3)

total net benefit   total benefit minus total cost. (4)

total product   the total quantity of a good or service produced with a given quantity of inputs. (5, 14)

total revenue   the total revenue obtained by selling a particular quantity of a good or service; equal to price multiplied by quantity sold. (5)

tragedy of the commons the tendency for common property resources to be overexploited because no one has an incentive to conserve the resource, while individual financial incentives promote expanded exploitation. (5, 14, 15)

transactions costs costs associated with a market transaction or negotiation, such as legal and administrative costs to transfer property or to bring disputing parties together. (3)

transboundary pollution pollution carried beyond the borders of a specific region or country and affecting those outside the region. (8, 19)

transferable pollution permits tradable permits that allow a firm to emit a certain quantity of a pollutant. (16, 17, 18)

travel cost method the use of statistical analysis to determine people's willingness to pay to visit a natural resource such as a national park or river; a demand curve for the resource is obtained by analyzing the relationship between visitation choices and travel costs. (6)

true income an adjusted measure of income obtained by subtracting that portion of total income that would have to be invested at long-term rates to guarantee an indefinitely continued flow of income at the same level. (8)

under-pricing prices of goods or services below the price that would result from taking full social costs into account. (15)

undersupply of public goods the tendency for public goods to be supplied at levels below the social optimum because of a low effective demand. (5)

uniformly mixed pollutants any pollutant emitted by many sources in a region resulting in relatively uniform concentration levels across the region. (16)

unstable equilibrium a temporary equilibrium of, for example, a renewable resource stock level, that can be altered by minor changes in conditions, resulting in a large change in stock levels. (14)

use value the value that people place on the use of a good or service. (6, 15)

user cost(s) opportunity costs associated with the loss of future potential uses of a resource, resulting from consumption of the resource in the present. (4, 8, 11, 12)

utility the level of satisfaction obtained from an activity. (3)

waste mining obtaining resources used in a production process from waste products instead of using virgin resources. (17)

water-abundant and water-scarce areas areas of the world where stable water supplies are either ample or limited; water scarcity has been defined as less than 1,000 cubic meters per capita of renewable supply. (15)

water cycle the cycle of evaporation and precipitation that continually supplies fresh water. (15)

watershed management the management of a watershed to preserve its ecological integrity; includes the management of agriculture, residential development, industry, and other human activities. (16)

weak sustainability the view that natural capital depletion is justified as long as it is compensated for with increases in humanmade capital; assumes that humanmade capital can substitute for most types of natural capital. (7, 8, 20)

welfare analysis an economic tool that analyzes the total costs and benefits of alternative policies to different groups, such as producers and consumers. (3)

willingness to accept (WTA) the minimum amount of money people would accept as compensation for an action that reduces their utility. (6)

willingness to pay (WTP) the maximum amount of money people are willing to pay for a good or service that increases utility. (6)

World Environmental Organization (WEO) a proposed international organization that would have oversight on global environmental issues. (19)

World Trade Organization (WTO) an international organization dedicated to the expansion of trade through lowering or eliminating tariffs and nontariff barriers to trade. (19)

Index